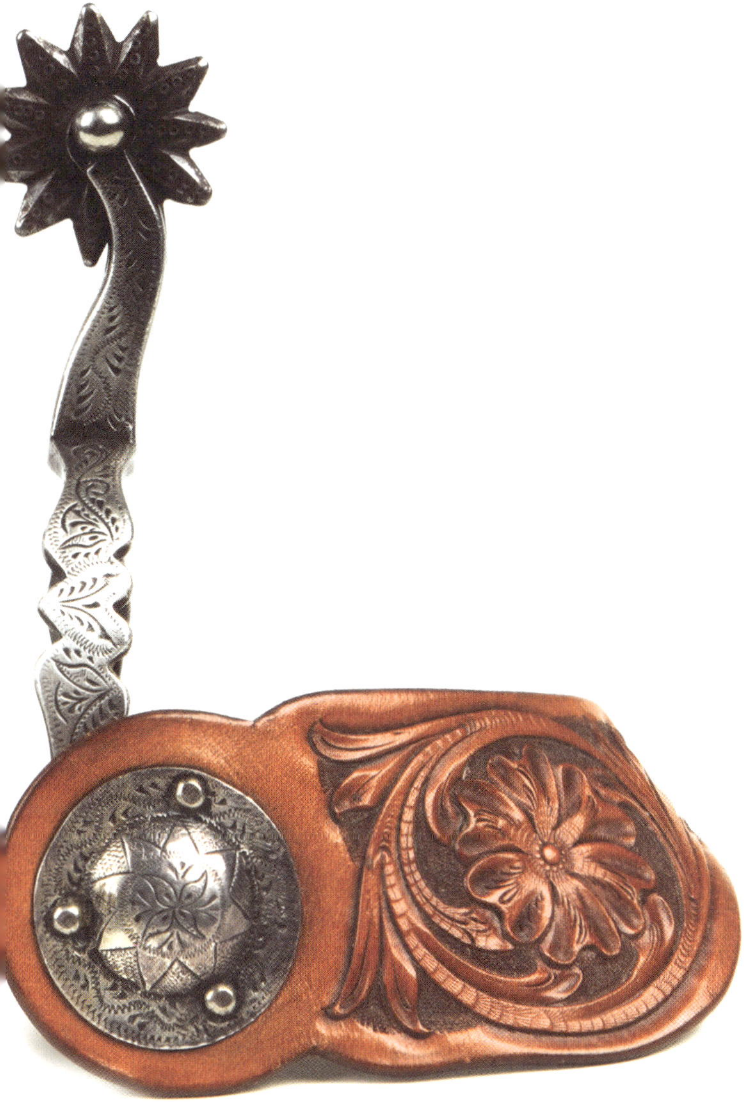

I0805699

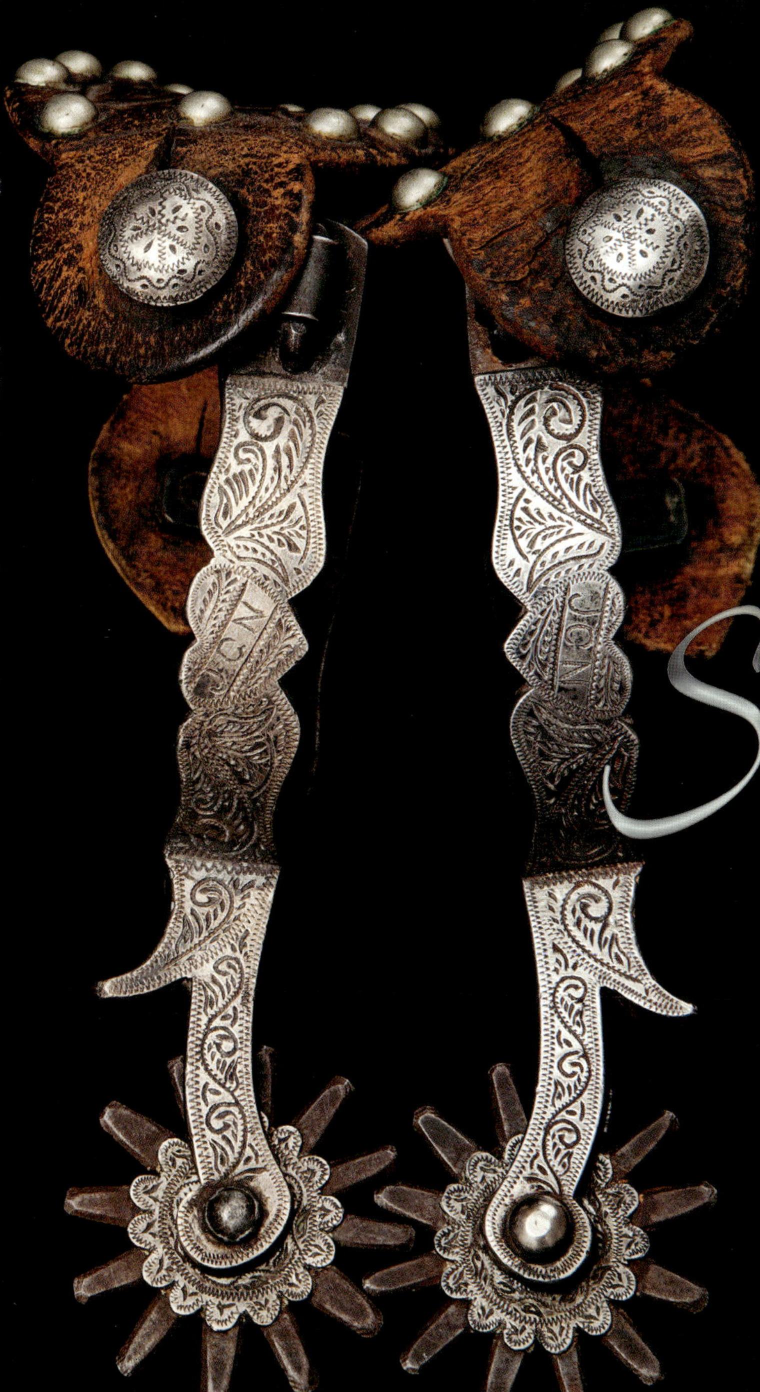

Eddy Hulbert Silversmith

Artistry in Dryhead Country, Montana

E. Helene Sage

Schiffer Publishing Ltd®
4880 Lower Valley Road • Atglen, PA 19310

Copyright © 2014 by E. Helene Sage

Library of Congress Control Number: 2014939238

All rights reserved. No part of this work may be reproduced or used in any form or by any means—graphic, electronic, or mechanical, including photocopying or information storage and retrieval systems—without written permission from the publisher.

The scanning, uploading, and distribution of this book or any part thereof via the Internet or via any other means without the permission of the publisher is illegal and punishable by law. Please purchase only authorized editions and do not participate in or encourage the electronic piracy of copyrighted materials.
"Schiffer," "Schiffer Publishing, Ltd. & Design," and the "Design of pen and inkwell" are registered trademarks of Schiffer Publishing, Ltd.

Designed by Justin Watkinson
Cover by Ro Shillingford
Type set in Helvetica Neue LT Pro/Zurich BT

ISBN: 978-0-7643-4726-9
Printed in United States of America

Published by Schiffer Publishing, Ltd.
4880 Lower Valley Road
Atglen, PA 19310
Phone: (610) 593-1777; Fax: (610) 593-2002
E-mail: Info@schifferbooks.com

For our complete selection of fine books on this and related subjects, please visit our website at www.schifferbooks.com. You may also write for a free catalog.

This book may be purchased from the publisher. Please try your bookstore first.

We are always looking for people to write books on new and related subjects. If you have an idea for a book, please contact us at proposals@schifferbooks.com.

Schiffer Publishing's titles are available at special discounts for bulk purchases for sales promotions or premiums. Special editions, including personalized covers, corporate imprints, and excerpts can be created in large quantities for special needs. For more information, contact the publisher.

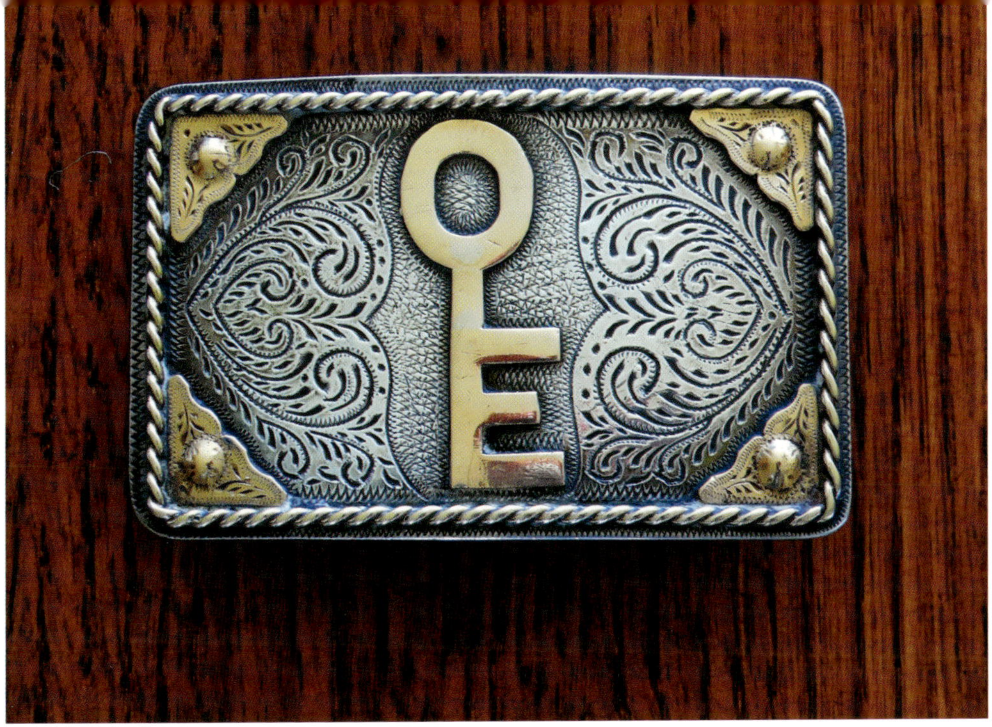

Engraved sterling silver belt buckle with 10K gold rope border, corners, and Ranch brand, "O hanging E." Made by Eddy Hulbert in 1952 for Henry R. Esp (b. 1900, d. 1989), a rancher from Lodge Grass, Montana. Esp was a "sheepman" who moved to the Crow Reservation in 1929 to become sheep foreman for the Antler Ranch. In 1949 he started a sheep and cattle ranch on Lodge Grass Creek, south of Lodge Grass, was later president of the Montana Woolgrowers Association, county commissioner, and a candidate for the state legislature. This buckle was accompanied by a matching pair of cufflinks. On the back of the silver belt buckle was engraved: HENRY R. ESP/FROM/ALVA/FEB. 5, 1952. (Alva was Henry's wife). *Courtesy Arne Esp. Photo by A. Esp.*

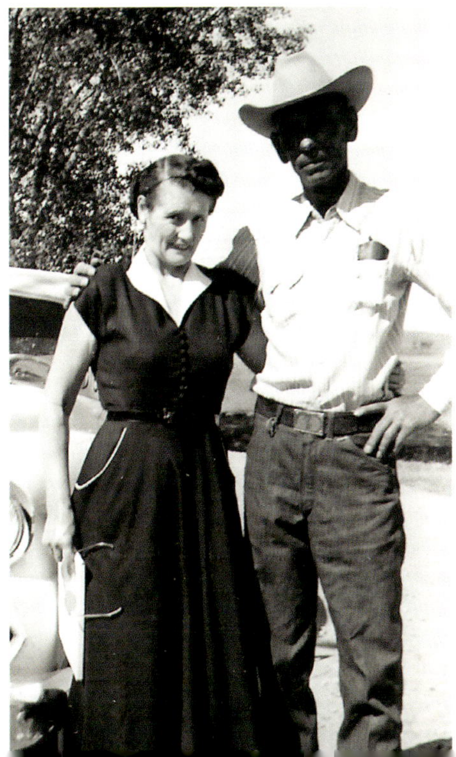

Henry R. Esp, wearing the buckle shown above, posing with his sister Alma. *Courtesy of Arne Esp, grandson of Henry R. Esp. Photographer unknown.*

Acknowledgments

The author is indebted to Shell Reid, whose book on Eddy Hulbert was the first study of this important silversmith. She was able to interview many of the "old timers" who knew Eddy in the Dryhead country where he worked and interacted with the local ranching community. Elmer Diederich first introduced me to Eddy Hulbert more than a decade ago by his selling me an engraved belt buckle with a Montana agate in the center. He has since enhanced my Hulbert collection with his rare and unusual finds, for which I am eternally grateful. I thank Bruce Bartlett (Rio Grande Trading Co.), Arne Esp (Hardin, Montana), Roman Gillitzer (Park City, Montana), Brian Lebel (Santa Fe, New Mexico), Jay Lyndes (Billings, Montana), Bob and Charla Nelson (The Nelson Museum of the West), Jim Nett (Great Falls, Montana), Michael NeVille (Cody, Wyoming), Mary Schmitt (Cayuse Western Americana), Joseph Sherwood (High Noon Western Americana), Bob Smith, Carl Webb, and Roger Wilmot (Laramie, Wyoming), for their insight, advice, and/or sharing of both knowledge and Hulbert artifacts, all of which contributed to the Hulbert inventory in this book. Brian Lebel graciously made space available at his Denver Old West Show & Auction for the photography of Hulbert silver, where Bill Manns (Santa Fe, New Mexico) and Johnny Williams (Paradise Valley, Arizona) patiently shot collections provided by friends and Hulbert collectors. Interviews with Arne Esp, Ray Huffman, Jay Lyndes, Jim Nett, and Michael NeVille were helpful and enlightening. Dave Claxton photographed much of the Klapmeier collection shown in Chapter 6, and Michael NeVille photographed the Cedarville Ranch buildings expressly for this book. I extend my sincere thanks to all these individuals.

I am grateful to Schiffer Publishing, Ltd., for their enthusiasm and expertise in the creation of beautiful and enduring books. Special thanks are due Nancy Schiffer for her insight and understanding of artistry in silver, and to Doug Congdon-Martin, the Premier Editor, who also photographed my collection of Hulbert silver.

Eileen Neligan prepared the final version of the text and, as always, made a smooth transition from my handwritten copy to a presentable manuscript.

I am indebted to my support group in Santa Fe that allowed me protected time for thinking, writing, and research: Debbie Lopez, Allen Swafford and Kent Kramer, Will, and Jesse and Bill Conant.

Dedication

This book is dedicated to Paul Bornstein, M.D. (1934-2013). His father buried the family silver in the garden of their home in Antwerp, Belgium, prior to their flight from the Nazis in 1940. Paul enjoyed beautiful silver, including the work of Eddy Hulbert; I shall always be grateful for his support and devotion.

Contents

INTRODUCTION

Eddy Hulbert and the Dryhead Country

The purpose of this book is to showcase the artistry of Eddy Hulbert, a Montana/Wyoming silversmith whose output was not only varied, but prodigious. Although Hulbert's life spanned two World Wars, his continued residence in the Dryhead country of southern Montana, near the Wyoming border (an area now encompassed within the Big Horn Canyon National Recreation Area), reflected much of the earlier times when ranching and cowboys were dominant themes in the American West. For someone of his place and time, Hulbert's life was not particularly unusual or remarkable, save for the contribution of his art, in the form of silver-decorated spurs, bits, and jewelry, much of it personalized and/or commissioned by the ranching communities in the proximity of his shop and home in Hillsboro. His engraving style was so distinctive, and his knowledge of bits and spurs, and the horses on which they were used, so extensive, that his reputation as a spur maker, loriner, and silversmith became a part of the heritage of the Northwest ranching tradition in the first half of the 20th century. Hulbert's custom orders, usually in the form of jewelry and belt buckles, have become keepsakes representing Montana history of that era.

The sole publication devoted to Eddy Hulbert was Shell Reid's excellent study, *Eddy Hulbert—Montana Silversmith* (1998). This book, written when several of Hulbert's acquaintances were still living, presented a personal view of Hulbert, his neighbors, his environs, and his life history. The reader is referred to this work for detailed information on these various topics. Table 1 is a chronology of the life of Eddy Hulbert and summarizes key events in his life and work. It provides a perspective in which to place Hulbert's work, as well as reference points for the progression of his art, from blacksmithing to fine jewelry.

Eddy Hulbert arrived at the Cedarvale Guest Ranch in Hillsboro, Carbon County, Montana, in 1911, at the age of 13. The area was referred to as Dryhead (or Dry Head, an arid rangeland that was said to derive its name from the pile of buffalo skulls accumulated at the base of a buffalo jump near Dryhead Creek; www.pryormountains.org/culturalhistory/homestead-era), and became his near-permanent home. A map of this area is shown in Figure 1-1. With the Pryor Mountains on the west, and the Crow Indian Reservation on the east, the region designated as the Big Horn Canyon National Recreation Area includes Hillsboro, Barry's Landing (part of the Cedarvale Guest Ranch), and the Lockhart Ranch (described below). Extending into northern Wyoming, the Bighorn (or Big Horn) River forms Bighorn Lake, on the western shore of which lie Kane and, farther west, Lovell, two towns frequented by Hulbert in his later years. The area around Hillsboro abounded in cattle and sheep ranches that provided a willing market for Hulbert's work. Importantly, the city of Billings, on the Yellowstone River, lay to the northwest of the "Big Dry." Hardin, on the Bighorn River, was directly north of Hillsboro and was joined to Billings by the present Route 90. This geographic triangle witnessed an important part of Eddy Hulbert's career.

TABLE 1. Chronology of the Life of Eddy Hulbert[1]

1898	Edmund (Eddy) Cummings Hulbert is born in Chicago, Illinois on March 8 to William M. Hulbert and Ann M. Cummings Hulbert.
1900	Ann Hulbert dies.
1911	William M. Hulbert dies. Eddy is left without funds, an education, and parental affection and guidance. Eddy is sent by a family member(s) to the Cedarvale Guest Ranch in Hillsboro, Carbon County, Montana. He is welcomed by the owners, Grosvenor "Doc" Barry and his wife Edith, and thereafter makes his home in this area of Montana (known as Dryhead).
1915-1920s	Eddy learns the blacksmithing trade and repairs Barry's boats, wagons, and farm machinery; he also is a farrier for the Cedarvale stock. His services extend to neighboring ranches and he becomes known as the "Hillsboro blacksmith."
1920	Doc Barry dies. Edith Barry, her son Claude St. John, and Eddy manage Cedarvale Ranch; Eddy is the "horse trader." Eddy also begins silversmithing.
1924	Eddy's silver-mounted stirrups and spurs are featured in Hamley's catalog No. 25 (Pendleton, Oregon).
1920s-1940s	Eddy's silverwork gains recognition in the Northwest; several saddleries advertise his bits, spurs, and stirrups: Hamley & Co., Fred Mueller Saddle & Harness Co. (Denver, Colorado), Otto F. Ernst, Inc. (Sheridan, Wyoming), and Connelly's Western Wear (Billings, Montana).
1937	Eddy moves to Cody, Wyoming for a short time.
1940s-1950s	Eddy devotes an increasing amount of time to the production of trophy/rodeo belt buckles, spurs, and jewelry. He personalized each item according to the event, ranch, and/or recipient's name or initials, often in gold.
1930s	Eddy develops a mail-order business and also sells his silverwork to neighbors and visitors at the guest ranches in the area.
Late 1940s	Eddy works as a tool dresser for an oil drilling company in Wyoming for several years.
Early 1950s	Eddy's stationery is marked "Kane, Wyoming," possibly reflecting a short residence there. Some of Eddy's pieces are displayed for sale at the Medicine Wheel Bar (Lovell, Wyoming).
1951	Edith Barry dies. Claude St. John, his wife Beverly, and their daughter Julie live with Eddy at Cedarvale.
1958	Eddy marries Mabel Bischoff in Red Lodge, Montana.
1960	Eddy dies on July 12 en route to a Lovell, Wyoming hospital, of a myocardial infarction. One year later, his wife dies and is buried next to him.

Footnotes:
1. Many of the details concerning Eddy Hulbert's life were gleaned from Reid, *Eddy Hulbert – Montana Silversmith*, published in 1998.

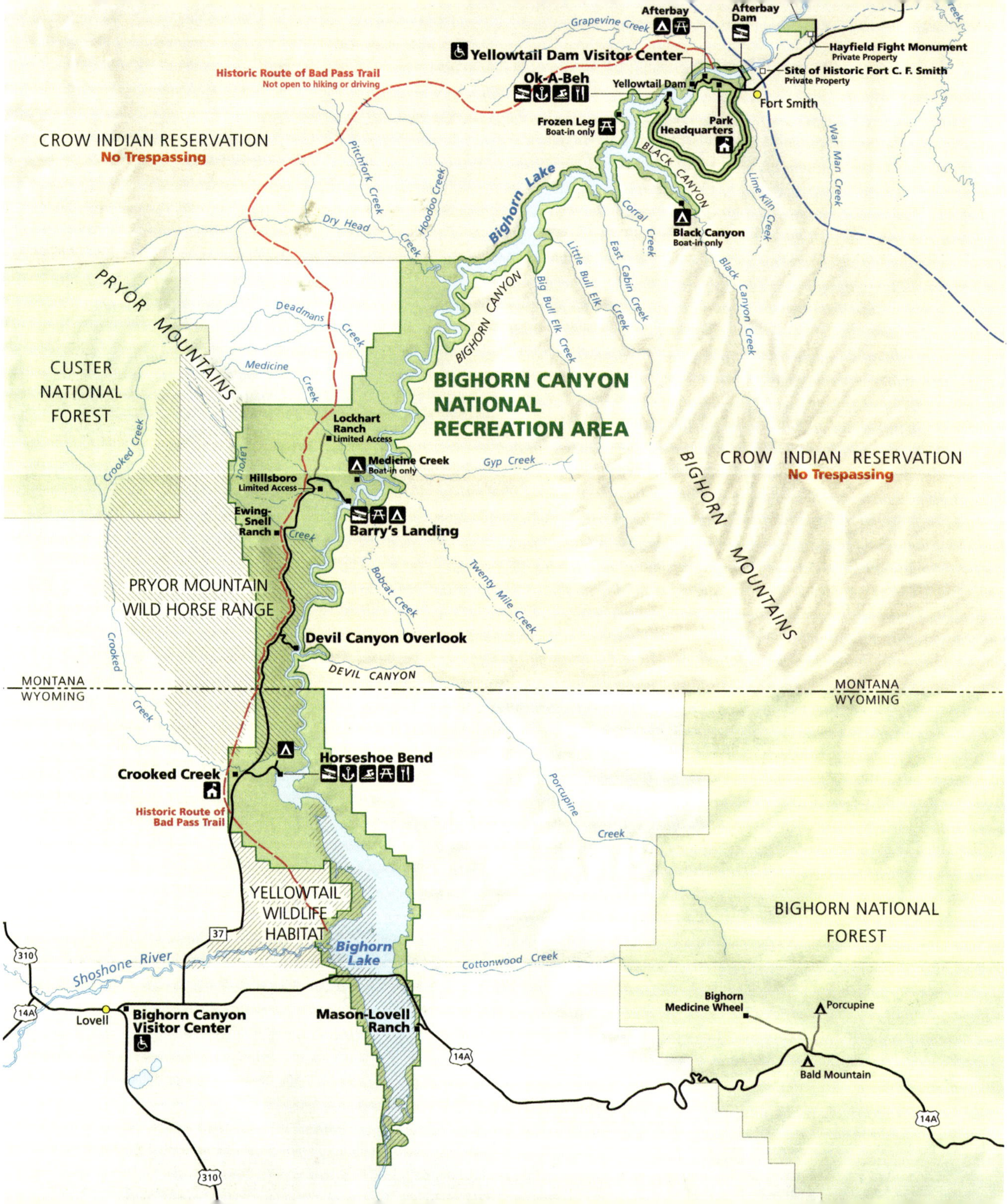

Figure 1-1. Map of Bighorn Canyon and the Dryhead area. In Montana, note Hillsboro and Barry's Landing, and in Wyoming, note Lovell; these areas were relevant to Eddy Hulbert's work and life. Kane, Wyoming (not shown on map), lies on Route 14A, directly east of Lovell and on the western edge of Bighorn Lake. *Courtesy of the National Park Service, U.S. Department of the Interior.*

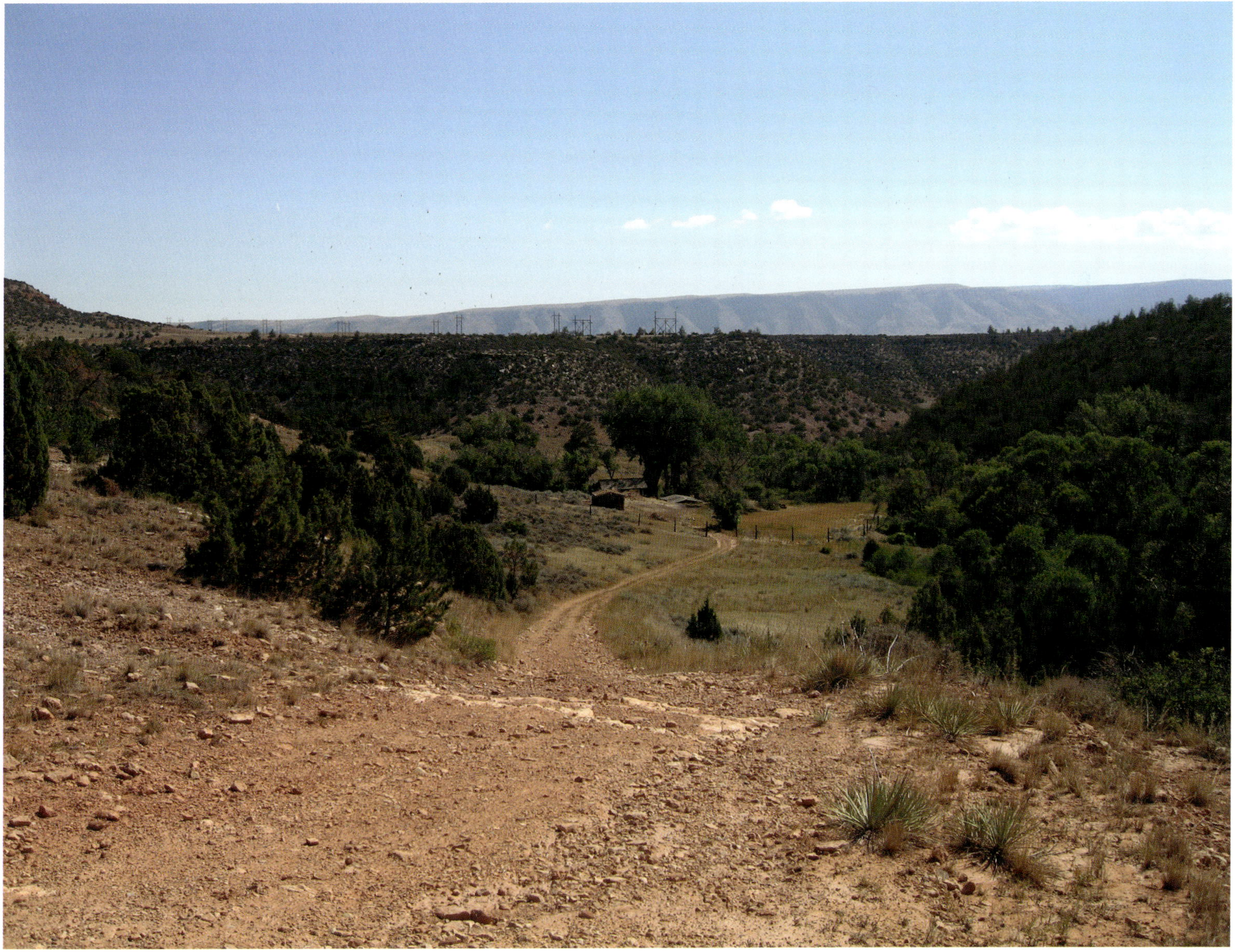

Figure 1-2. Hillsboro, Montana—The Dryhead country and location of Cedarvale Ranch, 2006. The Big Horn Mountains are shown in the background, and some of the ranch buildings appear in the foreground. The photo was taken facing east. *Courtesy of Arne Esp. Photo by A. Esp.*

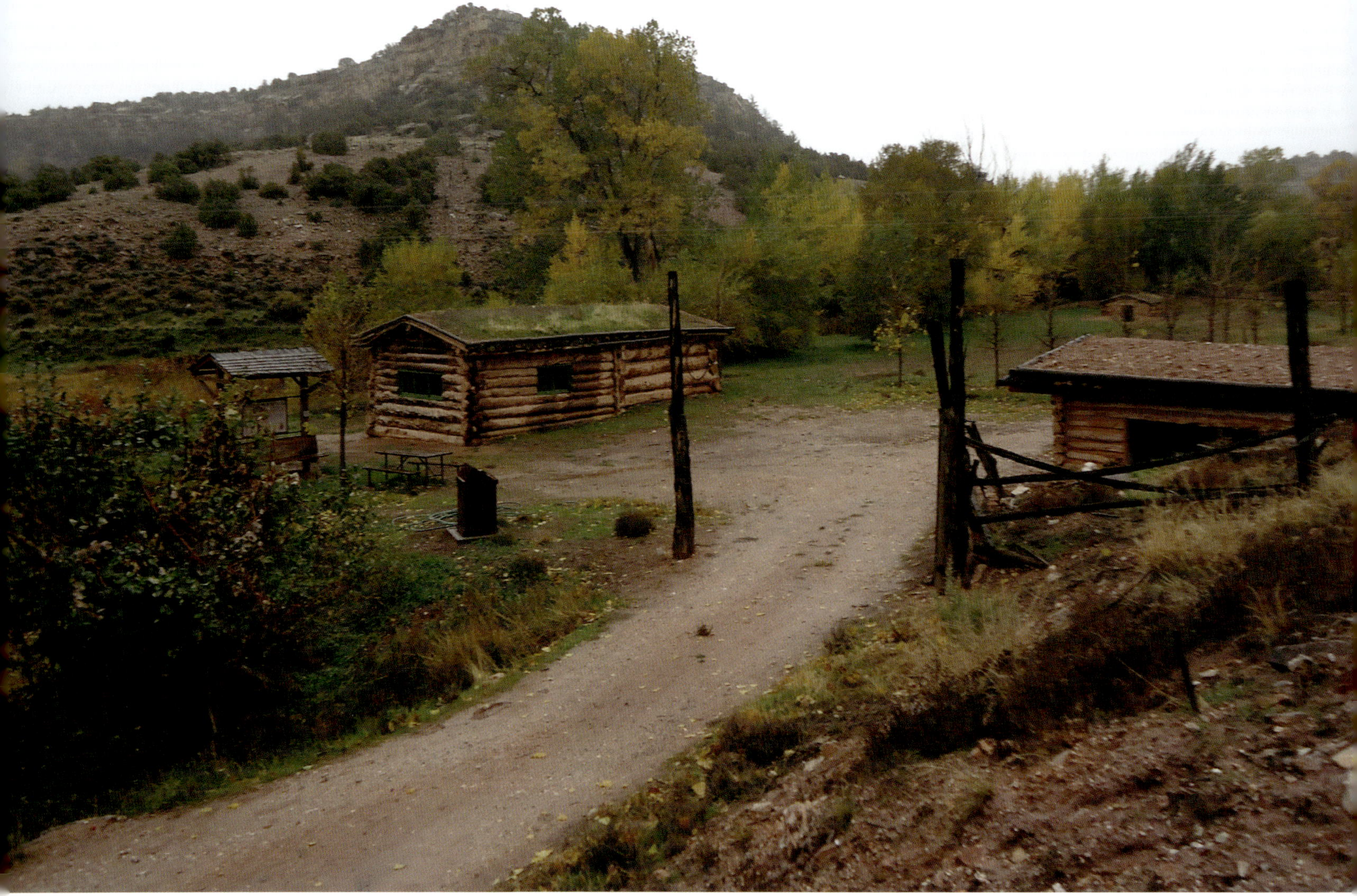

Figure 1-3. Hillsboro, Montana—Hulbert's Shop (on the left). A cabin or bunkhouse lies behind the shop, and a stone cellar, on the right. Photograph taken in 2013, facing southwest. *Courtesy of Michael NeVille. Photo by M. NeVille.*

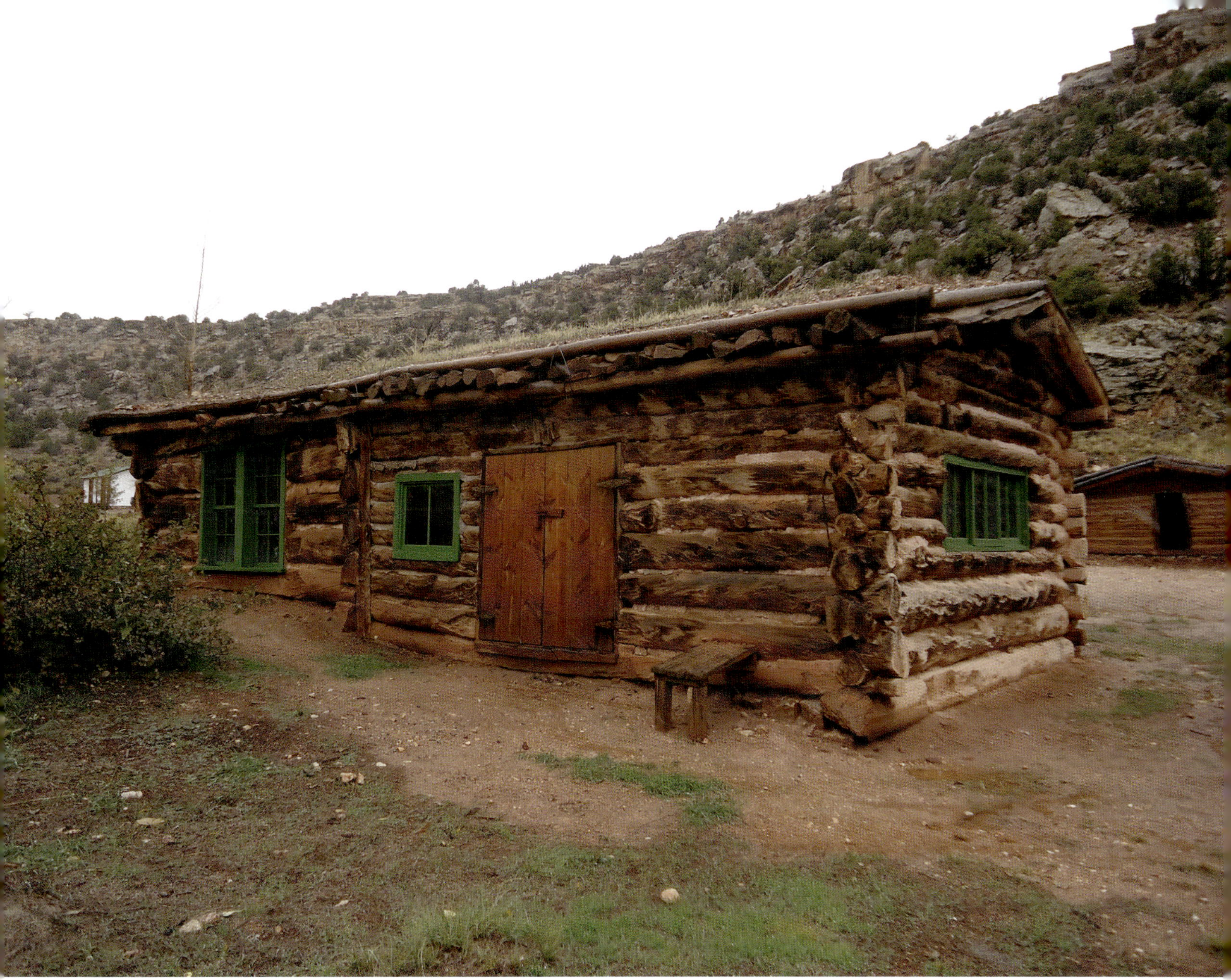

Figure 1-4. Hulbert's Shop. Exterior of the log cabin in which Eddy Hulbert did his work. Bunkhouse in back. Photograph taken in 2013. *Courtesy of Michael NeVille. Photo by M. NeVille.*

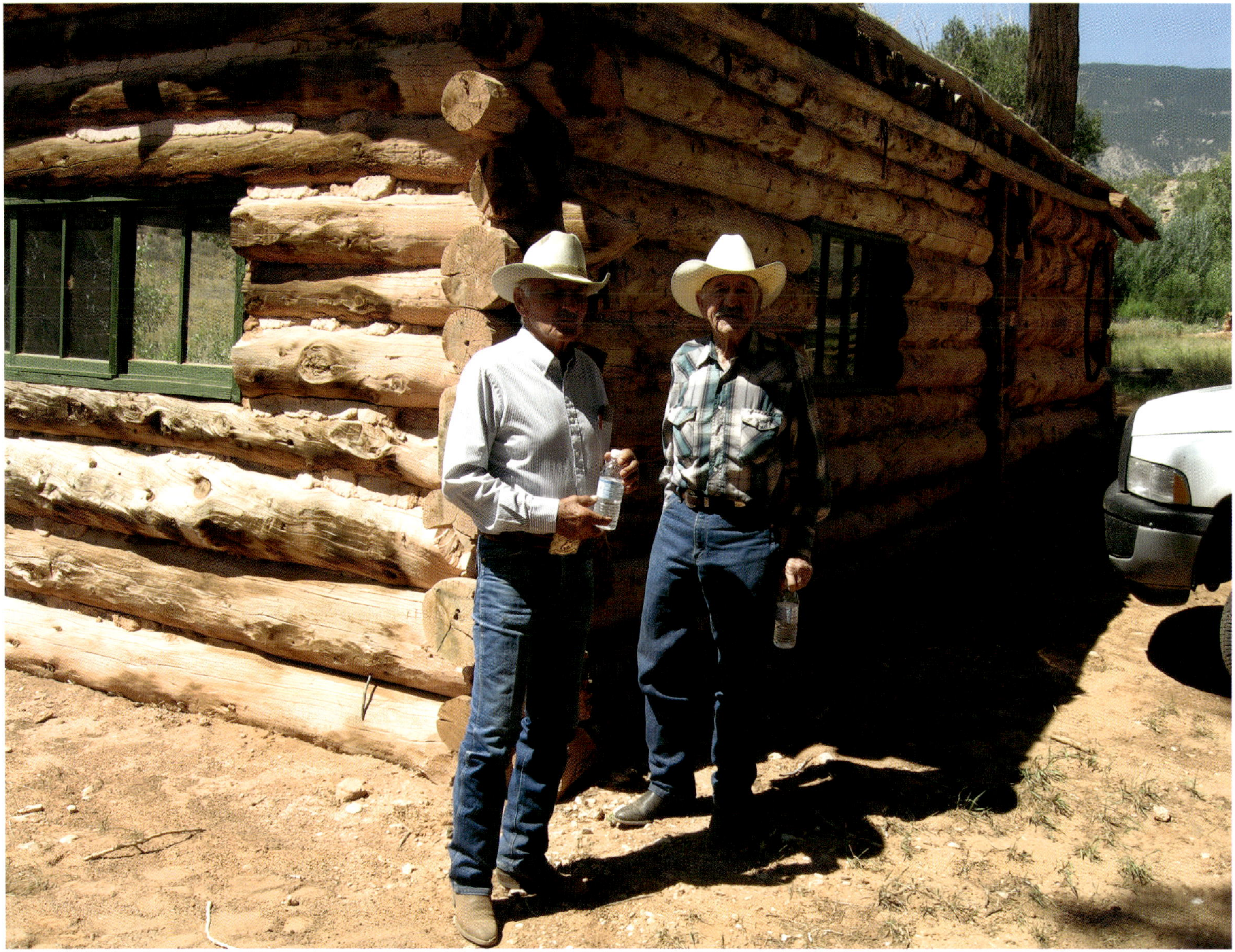

Figure 1-5. Hulbert's Shop. On the left is Henry (Hank) L. Esp (son of Henry R. Esp, see frontis photograph, and father of silversmith Arne Esp), standing next to his friend and fellow cowboy John Hammett outside Hulbert's shop. Hammett, who allegedly swam the Big Horn River from his lonely cow camp on Gyp Creek to visit with Hulbert, worked for the Antler Ranch. Both men are wearing Hulbert belt buckles. Photograph taken in 2006. *Courtesy of Arne Esp. Photo by A. Esp.*

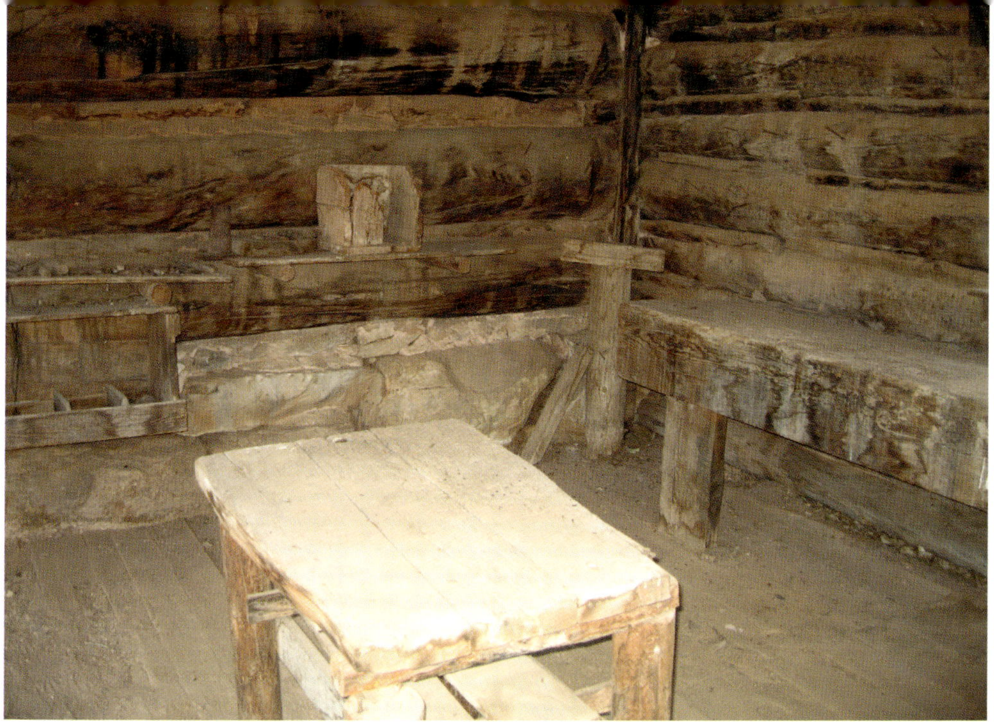

Figure 1-6. Hulbert's Shop. This photograph of the inside of Hulbert's log cabin shop was taken in 2006. Note the bins on the left and the stout table and benches. *Courtesy of Arne Esp. Photo by A. Esp.*

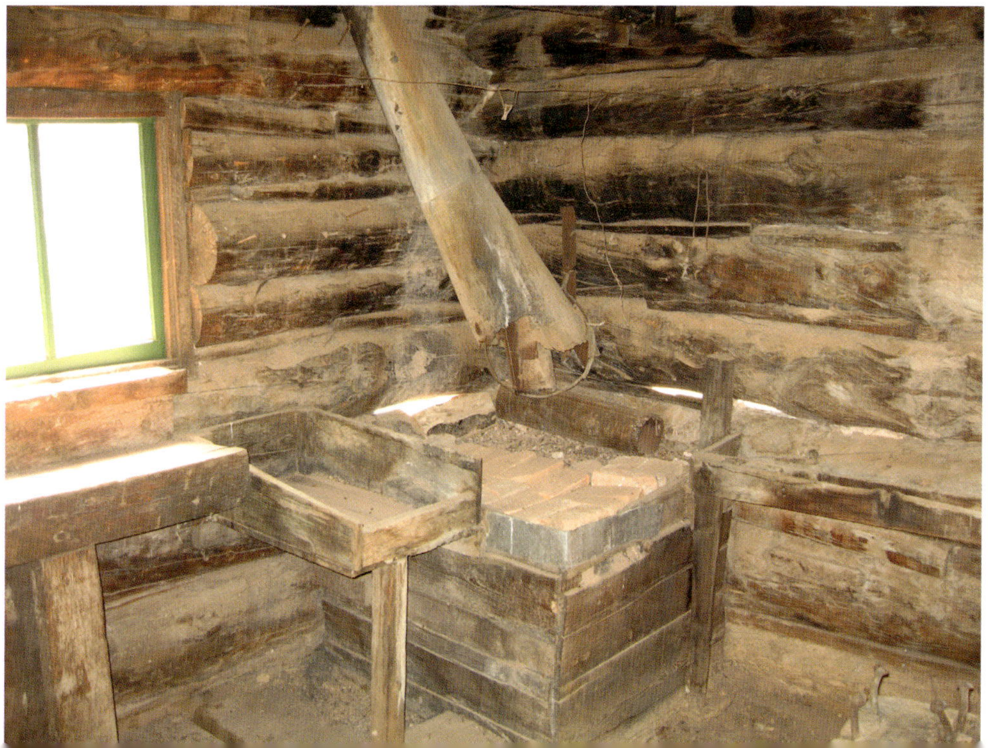

Figure 1-7. This photograph, taken in 2006, shows the forge and chimney where so many Hulbert creations were born. *Courtesy of Arne Esp. Photo by A. Esp.*

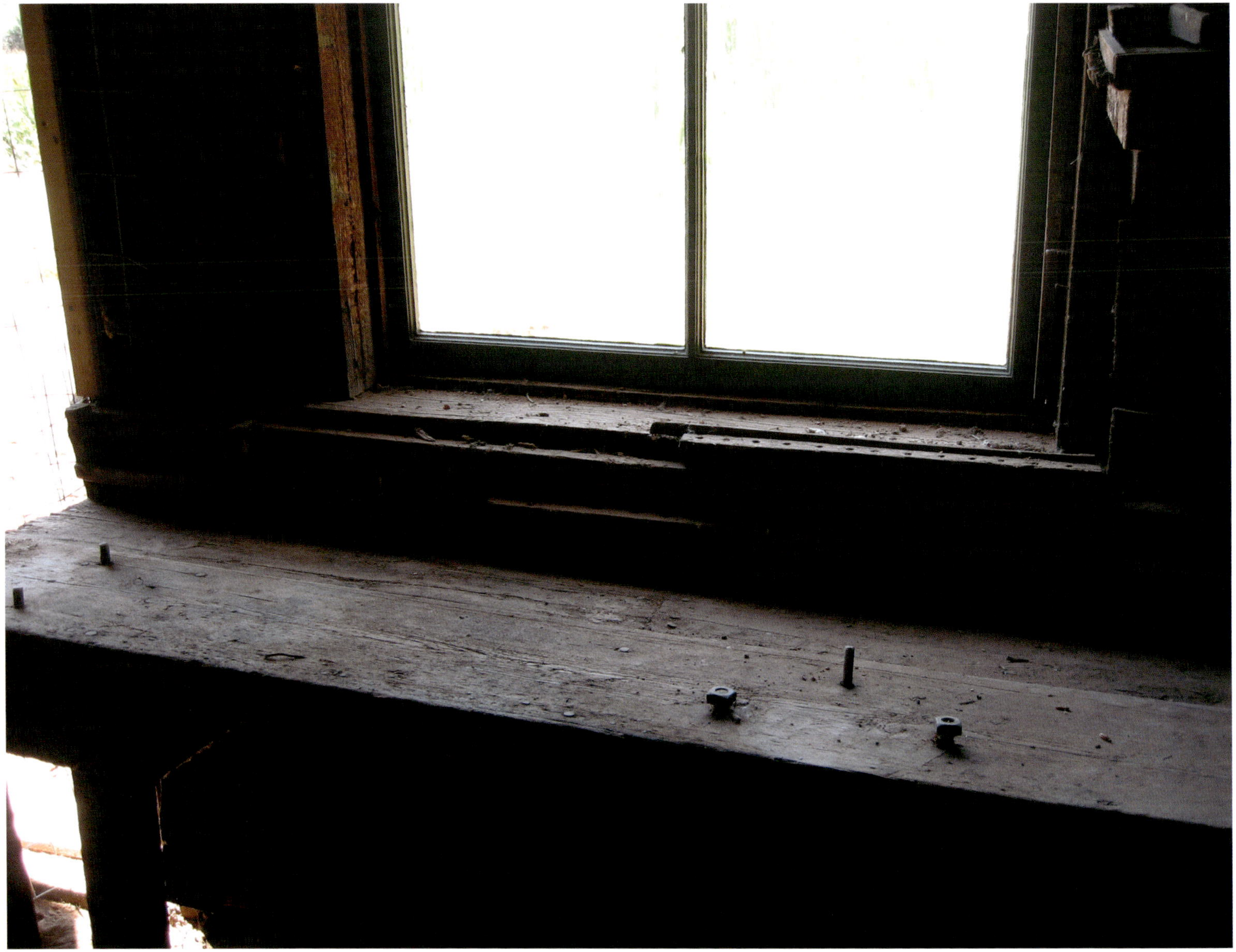

Figure 1-8. Hulbert's work bench was located just under a window for the natural light it provided. The photograph was taken in 2006. *Courtesy of Arne Esp. Photo by A. Esp.*

TABLE 2. Names of Individuals and Ranch Brands on Silver Designed by Eddy Hulbert[1]

Name/Initial/Brand	Identification[2]	Object
B	Beverly St. John ?	Conchos
B ST J	Beverly St. John	Belt buckle
Bar B Bar	Ranch brand	Spurs
BM	nd	Spurs, spur straps, conchos
BMJ	nd	Spurs & spur straps
BMS	Bertha Sisco, sister of Sammy Sisco	Belt buckle
CFC	Clarks Fork Cattle Co.	Necklace, bridle
CLARA	Wife of Billing's dentist?	Belt buckle
Diamond Bar	Brand, Diamond Bar Ranch, Cody, Wyoming	Spurs
DON	Don Abarr	Bit
EKS	nd	Spurs
GHB	nd	Spurs
HJC	Howard Carroll	Belt buckle
HS	Harry Sharp	Bridle rosettes
JB	Julia Brown, mother of Beverly St. John	Earrings
JCN	"Kid" Nichols, Diamond Bar Ranch, Cody, Wyoming	Spurs
JIM BRIDGER RODEO	1947, trophy	Hat band
JK	John Kapor, son of Sigrid Kapor	Bolo tie clasp
"Lazy JD"	Valley Ranch Brand	Spurs, bit
LT	nd	Bridle rosettes
M	Michele Kapor, daughter of Sigrid Kapor	Belt
O hanging E	Esp ranch brand	Belt buckle
RBL	nd	Spurs
Rudy Mudra	—	Leather belt with Hulbert buckle
SIG	Sigrid Kapor, Clarks Fork Cattle Co., Montana	Belt
SK	Sigrid Kapor	Jewelry
VERA	nd	Belt buckle
WALT SECREST	Cowboy	Two rodeo buckles
WJM	Woodson Moss	Spurs

Footnotes:
1. This list is limited to the silver items shown in this book; it is clear that many more were made, especially as horse show and rodeo trophies, as well as commissioned pieces.
2. nd, not determined.

Hulbert's output of bits and spurs was noteworthy, especially because he was a one-man outfit with primitive, self-made tools. Photographs of his shop at Hillsboro are shown in Figures 1-2 through 1-8. Taken long after all his tools were removed, one can yet appreciate the limited space and lighting in which Hulbert worked. Many of his customers were local cowmen, cowboys, and their families, and ranches such as the Valley Ranch ("Lazy JD" brand) of Valley, Wyoming, ordered their bits and spurs with their brand. In later years, Hulbert made trophy belt buckles for rodeos and personalized jewelry for his clients. A list of some of Hulbert's customers, as reflected in the initials, names, and brands on silver pieces shown in this book, can be found in Table 2. At best it is an abbreviated list, and many of the designated individuals remain unidentified.

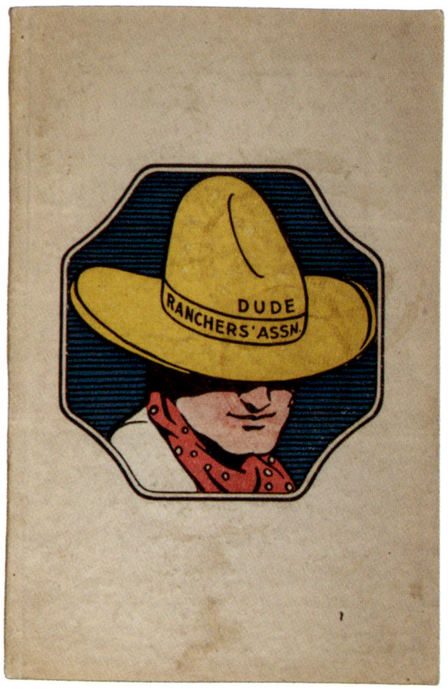

Figure 1-9. Advertising by Eddy Hulbert. Cover, Minutes of the Fourth Annual Dude Ranchers' Meeting, Held at Billings, Montana in the Northern Hotel Tea Room. November 18, 19, 20, 1929. S.E. Boyer & Co./Casper, Wyoming. *Courtesy of Jay Lyndes. Photo by J. Williams.*

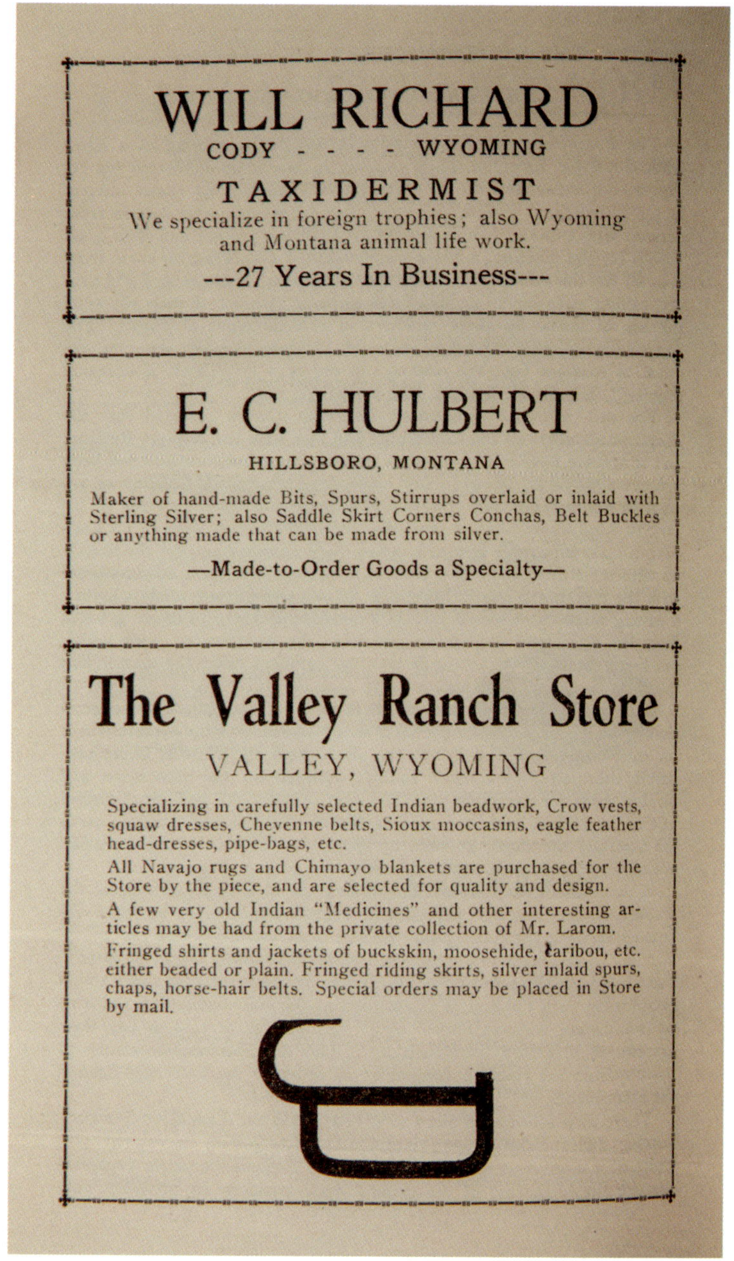

WILL RICHARD
CODY - - - - WYOMING
TAXIDERMIST
We specialize in foreign trophies; also Wyoming and Montana animal life work.
---27 Years In Business---

E. C. HULBERT
HILLSBORO, MONTANA
Maker of hand-made Bits, Spurs, Stirrups overlaid or inlaid with Sterling Silver; also Saddle Skirt Corners Conchas, Belt Buckles or anything made that can be made from silver.
—Made-to-Order Goods a Specialty—

The Valley Ranch Store
VALLEY, WYOMING
Specializing in carefully selected Indian beadwork, Crow vests, squaw dresses, Cheyenne belts, Sioux moccasins, eagle feather head-dresses, pipe-bags, etc.
All Navajo rugs and Chimayo blankets are purchased for the Store by the piece, and are selected for quality and design.
A few very old Indian "Medicines" and other interesting articles may be had from the private collection of Mr. Larom.
Fringed shirts and jackets of buckskin, moosehide, caribou, etc. either beaded or plain. Fringed riding skirts, silver inlaid spurs, chaps, horse-hair belts. Special orders may be placed in Store by mail.

Figure 1-10. Advertising by Eddy Hulbert inserted in Minutes (see Fig. 1-9). Note the ad (immediately below) for the Valley Ranch Store (Lazy JD brand), one of Hulbert's major customers (see Figure 1-13 and Chapters 2 and 3). *Courtesy of Jay Lyndes. Photo by J. Williams.*

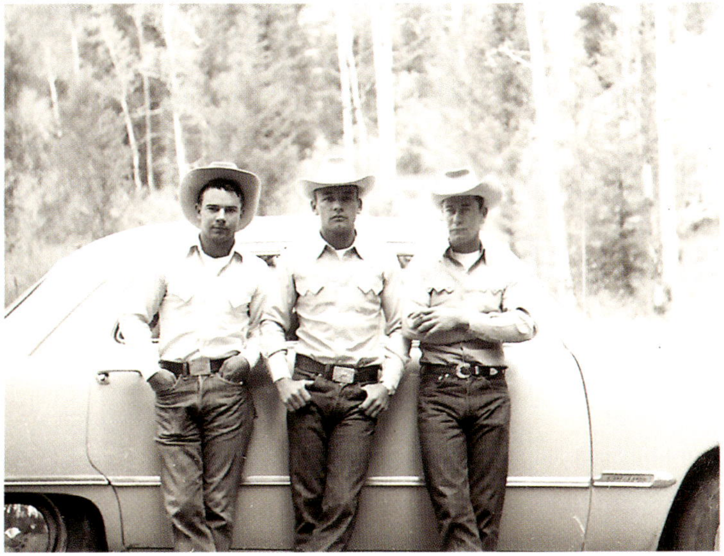

Figure 1-11. Scope of Hulbert's Work and Clientele. Three handsome rodeo cowboys—all wearing Eddy Hulbert belt buckles. From left to right: Donny Murdock, Hank Esp, and John Hammett, c. late 1940s/early 1950s. Compare the buckles on Esp and Hammett with those worn by these men in 2006, in front of Hulbert's shop (Figure 1-5). *Courtesy of Arne Esp. Photographer unknown.*

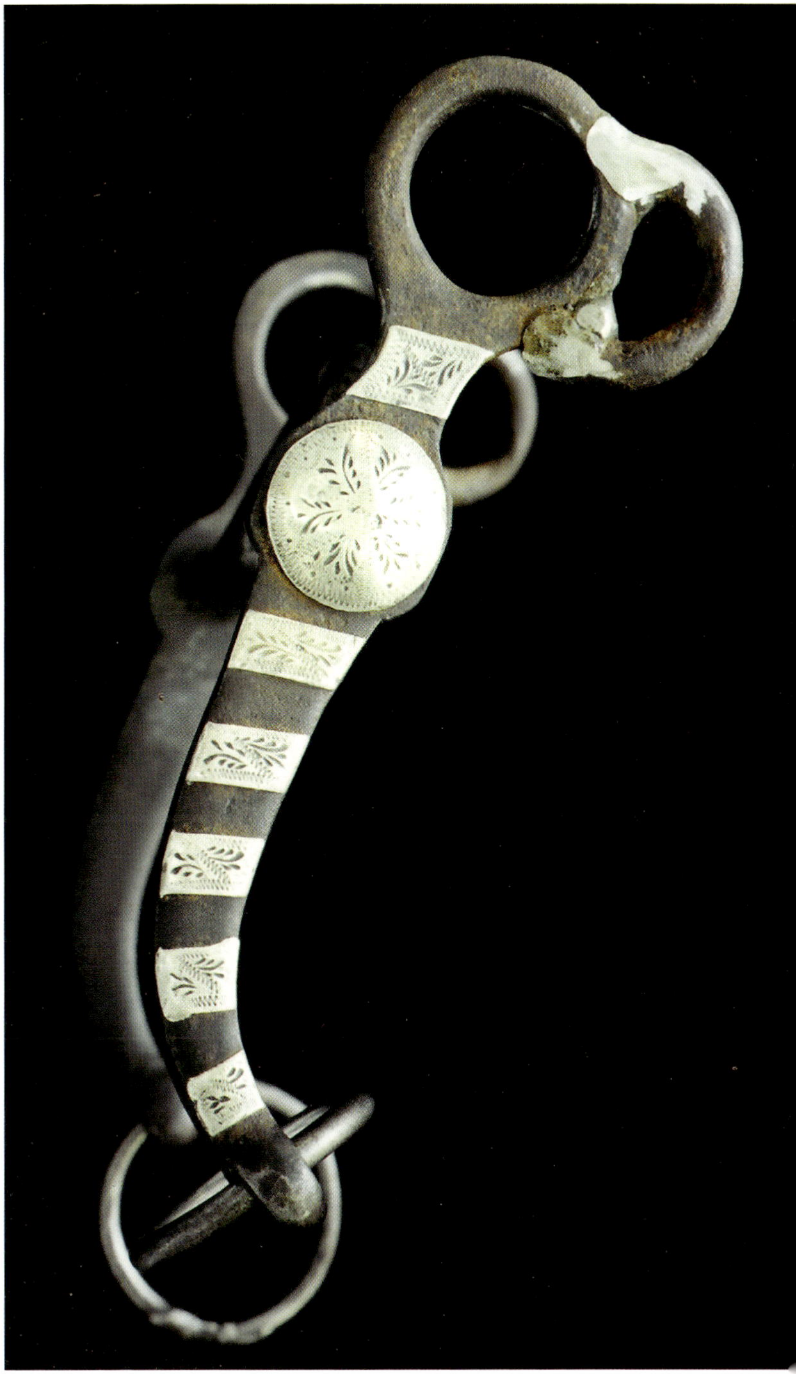

Figure 1-12. Scope of Hulbert's Work and Clientele. This "grazer" or grazing bit (see Chapter 3) was owned by John Hammett. The engraved silver banana cheek bit has seen hard use and shows (non-Hulbert) repairs on the loops next to the bridle rings (top). *Courtesy of Arne Esp. Photo by A. Esp.*

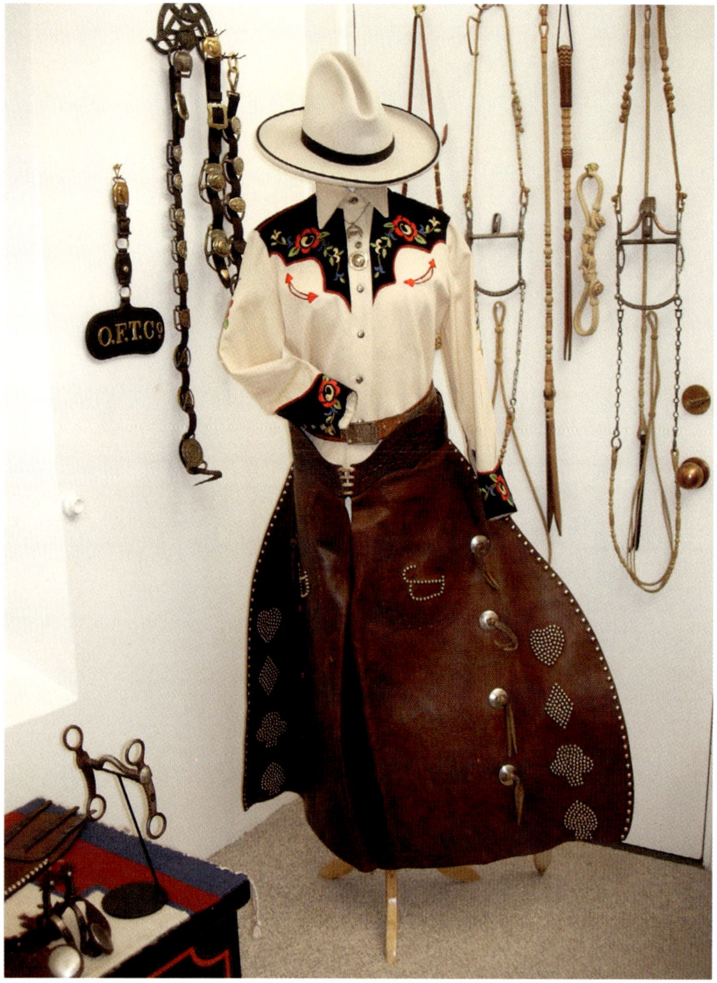

Figure 1-13. Scope of Hulbert's Work and Clientele. Shown on the model are an embroidered shirt with Hulbert-engraved silver buttons, a necklace with gold initials "CFC" (Clarks Fork Cattle Co., Dryhead, MT), engraved silver pin with gold heart, and an engraved banded silver belt with a square buckle (gold hearts, "SIG," and "CFC"). The Clarks Fork Cattle Co. was owned by Mike and Sigrid Kapor. More details on these items can be found in Chapters 3, 4, and 5. Also shown is a pair of ladies' brown leather batwing chaps with studded card suits and the Valley Ranch brand on the pockets, c. 1930-1940 (see Chapter 2 for details on the Valley Ranch). *Photo by author.*

Advertising was an important factor in the promotion and sale of Hulbert's work. Shown in Figures 1-9 and 1-10 is a 1929 brochure containing minutes from the Fourth Annual Dude Rancher's meeting (Billings), as well as Hulbert's ad for his silverwork ("overlaid or inlaid, always in Sterling"). Two phrases stand out as hallmarks of his career: "Anything made that can be made from silver," and "Made-to-order Goods a Specialty." An advertisement for the Valley Ranch Store appears below Hulbert's ad, and it is interesting that "silver inlaid spurs" form part of its inventory.

TABLE 3. Saddlery Catalogs Featuring Spurs, Bits, and Stirrups made by Eddy Hulbert[1]

Catalog (date)[2]	Item and number[3]
Hamley, #22 (1922)	np
Hamley, #25 (1925)	Spurs H54; stirrups H200
Hamley, #27 (1927)	Spurs H20, H25, H70
Hamley, #32 (1932)	Spurs H32, H70; bit 170; stirrups H200
Hamley, #35 (1935)	Bit 170
Hamley, #36 (1936)	np
Hamley, #42 (1942)	np
Ernst #11 (1930s)	Spurs E20, E25, E54, E70; bit 170; stirrups E200
Ernst, #13 (1930s)	Spurs 20-A, 25-A, 54-A, 70-A
Mueller, #52 (1930)	Spurs M20, M25, M54, M70; bit 170; stirrups M200
Mueller, #58 (1931)	Stirrups M200
Mueller, #70 (1934)	np

Footnotes:

1. There were probably other vendors that sold Hulbert stock, e.g., Connelly's Western Wear (Billings, MT) (Reid, 1998). The Table lists major saddleries and cowboy outfitters but is not all-inclusive.
2. Hamley and Company (Pendleton, OR); Otto F. Ernst, Inc. (Sheridan, WY); The Fred Mueller Saddle and Harness Company (Denver, CO).
3. np, not present.

Saddlery and tack store catalogs were even more critical to Hulbert's sales and exposure. Table 3 lists several different companies that featured Hulbert's spurs, stirrups, and/or bits in their catalogs: Hamley & Company (Pendleton, Oregon, 1924–1935), Otto F. Ernst, Inc. (Sheridan, Wyoming, 1930s), and the Fred Mueller Saddle & Harness Co. (Denver, Colorado, early 1930s). All of the items pictured in these catalogs appear in later chapters of this book.

Examples of the scope of Eddy Hulbert's work are shown in Figures 1-11 through 1-13. These pieces serve as an introduction to his engraving style as well as his breadth and expertise. The three young rodeo cowboys shown in Figure 1-11 are all wearing Hulbert belt buckles (Hank Esp's and John Hammett's buckles appear to be the same as those shown in Figure 1-5, still owned by these men more than 60 years later—see caption). Hank Esp, who still rides horseback and pilots an airplane, once

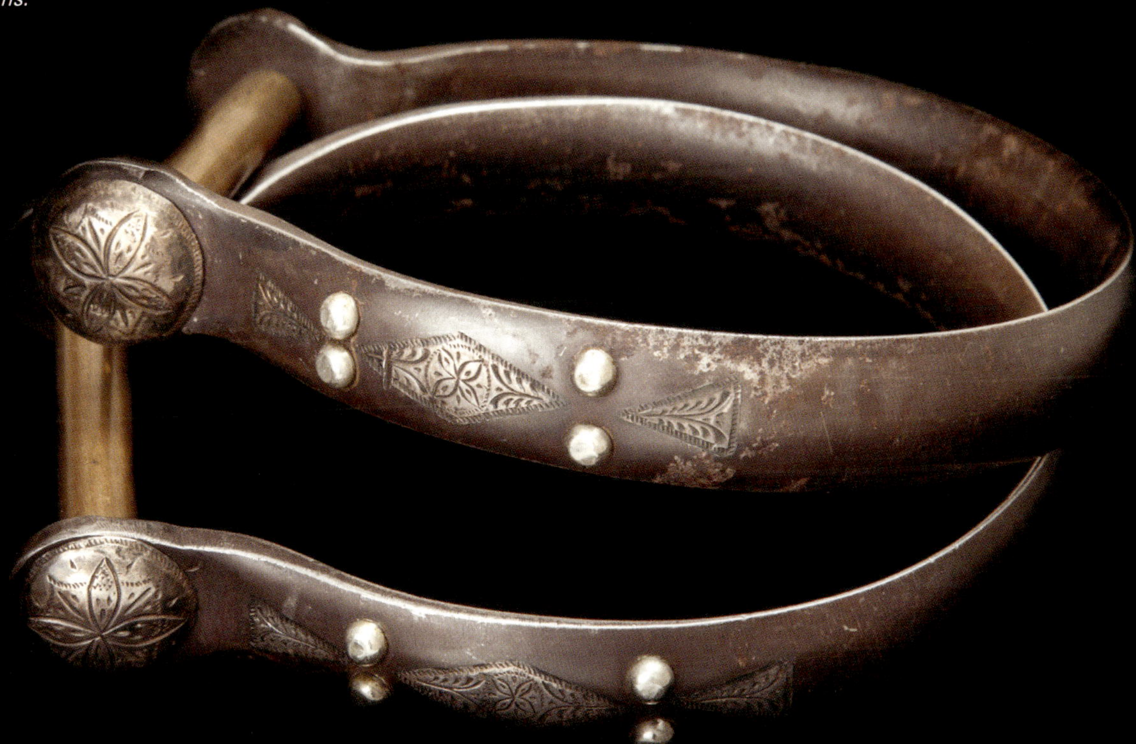

Figure 1-14. Saddle accessories by Hulbert. Hand-forged steel oxbow-style stirrups with engraved silver inlays. These signature stirrups were featured in several saddlery catalogs during the 1920s and 1930s. *Courtesy of the Nelson Museum of the West. Photo by J. Williams.*

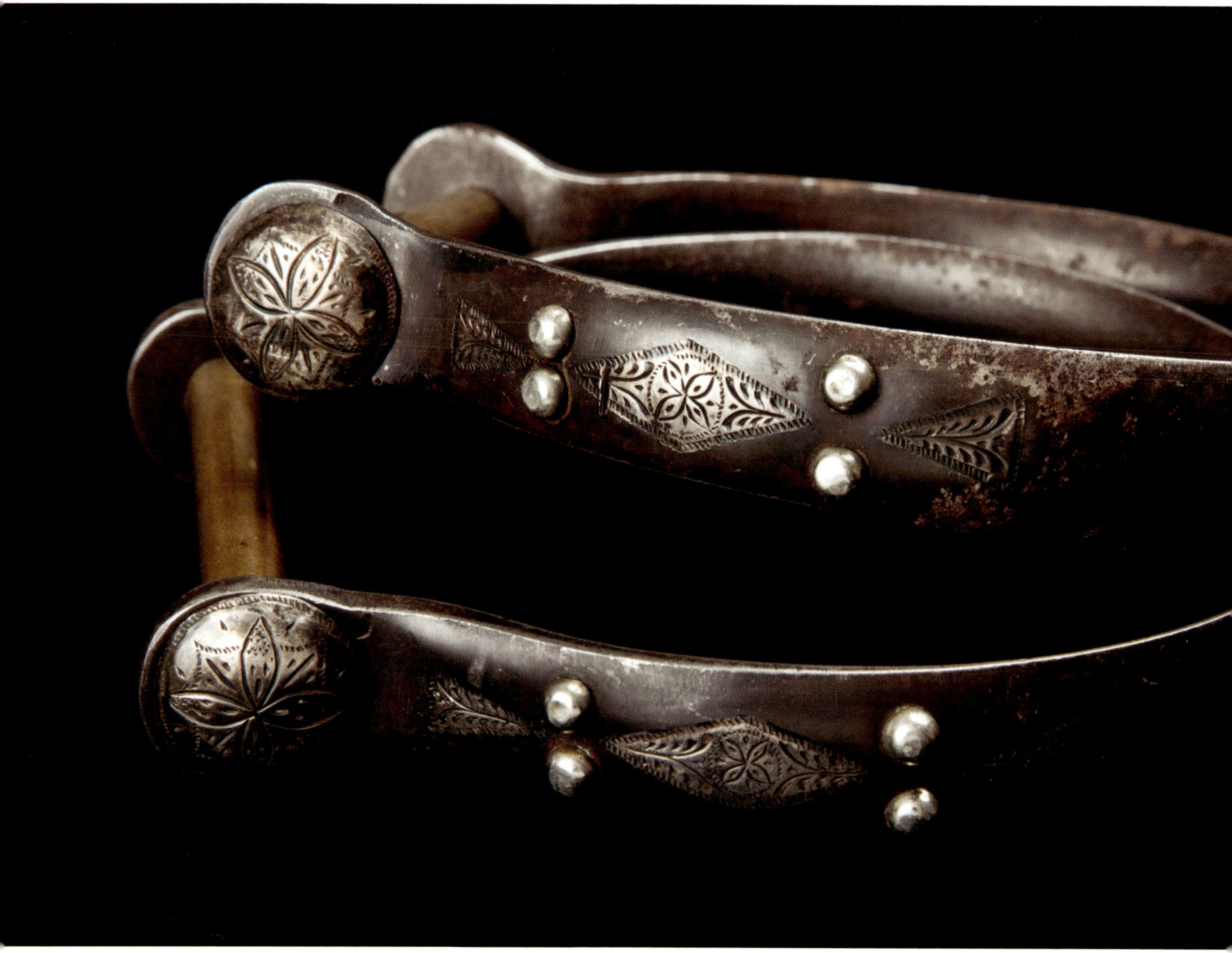

Figure 1-15. Stirrups by Hulbert: Enlarged view of Figure 1-14 showing engraved silver inlays, silver buttons, and silver bolt cap. *Courtesy of the Nelson Museum of the West. Photo by J. Williams.*

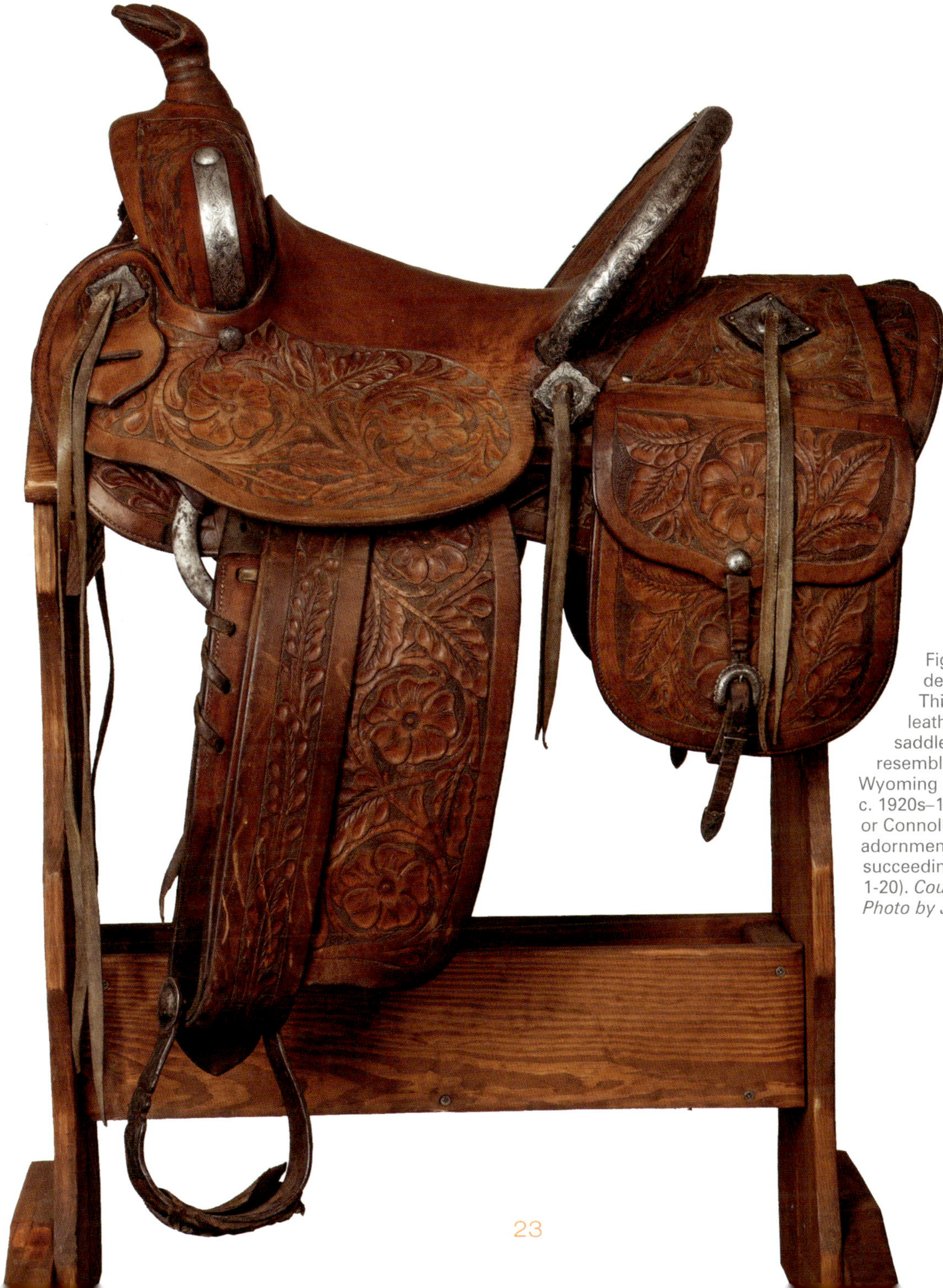

Figure 1-16. Saddle decorations by Hulbert. This handsome tooled leather saddle with matching saddle bags is unmarked but resembles work produced by Wyoming and Montana saddlemakers, c. 1920s–1940s, e.g., Otto Ernst or Connolly's. The Hulbert silver adornments are shown in the succeeding Figures (1-17 through 1-20). *Courtesy of Jay Lyndes. Photo by J. Williams.*

cowboyed for the Antler Ranch (as did his father, Henry R. Esp) and later established a cattle ranch west of Crow Agency, after his service in World War II. Both Hank and his son Arne ranch together on the Reservation, close to the Custer battlefield. Hammett was also employed by the Antler Ranch and would cross the Big Horn River from his camp on Gyp Creek to "visit" with his friend Eddy Hulbert.

The model in Figure 1-13 wears an embroidered Western-style shirt with silver buttons engraved by Hulbert. A silver necklace with the ranch designation "CFC" and a silver brooch are complemented by a silver-banded belt and an engraved buckle with "SIG" and "CFC" in gold letters. Mike and Sigrid Kapor owned the Clarks Fork Cattle Co. and clearly were clients of Hulbert's. Other examples of belt buckles and jewelry can be found in Chapters 4 and 5.

Saddle accessories formed another part of Hulbert's output. He was known for his hand-forged steel oxbow-style stirrups inlaid with engraved sterling silver. Shown in Figures 1-14 and 1-15, these stirrups were given the number 200, with a prefixed letter, in several saddlery catalogs.

Figures 1-16 through 1-20 showcase an interesting but unmarked saddle done in the Wyoming/Montana style, and decorated tastefully with Hulbert's contemporary silverwork (c. 1920s–1930s). Included in this ensemble are a silver-engraved cantle band, conchos highlighting the saddle strings (the diamond shape is unusual), buttons (to cover screws), and Ranger sets (buckle, keeper, and tip) on each saddlebag. The deep, bold, scroll-like engraving is characteristic of Hulbert's style and represents, more or less, his distinctive signature. Only a very few saddles decorated with Hulbert's silverwork are known. A photograph of what is believed

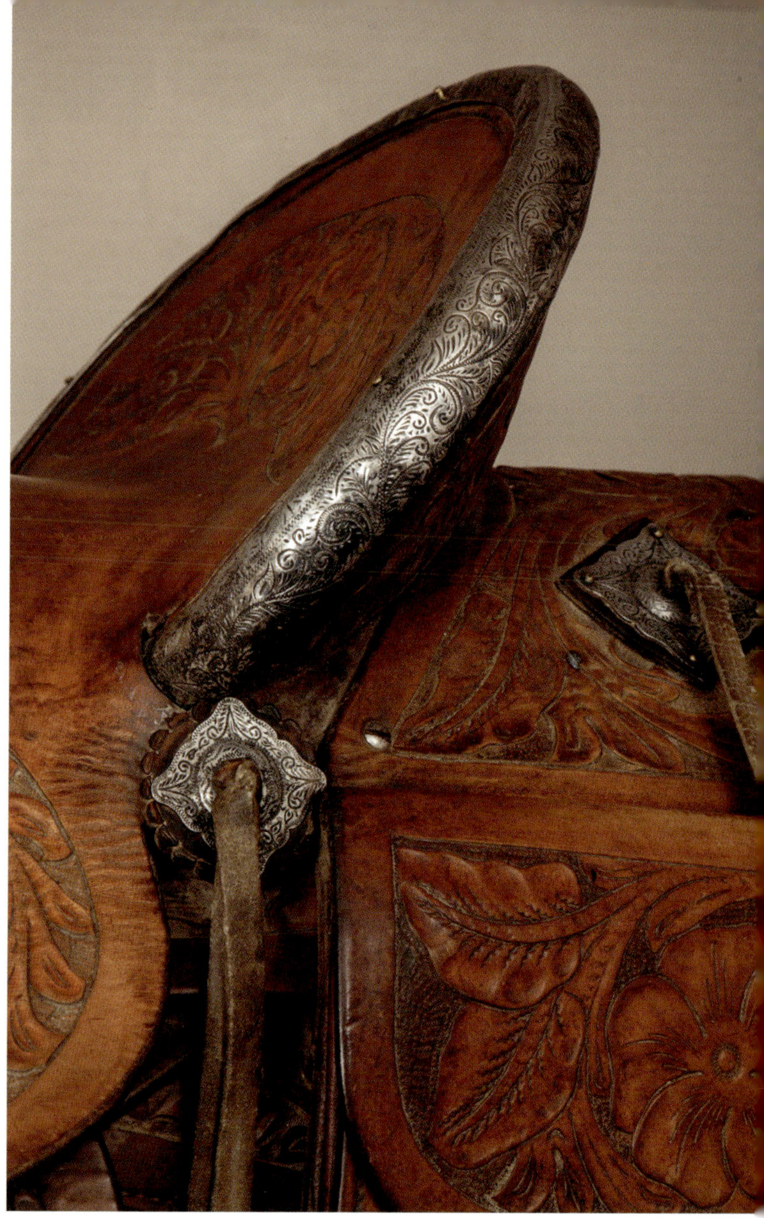

Figure 1-17. Saddle decorations by Hulbert. Cantle band and unusual diamond-shaped conchos; enlarged from Figure 1-16. *Courtesy of Jay Lyndes. Photo by J. Williams.*

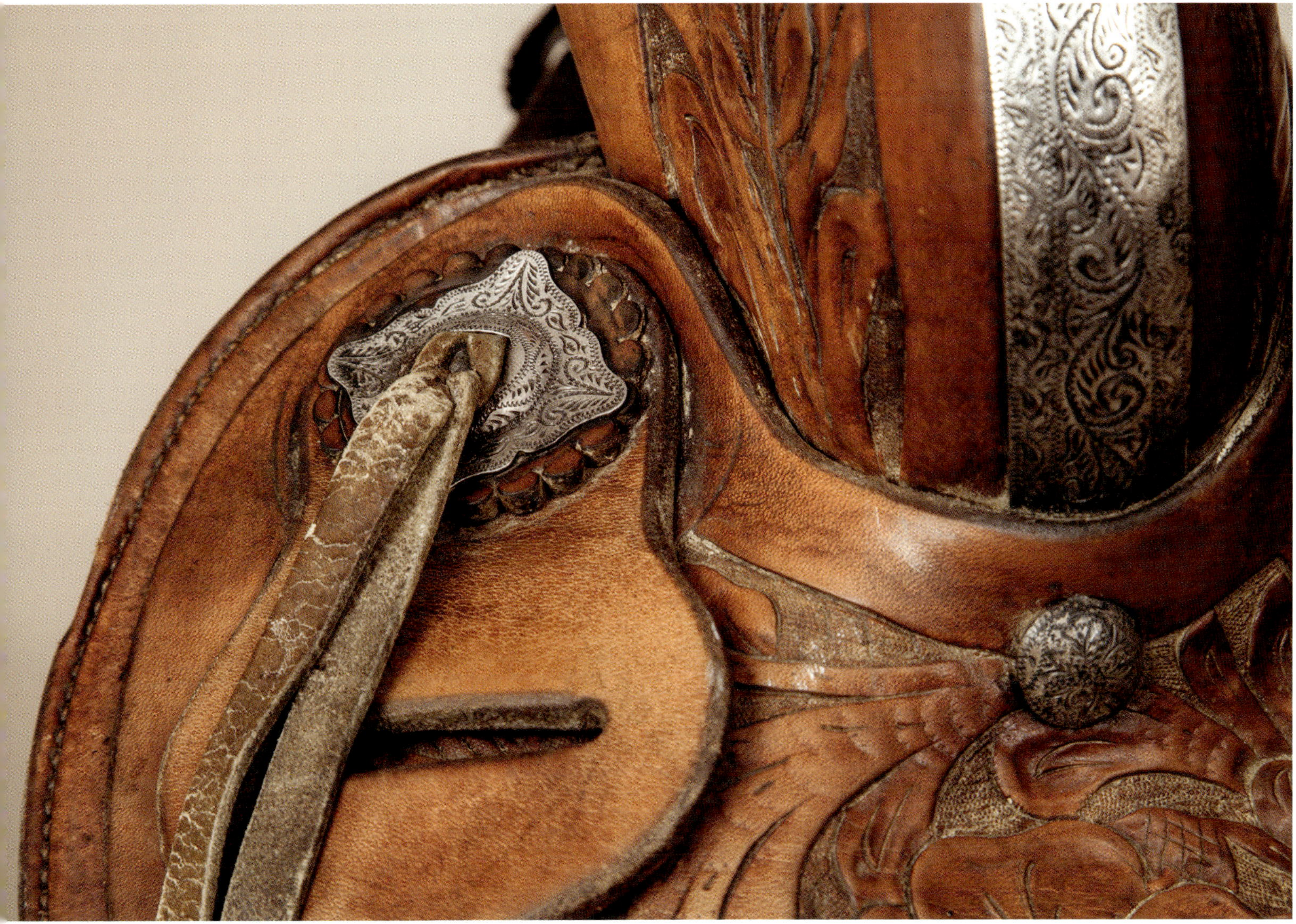

Figure 1-18. Saddle decorations by Hulbert. Pommel or fork band, silver button, and diamond-shaped saddle string concho; enlarged from Figure 1-16. *Courtesy of Jay Lyndes. Photo by J. Williams.*

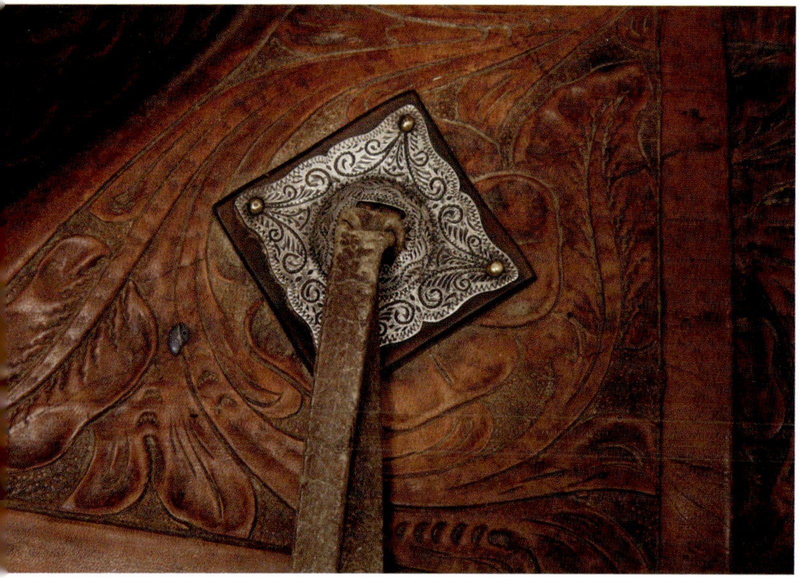

Figure 1-19. Saddle decorations by Hulbert. Diamond-shaped saddle string concho showing characteristic Hulbert style of bold engraving; enlarged from Figure 1-16. *Courtesy of Jay Lyndes. Photo by J. Williams.*

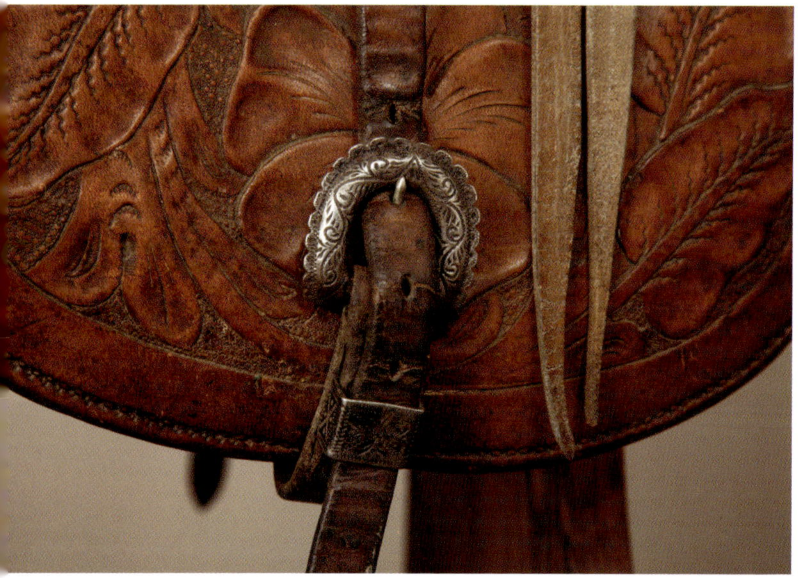

Figure 1-20. Saddle decorations by Hulbert. Buckle and keeper on saddle bag. The scalloped edge and bold engraving are Hulbert hallmarks; enlarged from Figure 1-16. *Courtesy of Jay Lyndes. Photo by J. Williams.*

to be the same saddle shown in Figures 1-16 through 1-20 was taken at a horse show in Billings, Montana, in 1940 (Figure 1-21). The floral-tooled leather saddlebags are identical, with the unusual diamond-shaped silver concho above the Ranger set. There are pommel and cantle silver bands, and the horn is canted at the same angle as the saddle shown in Figure 1-16. The stirrups with inlaid heart are clearly Hulbert. The martingale and bridle, a Parade set, were also made by Hulbert (see a similar set in Chapter 3). The inscription in the lower-right corner is "CHAPPLE'S–PETEK PHOTO." Chapple's was a drugstore in Billings, and Petek was a professional photographer (c. 1930s–1940s) who worked the rodeo/horse show circuits and was located in the photography department of the store.

The poem written by Jack Horan (Figure 1-22) accompanied the photo shown in Figure 1-21 and identifies the rider as Nibs Hartmam and the horse as Trifles. Penned in "cowboy English" to his friend, the faded yellow notebook paper shows sincere sentiment for the "old days" of the open range.

Eddy Hulbert had some interesting neighbors in the Dryhead area, many of whom are listed in Reid's book (1998). They are of interest here because some of them became Hulbert's customers who requested personalized items. For example, Don Abarr, whose bit is shown in Chapter 3, was born to a homesteading family in the Dryhead (Medicine Creek) area and graduated from the Dryhead School in May, 1936 (Abarr, 1989). He knew Hulbert and interacted with him as a cowboy and horse-trainer. In his book, *Hoofbeats on the Wind* (1989), he recounts a "horse deal" with Hulbert, in which (at the age of 14) he received a Hackney/Morgan black gelding branded "EH" on the left shoulder (named Omaha) as a payment for building a house and reservoir on Hulbert's homestead (Pete's Canyon). Unfortunately, the marriage Hulbert had planned with "the dude girl from Omaha" did not come about.

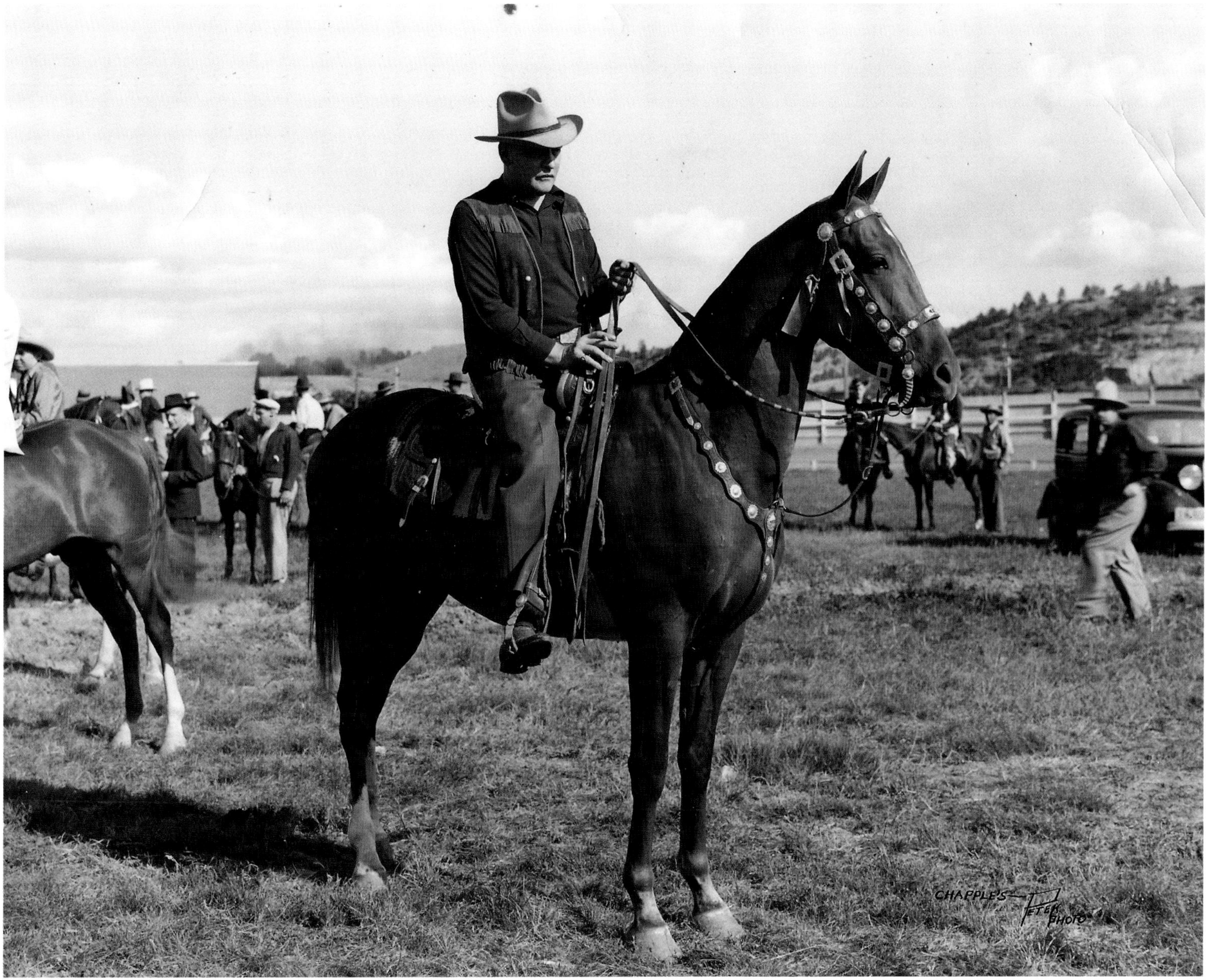

Figure 1-21. Hulbert saddle. This rare photo, inscribed "CHAPPLE'S—PETEK PHOTO" in the lower right corner, was taken at a Billings, Montana horse show in 1940. The saddle appears to be the one shown in Figures 1-16 through 1-20. Note the floral-tooled saddlebags with silver Ranger set and diamond-shaped concho, cantle, and pommel (fork) silver bands, and heart-inlaid stirrups. The floral-tooled leather and shape of the tree and horn confirm the identification. The silver on the parade bridle and martingale set are also Hulbert's work. *Courtesy of Jim Nett.*

Another interesting neighbor was the infamous Caroline Lockhart, a talented, complex, and rather difficult woman who ranched (L Slash Heart brand) in the Dryhead area in Wasson Canyon. Despite her being one of the founders of the Cody Stampede (Cody, Wyoming), she made enemies of most of the local ranchers, including Edith Barry, whom she termed "Old Satan" (diary entry of April 24, 1927—Hicks, 1984). She also referred to Eddy (Eddie) Hulbert as "The Ape," doubtless prompted by his physiognomy, despite the favors he performed on her behalf (diary entry of October 3, 1925—Hicks, 1984). An excellent study of this author and journalist with the acerbic, razor-sharp tongue, who failed to achieve recognition as the "Cattle Queen of Montana," is found in Furman (1994).

The NeVille family has a history in Dryhead contemporaneous with that of Eddy Hulbert's later years. Keith NeVille (1920–1974) bought a ranch there in 1950 and purchased several bits, spurs, and buckles custom-ordered from Hulbert. Mike NeVille, his son, met Hulbert in 1955 and again in 1959 at the St. Johns' house, under which Hulbert had engineered a creek to flow for cooling purposes during the hot summers of Hillsboro. A prized possession that has remained in the family was a silver-ferruled bridle that Mike's sister used on their Arabian stud for appearances in local parades and rodeos. A photograph of this bridle, as well as other pieces made by Hulbert for the NeVilles, is shown in Reid (1998).

One might speculate on the reasons Hulbert's work had virtually been ignored in the literature until Reid's book appeared in 1998. Jane Pattie's superb study, *Cowboy Spurs and their Makers*, does not mention him (Pattie, 1994). Hicks (1984) misspells Hulbert's name and terms his two-stroke engine, outside his Hillsboro shop, an "interesting contraption; the purpose of which is now a mystery." Yet Hulbert's bits and spurs were not only used by working cowboys and ranchmen, but his trophy buckles and jewelry were also in demand and widely appreciated throughout the communities of Carbon County and Billings, Montana. Certainly much of his work was collected and saved for posterity. Several books published in the 1990s that were devoted to cowboy collectibles do mention Hulbert: all issues (1-6) of the Hutchinses' *Old Cowboy Saddles and Spurs* state that "Edward C. Hulbert made spurs in the 1920s and 30s [sic] in Kane, Wyoming. He was known for his nice quality silver mounted spurs. He marked them 'E.H.' (with a rounded shape)." Some of these inaccuracies were corrected in the seventh edition by Graham and Graham (2003): "Edmond Cummings Hulbert was born in 1898. He was self-taught and made most of his spurs in Hillsboro, MT. 1920s–1940s. Hulbert died on July 12, 1960. He marked his spurs 'EH' (with a rounded shape)." A single pair of Hulbert spurs is pictured in Mackin's encyclopedic collectibles guide (1995) and are described thus: "These beautifully crafted silver and gold overlaid and inlaid spurs are marked 'E.H.' for Wyoming maker, Ed Hulbert. They combine the swing button Texas bands with a stylish California shank." These spurs, with their gold initials "CPC," were presumably made for the owner; similar styles can be seen in Chapter 2.

In the following four chapters, Hulbert's work has been grouped according to the items that he designed, fashioned, and embellished: spurs, bits and bridles, belts and belt buckles, and jewelry. The generosity of several collectors has made it possible to show a wide variety of Hulbert's engraving styles and artistry. Chapter 6 describes two of Hulbert's contemporaries, Ed Klapmeier and C.E. O'Such, both of Miles City, Montana. Parallels and differences in their work will become obvious. The beauty of these utilitarian as well as decorative silver pieces cannot escape one's appreciation and admiration.

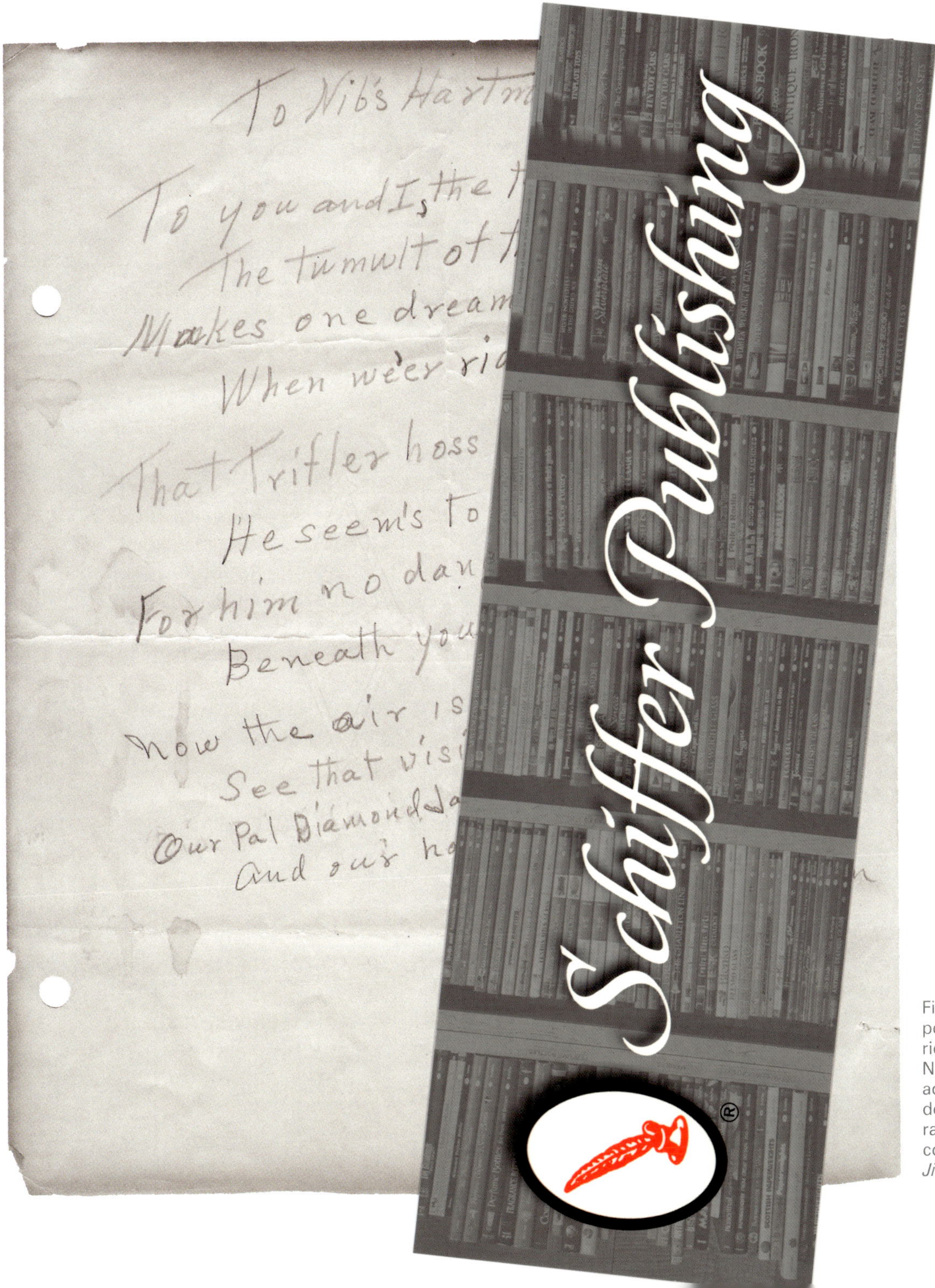

Figure 1-22. Hulbert saddle—poem. This poem, written by Jack Horan, identifies the rider shown in the photo (Figure 1-21) as Nibs Hartmam and the horse as Trifles. It accompanied the photograph and shows deep feeling for the "old days" of the open range. Horan is the author of a book of cowboy poems, *Burnt Leather. Courtesy of Jim Nett.*

Spurs

Judging by the length of this chapter, relative to the other chapters, one might conclude that Eddy Hulbert produced more spurs than any other item. Possibly, but there are no inventories or other records to guide us in this respect. It is clear that he made spurs over the duration of his career (a pair dated "1960," the year of his death, is shown in Figure 2-78), whereas jewelry pieces, especially the custom-ordered or commissioned varieties, were made later in his career, and obviously as a limited or single output. Spurs, as well as bits, were utilitarian objects needed by cowboys, ranchers, and horsemen; their design, beauty, and in some cases, personal designations also made them collectors' items that were retained over several generations of ranching families. That some styles of Hulbert's spurs were marketed commercially by saddlery/harness outlets would indicate that a supply or inventory of these pieces would have had to be on hand. Many, if not most, of these spurs were not marked with the characteristic "EH," cut with a rounded tool.

Hulbert's spurs were of the "Northern Plains" type, a designation broadly classified as a combination of California and Texas styles (Pattie, 1994). Because the design of the spur had to match the needs of the cowboy, as dictated by the geography of the range, weather conditions, type of boot worn, size and training of the horses ridden, and general level of use, regional differences developed that were implemented by local spurmakers. For example, spurs of Wyoming and Montana were typically of one-piece construction (see below), rather than the two-piece varieties typical of California, though were often decorated with engraved silver inlays or overlays and conchos, more reminiscent of the California style. These are generalizations for which many exceptions can be found—some highly artistic and collectible spurs of the Northern Plains area were made by the Qualey Brothers (Grangeville, Idaho), Phillips and Gutierrez (Cheyenne, Wyoming), and Schnitger (Gillette, Wyoming). Some collectors have claimed that Hulbert was influenced by spurmakers at the Cañon City Prison (Cañon City, Colorado) (see Maul and Ferguson, 1995, for a description of this style). However, any real similarities between Cañon City and Eddy Hulbert are more likely to be coincidental.

A brief description of the construction of hand-forged, one-piece, silver-decorated spurs, as Eddy Hulbert made, is necessary, beginning with the parts of a spur (as referred to in Figure captions): 1) the *heelband* is generally the widest part of the spur and wraps around the heel of the boot; 2) the *shank* projects outward from the center of the heelband and accommodates the *rowel*, which is a wheel-like disc with spokes that rotate on a pin set between both sides of the shank and would contact the body of the horse; 3) *rowels* can be made in several different patterns, including (self-explanatory) a *sawtooth*, a *star*, *spokes*, and (most commonly) a *toothed* variety with any number of points, e.g., a 12-point rowel; 4) the *chap guard* is a projection off the upper surface of the shank that prevents the rider's chap cuffs from engaging the rowel; 5) *buttons* appear at the boot-ends of the heelbands for the attachment of the spur straps. They can be stationary or attached to a metal staple or loop that enables them to "swing" (*swinging buttons*, set straight or angled).

Hulbert was trained (but mostly self-taught) as a blacksmith at the Cedarvale Ranch. He therefore had knowledge of the use of a forge and the cutting and shaping of iron and other metals. He was also able to make or modify most of his tools (chisels, engraving tools, hammers, saws, punches, drills, awls, and files) and machinery (forge, bandsaw, polisher, vices). Many people over the years have commented on the apparent paradox between his sophisticated workmanship and the primitive conditions under which his pieces were created.

A detailed summary of one-piece spur construction as practiced by Hulbert, and by a more contemporary maker, has been provided by Reid (1998) and Pattie (1994), respectively. Briefly, an iron (or steel) bar approximately 5″ long is split down the middle for most of its length, and the two resulting halves are shaped at right angles to the uncut part, to form a T-shape. After the piece is heated, the split sides are flattened (hammered by hand) over a mold to form the two heelbands. The unsplit section becomes the shank, which is shaped according to design (e.g., a chap guard can be drawn off) and split to accept the rowel and its pin. Holes are drilled for the rowel pin and, if needed, staples (for the swinging button) and heel chains.

By this point the spur has been filed and sanded to remove rough edges and hammer marks, and has been heated in the forge to temper/strengthen it. Hulbert used patterns for his rowels, which were punched out of heated metal and later hand-filed and at times decorated with punch marks and/or engraved discs. These rowel patterns are shown in Figure 2-10 and also in Reid (1998). It is likely that Hulbert also cut metal discs by hand (saw) and thereby created his own designs. The final step was the inlaying or overlaying of silver—on the heelband edges, buttons, shank, and sometimes on the inner circumference of the rowel (*rowel disc* or *cover*). The silver to be used was cut into the desired shape and fitted into a chiseled-out depression on the spur area to be inlaid.

The silver piece was crimped down for a secure fit such that water and hence, rust, would not compromise the mounting. Hulbert might have used a silver solder as well, but there are many aspects of his procedures that are not clear. For overlays, the silver was positioned on the surface of the spur, e.g., the heelband, and set permanently with a type of solder. Silver discs were set on top of bolt heads or similar metal shapes to decorate stationary or swinging buttons. The silver mounts were ready for engraving, and in some cases, gold letters or ranch brands were added as final touches. It is believed that Hulbert's engraving was, for the most part, freehand. It is possible, however, that for some pieces he used a pre-drawn pattern of his own design.

Advertisements for Hulbert Spurs—Standard Patterns

As listed in Table 3, several saddlery and tack stores carried Hulbert's work. This inventory was limited to his oxbow stirrups, a few bits, and to three or four styles of his spurs. Figure 2-1 is a page from the Otto F. Ernst, Inc. catalog (1930s) that featured four styles of spurs, with the proviso that the customer could substitute his own preference regarding shank and rowels. Three of these spurs appear in the Hamley & Company catalog (1927) (Figure 2-2), again with variations if desired (e.g., straight, turned up, or swinging buttons; shank; rowels). Hamley's advertisement is a ringing endorsement of Hulbert's work:

> The three spurs shown below were designed by Montana cowboys and made strictly according to their specifications. Reports from that part of the country are to the effect that these spurs are "just right." They say they are the proper weight, proper size bands, right length shanks, and that they hang as a spur should hang.

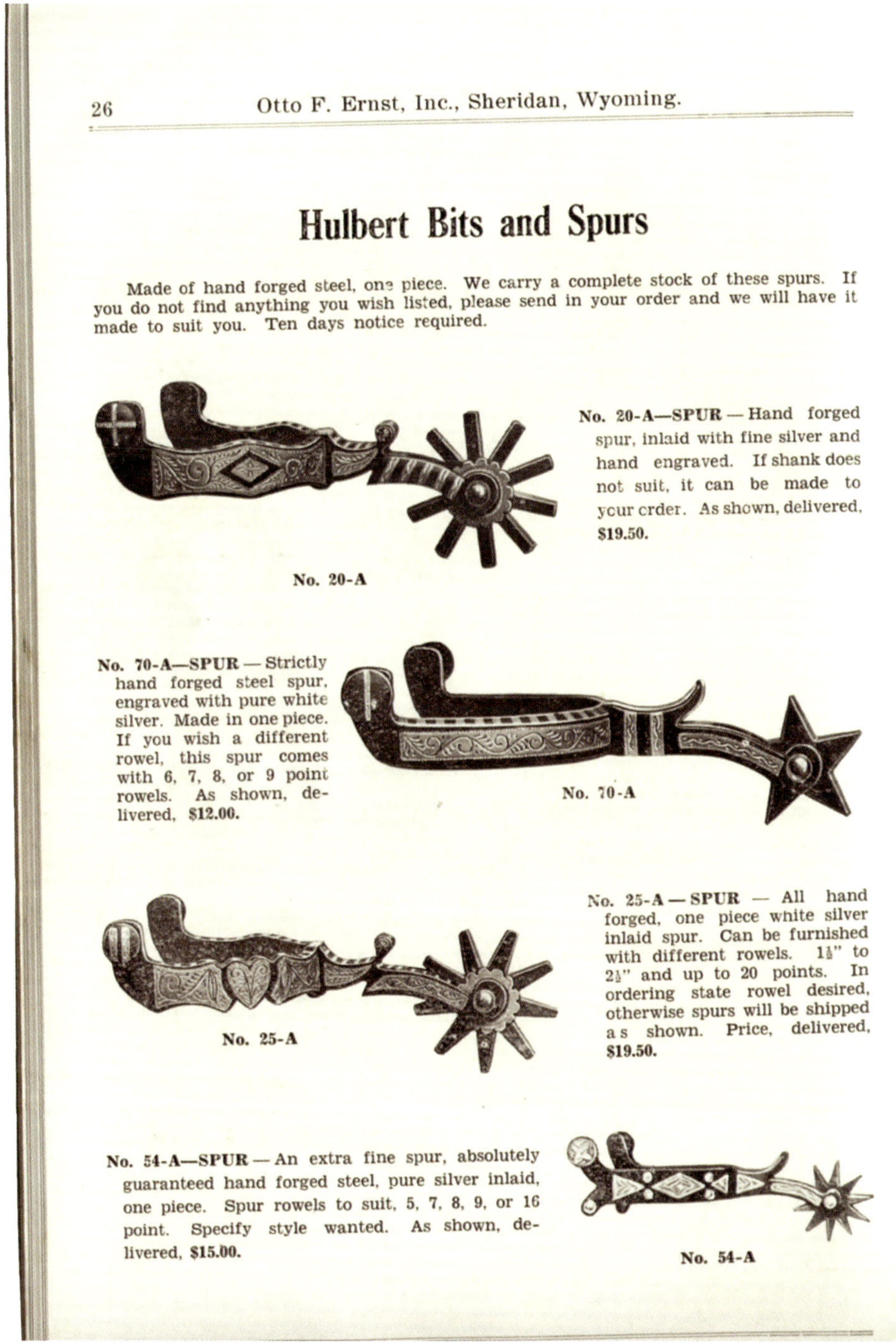

26 Otto F. Ernst, Inc., Sheridan, Wyoming.

Hulbert Bits and Spurs

Made of hand forged steel, one piece. We carry a complete stock of these spurs. If you do not find anything you wish listed, please send in your order and we will have it made to suit you. Ten days notice required.

No. 20-A

No. 20-A—SPUR—Hand forged spur, inlaid with fine silver and hand engraved. If shank does not suit, it can be made to your order. As shown, delivered, **$19.50.**

No. 70-A—SPUR—Strictly hand forged steel spur, engraved with pure white silver. Made in one piece. If you wish a different rowel, this spur comes with 6, 7, 8, or 9 point rowels. As shown, delivered, **$12.00.**

No. 70-A

No. 25-A

No. 25-A—SPUR—All hand forged, one piece white silver inlaid spur. Can be furnished with different rowels. 1½" to 2½" and up to 20 points. In ordering state rowel desired, otherwise spurs will be shipped as shown. Price, delivered, **$19.50.**

No. 54-A—SPUR—An extra fine spur, absolutely guaranteed hand forged steel, pure silver inlaid, one piece. Spur rowels to suit, 5, 7, 8, 9, or 16 point. Specify style wanted. As shown, delivered, **$15.00.**

No. 54-A

Figure 2-1. Advertisements for Hulbert Spurs. Four popular styles of Hulbert spurs are shown on page 26 of a 1930s catalog distributed by Otto F. Ernst, Inc., Sheridan, Wyoming, examples of which appear in succeeding figures. *Courtesy of Joseph Sherwood.*

Examples of these "catalog" spurs appear in succeeding figures. Figures 2-3 through 2-9 show in detail a pair of Hulbert "heart"-style spurs that differ in several respects from Hamley's H25 model. Engraving details and the "EH" mark are described in the respective captions. A collection of rowel patterns used by Hulbert is shown in Figure 2-10.

A variation of the "diamond" pattern spur H20 (Hamley's designation) appears in Figure 2-11, and of pattern H70, in Figures 2-12 and 2-13. The marked pair (Figure 2-13) was probably not purchased from a saddlery catalog. More catalog-featured spurs, or variations thereof, are shown in Figures 2-15 and 2-16 ("geometric," Ernst's No. 54-A), and in Figure 2-17 ("diamond," H20). A "bar" pattern spur was also popular among Hulbert's clientele, as shown in Figure 2-14.

The next group of figures is a collection of Hulbert's advertising cards and correspondence. His "#40" spur (Figures 2-18 and 2-19), Nos. H20 and H25 (Figures 2-24 and 2-25), No. 170 (closely resembling Hamley's H70 spur) (Figures 2-26 and 2-27), and No. 50 ("bar inlay") (Figures 2-28 and 2-29), are shown with their accompanying descriptions.

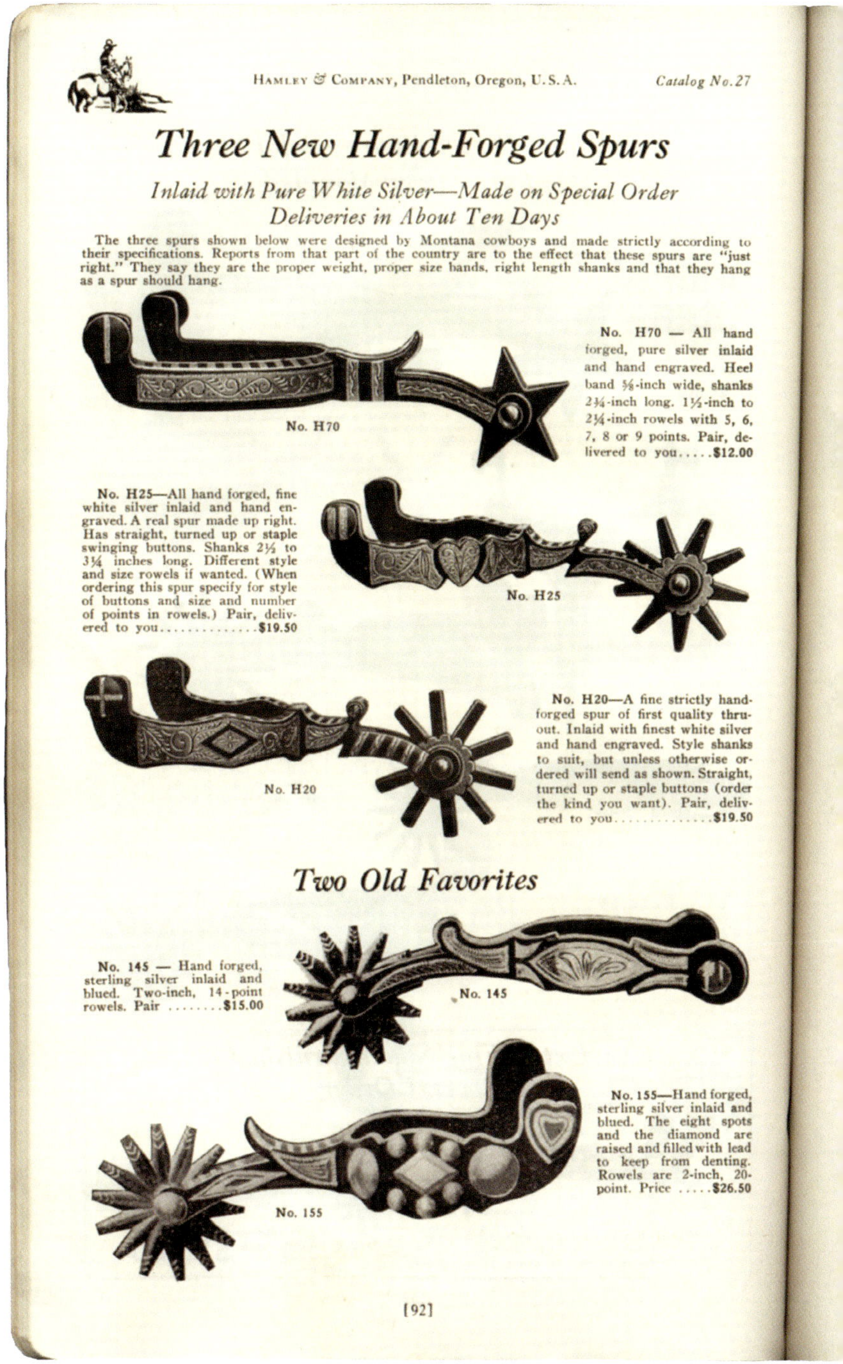
HAMLEY & COMPANY, Pendleton, Oregon, U.S.A. — Catalog No. 27

Three New Hand-Forged Spurs

Inlaid with Pure White Silver—Made on Special Order
Deliveries in About Ten Days

The three spurs shown below were designed by Montana cowboys and made strictly according to their specifications. Reports from that part of the country are to the effect that these spurs are "just right." They say they are the proper weight, proper size bands, right length shanks and that they hang as a spur should hang.

No. H70

No. H70 — All hand forged, pure silver inlaid and hand engraved. Heel band ⅝-inch wide, shanks 2¾-inch long. 1½-inch to 2¼-inch rowels with 5, 6, 7, 8 or 9 points. Pair, delivered to you.....$12.00

No. H25—All hand forged, fine white silver inlaid and hand engraved. A real spur made up right. Has straight, turned up or staple swinging buttons. Shanks 2½ to 3¼ inches long. Different style and size rowels if wanted. (When ordering this spur specify for style of buttons and size and number of points in rowels.) Pair, delivered to you..............$19.50

No. H25

No. H20

No. H20—A fine strictly hand-forged spur of first quality thruout. Inlaid with finest white silver and hand engraved. Style shanks to suit, but unless otherwise ordered will send as shown. Straight, turned up or staple buttons (order the kind you want). Pair, delivered to you..............$19.50

Two Old Favorites

No. 145 — Hand forged, sterling silver inlaid and blued. Two-inch, 14-point rowels. Pair $15.00

No. 145

No. 155—Hand forged, sterling silver inlaid and blued. The eight spots and the diamond are raised and filled with lead to keep from denting. Rowels are 2-inch, 20-point. Price $26.50

No. 155

[92]

Figure 2-2. Advertisements for Hulbert Spurs. Three styles (H20, H25, and H70) (also seen in Figure 2-1) are shown on page 92 of Hamley & Company's catalog No. 27 (1927). *Courtesy of Joseph Sherwood.*

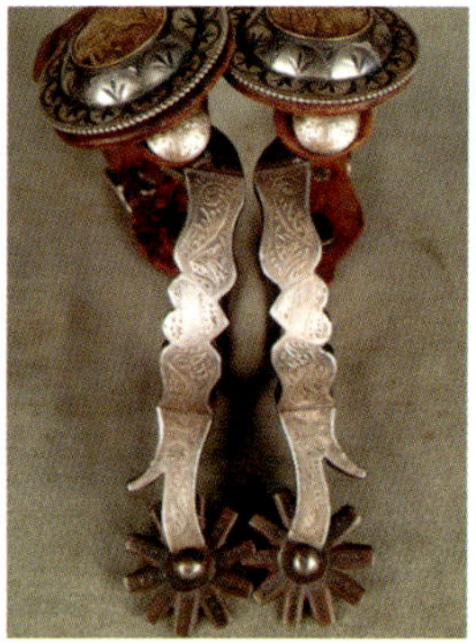

Figure 2-3. Hulbert "Heart"-style Men's Spurs. The heelbands of these spurs resemble style H25 (Figure 2-2), but there is no demarcation between the silver heart and flanking pieces (shown here as overlays), and the shanks and chap guards are clearly different. *Courtesy of B. Bartlett.*

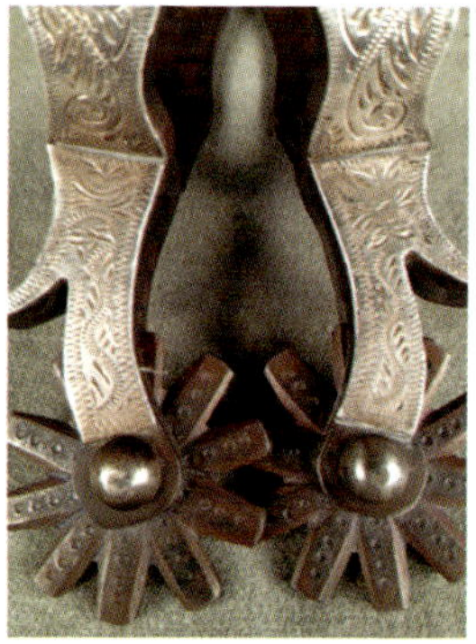

Figure 2-5. Heart Spurs (Figure 2-3) showing engraving detail on shanks and decorated 10-point rowels. *Courtesy of B. Bartlett.*

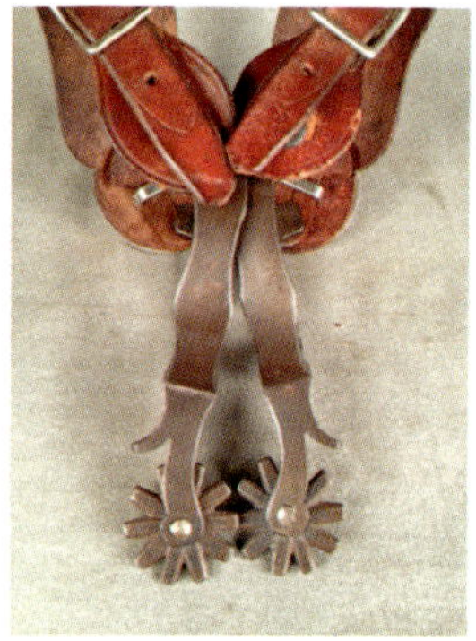

Figure 2-7. Heart Spurs (Figure 2-3) showing inside, plain heelbands and rowels. *Courtesy of B. Bartlett.*

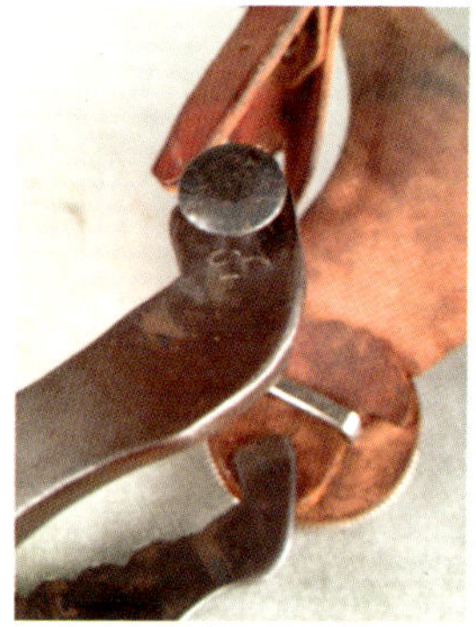

Figure 2-9. Heart Spurs (Figure 2-3) showing Eddy Hulbert's characteristic mark (EH, in curved letters) on the heelband close to the button. *Courtesy of B. Bartlett.*

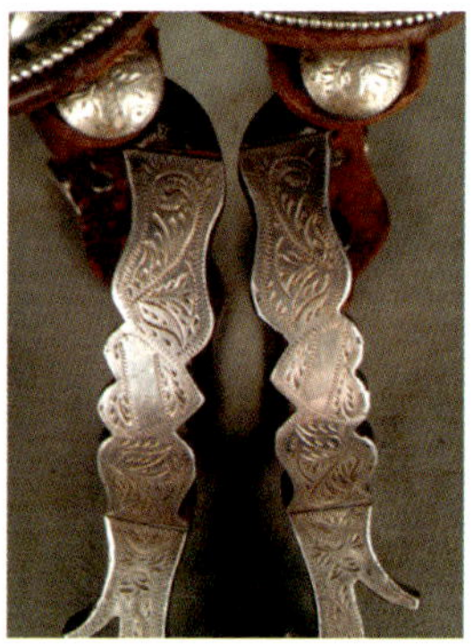

Figure 2-4. Heart Spurs (Figure 2-3) showing engraving detail on silver overlays. *Courtesy of B. Bartlett.*

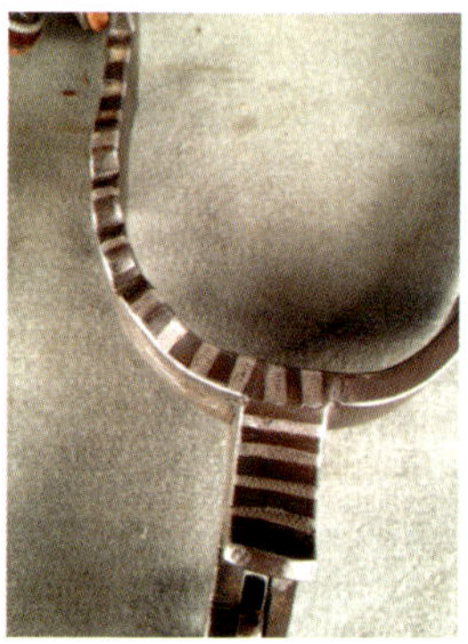

Figure 2-6. Heart Spurs (Figure 2-3) showing engraved silver inlays on under-edge of heelband and chap guard. Note that this pair of spurs is single-mounted, with the silver only on the outside heelband. *Courtesy of B. Bartlett.*

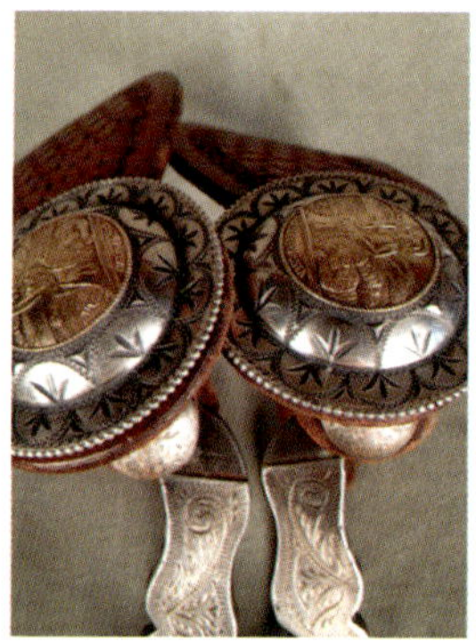

Figure 2-8. Heart Spurs (Figure 2-3) showing conchos fitted to spur straps, attached to the heel buttons. Note that these conchos are not by Hulbert but resemble a California style with a foreign coin in the center. *Courtesy of B. Bartlett.*

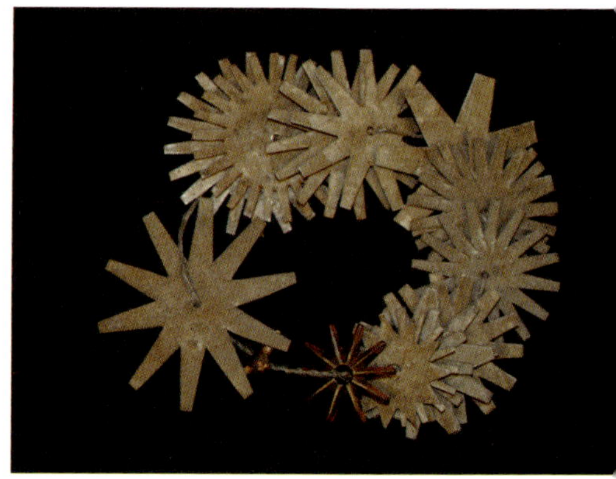

Figure 2-10. A collection of Rowel Patterns used by Hulbert. *Courtesy of R. Wilmot. William Manns photo.*

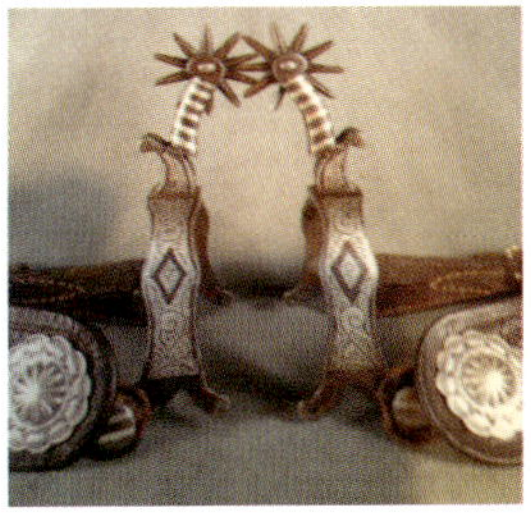

Figure 2-11. Hulbert Spurs, a Variation of "Diamond" Pattern H20 (Figure 2-2). These men's spurs are unmarked but are clearly Hulbert's work. They feature offset shanks, silver inlay, and Cheyenne split heelbands drilled for tie-downs. *Courtesy of C. Webb. Photo by B. Bartlett.*

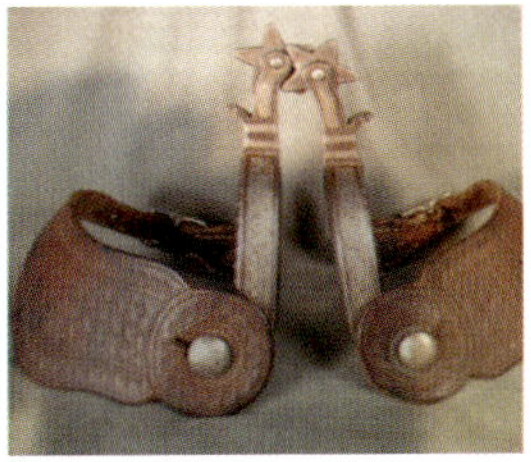

Figure 2-13. Hulbert Spurs, a Variation of Pattern H70 (Figure 2-2). This pair of silver-inlaid spurs is marked "EH" and features five-point star rowels. The dimensions of the shanks differ slightly from those of H70, and the buttons are plain. *Courtesy of C. Webb. Photo by B. Bartlett.*

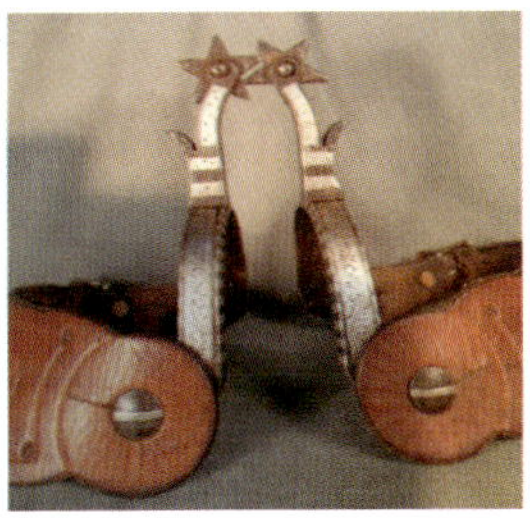

Figure 2-12. Hulbert Spurs, Pattern H70 (Figure 2-2). Also unmarked, these silver-inlaid spurs feature five-point star rowels. *Courtesy of C. Webb. Photo by B. Bartlett.*

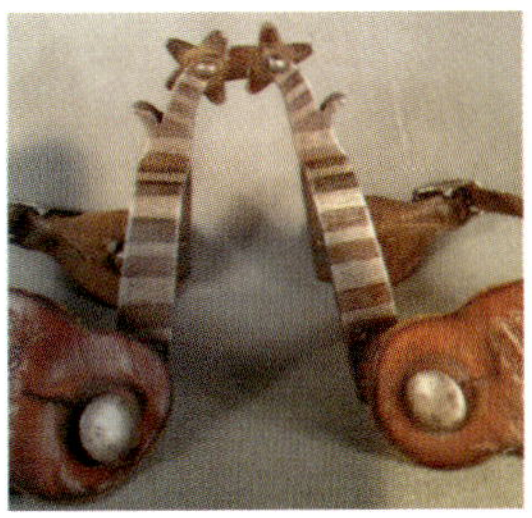

Figure 2-14. Hulbert Spurs, "Bar" Pattern, fitted with five-point Star Rowels. This marked pair features 5/8" silver-inlaid heelbands and silver-inlaid top edges. The swinging buttons are angled, and there is a drilled hole just below them to accommodate tie-downs or chains. *Courtesy of C. Webb. Photo by B. Bartlett.*

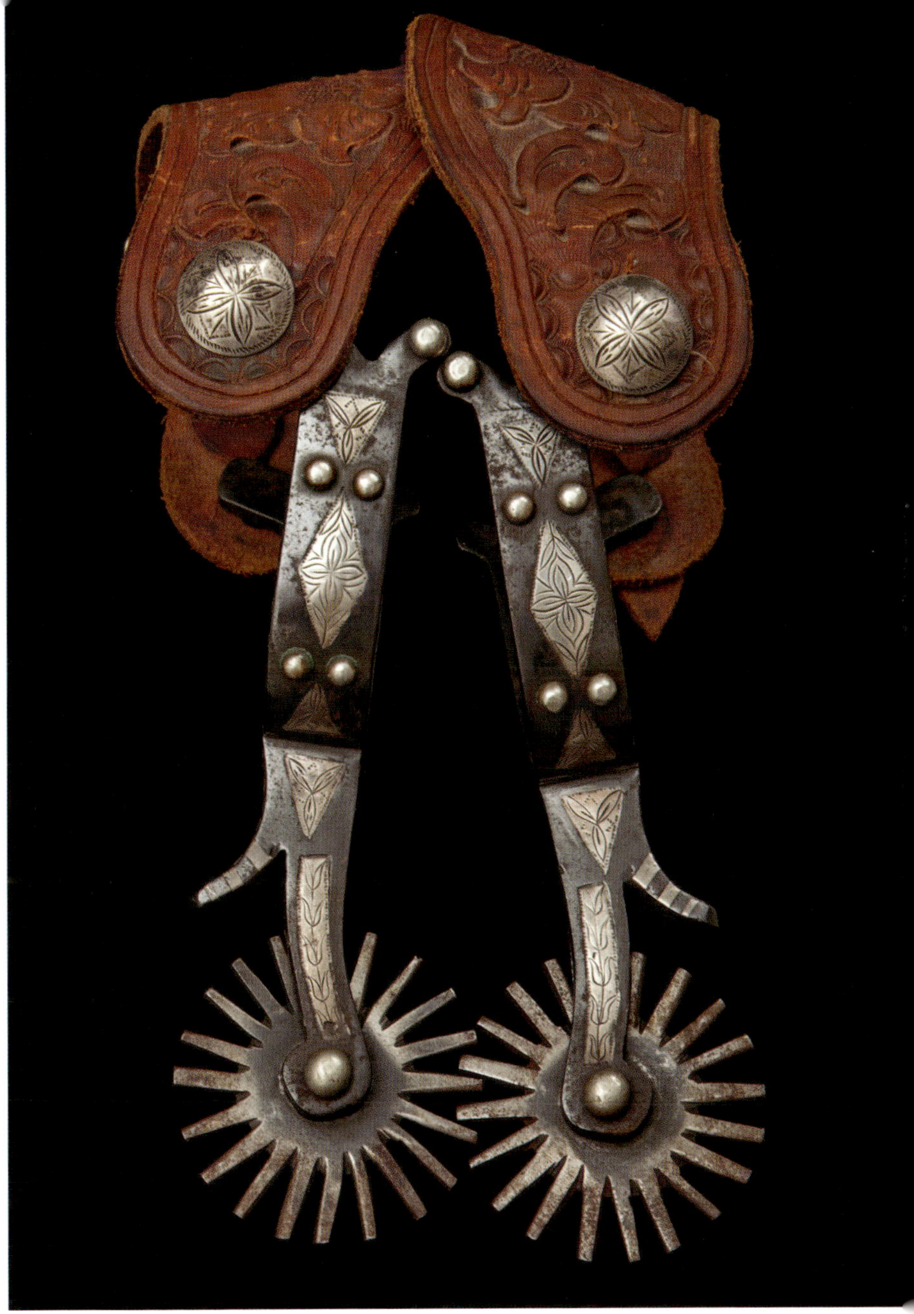

Figure 2-15. Hulbert Men's Spurs in Geometric Pattern 54A (Figure 2-1). These spurs show silver inlaid diamonds and triangles highlighted by small silver buttons, and split Cheyenne heelbands. The chap guards are also inlaid. These spurs were formerly owned by "Kid" Nichols of the Diamond Bar Ranch, Cody, Wyoming. *Courtesy of J. Lyndes. Photo by J. Williams.*

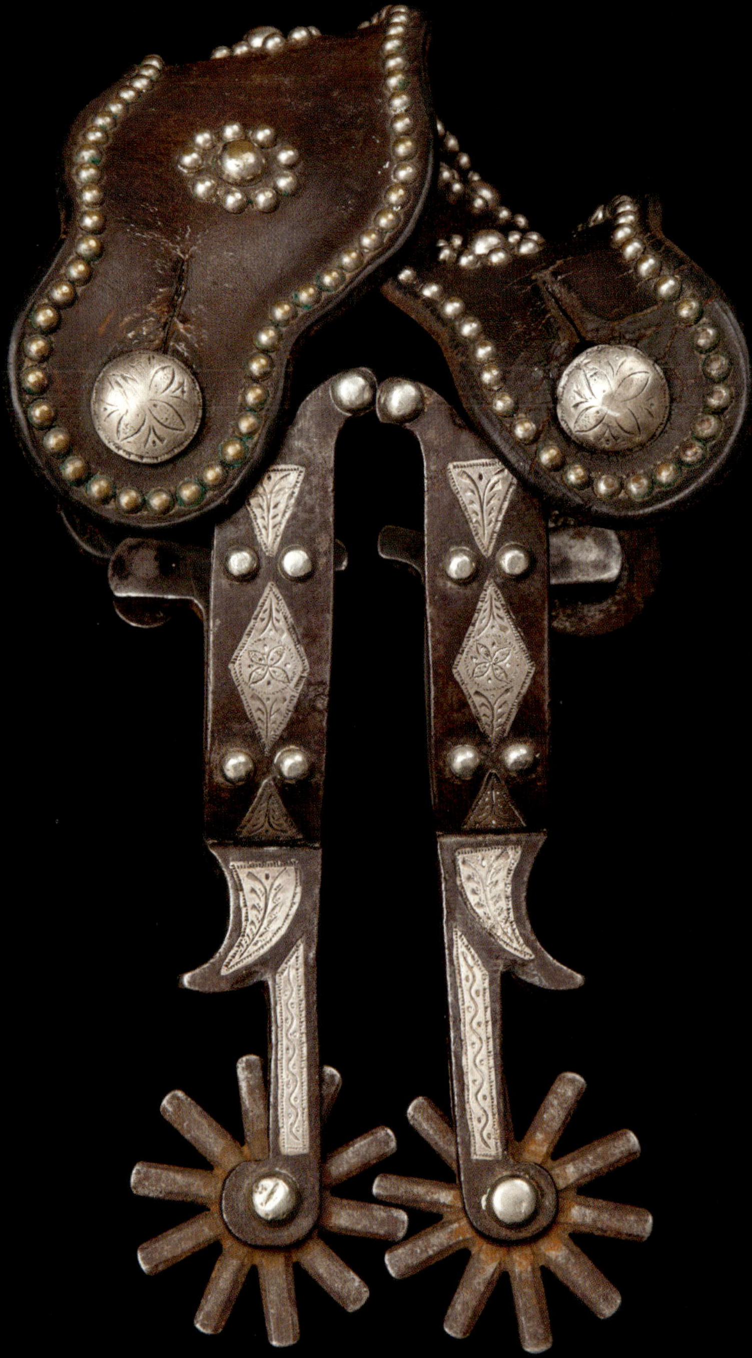

Figure 2-16. Hulbert Men's Spurs in Geometric Pattern 54A (Figure 2-1). Although these spurs closely resemble those shown in Figure 2-15, note that the shanks are straight and the inlays on the chap guards are different. *Courtesy of J. Lyndes. Photo by J. Williams.*

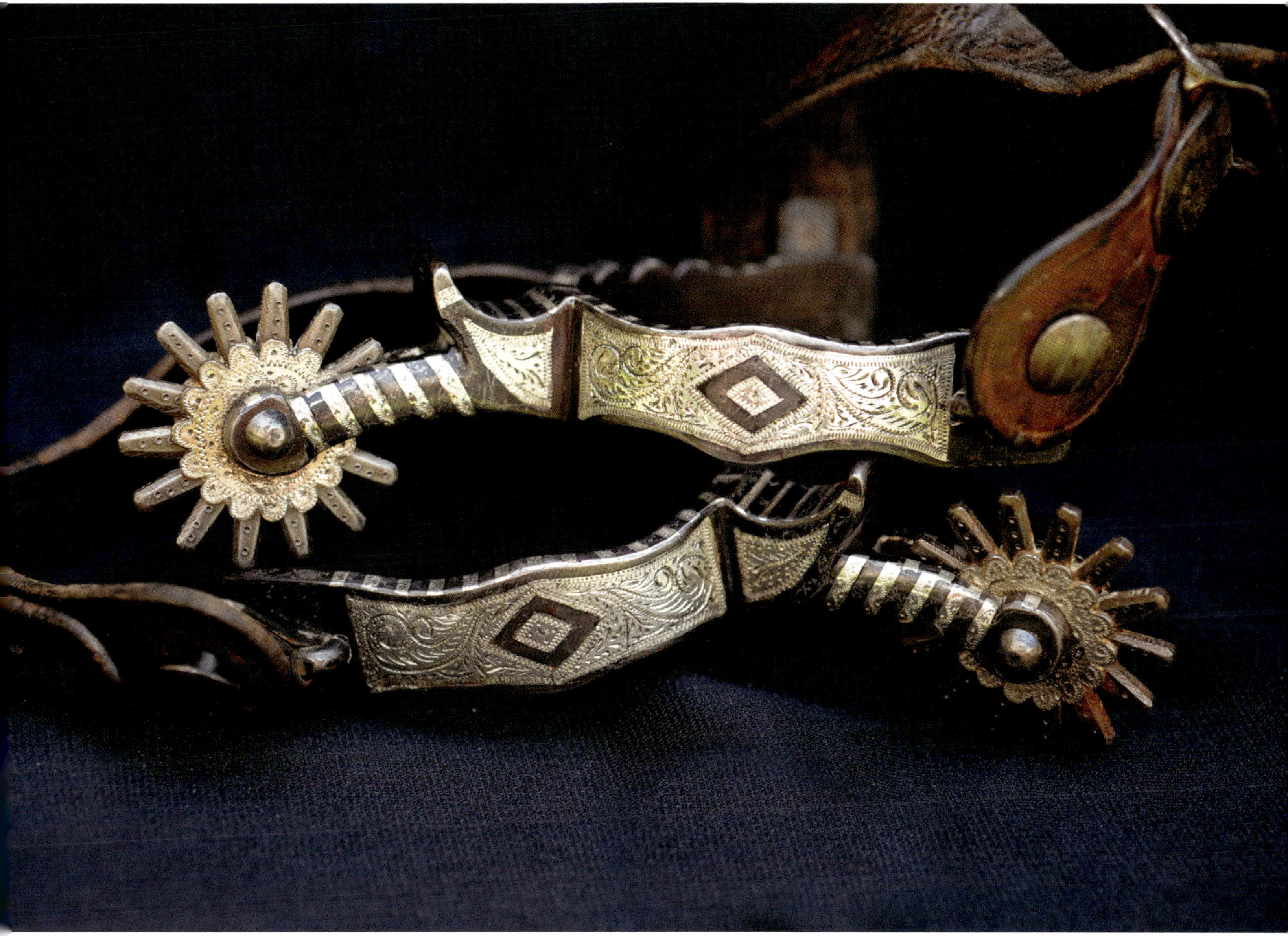

Figure 2-17. Hulbert Men's Spurs, "Diamond" Pattern H20 (Figure 2-2). This very fancy pair of engraved silver-inlaid spurs recapitulates closely the examples shown in both the Hamley and Ernst catalogs. The chap guard is a more conservative style without the end bulb, and the buttons reflect a custom order. Note the silver decoration at the base of the rowels. *Courtesy of R. Wilmot. William Manns photo.*

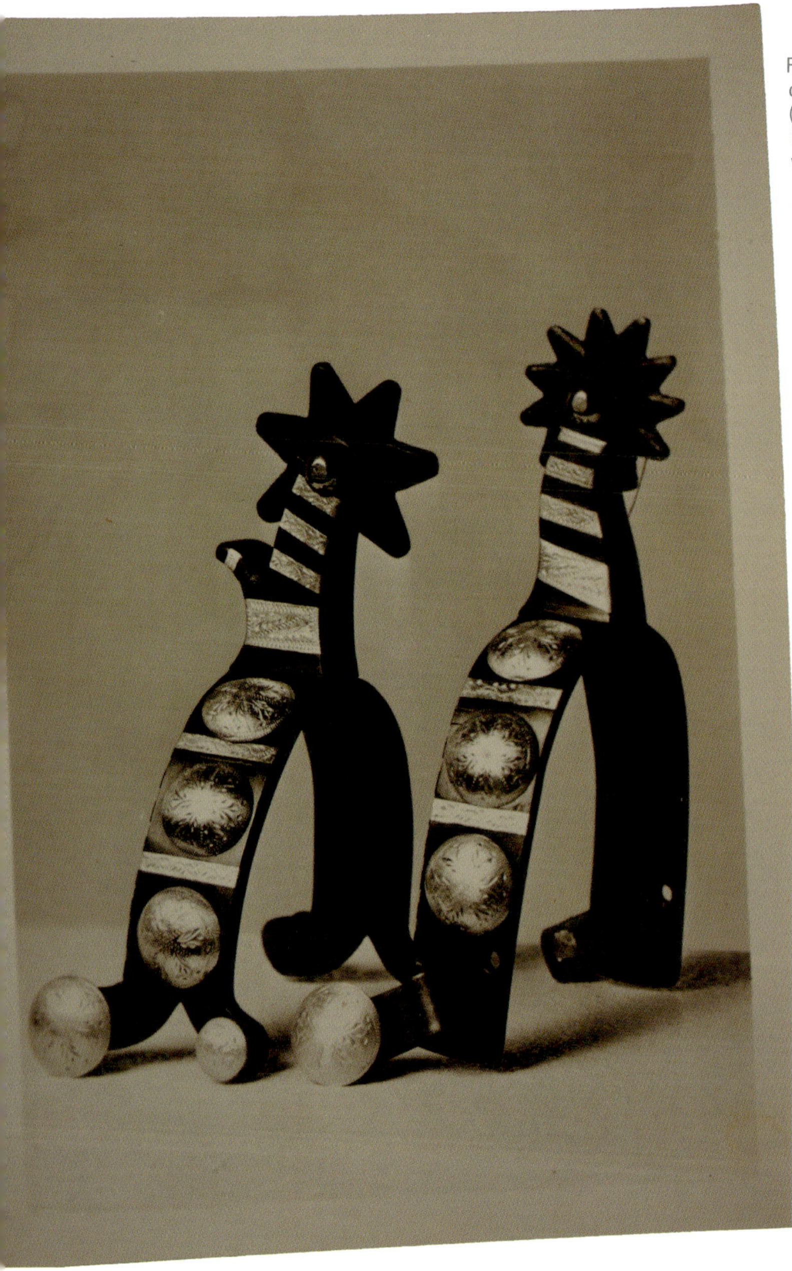

Figure 2-18. Advertising (studio) card—Hulbert No. 40 Spur. This card (5" H x 3.5" W) shows "3-Button Mount" spurs. The spur on the left was "Made double button with chap guard," and the one on the right, "with 'Goose Neck' shank" (see Figure 2-19 for Hulbert's written description verso). *Courtesy of R. Wilmot. William Manns photo.*

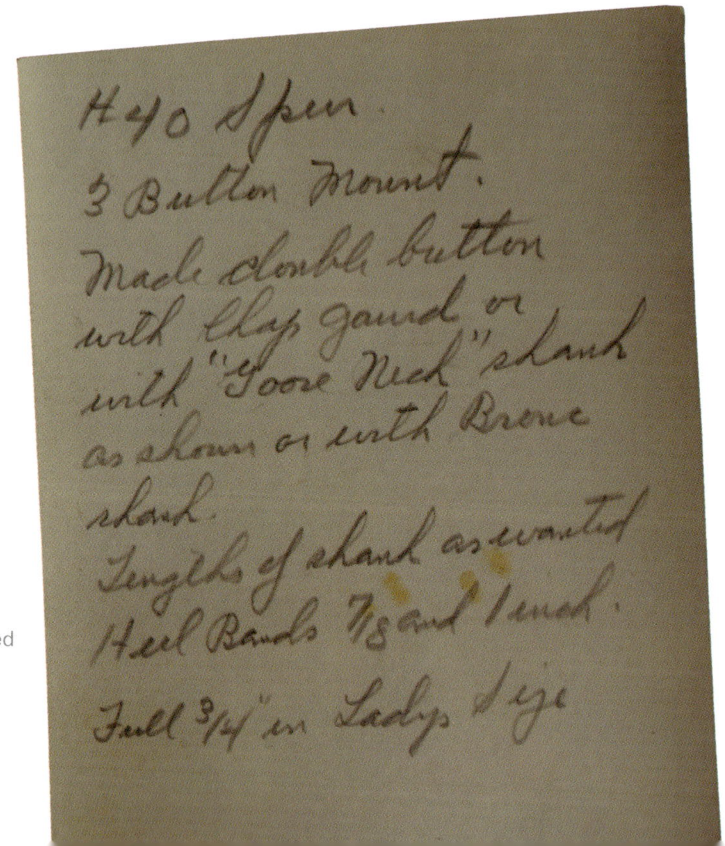

H40 Spur.
3 Button Mount.
Made double button
with Chap guard or
with "Goose Neck" shank
as shown or with Bronc
shank.
Lengths of shank as wanted
Heel Bands 7/8 and 1 inch.
Full 3/4" in Ladys Size

Figure 2-19. Advertising card, verso of Figure 2-18. Hulbert has mentioned several variations available in these spurs, including a "Ladys Size." *Courtesy of R. Wilmot. William Manns photo.*

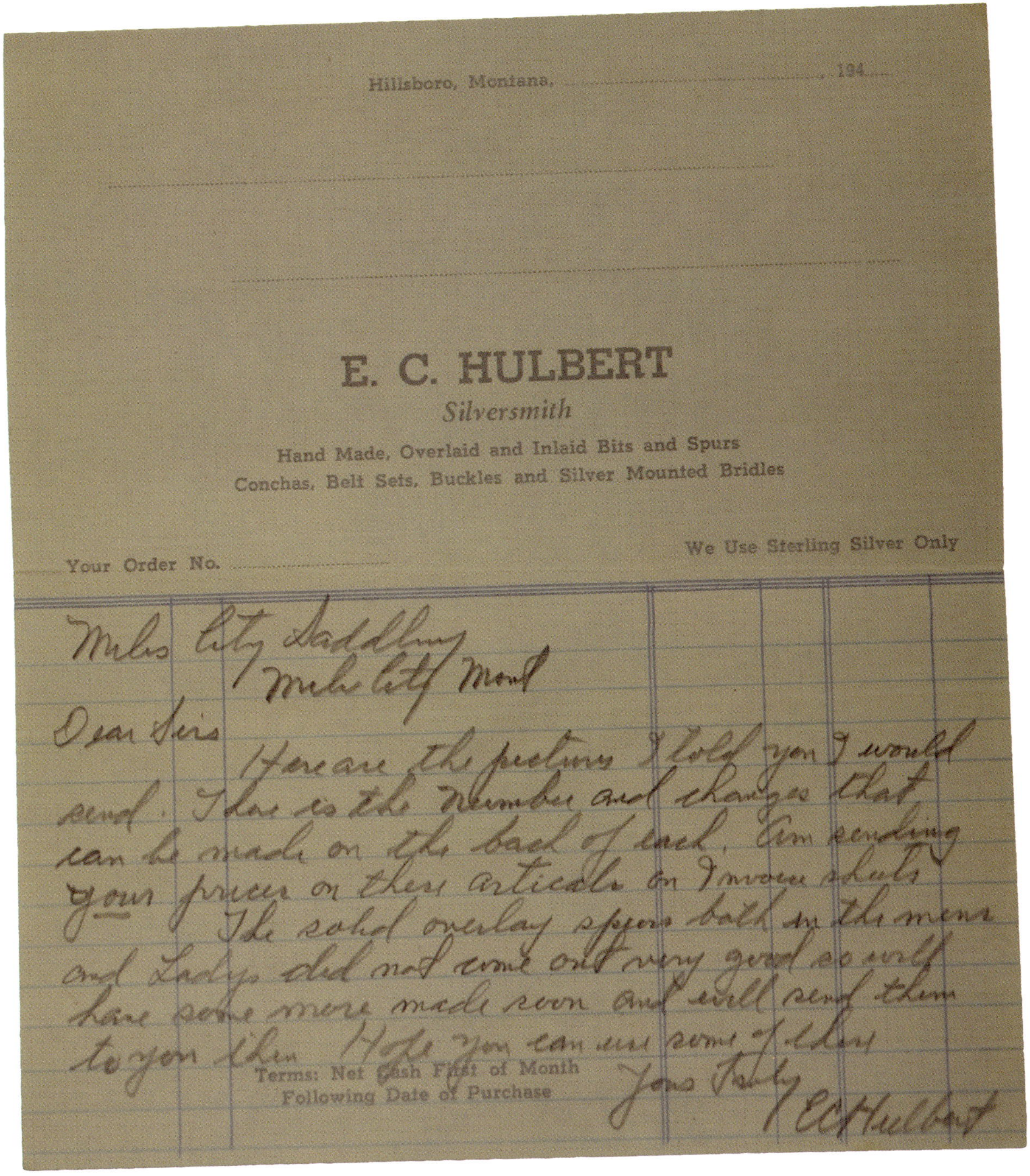
Hillsboro, Montana, ..., 194....

E. C. HULBERT

Silversmith

Hand Made, Overlaid and Inlaid Bits and Spurs

Conchas, Belt Sets, Buckles and Silver Mounted Bridles

Your Order No. ....

We Use Sterling Silver Only

Miles City Saddlery
Miles City Mont

Dear Sirs

Here are the pictures I told you I would send. There is the Number and changes that can be made on the back of each. Am sending your prices on these articals on Invoice sheets

The solid overlay spurs both in the mens and Ladys did not come out very good so will have some more made soon and will send them to you then. Hope you can use some of these

Yours Truly

E C Hulbert

Terms: Net Cash First of Month
Following Date of Purchase

Figure 2-20. Correspondence between Eddy Hulbert and Miles City Saddlery (Miles City, Montana). From Hillsboro, Montana, Hulbert describes the photographs (cards) that he is sending for consideration by this famous saddlery. *Courtesy of R. Wilmot. William Manns photo.*

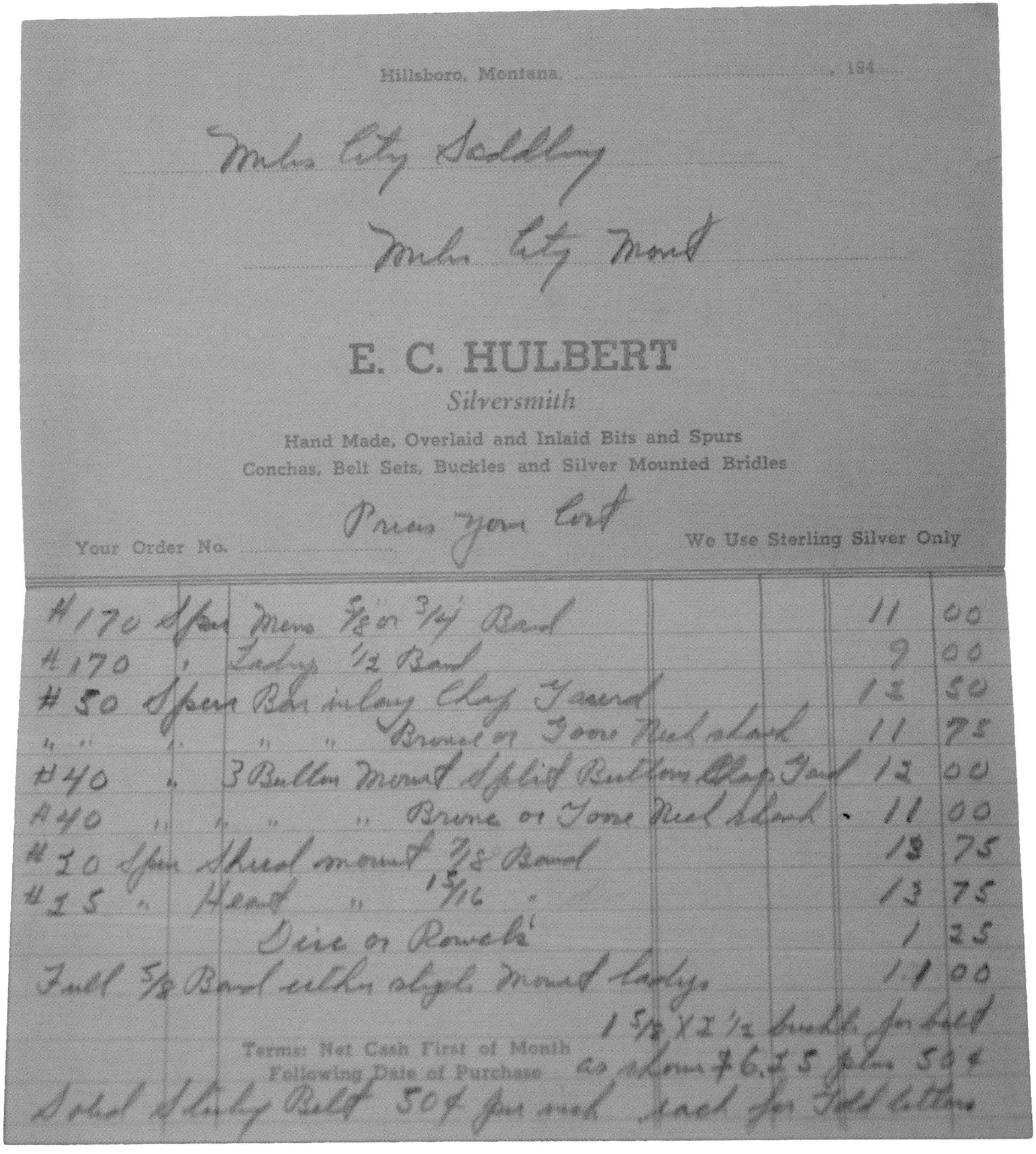

Hillsboro, Montana, ..., 194...

Miles City Saddlery

Miles City Mont

E. C. HULBERT

Silversmith

Hand Made, Overlaid and Inlaid Bits and Spurs

Conchas, Belt Sets, Buckles and Silver Mounted Bridles

Prices your cost

Your Order No. .... We Use Sterling Silver Only

#170 Spur Mens 5/8" or 3/4" Band	11	00
#170 " Ladys 1/2 Band	9	00
#50 Spur Bar inlay Clasp Guard	12	50
" " " " " Bronze or Goose Neck shank	11	75
#40 " 3 Button Mount Split Button Clasp Guard	12	00
#40 " " " " Bronze or Goose Neck Shank	11	00
#10 Spur Shield mount 7/8" Band	13	75
#15 " Heart " 15/16	13	75
Dice or Rowels	1	25
Full 5/8 Band either style mount ladys	11	00

1 5/8 X 1 1/2 buckle for belt as shown $6.15 plus 50¢

Terms: Net Cash First of Month Following Date of Purchase

Solid Sterling Belt 50¢ per inch each for Gold letters

Figure 2-21. Correspondence between Eddy Hulbert and Miles City Saddlery. This invoice, which accompanied the letter shown in Figure 2-20, lists several models of Hulbert spurs with their wholesale prices. *Courtesy of R. Wilmot. William Manns photo.*

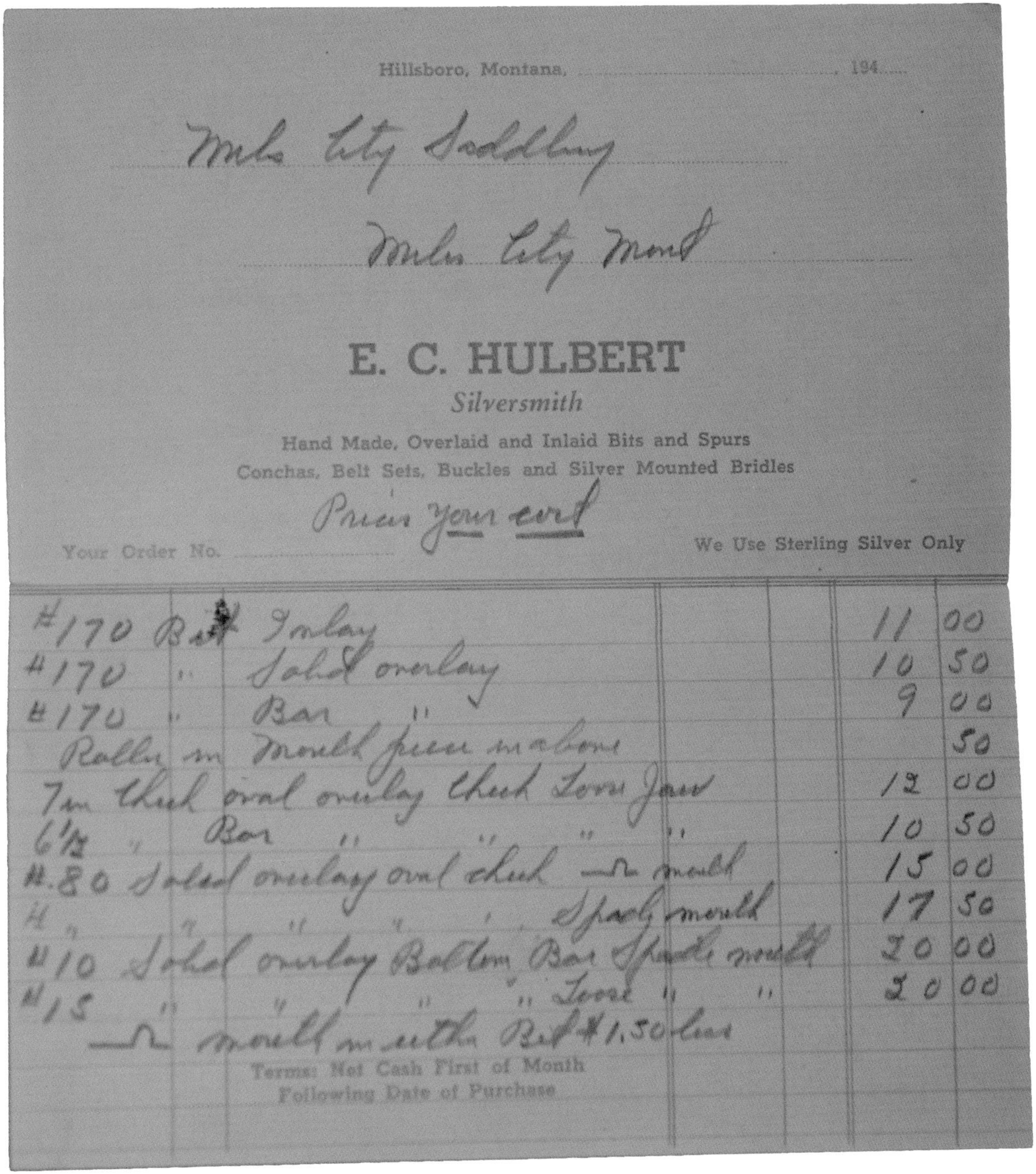

Hillsboro, Montana, ... 194....

Miles City Saddlery

Miles City Mont

E. C. HULBERT

Silversmith

Hand Made, Overlaid and Inlaid Bits and Spurs

Conchas, Belt Sets, Buckles and Silver Mounted Bridles

Prices your cost

Your Order No. .... We Use Sterling Silver Only

Item	Price	
#170 Bit Inlay	11	00
#170 " Solid overlay	10	50
#170 " Bar "	9	00
Roller in mouth piece in above		50
7 in cheek oval overlay cheek Loose Jaw	12	00
6½ " Bar " " " "	10	50
#80 Solid overlay oval cheek ⌒ mouth	15	00
# " " " " Spade mouth	17	50
#10 Solid overlay Bottom Bar Spade mouth	20	00
#15 " " " " Loose " "	20	00
⌒ mouth in either Bit #1.50 less		

Terms: Net Cash First of Month Following Date of Purchase

Figure 2-22. Correspondence between Eddy Hulbert and Miles City Saddlery. This invoice, presumably included with that in Figure 2-21, lists several styles of Hulbert bits, with accompanying wholesale prices. Details on these and other bits can be found in Chapter 3. *Courtesy of R. Wilmot. William Manns photo.*

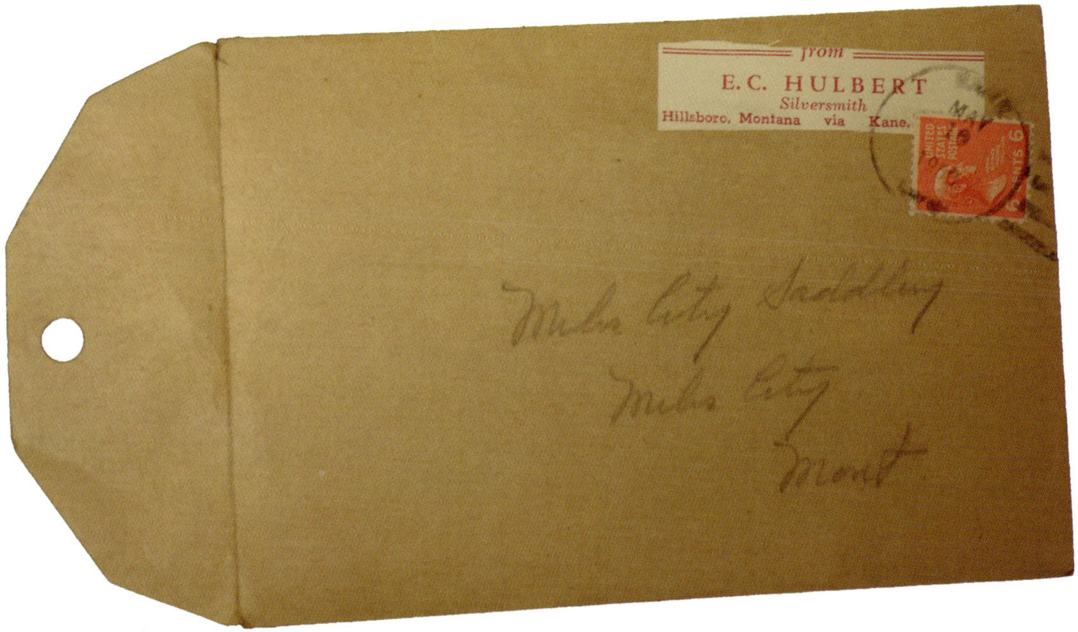

Figure 2-23. Correspondence between Eddy Hulbert and Miles City Saddlery. Envelope bearing Hulbert's return address: Hillsboro, Montana via Kane (Wyoming). The cancel date appears to be May 18, 1950. *Courtesy of R. Wilmot. William Manns photo.*

A popular style of Hulbert spur was the "3-Button" pattern, shown in Figures 2-30 through 2-33. Note the ornate rowels with their engraved silver discs or covers (Figure 2-31). The "heart" pattern was possibly the most popular, however, and Hulbert crafted many variations of this theme. Overlays and inlays are shown in Figures 2-34 through 2-37. Other, less common, patterns were the "diamond" (Figures 2-38 and 2-39), "shield" (Figure 2-40), and "band" (Figures 2-41 and 2-42). Two very impressive "bar" pattern spurs are shown in Figures 2-43 and 2-44. The former are inlaid with engraved silver and have fancy punched eighteen-point rowels. The latter are somewhat less elaborate (e.g., the bars are all of a single width, and the rowels are plain). However, the heart-shaped conchos decorating the spur straps are very impressive, with the engraved initials "BM" as part of the design (Figure 2-45).

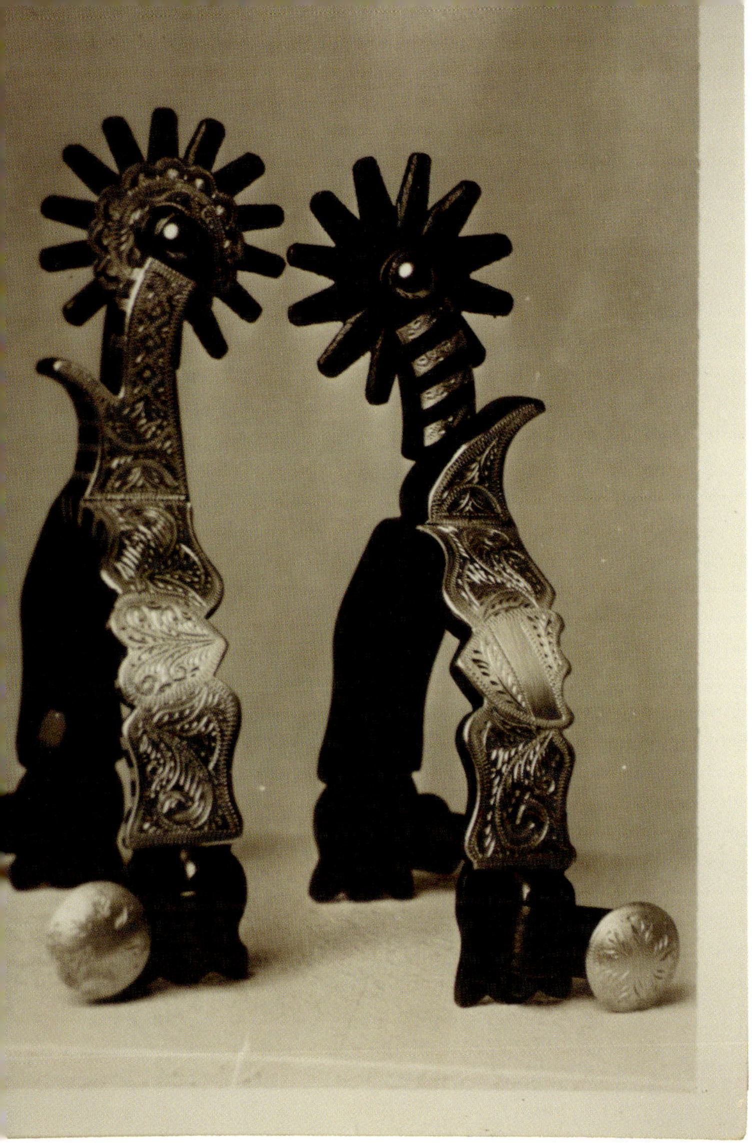

Figure 2-24. Advertising card—Hulbert No. H25 (left) and H20 (right) Spurs. These two examples show solid overlays in an engraved silver heart pattern or shield pattern. Note the different patterns on the shanks (overlay on left, and inlay on right). Card, 5″ H x 3.5″ W. *Courtesy of R. Wilmot. William Manns photo.*

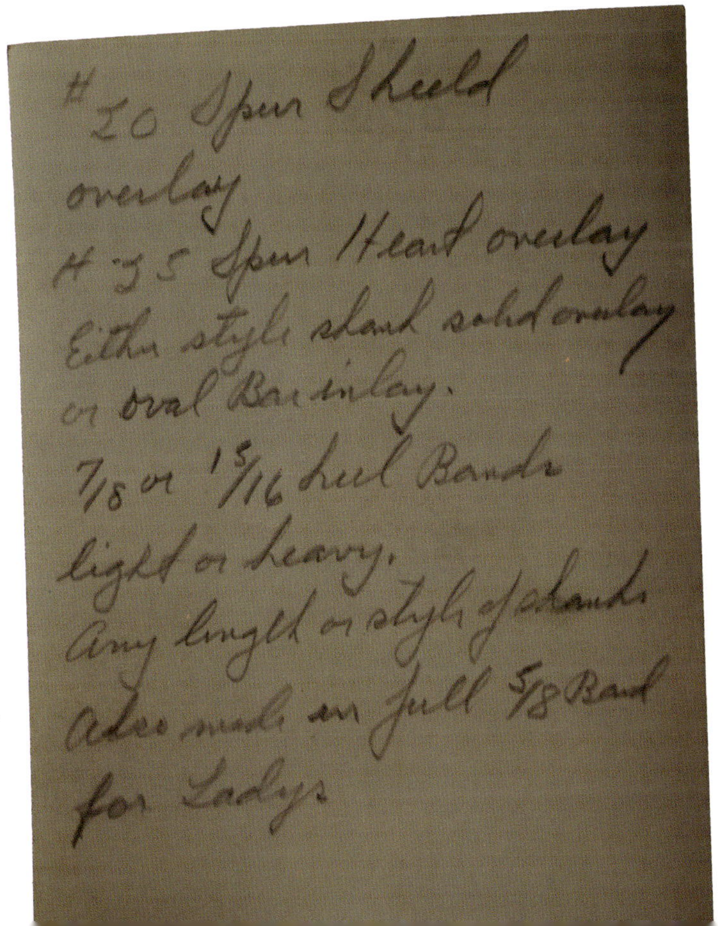

#20 Spur Shield
overlay
H 25 Spur Heart overlay
Either style shank solid overlay
or oval Bar inlay.
7/8 or 15/16 heel Bands
light or heavy.
Any length or style of shanks
Also made in full 5/8 Band
for Ladys

Figure 2-25. Advertising card—Hulbert No. H25 and H20 Spurs. Verso of Figure 2-24. Hulbert offered a variety of modifications in his spurs, as can be seen in his written description. For example, the heelbands ranged from 5/8″ (ladies') to 7/8″ or 15/16″, light or heavy, for men. *Courtesy of R. Wilmot. William Manns photo.*

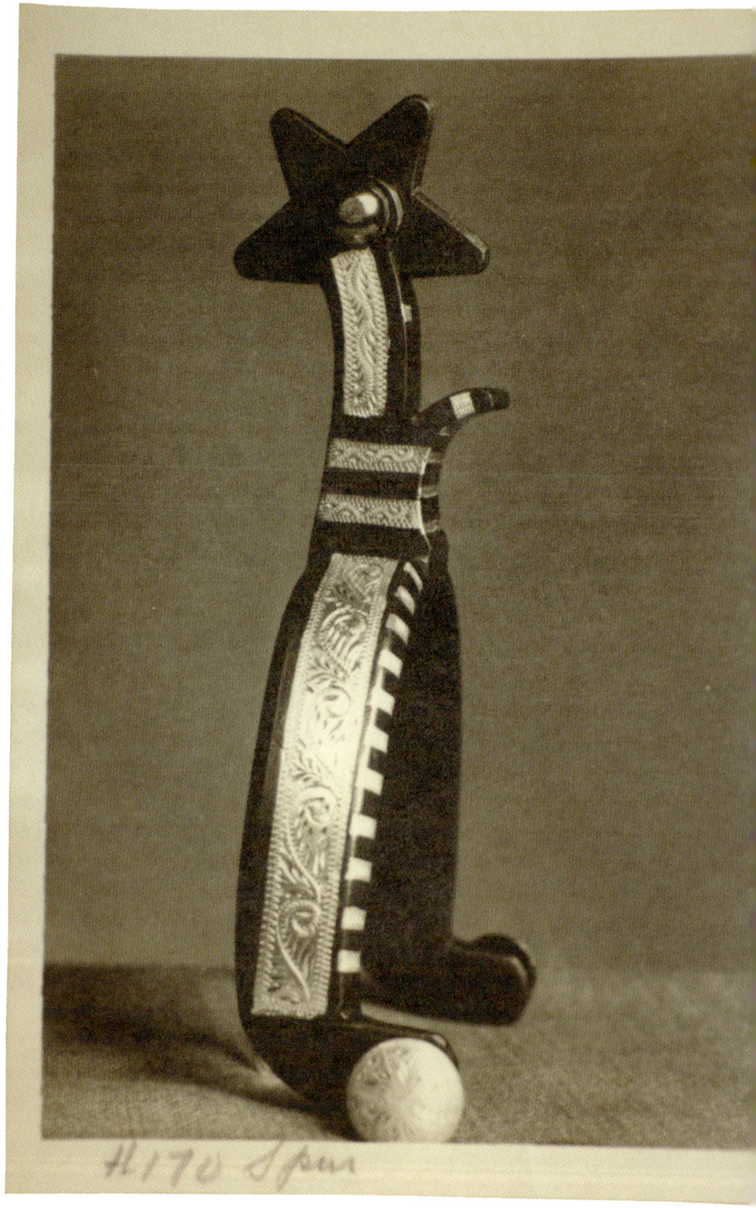

Figure 2-26. Advertising card—Hulbert No. 170 Spur. This spur resembles very closely Spur H70 (Figure 2-2) in the Hamley catalog. Note that Hulbert's number at the bottom of the card is "H170." He describes this pair as a "solid inlay" with "full striped edges" (see Figure 2-27). Although rowels and shank lengths were "as wanted," staple swinging buttons were "extra." Card, 5" H x 3.5" W. *Courtesy of R. Wilmot. William Manns photo.*

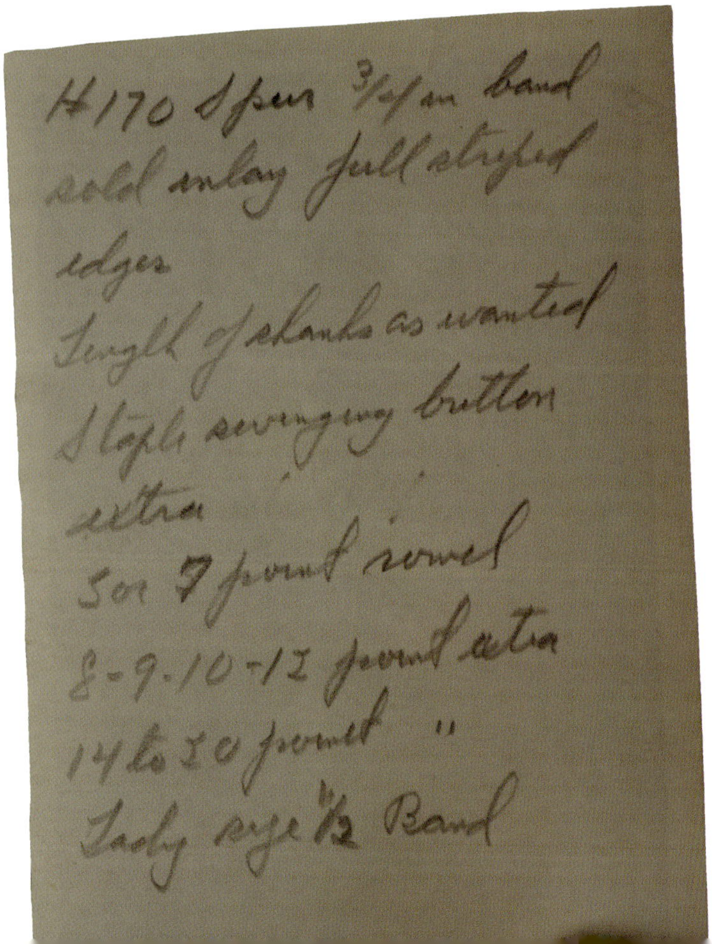
H170 Spur 3/4 in band
sold inlay full striped
edges
Length of shanks as wanted
Staple swinging button
extra
5 or 7 point rowel
8-9-10-12 point extra
14 to 20 point "
Lady size 1/2 Band

Figure 2-27. Advertising card—Hulbert Spur #170, verso. A list of possible modifications for the spur shown in Figure 2-26 included extra charges for rowels with increasing numbers of points, and a 1/2" heelband for a lady's spur. *Courtesy of R. Wilmot. William Manns photo.*

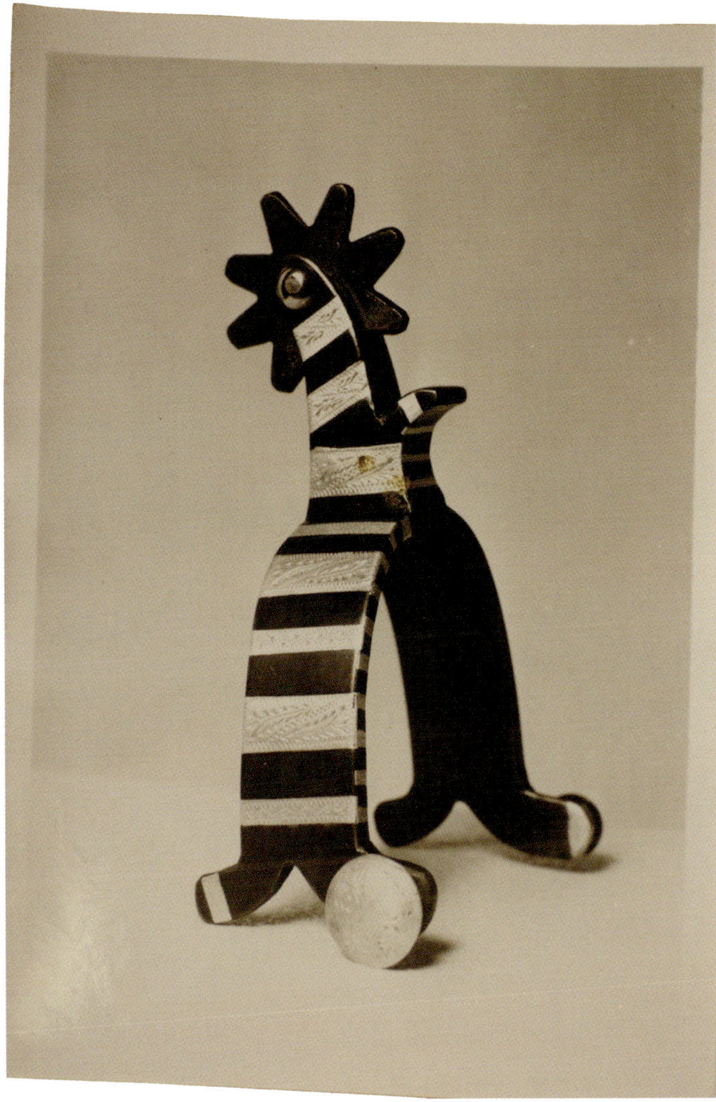

Figure 2-28. Advertising card—Hulbert Spur No. 50, "Bar Inlay." This handsome spur was made with engraved silver-inlaid bars of alternating widths on the split heelband. The bands ranged from 3/4" to 1" in width (5/8" or 3/4" for ladies'), and the shanks ("Goose Neck or Bronc") could be made in any desired length. Card, 5" H x 3.5" W. *Courtesy of R. Wilmot. William Manns photo.*

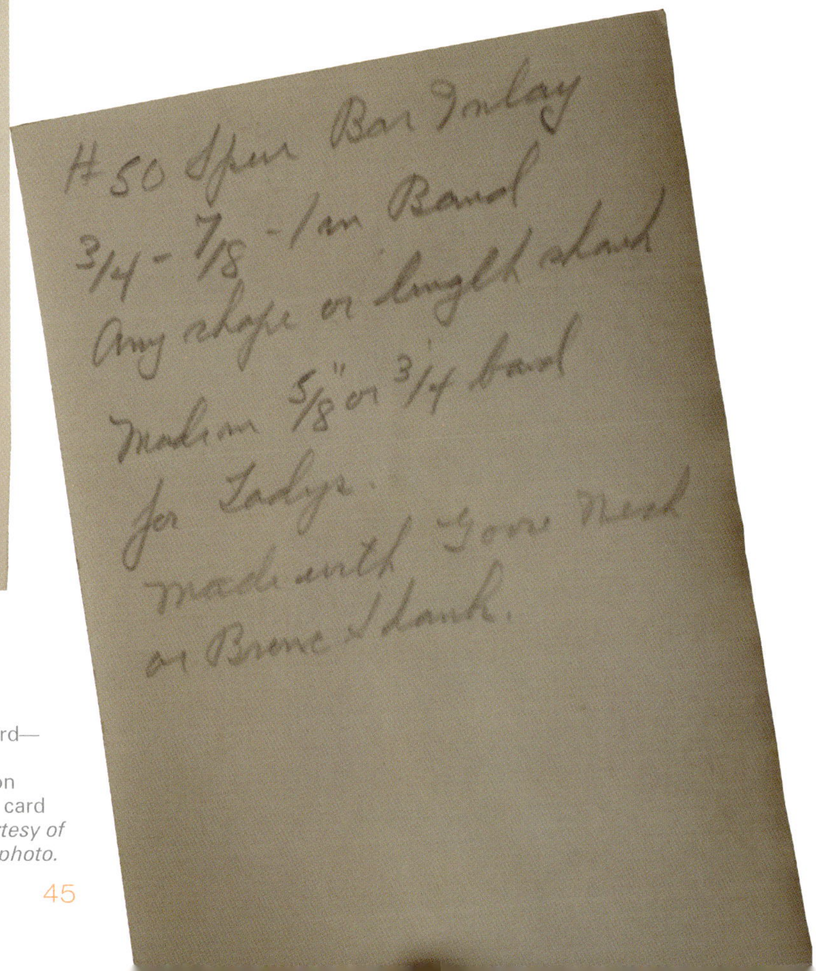

Figure 2-29. Advertising card—Hulbert Spur No. 50 verso. Hulbert's written description appears on the back of the card shown in Figure 2-28. *Courtesy of R. Wilmot. William Manns photo.*

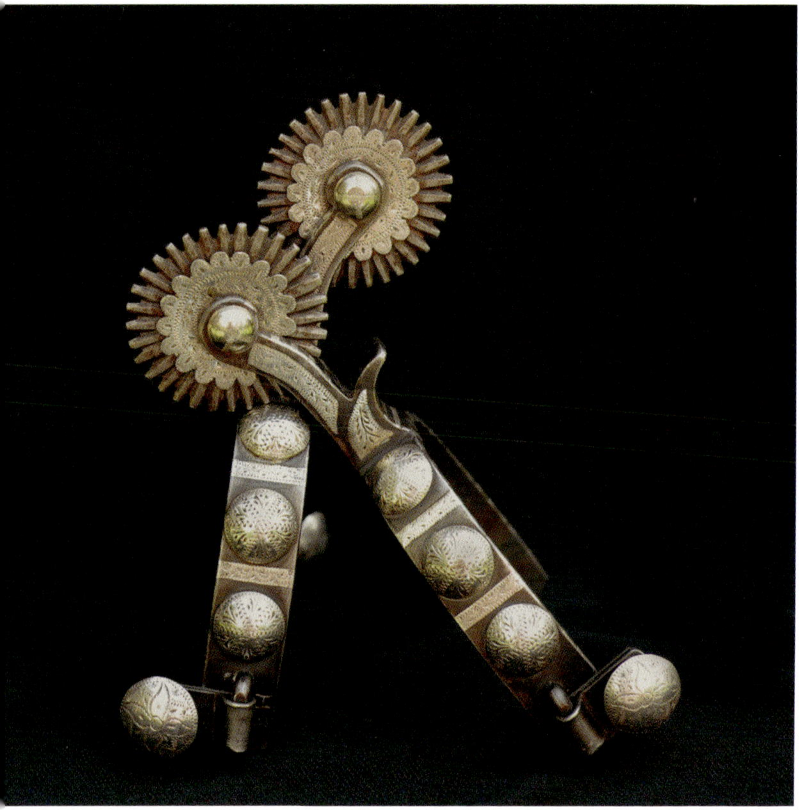

Figure 2-30. Hulbert men's spurs—3-Button Pattern. These beautifully-executed spurs are in excellent condition and include ornate silver discs on the rowels and swinging silver-capped buttons. *Courtesy of R. Wilmot. William Manns photo.*

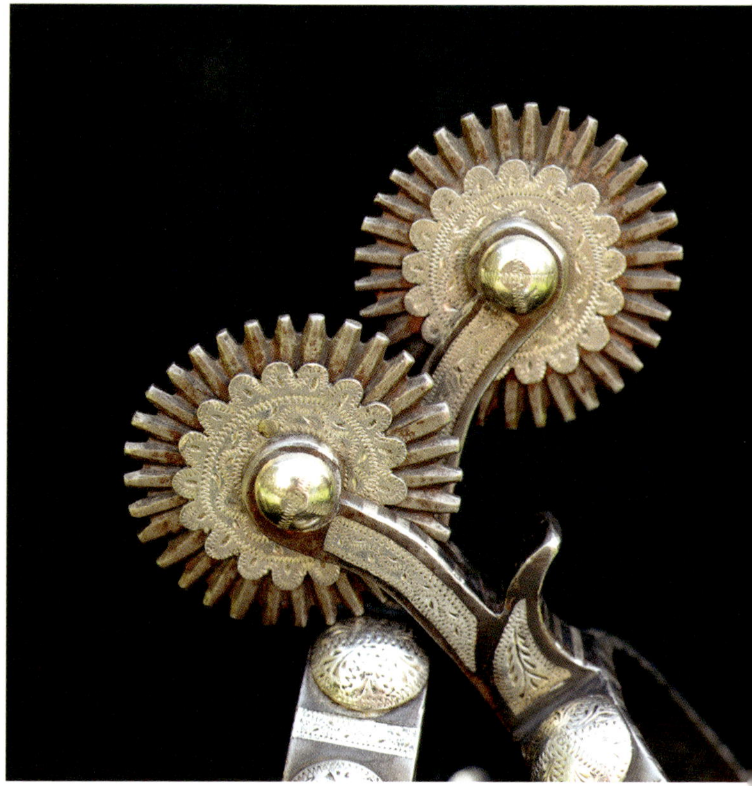

Figure 2-31. Hulbert spurs—3-Button Pattern. The silver discs on the rowels are shown here with the characteristic Hulbert hand-engraving, enlarged from Figure 2-30. *Courtesy of R. Wilmot. William Manns photo.*

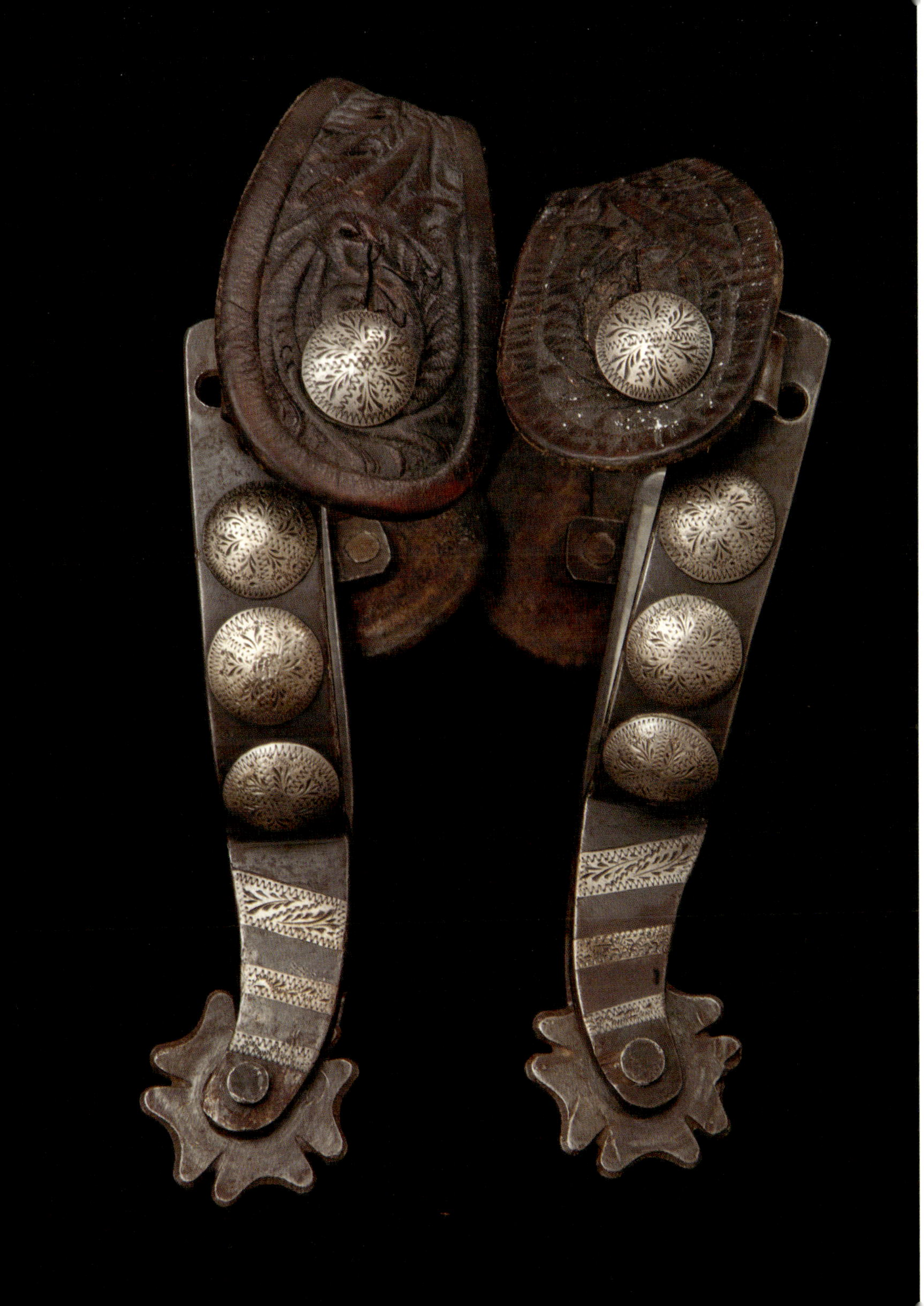

Figure 2-32. Hulbert spurs—3-Button Pattern. This "working" pair of spurs (compare with the pair shown in Figure 2-33) features three silver buttons, with no spacer bars between them, no chap guard, and interesting cloverleaf rowels. *Courtesy of J. Lyndes. Photo by J. Williams.*

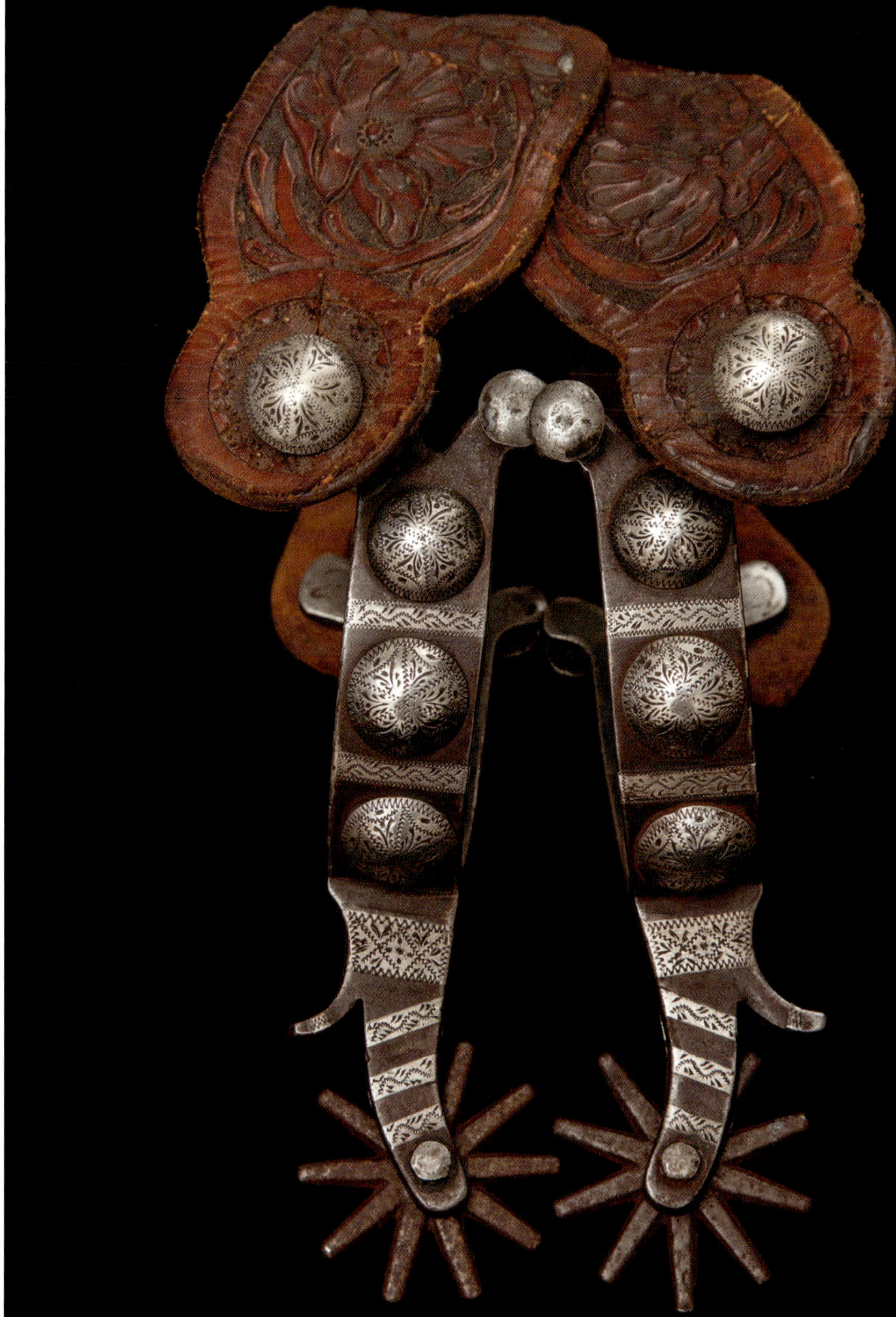

Figure 2-33. Hulbert spurs—3-Button Pattern. A fancy pair in this style, with silver inlays separating the silver buttons, highlighting the shanks and chap guards, and covering the buttons on the split heelbands. Note the chasing on the rowels. *Courtesy of J. Lyndes. Photo by J. Williams.*

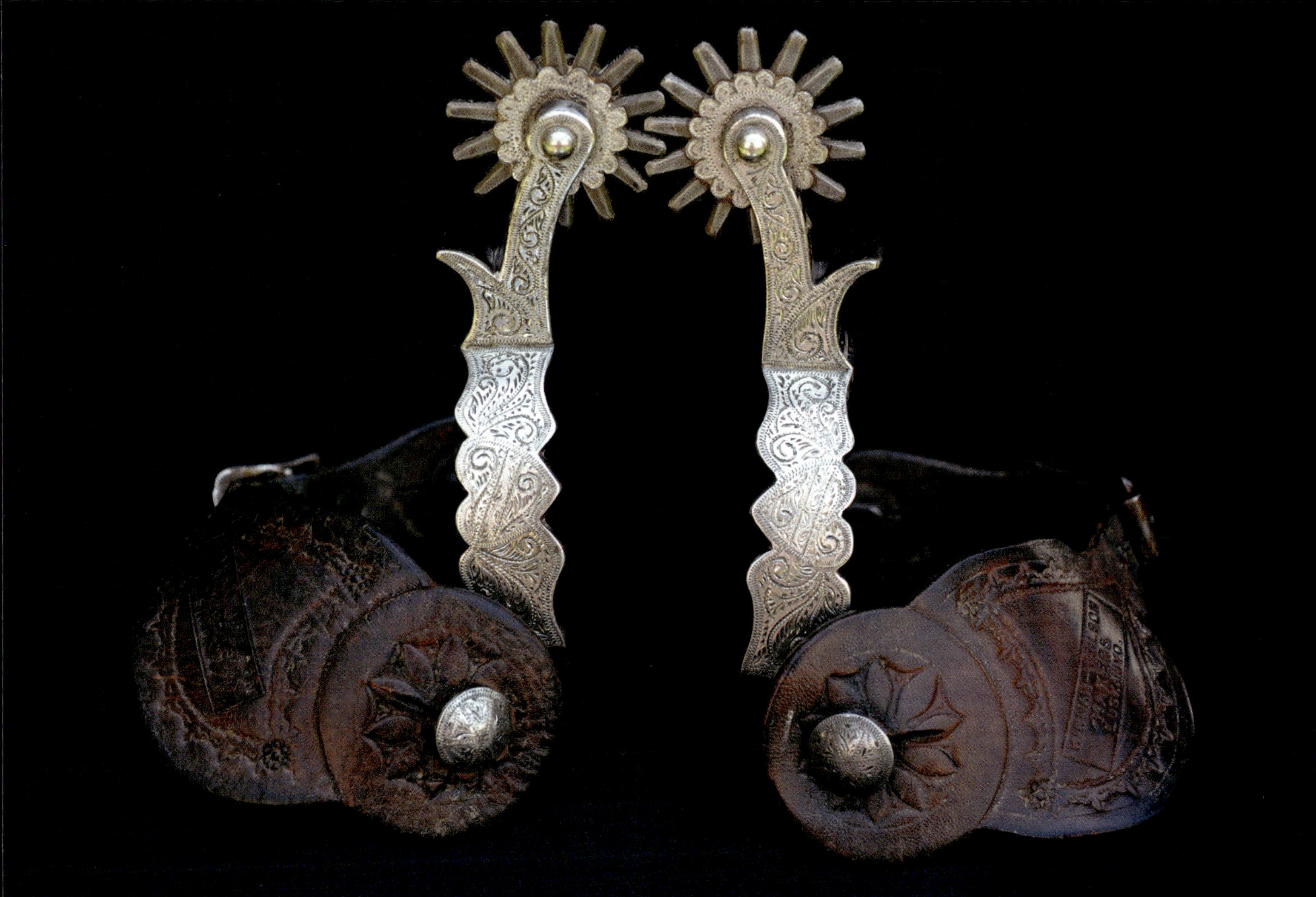

Figure 2-34. Hulbert spurs—Heart Pattern. Silver overlaid spurs with engraved buttons, shanks, and discs on 14-point rowels, with period straps by a Wyoming maker (see Figure 2-35). *Courtesy of R. Wilmot. William Manns photo.*

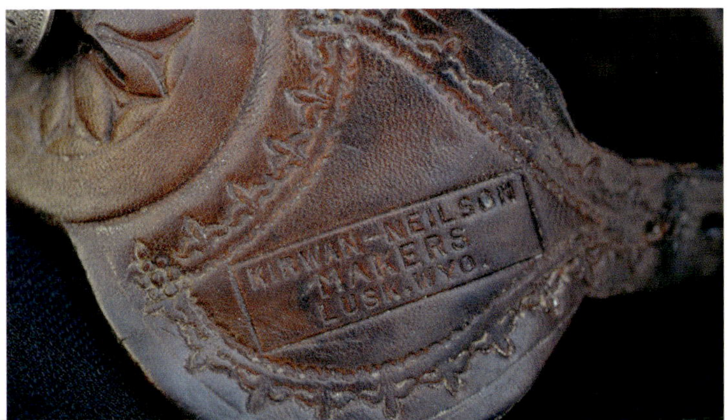

Figure 2-35. Spur straps on Hulbert spurs (Figure 2-34). The maker mark/stamp is "KIRWAN-NEILSON/ MAKERS/LUSK, WYO." *Courtesy of R. Wilmot. William Manns photo.*

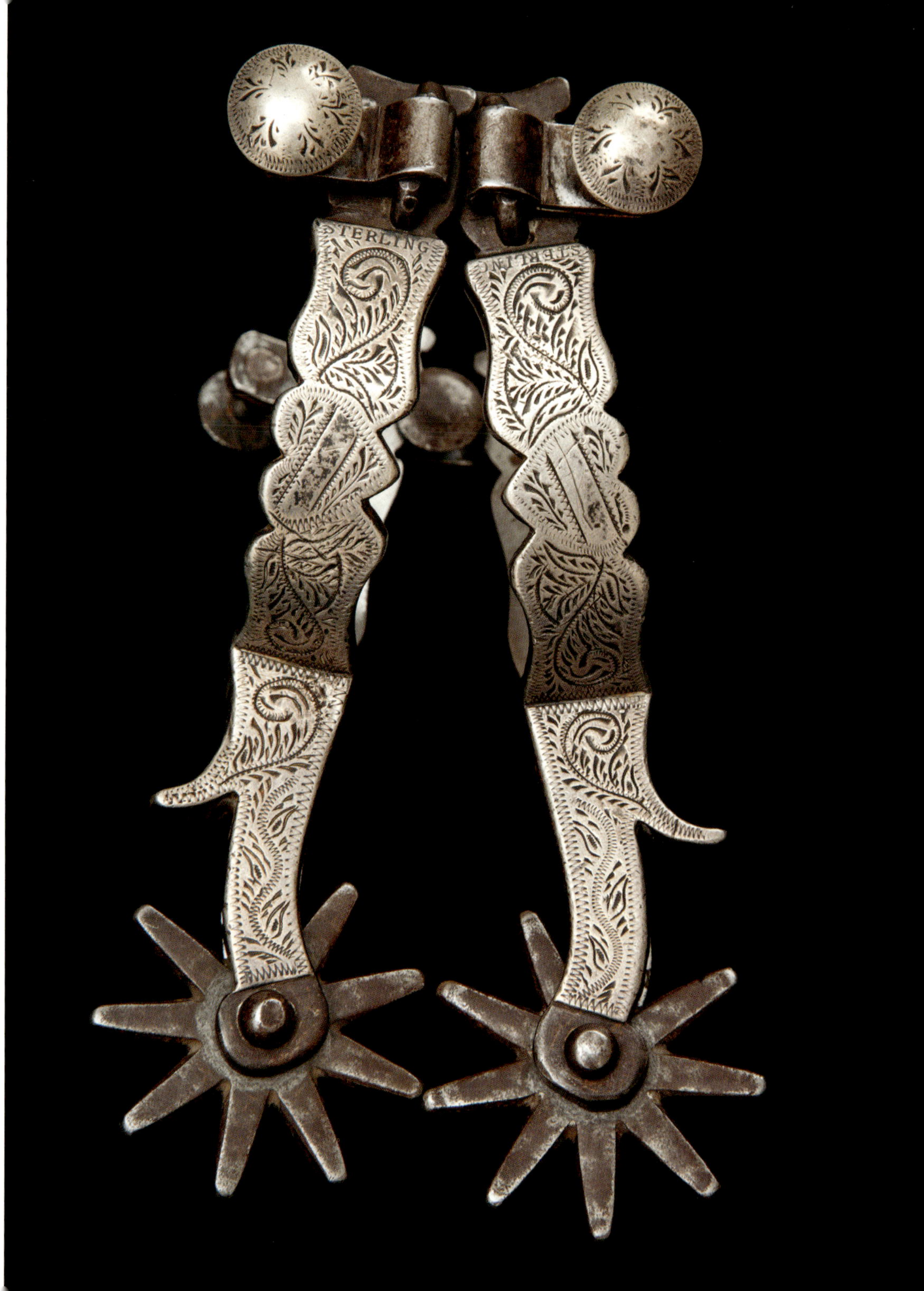

Figure 2-36. Hulbert spurs—Heart Pattern. Engraved silver overlaid, one-piece spurs with silver-covered swinging buttons and plain 9-point rowels. *Courtesy of J. Lyndes. Photo by J. Williams.*

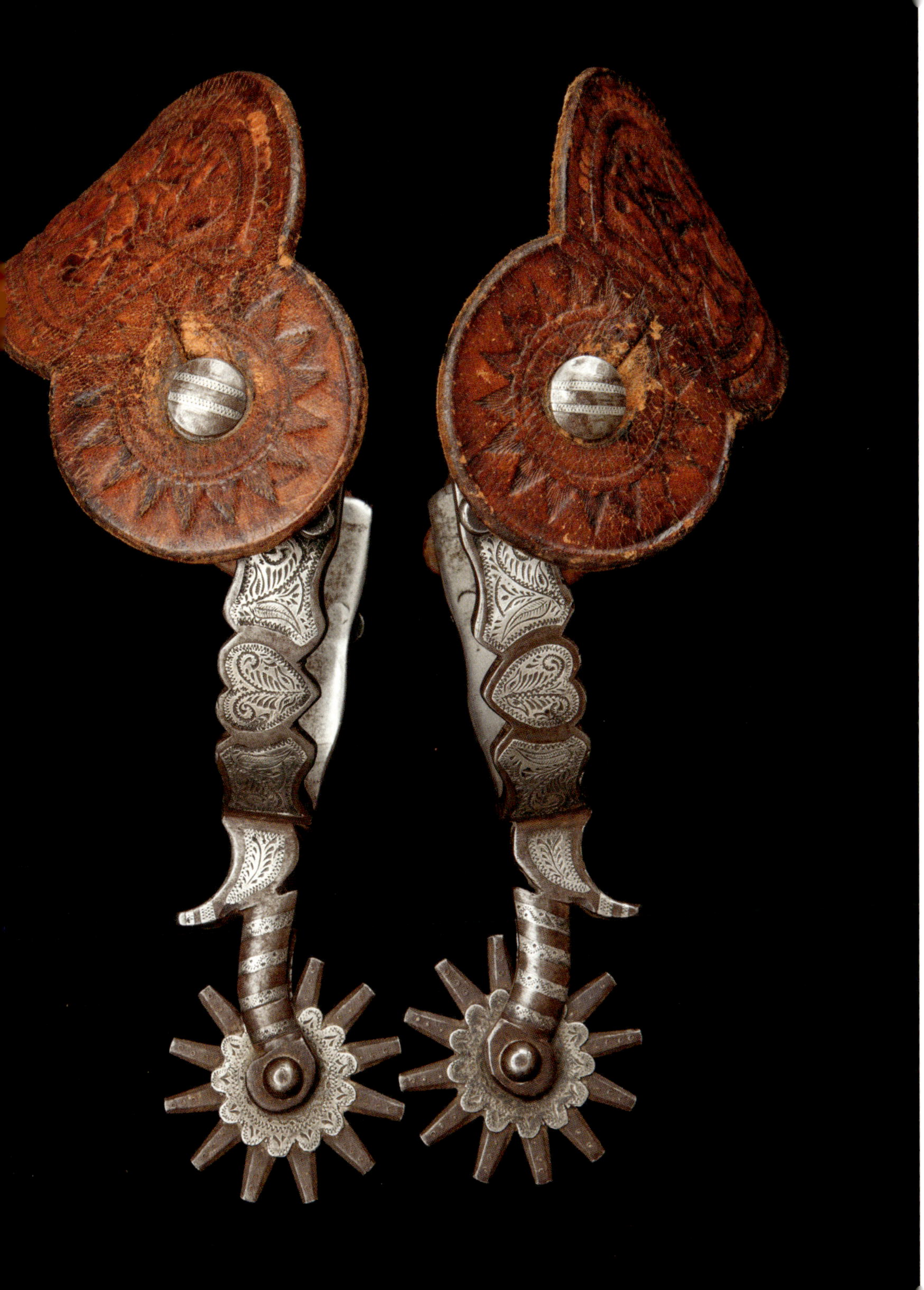

Figure 2-37. Hulbert spurs—Heart Pattern. These spurs resemble closely No. H25 (Figure 2-2), with separately inlaid silver heart and flanking pieces on heelbands and chap guards, and banded inlays on the shanks. Note discs on chased 12-point rowels. *Courtesy of the Nelson Museum of the West. Photo by J. Williams.*

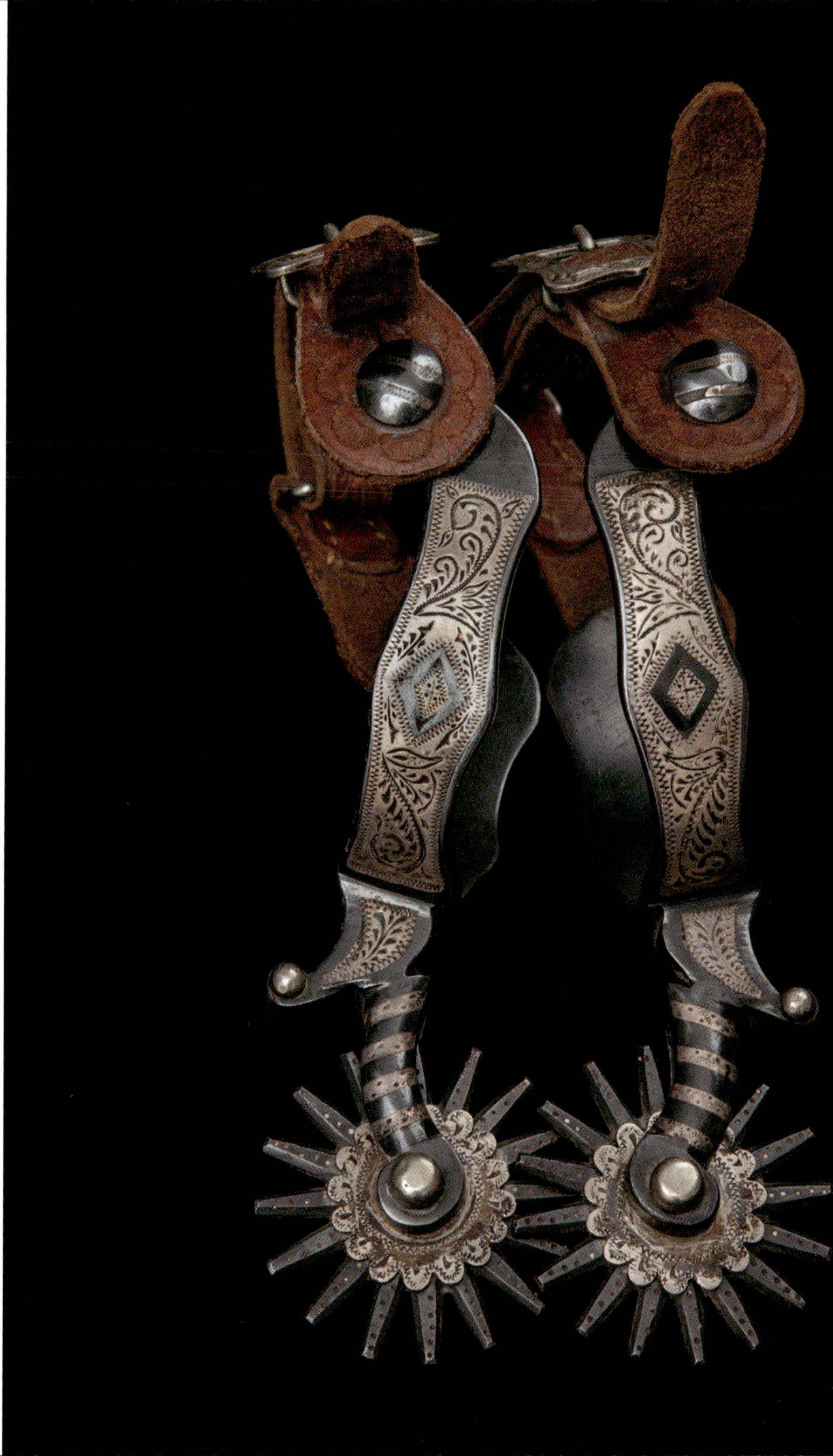

Figure 2-38. Hulbert spurs—Diamond Pattern. A pair very similar to No. H20 (Figure 2-2), these beautifully crafted spurs show the silver diamond inlay on the heelbands, discs on the 16-point chased rowels, banded shanks, and small buttons on the tips of the chap guards. *Courtesy of J. Lyndes. Photo by J. Williams.*

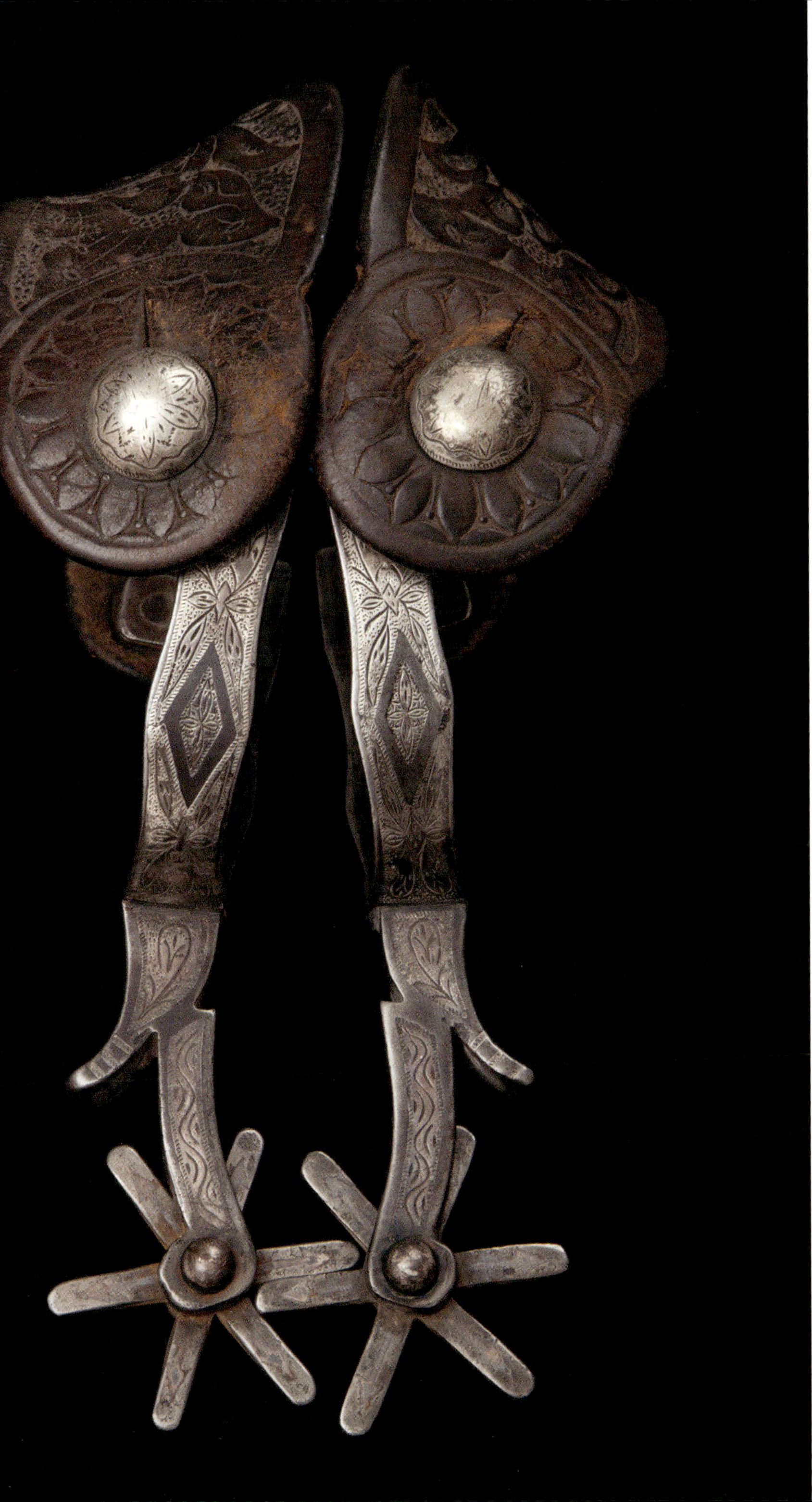

Figure 2-39. Hulbert spurs—Diamond Pattern. A variation of the design shown in Figure 2-38, this pair features an elongated diamond, extended shanks, and chased 6-point rowels. *Courtesy of J. Lyndes. Photo by J. Williams.*

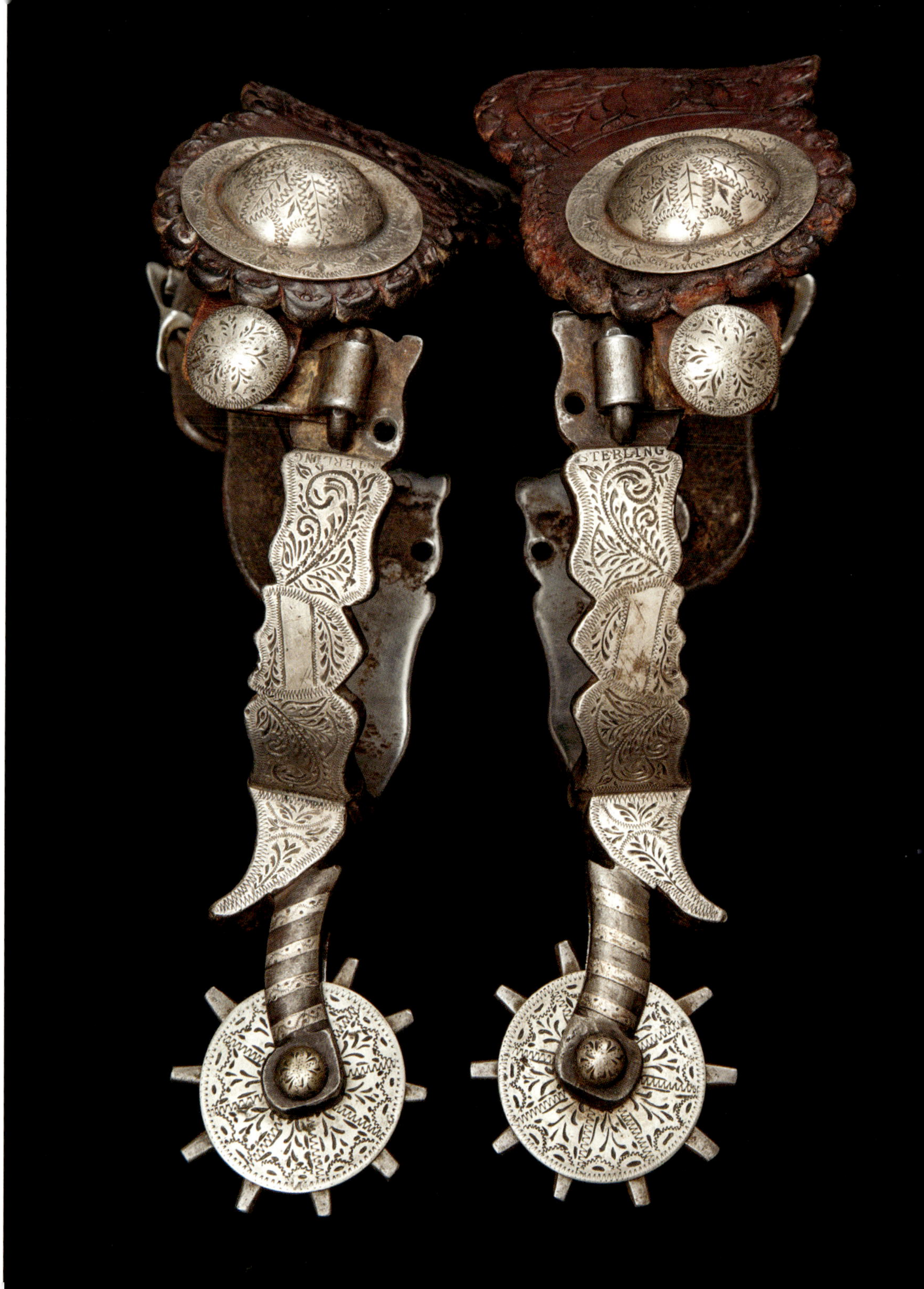

Figure 2-40. Hulbert spurs—Shield Pattern. An impressive pair of engraved silver-overlaid spurs with a shield in the center of the heelbands, banded shanks, and huge silver discs covering most of the 10-point rowels. The conchos on the spur straps appear to be engraved by Hulbert. *Courtesy of J. Lyndes. Photo by J. Williams.*

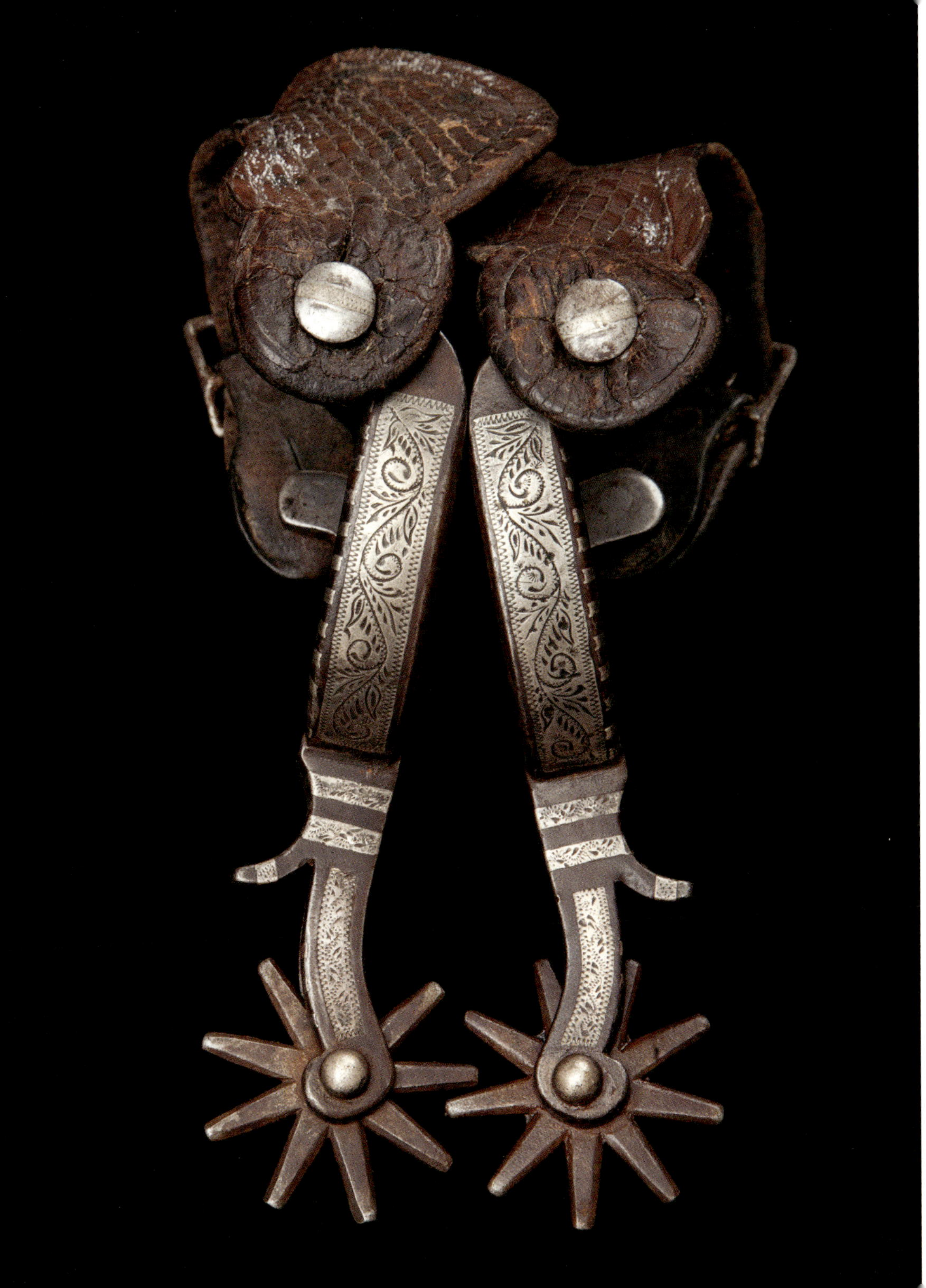

Figure 2-41. Hulbert spurs—Band Pattern. These spurs are nearly exact duplicates of No. H70 (Figure 2-2) and exhibit an engraved heelband, buttons with a single-silver stripe, and inlays on the top edges. *Courtesy of J. Lyndes. Photo by J. Williams.*

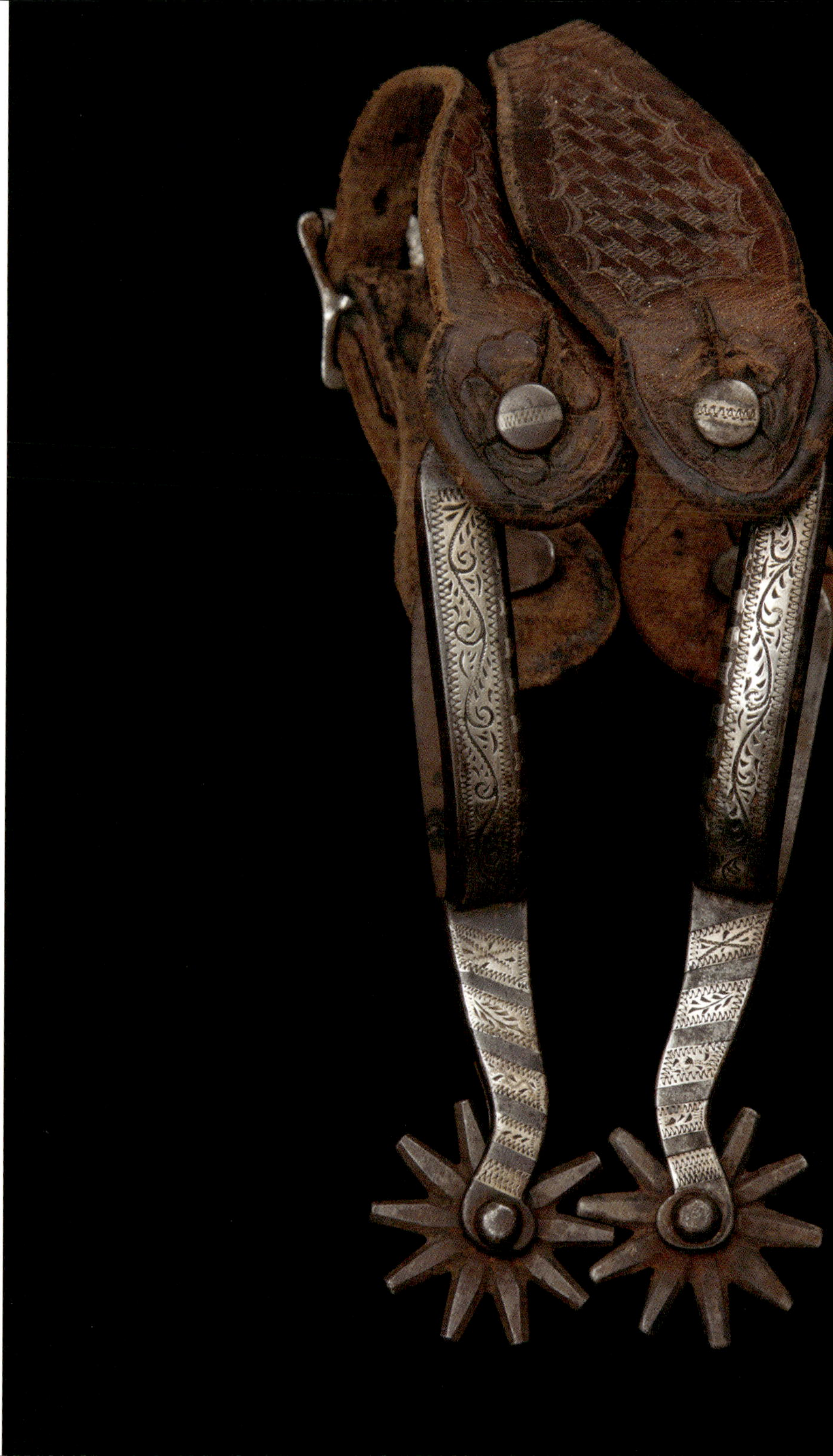

Figure 2-42. Hulbert spurs—Band Pattern Variation. The size and scale of this pair indicate that it might have been a custom order for a woman. The shanks are distinctive, and the heelbands show silver inlays on the top edge. *Courtesy of J. Lyndes. Photo by J. Williams.*

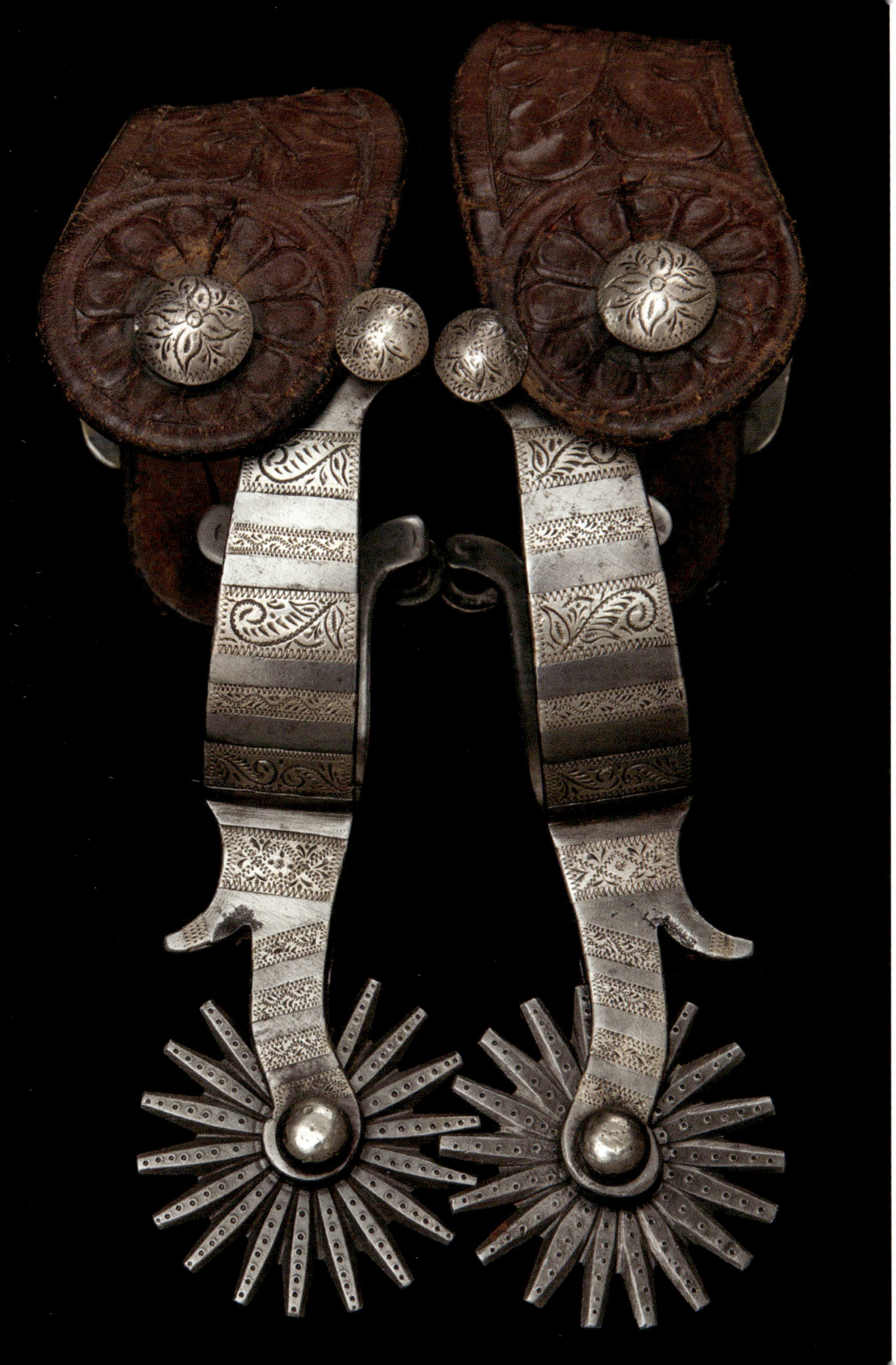

Figure 2-43. Hulbert spurs—Bar Pattern. This superbly-crafted pair of spurs, with engraved silver bars of different widths across the heelbands and shanks, exhibits split heelbands decorated with engraved silver button covers and intricately chased 18-point rowels. *Courtesy of J. Lyndes. Photo by J. Williams.*

Figure 2-44. Hulbert spurs—Bar Pattern with custom conchos. The silver bars on the heelbands of these men's single-mounted spurs are uniform in size, and the wide heelbands are split, with an outer silver-covered button. The 16-point rowels are plain iron. Note the heart-shaped silver conchos on the spur straps. *Photo by D. Congdon-Martin.*

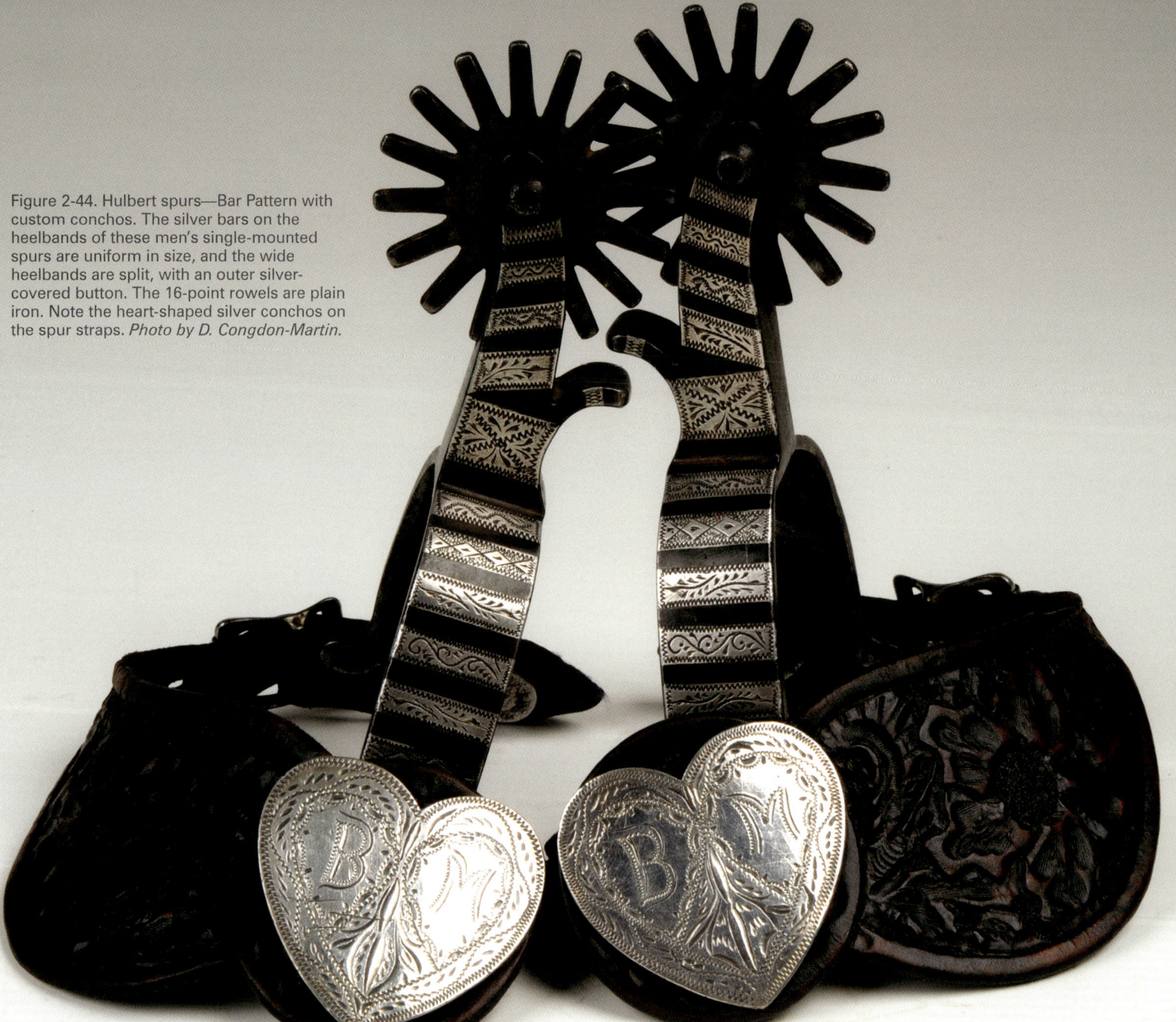

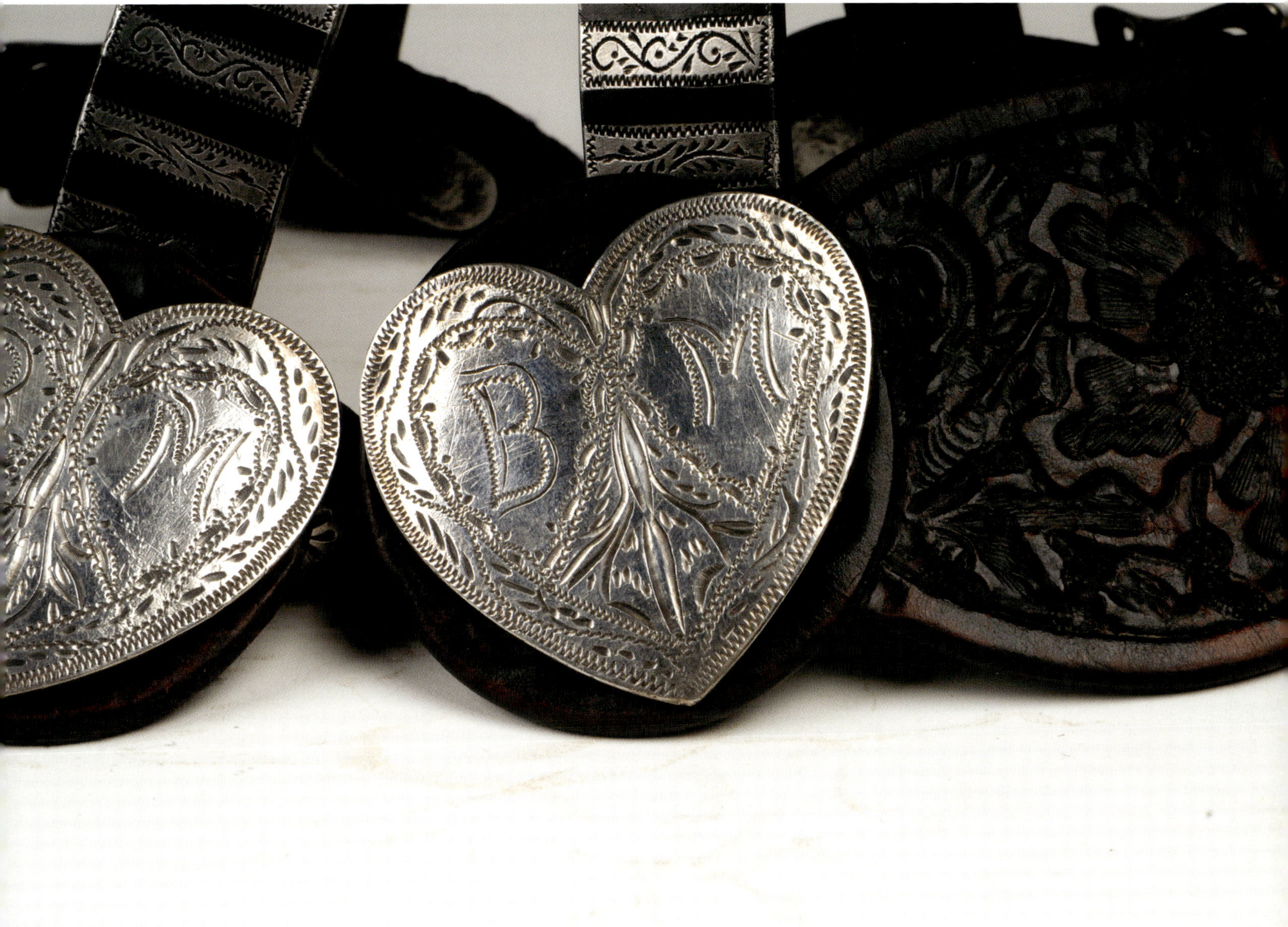

Figure 2-45. Personalized heart conchos on spurs (Figure 2-44). These conchos are elaborately engraved with the initials "B" and "M". *Photo by D. Congdon-Martin.*

Unusual Spurs and Interesting Variations

Hulbert made beautiful "ladies'" spurs—he understood that cowgirls required more refined, lighter weight, shorter heelband spurs that, in some cases, were personalized according to the woman's preference. A heart pattern variation, clearly made for a cowgirl, bears a rare mark ("H"). The straps were outfitted with Hulbert-engraved silver conchos and Ranger buckle sets, an altogether elegant pair (Figures 2-46 through 2-48). A rare pair of "snake" pattern spurs is shown in Figures 2-49 and 2-50. The reptile is coiled around to form the heelband and has a rather elongated snout. The straps are of the same period and are marked "OTTO F. ERNST/ MAKER/SHERIDAN, WYO." The engraving on the spurs in Figure 2-51 appears to be by Eddy Hulbert, yet the spur itself is marked "VISALIA STOCK SADDLE CO./SAN FRANCISCO," a quality saddler known for its fine line of products, including spurs (Figure 2-52). In this case, Hulbert might have enhanced these spurs for a local cowman, or perhaps replaced the original, damaged silver with his own work.

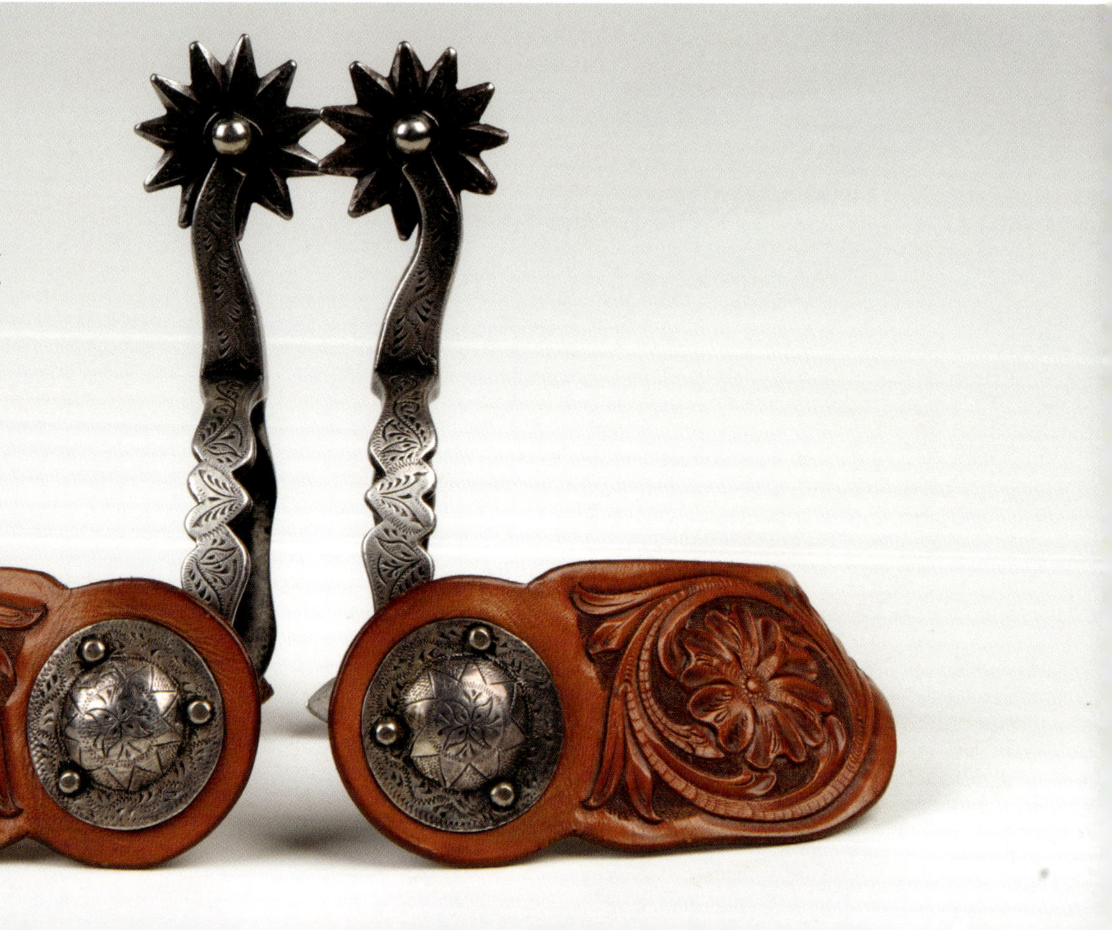

Figure 2-46. Hulbert spurs—Heart Pattern variation. These outstanding single-mounted spurs, c. 1930s–1940s, were clearly made for a cowgirl. They are unusual, in that the Hulbert mark is a single "H" in block letters under both buttons (see Figure 2-48). The spurs are fitted with fully-tooled straps with sterling silver-engraved matching Hulbert conchos (see Figure 2-47) and matching Ranger buckle sets (see Figure 2-48). The star-shaped, 10-point rowels are punch-decorated. *Photo by D. Congdon-Martin.*

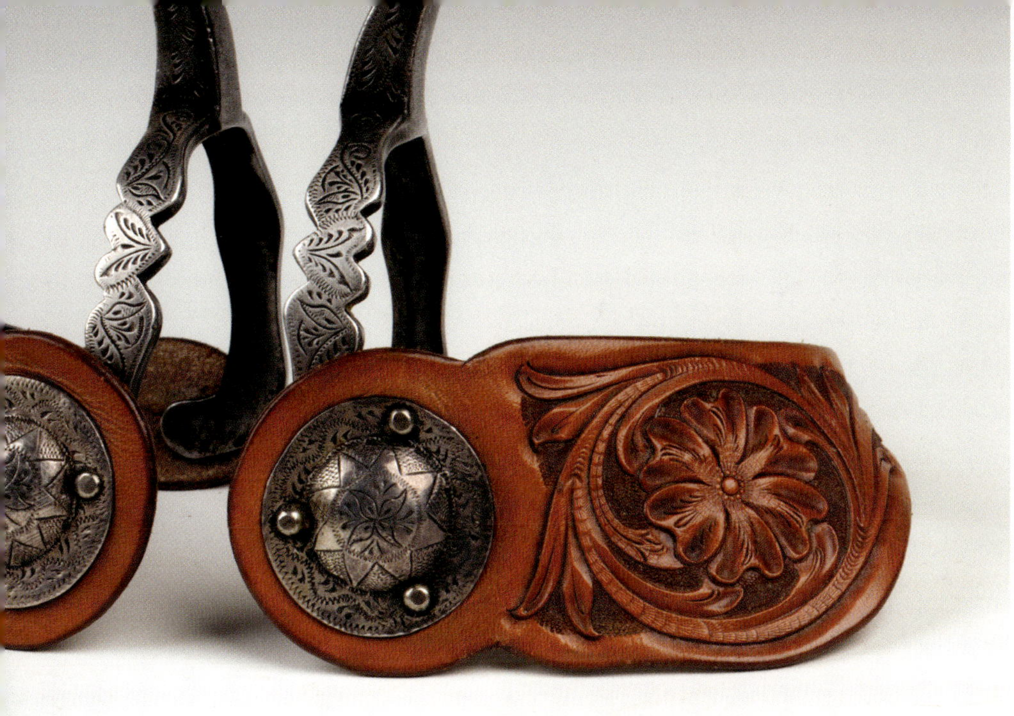

Figure 2-47. Hulbert conchos—Enlarged view of Figure 2-46. Note the pristine condition of the silver and the straps. *Photo by D. Congdon-Martin.*

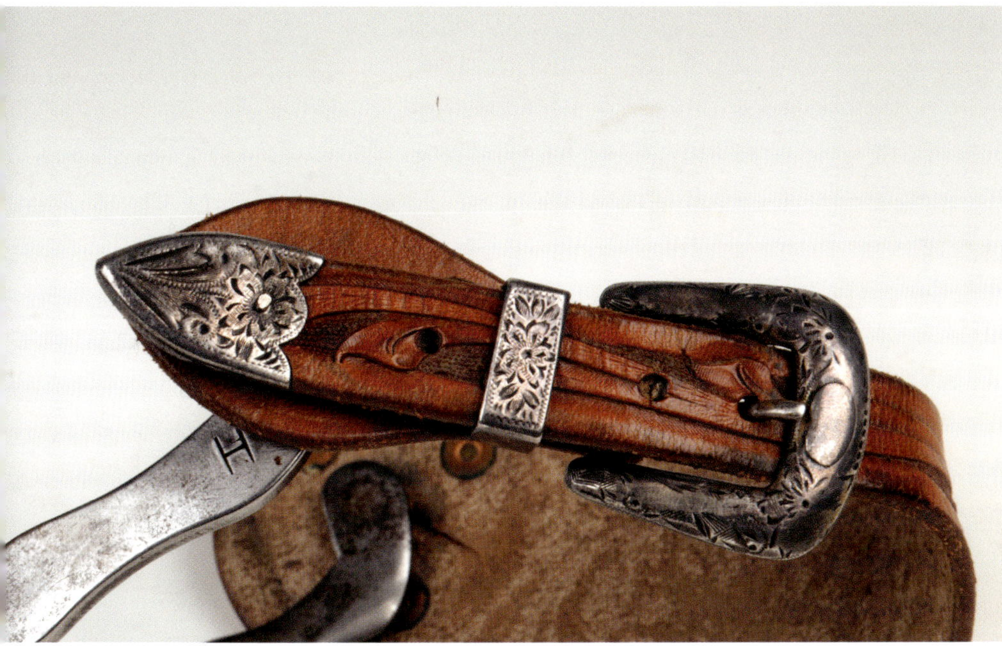

Figure 2-48. Hulbert Ranger set on spur straps—Enlarged view of Figure 2-46. This small Ranger set complements the straps on these elegant, petite spurs. Note the "H" mark in block letters on the end of the unmounted heelband. *Photo by D. Congdon-Martin.*

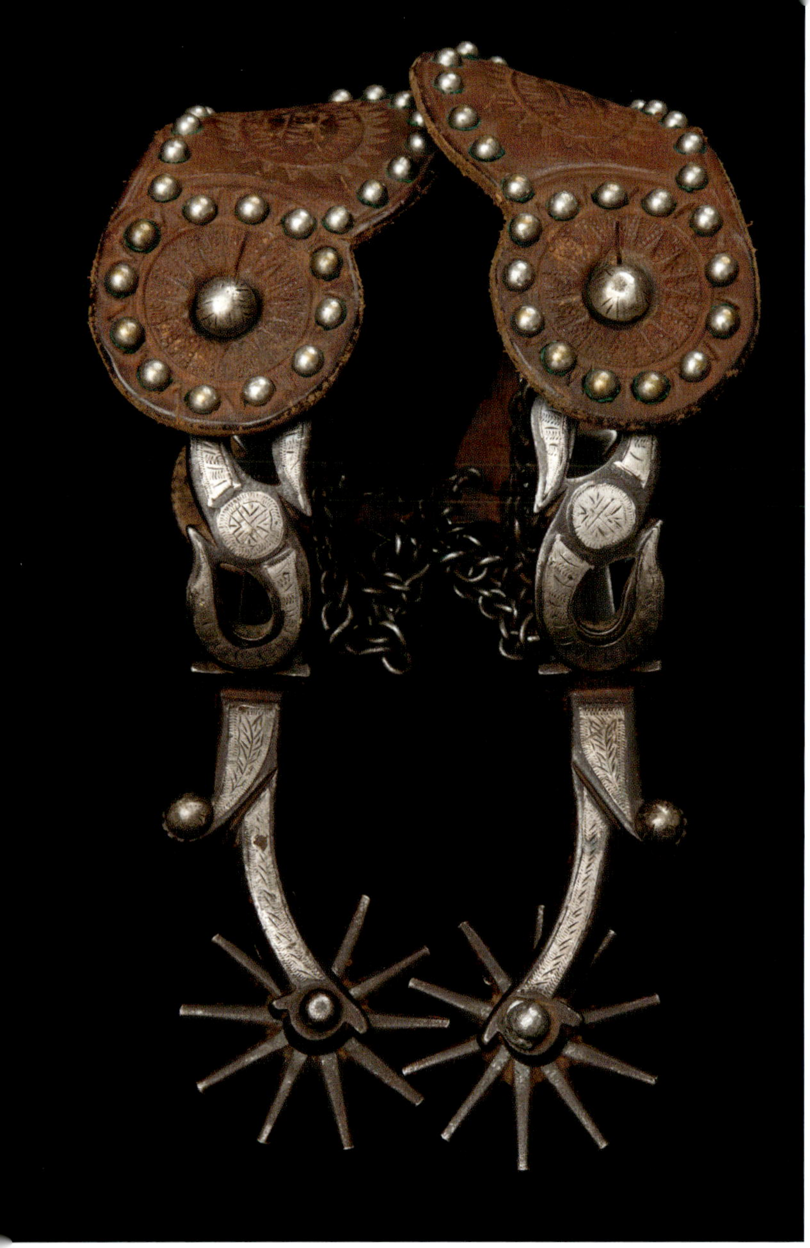

Figure 2-49. Hulbert spurs—"Snake" Pattern. This pattern of a coiled snake in silver inlay is exceedingly rare. The spurs have extra-long silver-inlaid shanks with silver buttons on the tips of the chap guards. The period straps are from the Ernst Saddlery (see Figure 2-50). Courtesy of J. Lyndes. Photo by J. Williams.

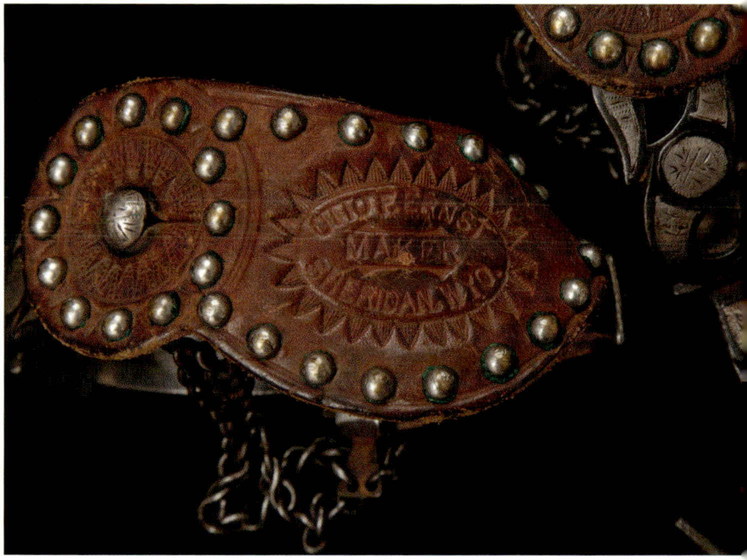

Figure 2-50. Spur straps on spurs shown in Figure 2-49. The mark is clearly stamped: "OTTO F. ERNST/MAKER/SHERIDAN/WYO." Note the pointed nose that Hulbert gave the snake. *Courtesy of J. Lyndes. Photo by J. Williams.*

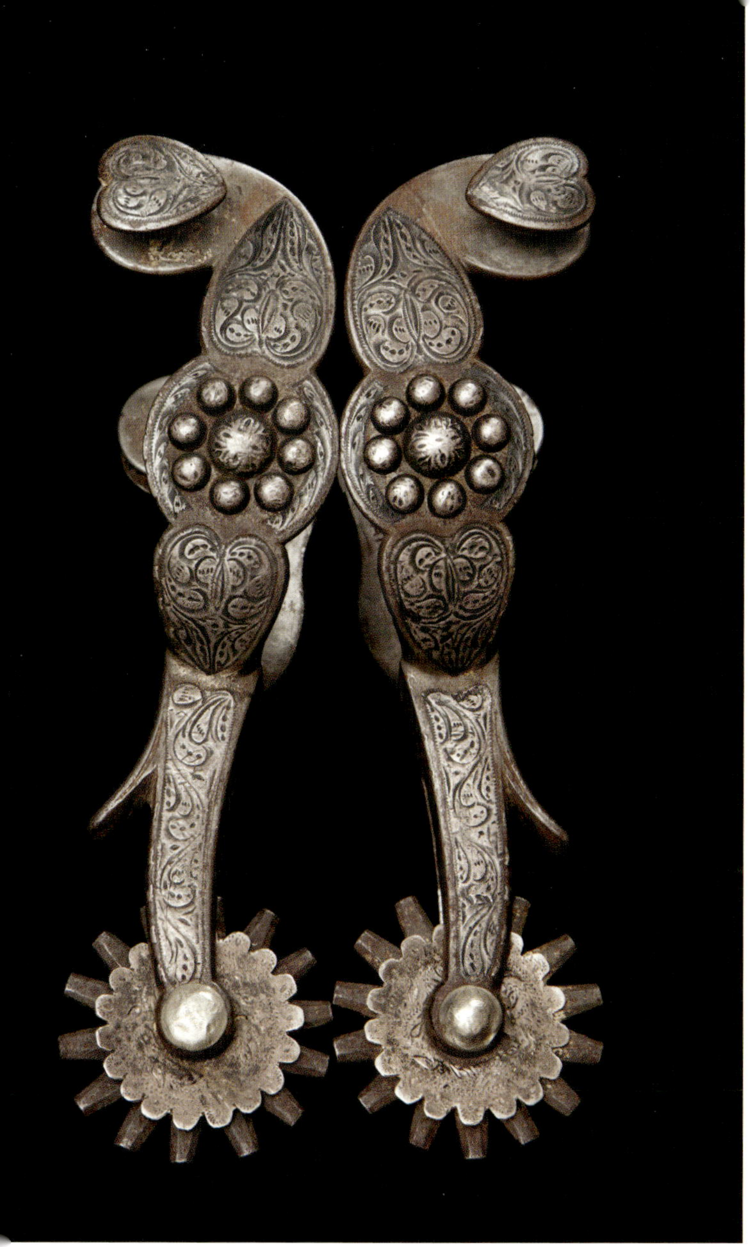

Figure 2-51. Hulbert silver on Visalia spurs. It was not unusual to have shop-made spurs decorated with silver by another maker, or to have a recognized silversmith replace silver on a worn or damaged set of spurs. Shown here is a pair of spurs made by the Visalia Stock Saddle Co. (San Francisco), but mounted with Hulbert-engraved silver on the shanks, heelbands, rowel discs, and heart-shaped buttons. See Figure 2-52 for mark. *Courtesy of J. Lyndes. Photo by J. Williams.*

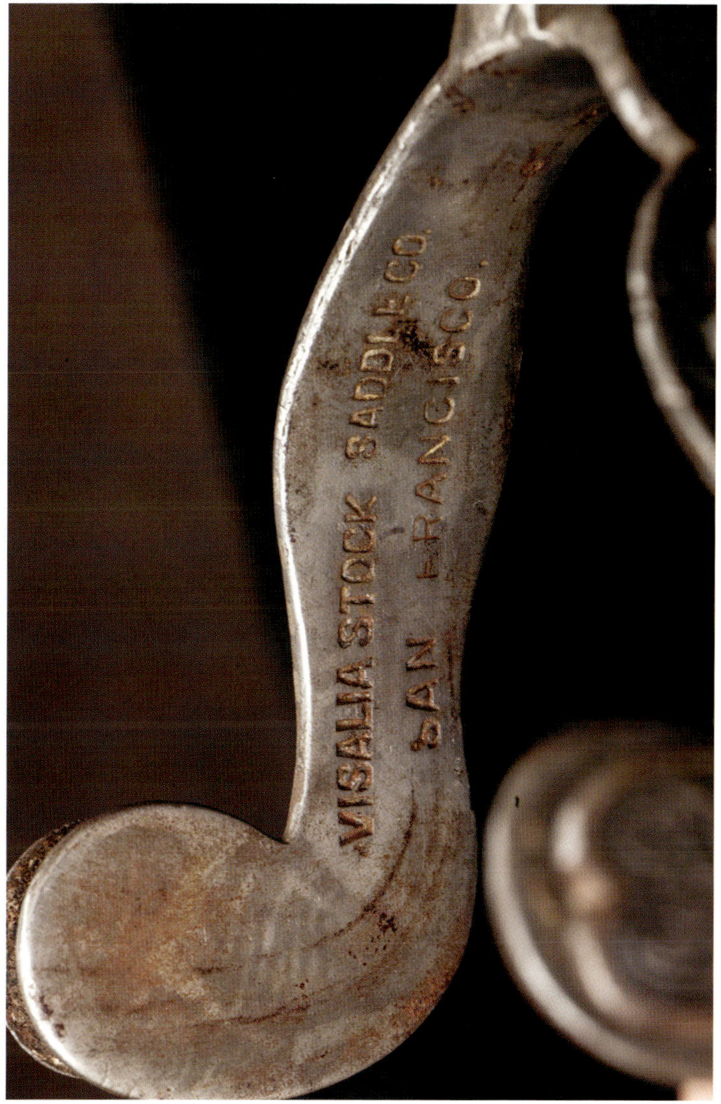

Figure 2-52. Visalia-marked spurs with Hulbert silver as shown in Figure 2-51. The characteristic mark: "VISALIA STOCK SADDLE CO./SAN FRANCISCO," appears on the inside of the heelband. *Courtesy of J. Lyndes. Photo by J. Williams.*

Custom Orders

Much of Hulbert's later work was commissioned or custom-ordered by rodeos or horse shows as prizes or by individuals wanting their initials or ranch brands on their spurs. A stunning example of a pair of custom-ordered spurs is shown in Figures 2-53 through 2-57. These are double-mounted (silver on both sides of the heelband) with the initials "BMJ" on the inner side and decorated hearts and circles on the outside. The original straps with Hulbert-engraved silver initials "BJ" are shown in detail in Figure 2-54, and the accompanying conchos in Figure 2-57. "Snowflake" rowels and quatrefoil silver buttons (Figure 2-55) add to the elegance of these showy spurs. A similar pair, but with the initials "RBL" and different shanks, is shown in Figure 2-58. These spurs are believed to have been the property of Rosella B. Boe Lemmon, wife of famous rancher, land and town developer, bank president, and founder of Lemmon, South Dakota, George Edward "Ed" Lemmon. Rosella married Lemmon in 1900 in Edgemont, South Dakota, and participated in many aspects of the Lemmon ranching operation that included driving cattle and construction of dipping tanks (Sanderson, 2011; Yost, 1969; Schmidt, 2007). She clearly enjoyed the finer side of life as well as the Western traditions embodied in her husband's ranching efforts, which ended in 1923 due to financial hardships. Divorced in 1927, Rosella moved to Sturgis and died in 1964 (Sanderson, 2011).

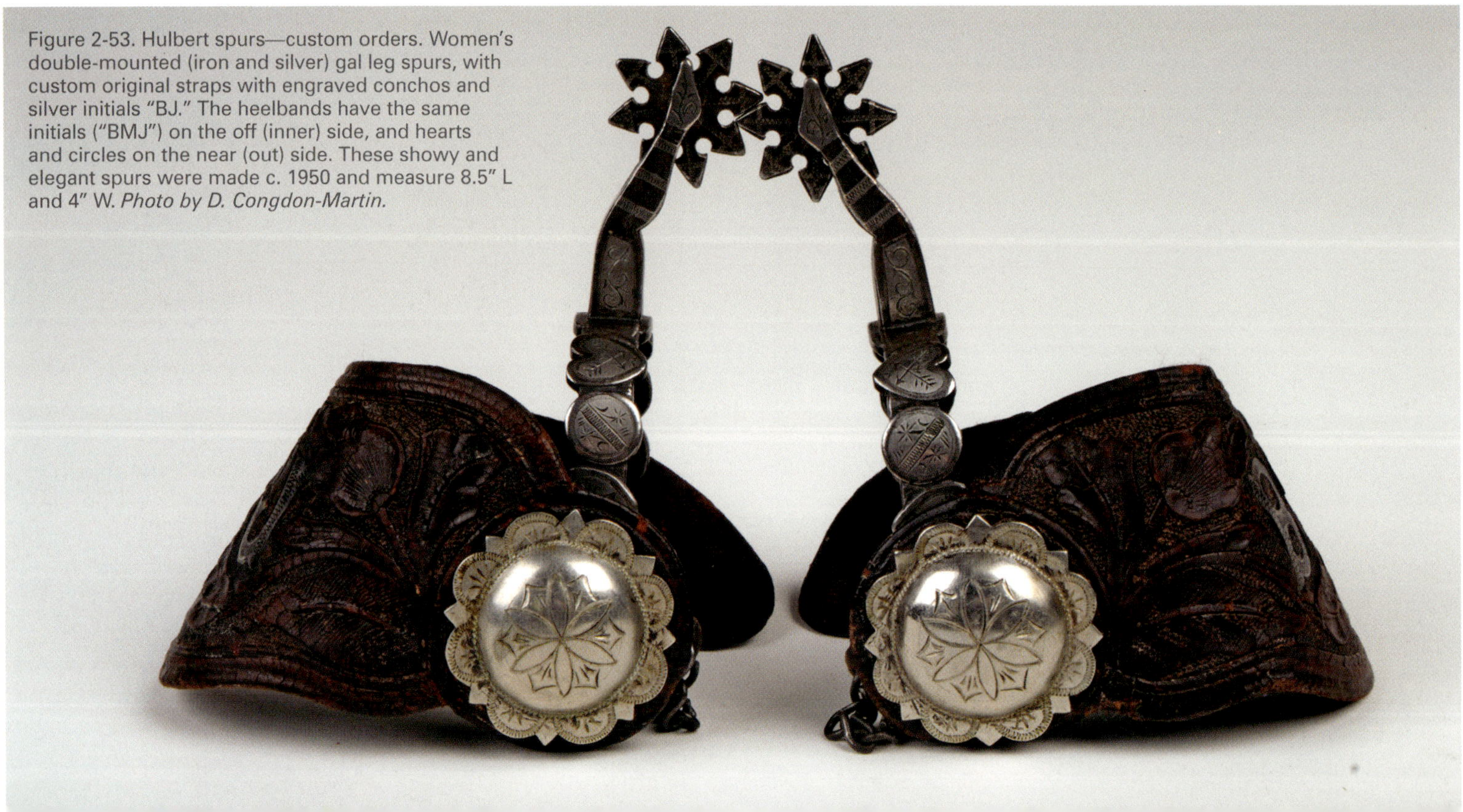

Figure 2-53. Hulbert spurs—custom orders. Women's double-mounted (iron and silver) gal leg spurs, with custom original straps with engraved conchos and silver initials "BJ." The heelbands have the same initials ("BMJ") on the off (inner) side, and hearts and circles on the near (out) side. These showy and elegant spurs were made c. 1950 and measure 8.5" L and 4" W. *Photo by D. Congdon-Martin.*

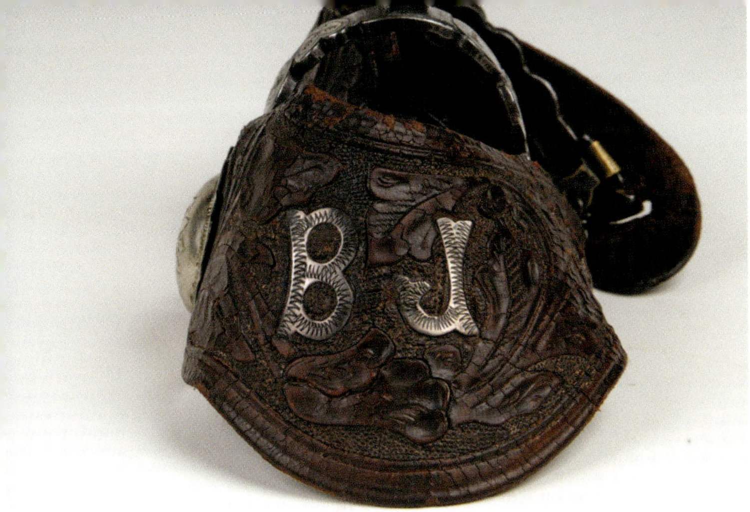

Figure 2-54. Hulbert spurs—custom orders. Enlarged view of Hulbert's silver initials on spur straps fitted onto spurs shown in Figure 2-53. *Photo by D. Congdon-Martin.*

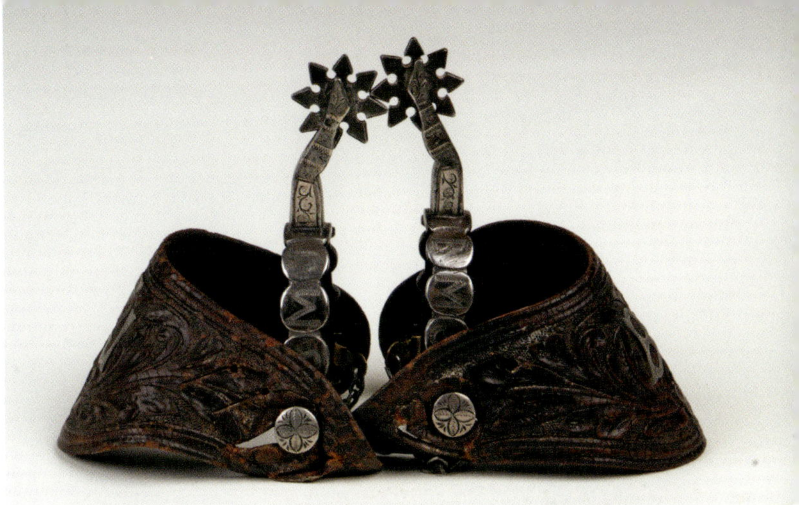

Figure 2-55. Hulbert spurs—custom orders. Off side of spurs shown in Figure 2-53. Initials, snowflake rowels, and quatrefoil silver buttons are evident. *Photo by D. Congdon-Martin.*

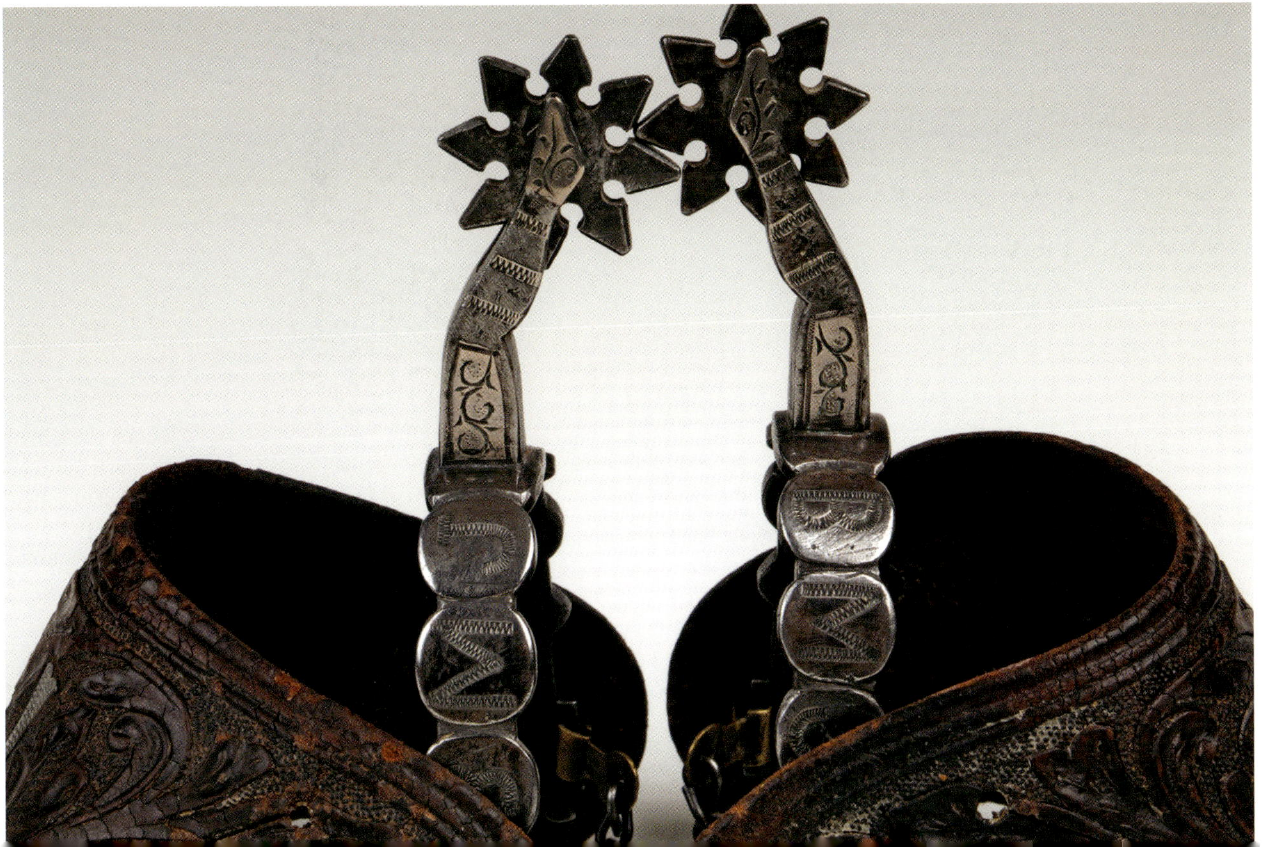

Figure 2-56. Hulbert spurs—custom orders. Enlarged view of spurs in Figure 2-55 showing initials and unusual engraving on the gal leg shanks. *Photo by D. Congdon-Martin.*

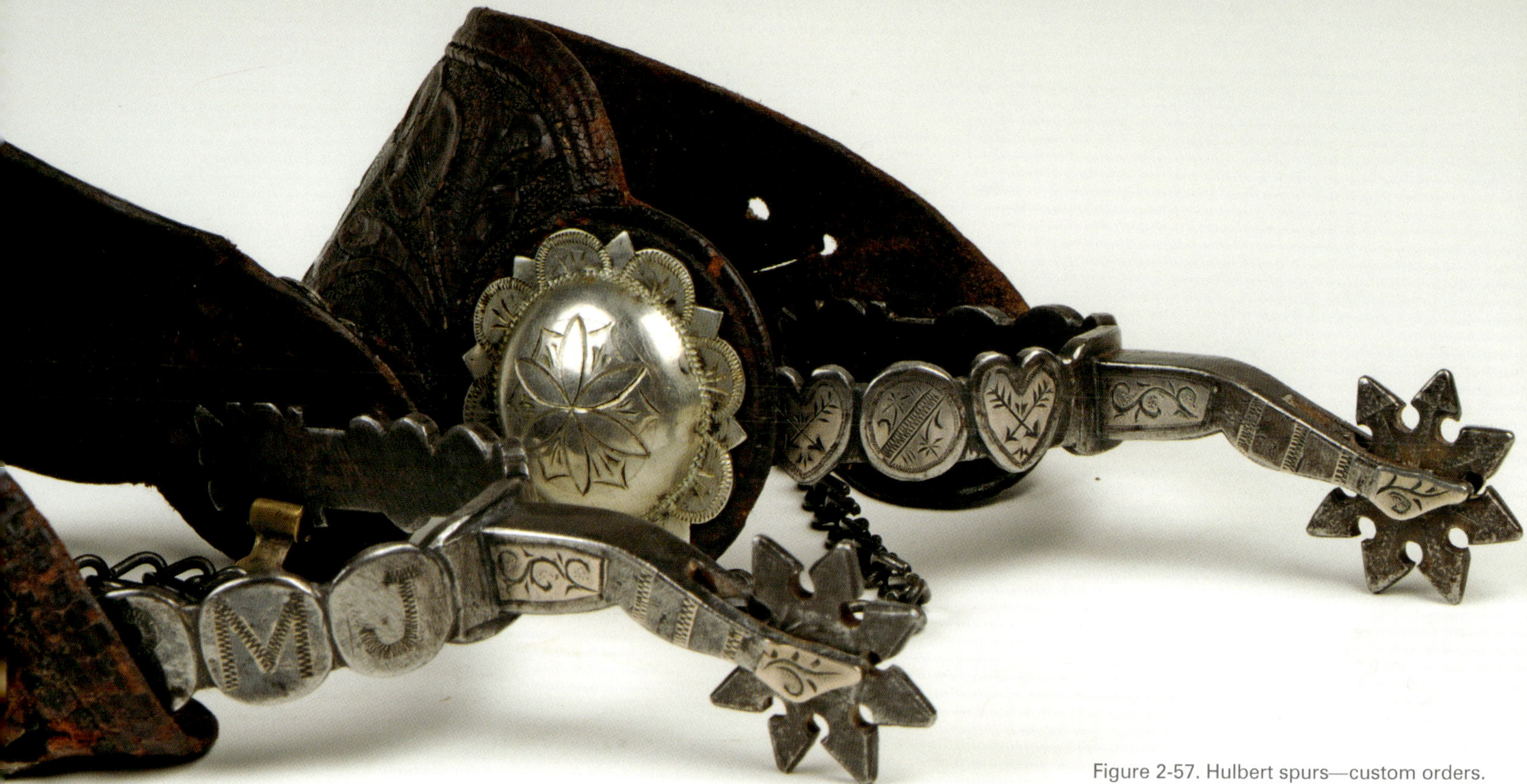

Figure 2-57. Hulbert spurs—custom orders. Spurs (Figure 2-53) showing gal leg shanks with "garters" and engraved slippers. Note the conchos and unusual engraved silver pieces on the inner and outside heelbands. *Photo by D. Congdon-Martin.*

Spurs with engraved initials on more or less standard patterns were also popular. A woman's pair of silver-overlaid double mounts with the initials "EKS" is shown in Figures 2-59 and 2-60, and a second pair with the initials "JCN,"owned by Wyoming rancher James "Kid" Nichols (1883–1962) (Patrick, 1969), in Figure 2-61. In both sets, the initials were engraved across the center on the heelband. Two pairs of initialed men's spurs, with engraved "WJM" and inlaid "GHB" (Figures 2-62 and 2-63, respectively), present an interesting contrast. The former, made for Woodson Moss, a rancher in the Dryhead country, are attractive and showy, with very sharp rowels, whereas the latter pair is heavy and worn, with blunt star rowels, and part of a "working" cowboy's outfit. Hulbert also made conchos and buckle (Ranger) sets for spur straps. Figures 2-64 and 2-65 depict a beautiful pair with the gold initial "B" overlaid onto the engraved silver conchos. These might have been made for Beverly St. John (see Chapter 4, and Reid, p. 53).

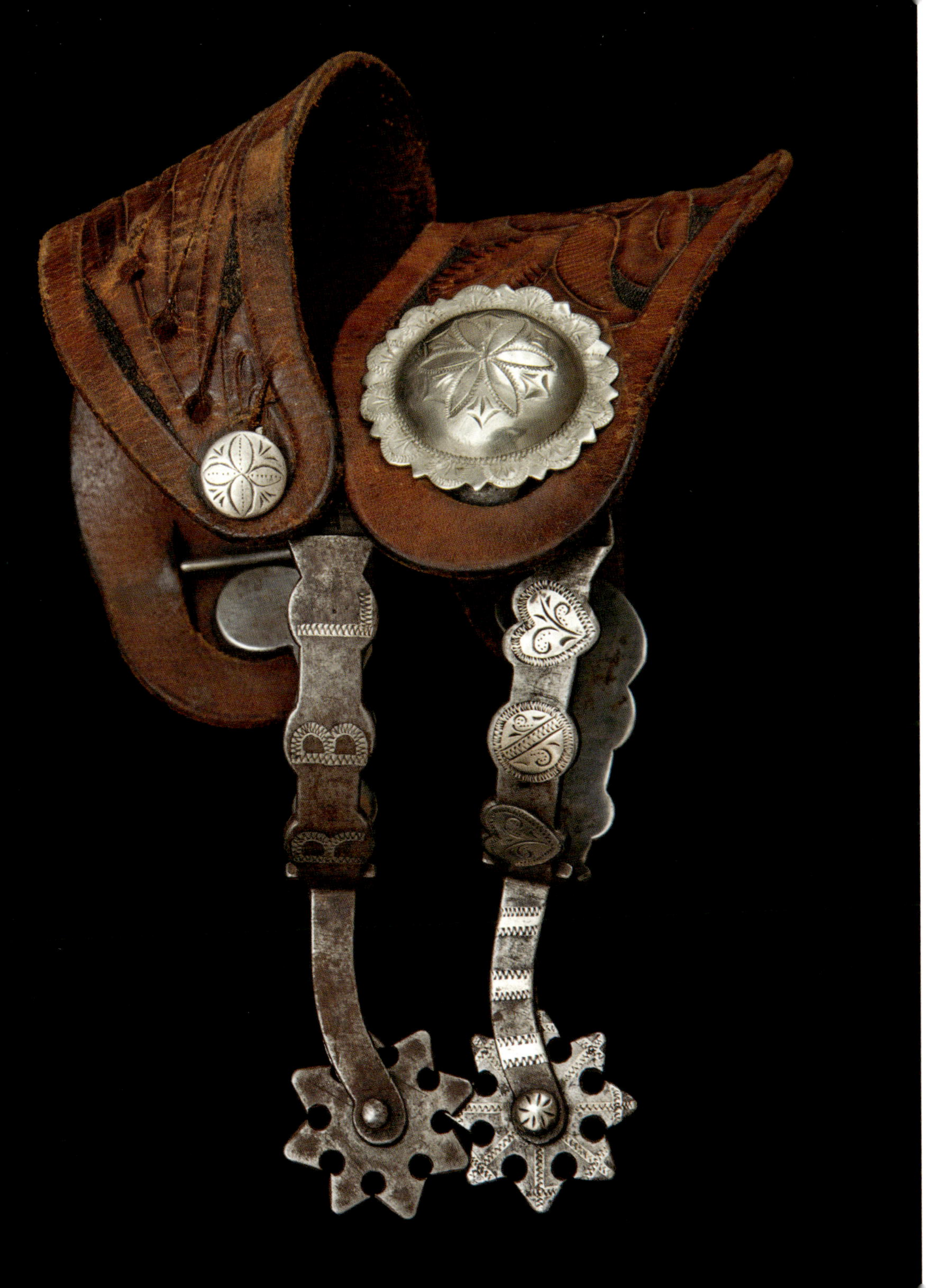

Figure 2-58. Hulbert spurs—custom orders. This pair of women's spurs resembles those shown in Figure 2-53, with the circle and heart-engraved heelbands, chased snowflake rowels, and silver button covers and conchos. However, the initials are different ("RBL") and the shanks are not crafted in the gal leg shape. These spurs are believed to have belonged to Rosella B. Lemmon, wife of rancher and land developer George E. Lemmon, South Dakota (see text for details). *Courtesy of J. Lyndes. Photo by J. Williams.*

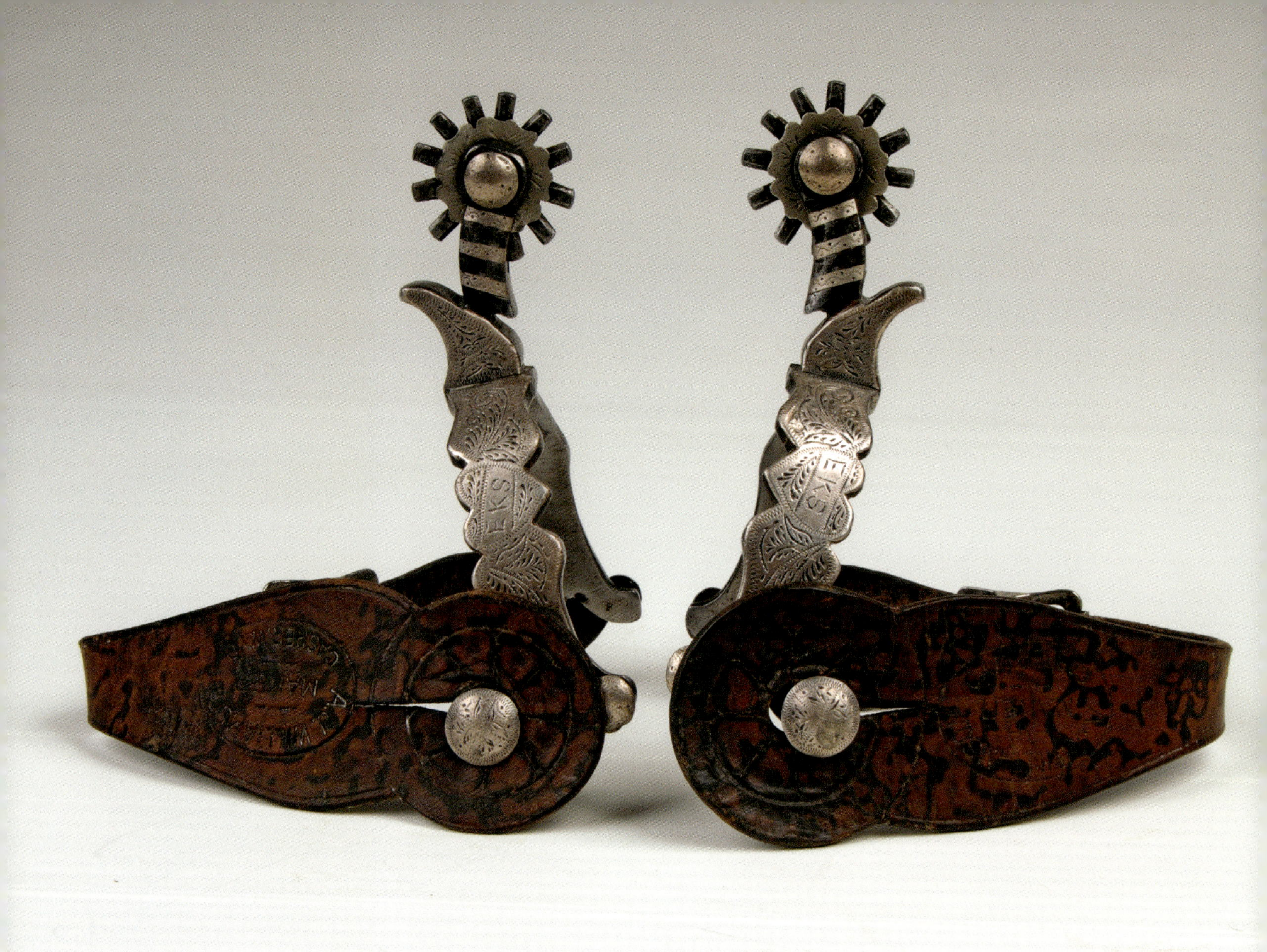

Figure 2-59. Hulbert spurs—custom orders. Shown are a double-mounted women's pair of engraved silver spurs with Cheyenne heelbands and covered (disc) 12-point rowels. The spurs have silver buttons, top edge inlays, and a heart on each heelband with the initials "EKS." The spur straps are marked "A.J. WILLIAMSON/MAKER/CASPER, WYO." *Photo by D. Congdon-Martin.*

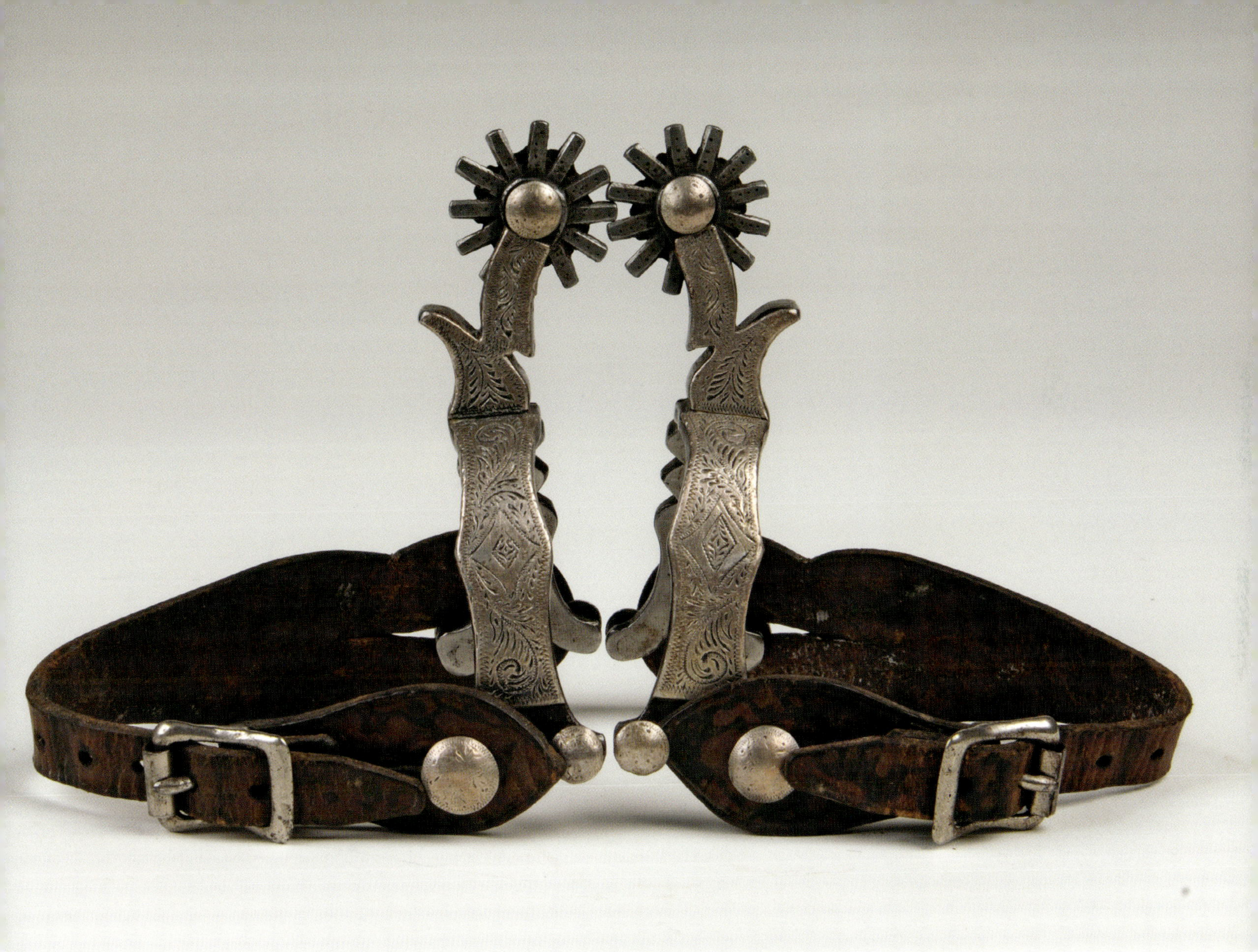

Figure 2-60. Hulbert spurs—custom orders. Opposite (inner) sides of spurs in Figure 2-59, showing silver overlaid double mounts. *Photo by D. Congdon-Martin.*

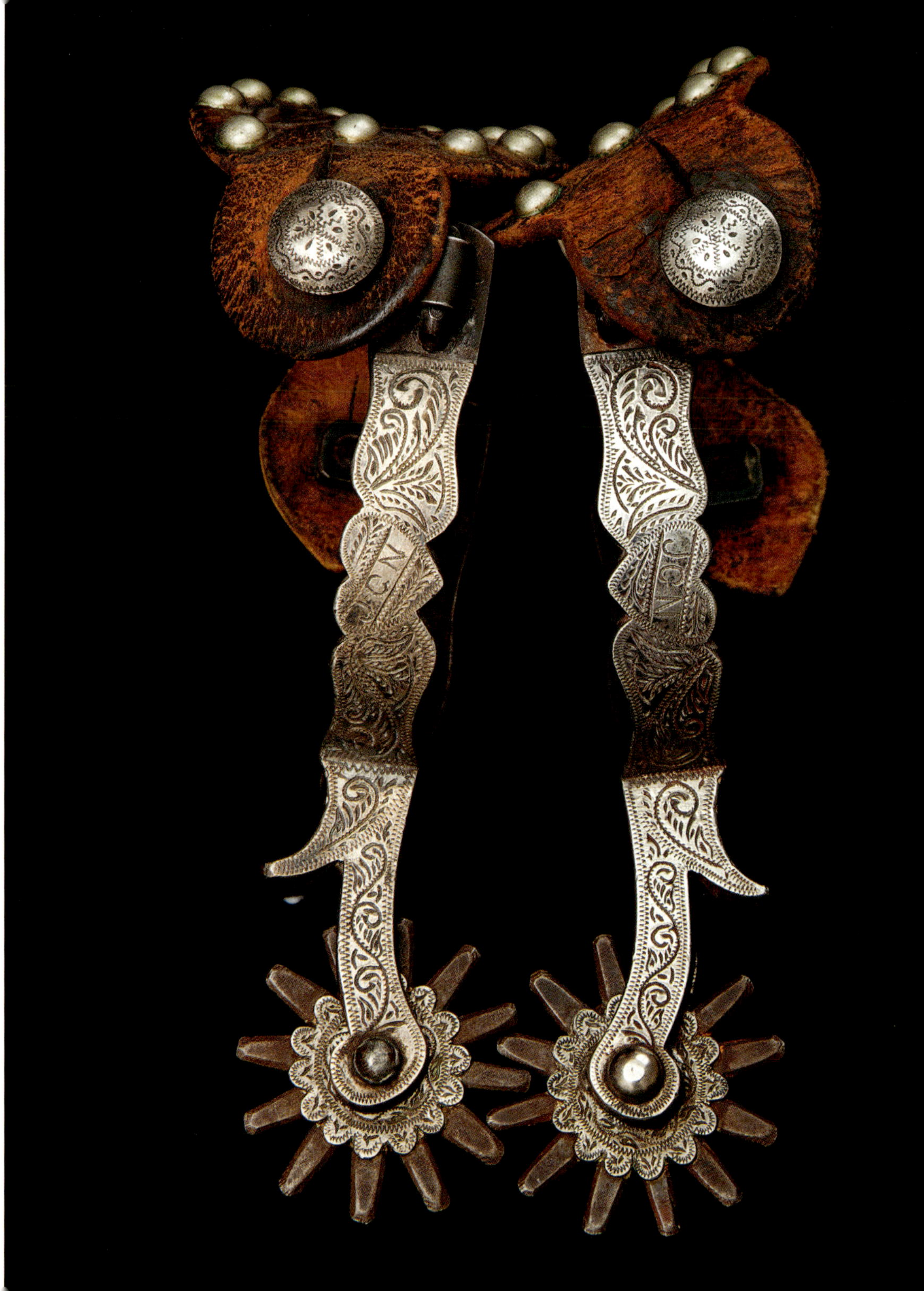

Figure 2-61. Hulbert spurs—custom orders. An elaborate pair in the heart pattern with the initials "JCN" engraved across the center hearts. An unusual feature of these spurs is the silver overlay on one side of the heelband, and an inlaid ranch brand on the other side (see Figure 2-76). The engraved silver button covers and discs on the 12-point rowels complete this set of spurs, formerly owned by "Kid" Nichols, of the Diamond Bar Ranch (Cody, Wyoming). *Courtesy of J. Lyndes. Photo by J. Williams.*

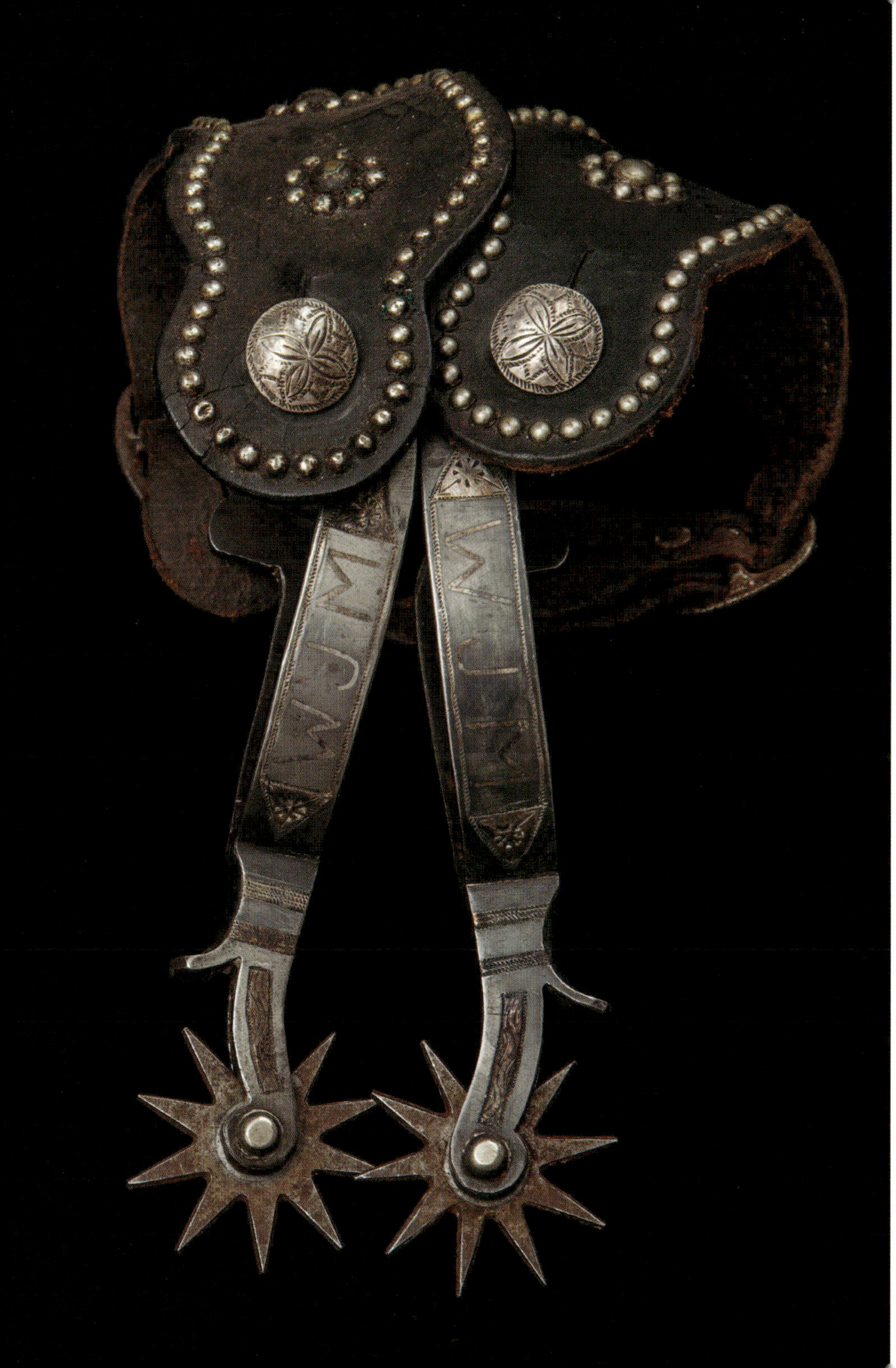

Figure 2-62. Hulbert spurs—custom orders. This rather plain but attractive pair of men's spurs has the initials "WJM" engraved prominently across the heelbands. They were made for Woodson Moss, a rancher in the Dryhead area of Montana or Wyoming. The 10-point rowels appear original yet are very sharp. *Courtesy of J. Lyndes. Photo by J. Williams.*

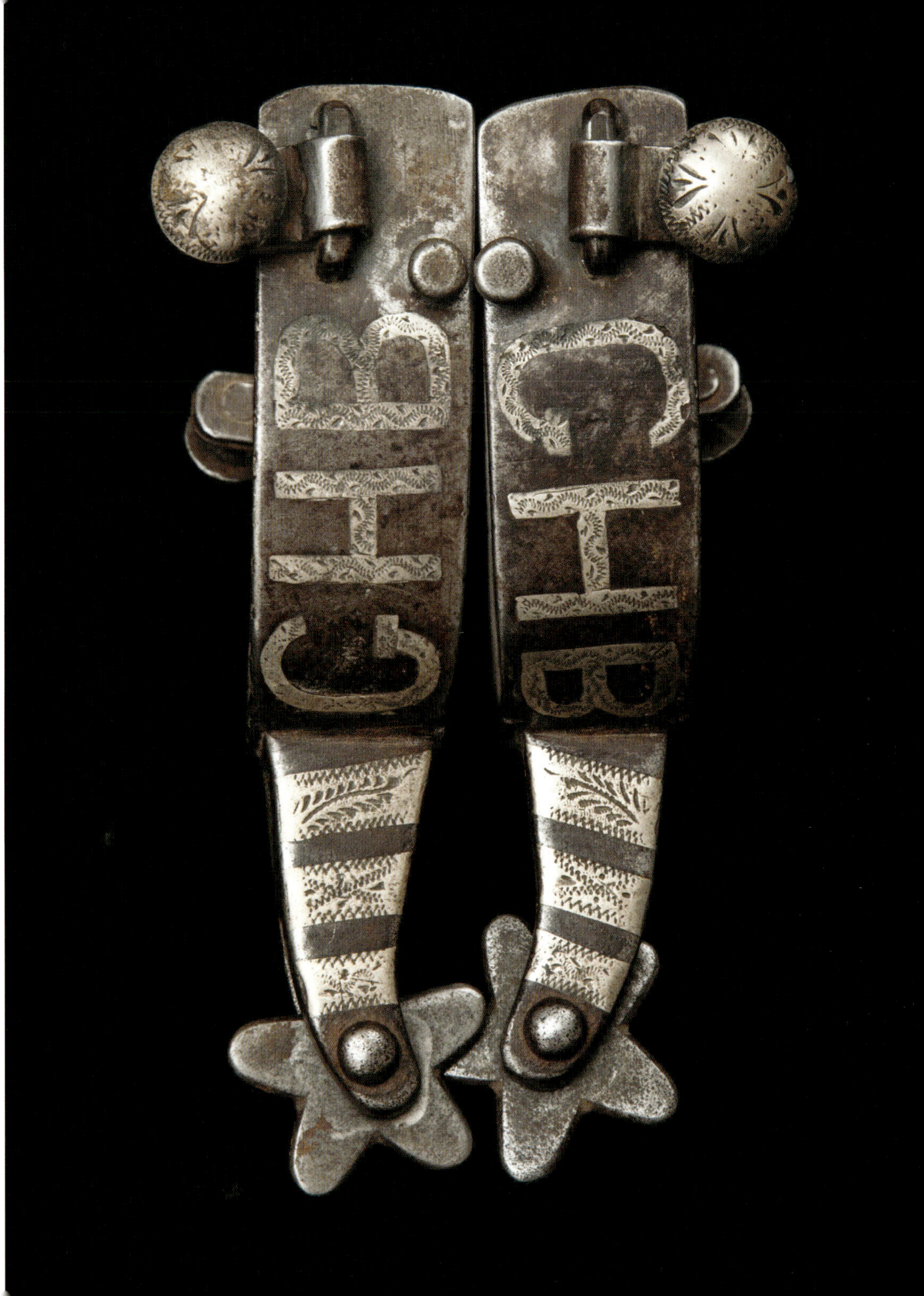

Figure 2-63. Hulbert spurs—custom orders. This heavy pair of working cowboy spurs shows much period use and wear, but the initials "GHB" remain clear and bold. Bar-inlaid shanks, 5-point star rowels, and silver-covered swinging buttons complete the set. *Courtesy of J. Lyndes. Photo by J. Williams.*

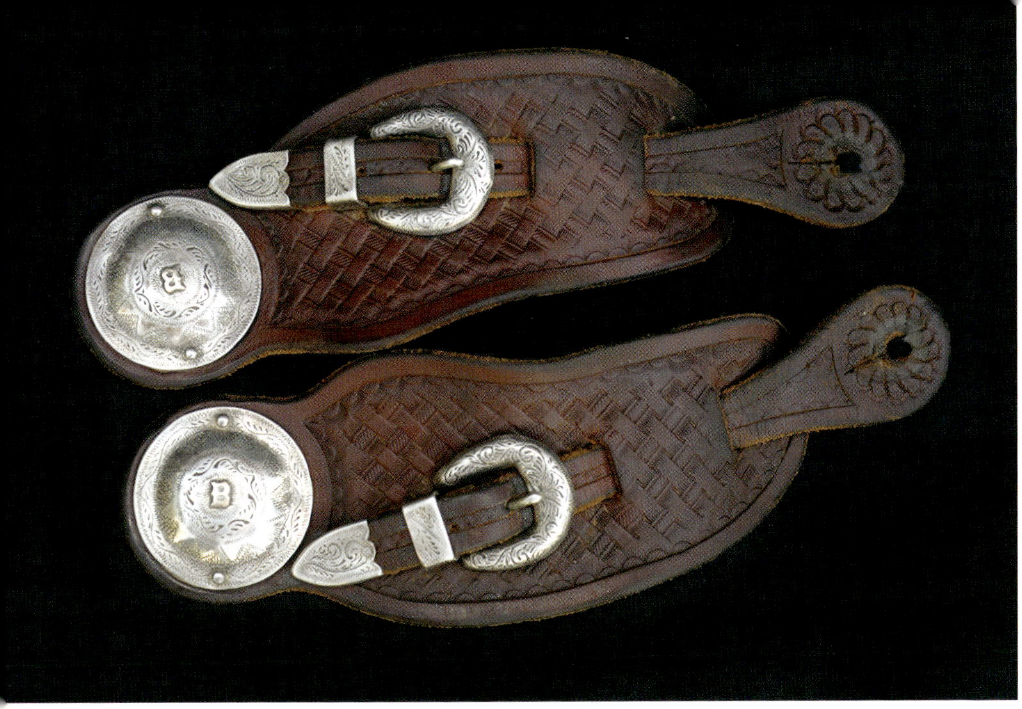

Figure 2-64. Hulbert spurs—straps with personalized conchos. These basket-stamped spur straps were fitted with engraved silver Ranger sets and conchos, the latter with a gold initial "B" in the center. *Courtesy of R. Wilmot. William Manns photo.*

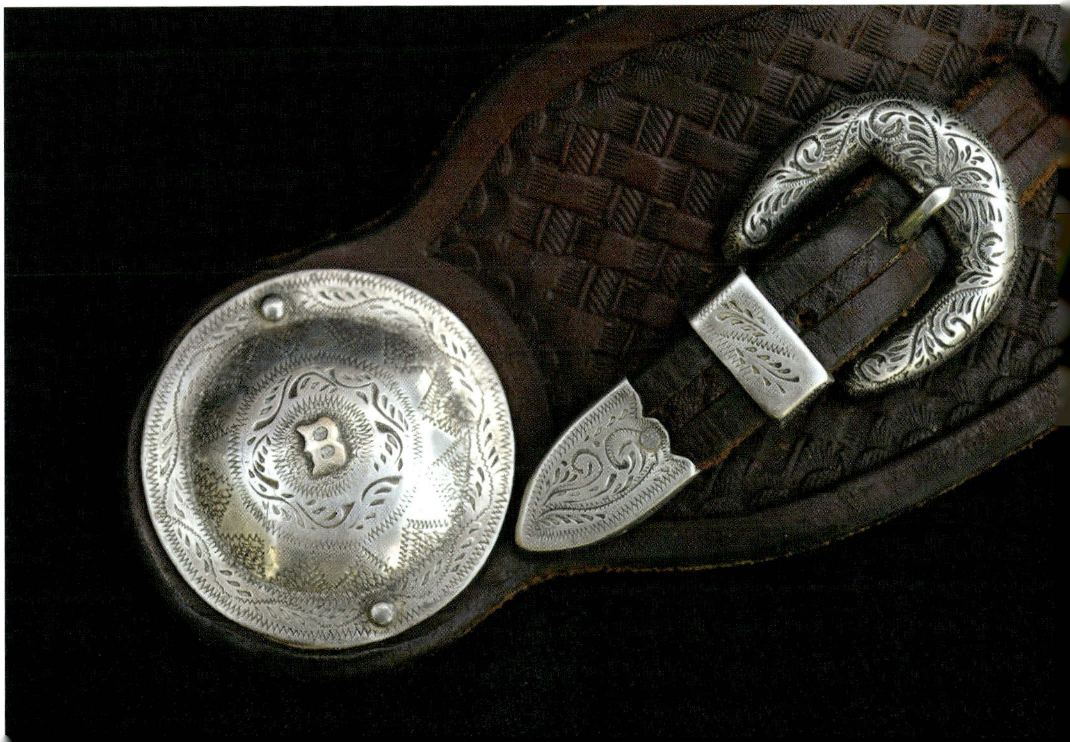

Figure 2-65. Hulbert spurs—straps with personalized conchos. An enlarged view of the Ranger set and conchos shown in Figure 2-64. Hulbert typically used gold letters overlaid/soldered onto his engraved silver. *Courtesy of R. Wilmot. William Manns photo.*

Custom Orders – Ranches

The Valley Ranch, a famous dude ranch located on the South Fork of the Shoshone River, Cody, Wyoming, used the "Lazy JD" brand and commissioned Hulbert's silver work for their Ranch store, most or all of which bore their brand. An example of the silver-inlaid "Lazy JD" brand on a pair of Hulbert's spurs, with similarly-branded straps, is shown in Figures 2-66 and 2-67. This pair was part of a four-piece ensemble belonging to Irma Larom, wife of Larry Larom, who founded the Valley Ranch in 1915 with his Princeton University friend, Winthrop Brooks (later president of Brooks Brothers clothier). Irving Hastings (Larry) Larom (1889–1973) was a dynamic presence in the Yellowstone National Park area and was the first president of the Dude Ranchers Association in 1926 (en.wikipedia.org.wiki/Larry_Larom). Two of the other items claimed to have belonged to Irma Larom are shown in Figures 2-68 and 2-69; the batwing chaps and bronc belt both have the "Lazy JD" brand and

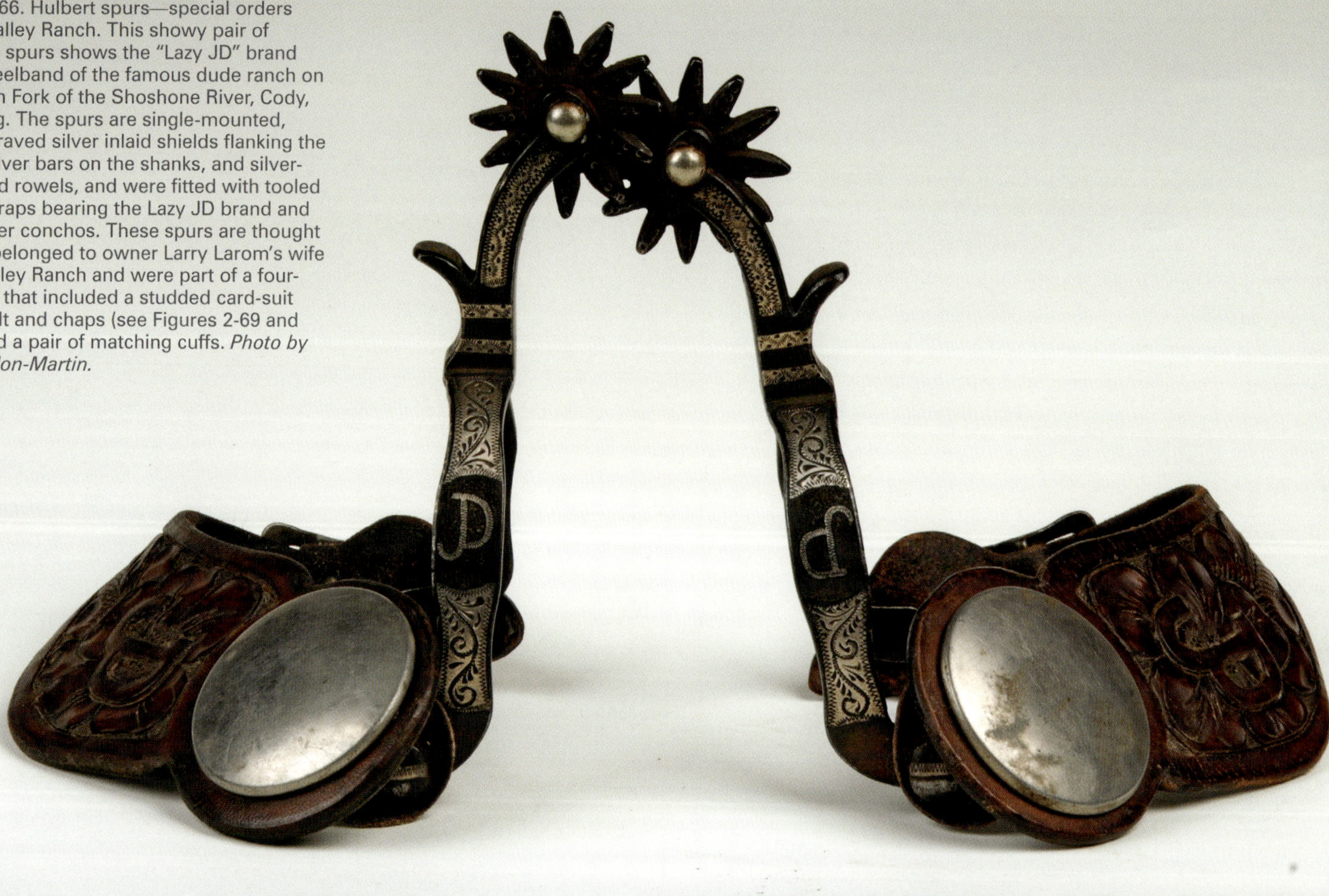

Figure 2-66. Hulbert spurs—special orders for the Valley Ranch. This showy pair of women's spurs shows the "Lazy JD" brand on the heelband of the famous dude ranch on the South Fork of the Shoshone River, Cody, Wyoming. The spurs are single-mounted, with engraved silver inlaid shields flanking the brand, silver bars on the shanks, and silver-decorated rowels, and were fitted with tooled brown straps bearing the Lazy JD brand and plain silver conchos. These spurs are thought to have belonged to owner Larry Larom's wife at the Valley Ranch and were part of a four-piece set that included a studded card-suit bronc belt and chaps (see Figures 2-69 and 2-68), and a pair of matching cuffs. *Photo by D. Congdon-Martin.*

were further embellished with studded card suits. Figure 2-70 is a photograph of a pair of nicely-executed men's spurs with rocker-engraved "Lazy JD" brands inlaid on the heelbands. In contrast, the same engraved, inlaid brand appears on a more refined pair, possibly made in a ladies' size, with large plain conchos on "Lazy JD" spur straps (Figures 2-71 and 2-72). Although we do not know which saddlemaker tooled these straps, they were certainly a commissioned order for the Valley Ranch.

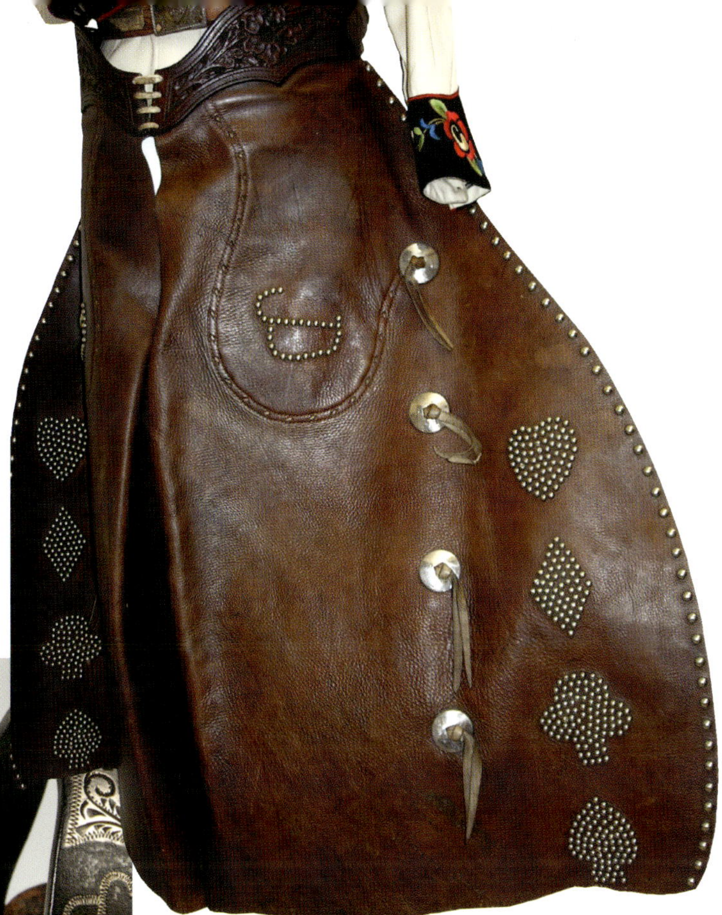

Figure 2-68. Valley Ranch batwing chaps. Brown leather women's batwing chaps with studded card suits, trim, and Lazy JD brand on pockets, c. 1930–1940. These chaps were part of the ensemble that included the spurs shown in Figure 2-66. *Photo by author.*

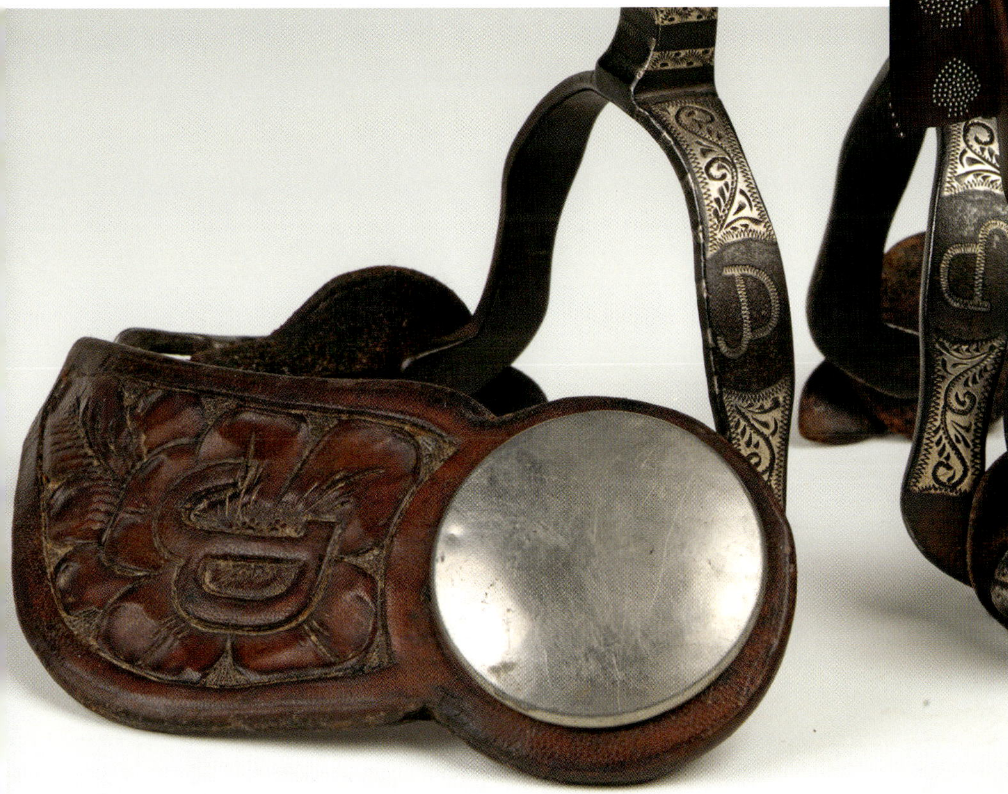

Figure 2-67. Hulbert spurs—special orders for the Valley Ranch. Shown is an enlarged view of the Lazy JD brand on one spur and strap from Figure 2-66. Note rocker engraving on the brand. *Photo by D. Congdon-Martin.*

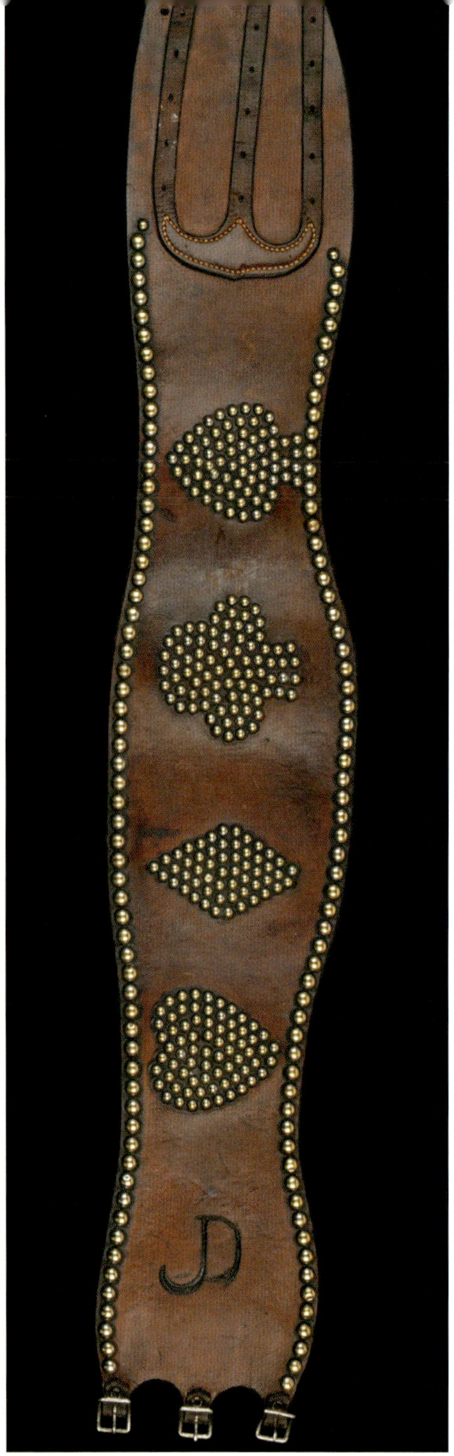

Figure 2-69. Valley Ranch bronc belt. Brown leather women's bronc belt with studded card suits and Lazy JD brand burned in. This belt was part of the ensemble that included the spurs (Figure 2-66) and chaps (Figure 2-68). *Photo by D. Congdon-Martin.*

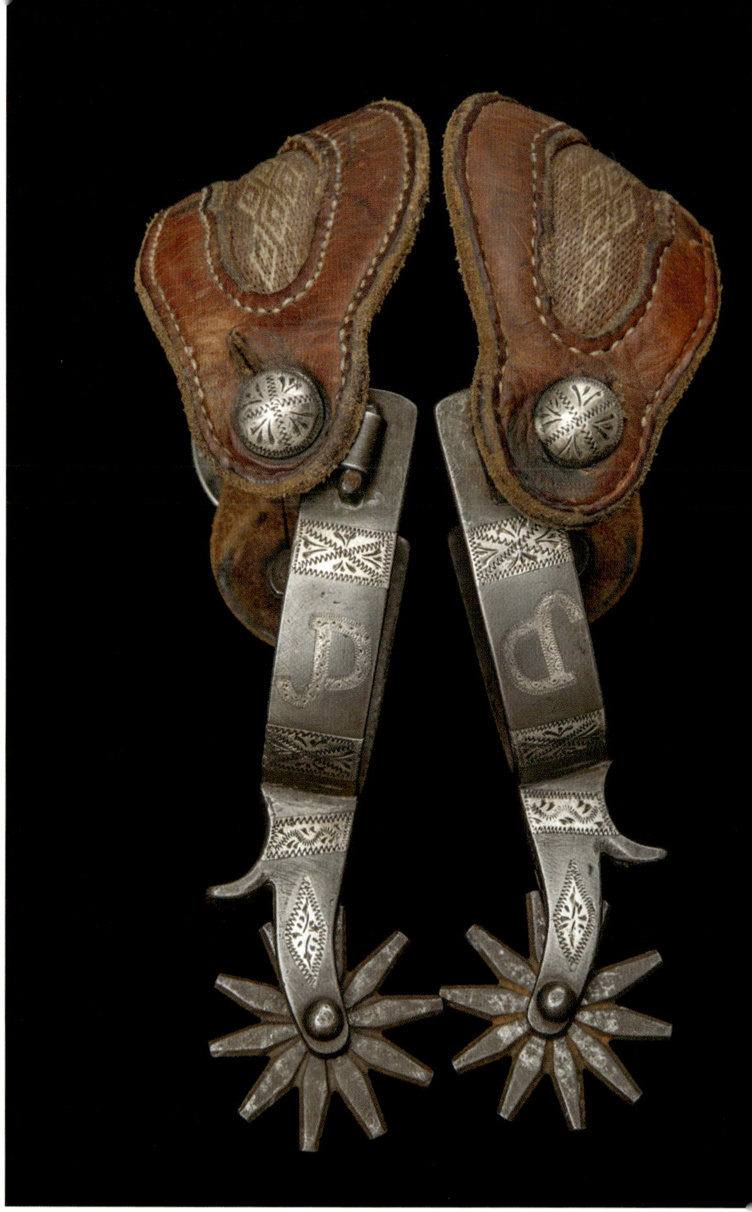

Figure 2-70. Hulbert spurs—custom orders. This pair of cowboy spurs shows engraved silver inlays and the Lazy JD brand. Chap guards, engraved silver button covers, swinging buttons, and 10-point rowels complete the set. The leather straps have horsehair insets. *Courtesy of J. Lyndes. Photo by J. Williams.*

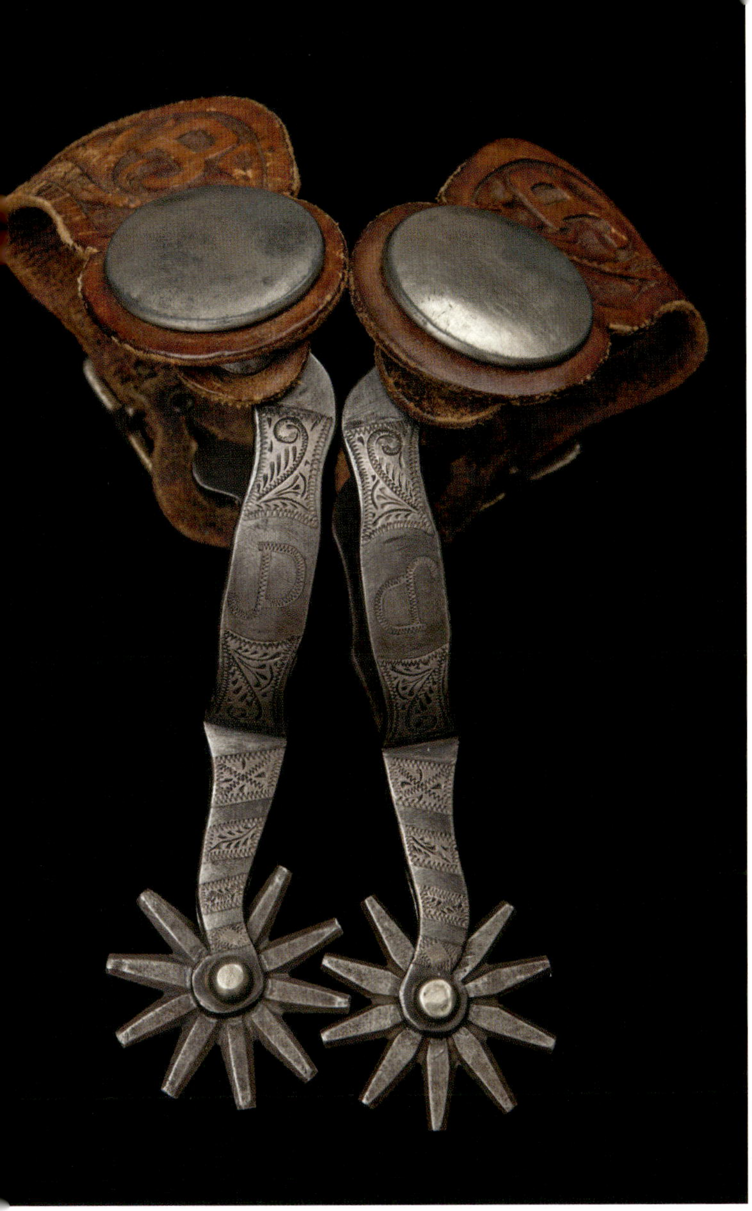

Figure 2-71. Hulbert spurs—custom orders. Possibly a woman's pair of nicely-inlaid silver spurs with the Lazy JD brand on the heelbands. The curved shanks lack chap guards and are fitted with 10-point plain rowels. *Courtesy of J. Lyndes. Photo by J. Williams.*

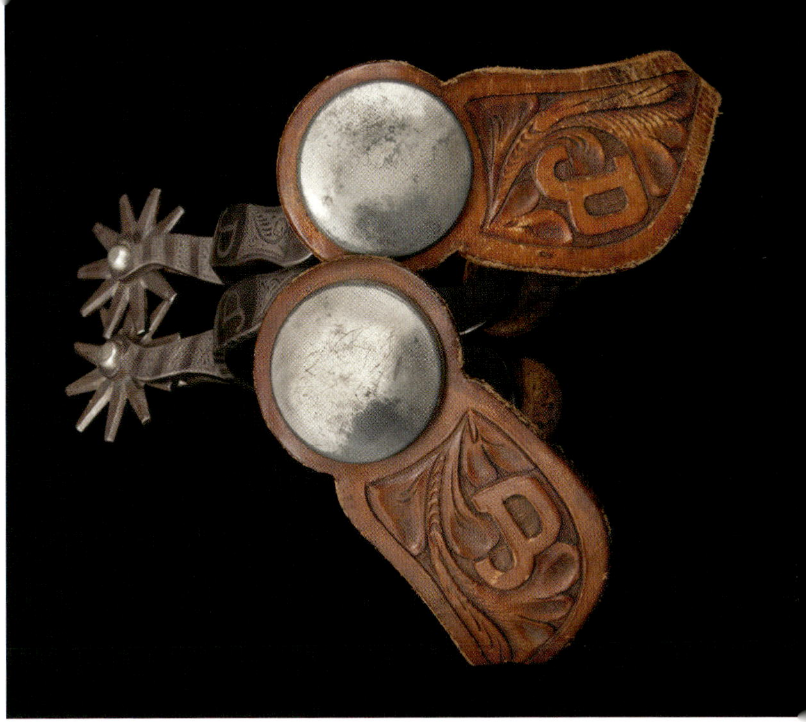

Figure 2-72. Hulbert spurs—custom orders. The spurs shown in Figuare 2-71 were matched with a custom pair of tooled brown straps carrying the Lazy JD brand and huge conchos. *Courtesy of J. Lyndes. Photo by J. Williams.*

The final pair of Hulbert spurs made for this rather elegant dude ranch is shown in Figure 2-73. "VALLEY WYO," in silver, rocker-engraved letters, was inlaid on the heelbands of these interesting spurs with unusual seven-point rowels and the Ranch brand on the silver button covers.

Custom-ordered Hulbert spurs bearing other ranch brands are shown in Figures 2-74 through 2-76. An unusual pair, with extended shanks, minimal chap guards, and slender bands, bears in gold letters "KB" and the brand "Bar B Bar" (Figure 2-74). A more ornate, overlaid pair of spurs in the "shield" pattern (Figure 2-75) has the brand "Lazy J/inverted T" (?) in gold letters on the heelbands. Figure 2-76 shows spurs with the "Diamond Bar" brand on the heart pattern silver overlay, with the

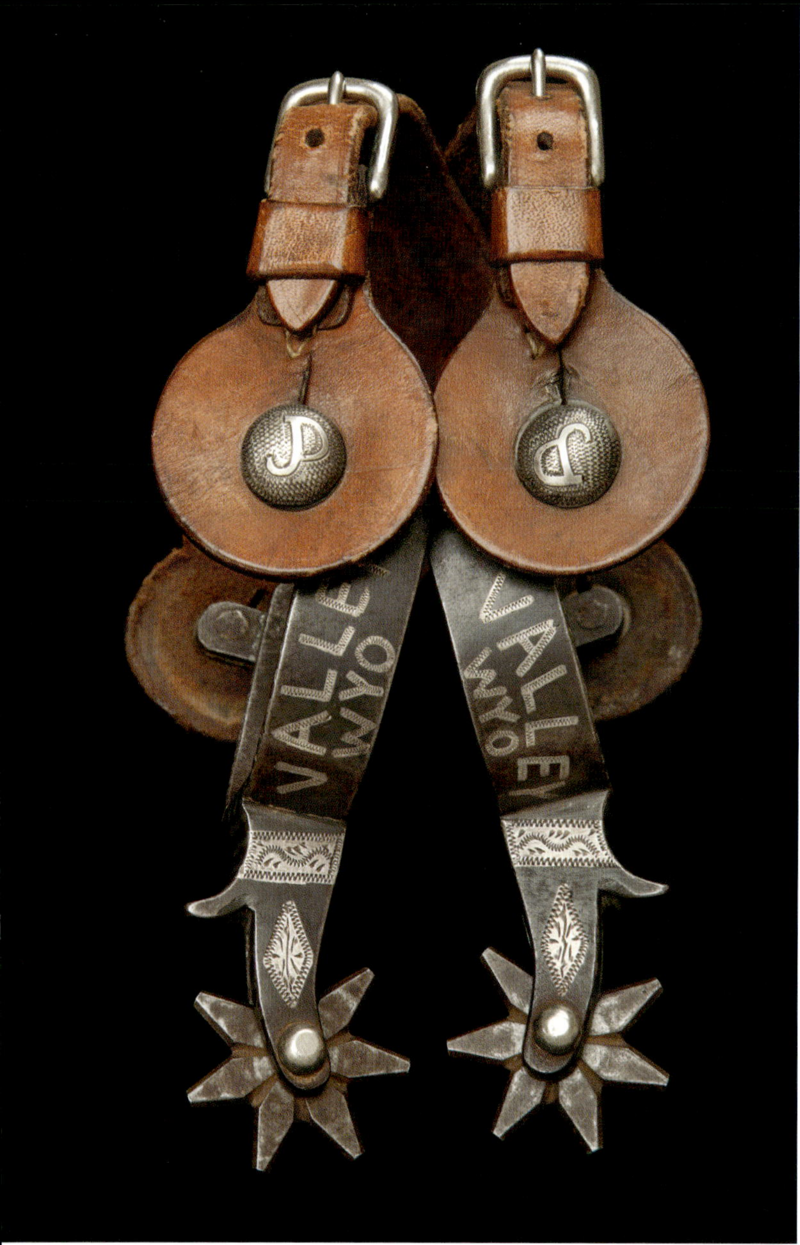

Figure 2-73. Hulbert spurs—custom orders. These outstanding spurs exhibit the ranch name and location ("VALLEY/WYO") inlaid in silver on the heelbands. The Lazy JD brand has been engraved on the silver button covers. Unusual 7-point rowels complement the silver-inlaid shanks. *Courtesy of B. Smith. Photo by J. Williams.*

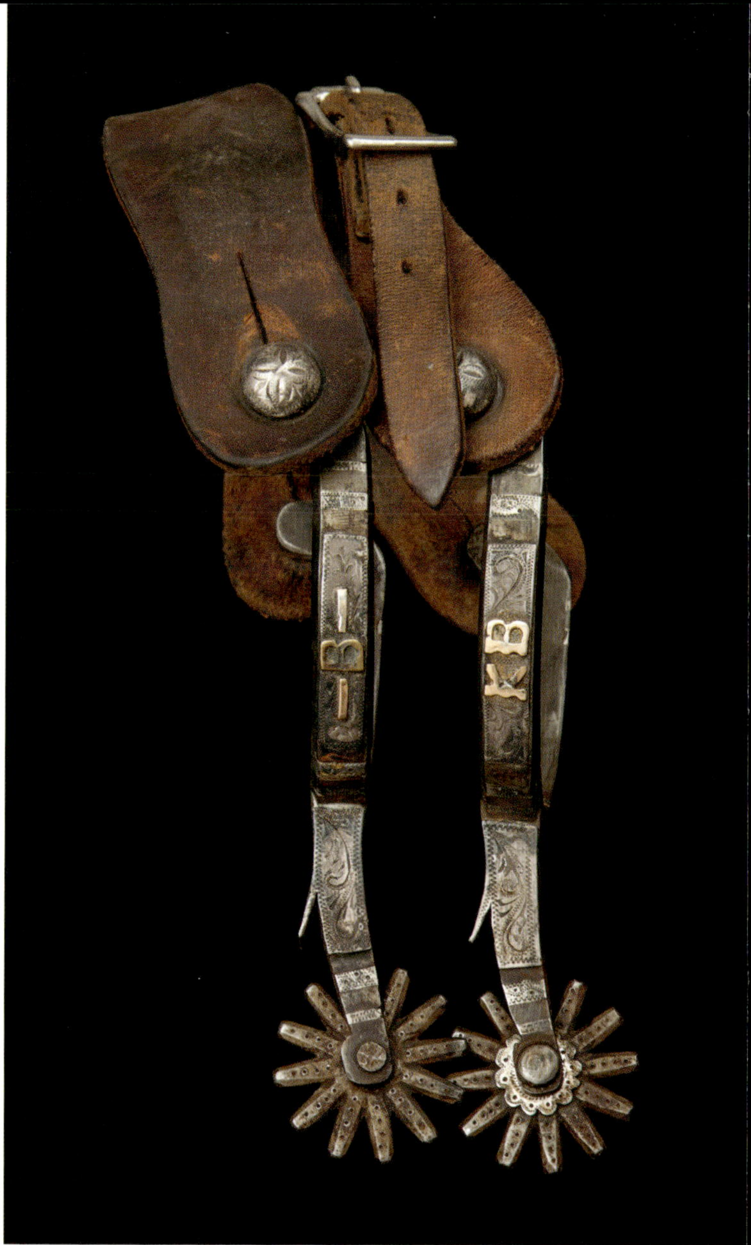

Figure 2-74. Hulbert spurs—custom orders. The heelbands on these double-mounted spurs bear the initials in gold "KB" and the ranch brand (in gold) "Bar B Bar." Possibly a woman's pair, these spurs were made with extended shanks, minimal chap guards, and punched 12-point rowels with silver discs. *Courtesy of J. Lyndes. Photo by J. Williams.*

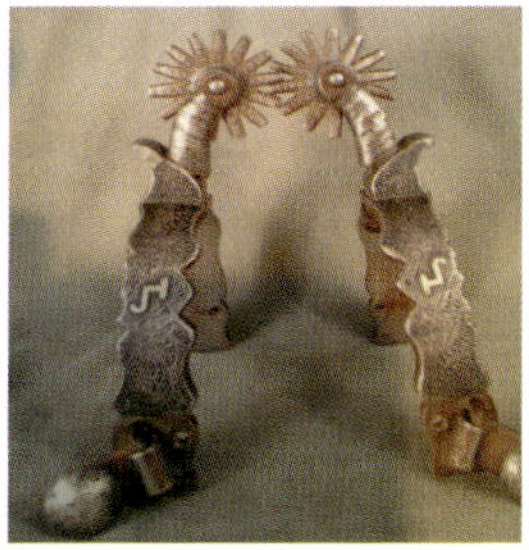

Figure 2-75. Hulbert spurs—custom orders. An outstanding pair of marked spurs showing the owner's brand mounted in gold on the heelbands. The shield pattern is fully overlaid between the heelbands and shanks, and the shanks are inlaid below the chap guards. The 14-point rowels are punch-decorated, and the swinging buttons are set at a 45-degree angle. *Courtesy of C. Webb. Photo by B. Bartlett.*

owner's initials "JCN" opposite (see Figure 2-61, and p. 66). The "rolling log" or swastika on the well-used spurs in Figure 2-77 is unusual. Because of the assumption of this ancient symbol by the Third Reich, it is likely that the spurs were ordered in the early 1930s; indeed, their style and workmanship indicate this earlier date.

A pair of Eddy Hulbert's trophy spurs is shown in Figure

Figure 2-76. Hulbert spurs—custom orders. The inlaid "Diamond Bar" ranch brand is shown on this heart-pattern, engraved silver overlaid pair of spurs, the opposite sides of which, bearing the initials "JCN," are shown in Figure 2-61. These spurs belonged to James "Kid" Nichols (1883–1962), of the Diamond Bar Ranch (Cody, Wyoming). *Courtesy of J. Lyndes. Photo by J. Williams.*

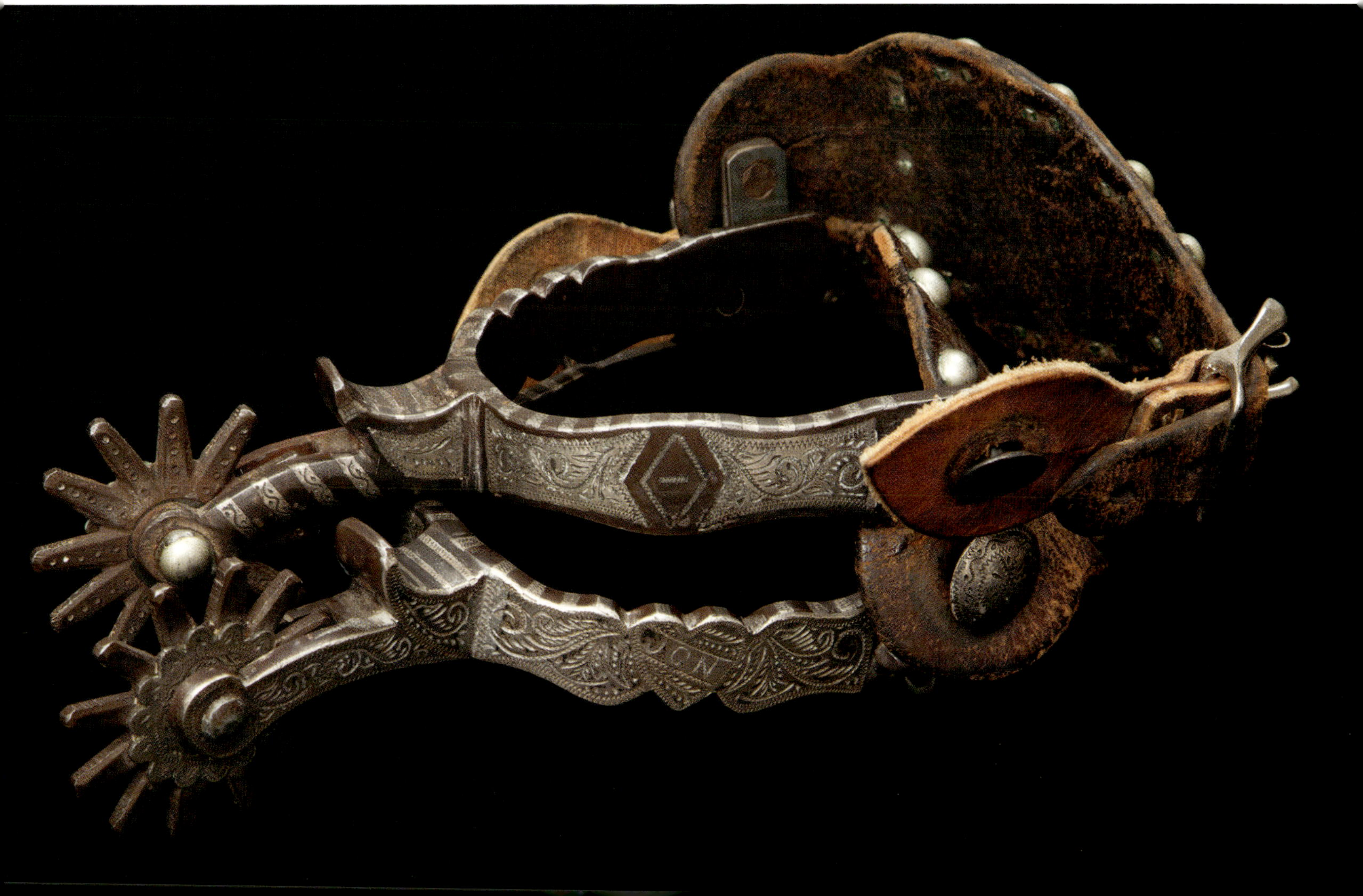

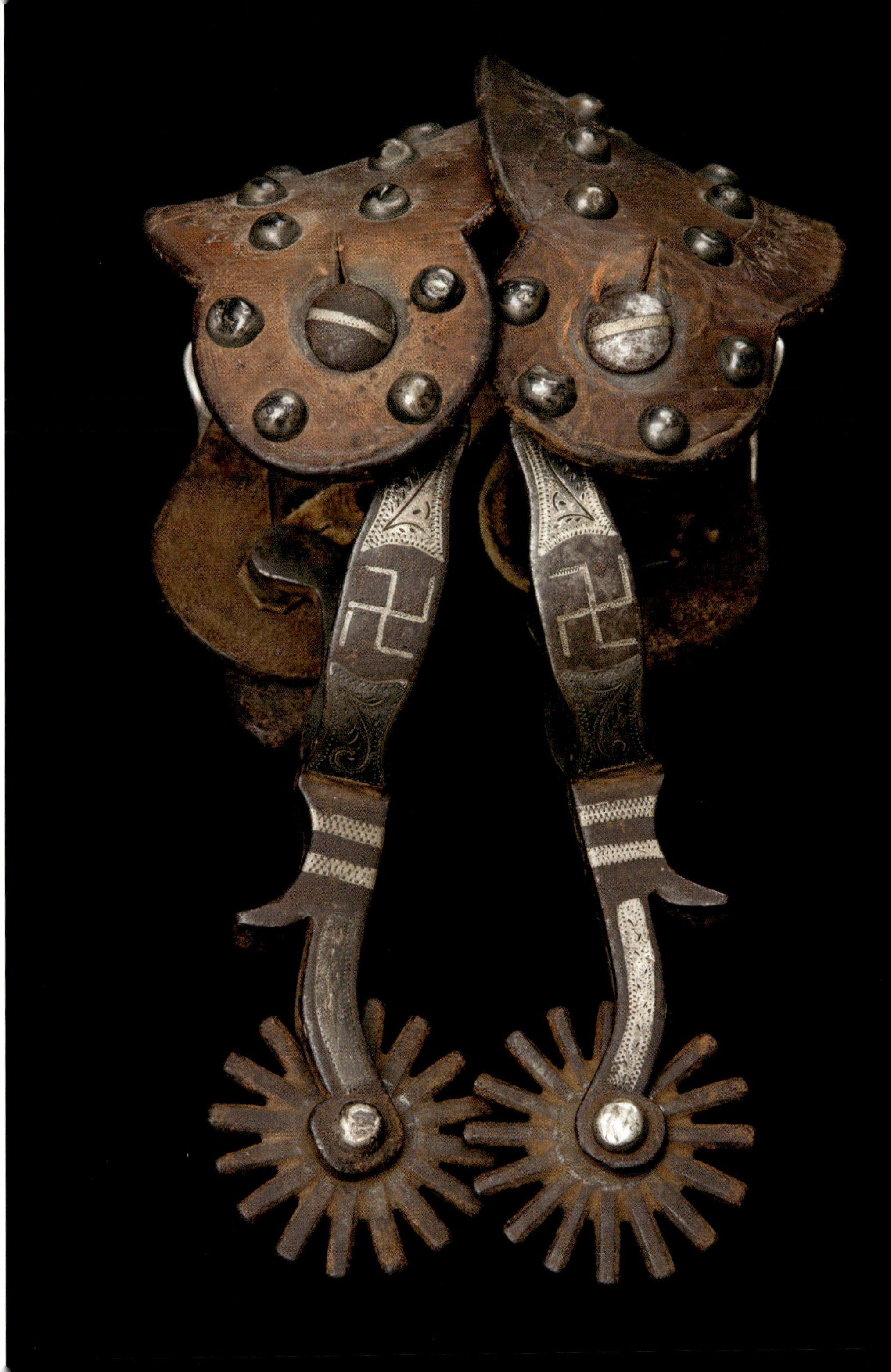

Figure 2-77. Hulbert spurs—custom orders. The inlaid "rolling log" or swastika on this pair of c.1930s working cowboy spurs is flanked by engraved silver inlays. The extra-long shanks are also inlaid and bear 16-point, undecorated rowels. A single silver bar has been inlaid across the button. It is likely that this pair was ordered in the 1930s prior to the rise of the Third Reich. *Courtesy of J. Lyndes. Photo by J. Williams.*

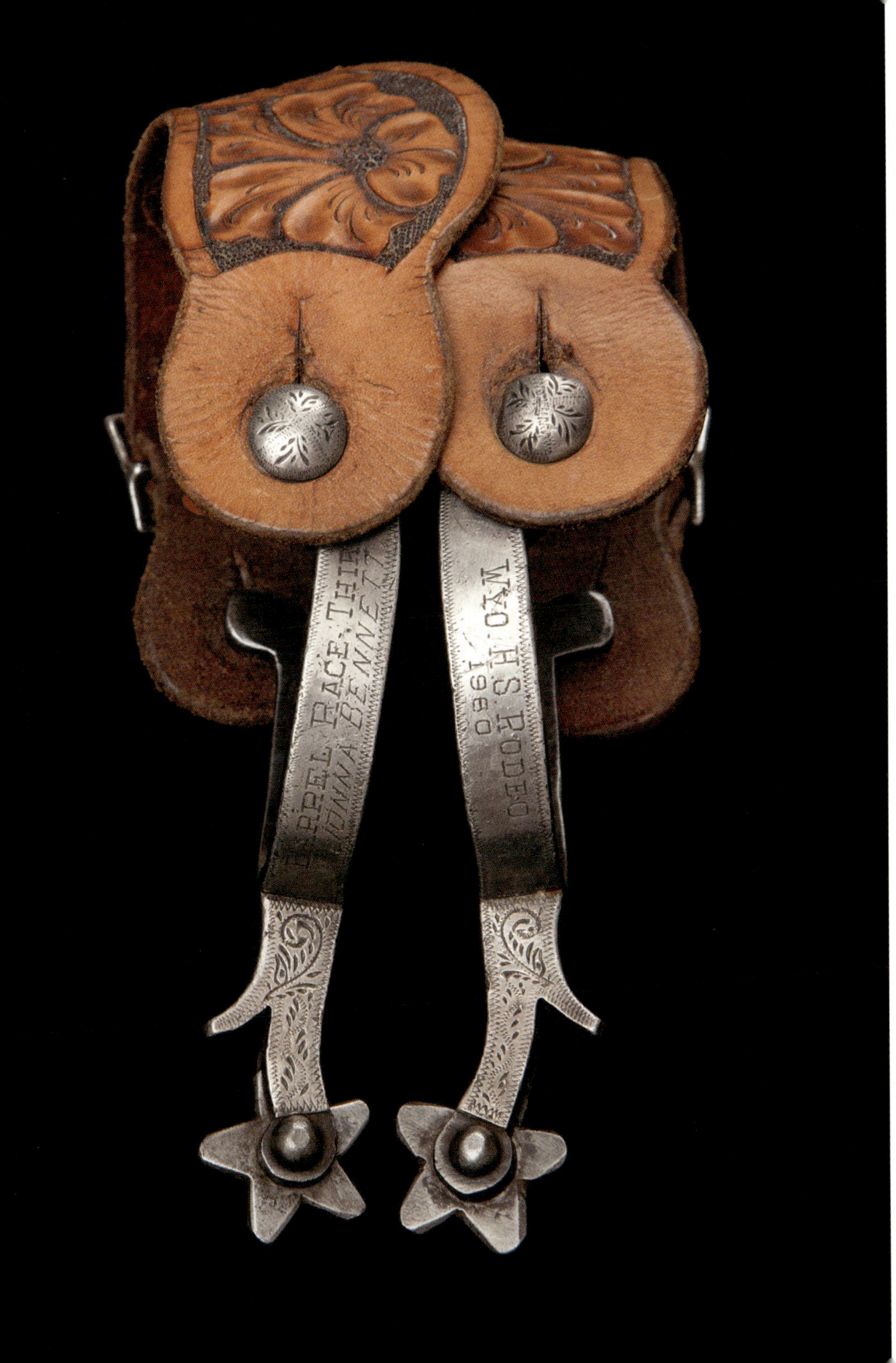

Figure 2-78. Hulbert spurs—custom orders. Hulbert made several trophy items, including spurs. This pair was engraved for "JONNA BENNETT/BARREL RACE, THIRD PLACE." The opposing heelband identifies the "WYO. H.S. RODEO/1960" ("H.S."—high school). This order might have been one of the last pairs of spurs that Hulbert made before his death in July, 1960. *Courtesy of M. Schmitt. Photo by J. Williams.*

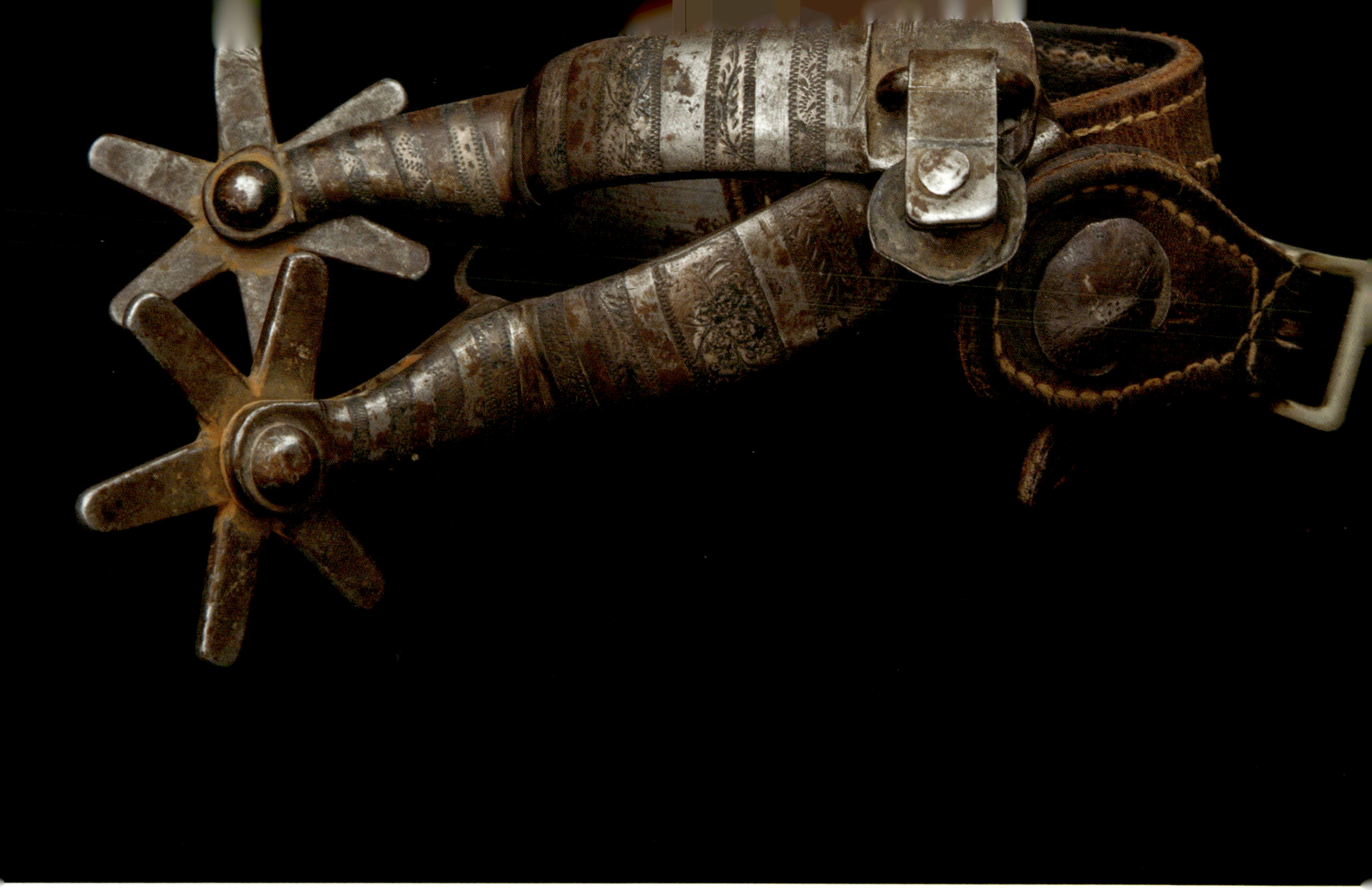

Figure 2-79. Hulbert spurs—a working cowboy's pair. These bar pattern silver-inlaid spurs with swinging buttons and 6-point rowels show wear and heavy period use. They belonged to a working cowboy, Slim Cheney, of Bozeman, Montana, who wrote the note shown in Figures 2-80 and 2-81, asking for a $10 loan with the spurs as collateral. The spurs were never redeemed. *Courtesy of J. Lyndes. Photo by J. Williams.*

2-78. They were won (third place) by a young woman, "Jonna Bennett," in a barrel race in the Wyoming High School Rodeo, in 1960. A fine award for a third place win, these spurs were among the very last that Hulbert made before his death in 1960.

This chapter ends with a "working pair" of Eddy Hulbert spurs, owned and used by a cowboy named Slim Cheney, of Bozeman, Montana. The spurs are the silver inlaid "bar" pattern, with swinging buttons and rather blunt, six-point spoke rowels (Figure 2-79). Cheney was out of work and wrote the note shown in Figures 2-80 and 2-81 requesting a $10 loan on his cherished spurs. He promised to return the money (and pick up his spurs) when a ranching outfit hired him. Cowpunchers' jobs were difficult to find in those later days, and sadly, the spurs were never redeemed. A noted collector of Hulbert's work has claimed these spurs (and the accompanying note) to be "among his favorite." Indeed, Eddy Hulbert's spurs found homes with clientele ranging from the working cowboy to the wealthy dude ranch visitor.

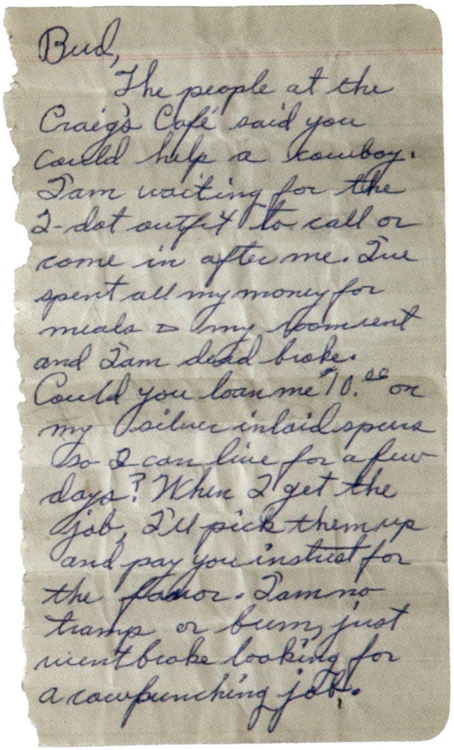
Bud,
The people at the
Craig's Café said you
could help a cowboy.
I am waiting for the
2-dot outfit to call or
come in after me. I've
spent all my money for
meals & my [illegible]
and I am dead broke.
Could you loan me $10.00 on
my silver inlaid spurs
so I can live for a few
days? When I get the
job, I'll pick them up
and pay you instead for
the favor. I am no
tramp or bum, just
went broke looking for
a cowpunching job.

Figure 2-80. Hulbert spurs—a working cowboy's pair. Note written to "Bud" by Slim Cheney, who requested a $10 loan against the spurs shown in Figure 2-79. Work as an early 20th century cowpuncher was on a job-by-job basis and rarely lasted throughout the year. *Courtesy of J. Lyndes. Photo by J. Williams.*

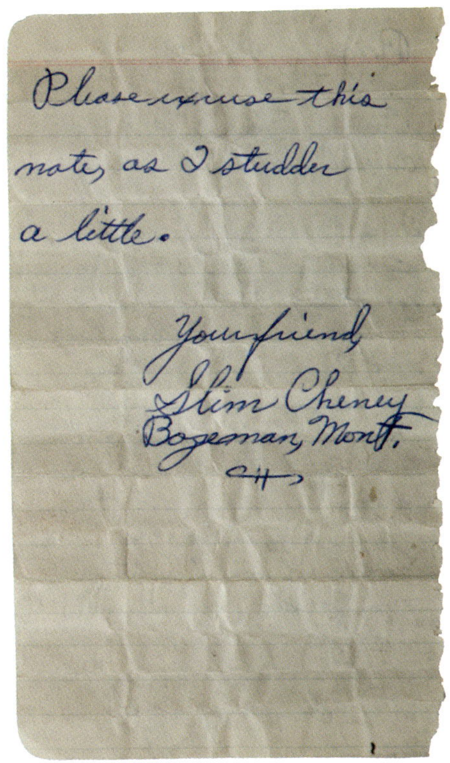
Please excuse this
note, as I studder
a little.

Your friend,
Slim Cheney
Bozeman, Mont.

Figure 2-81. Hulbert spurs—a working cowboy's pair. Verso of note written by Slim Cheney (Figure 2-80). *Courtesy of J. Lyndes. Photo by J. Williams.*

Bits and Bridle Ornaments

Eddy Hulbert made serviceable, "working" bits that were nevertheless very attractive in their simplicity because of the silverwork that decorated and distinguished them. A unique contribution was the removable mouthpiece, by which one could change the type of bit (e.g., from a simple curb or grazing bit, to a half-breed with port in the center, to a spade with a more elaborate port that fit against the roof of the horse's mouth). Examples of these mouthpieces can be found in the succeeding figures. There is no doubt that Hulbert made a number of bits (many of which had fixed mouthpieces) that were sold in the Dryhead/Billings area.

This chapter begins with a rare collection of advertising cards depicting different styles of bits, Hulbert's numbers for them, and his description of their features and modifications that were available (Figures 3-1 through 3-12). "Bit No. 15," a loose-jaw spade (the cheeks of the bit rotate around the mouthpiece, as opposed to their being fixed and immovable), was made with an attractive silver overlay on the cheeks and slobber bar (the horizontal piece at the bottom of the bit, sometimes referred to as a lip bar) (Figures 3-1 and 3-2). In contrast, Figures 3-3 through 3-6 show low-port grazing bits (No. 170) with different varieties of silver overlay. This style is referred to as "banana cheek" and was featured in several saddlery catalogs (see captions). Note the engraved silver conchos and edge inlays on the bit in Figure 3-3. Hulbert's bit No. 10, a spade with solid silver overlay, is shown and described in Figures 3-7 and 3-8, and two banana cheek, loose-jaw bits with crescent and shield or crescent and bar decorations near the mouthpiece can be seen in Figures 3-9 and 3-10. The last advertising card in this series shows Hulbert's bit No. 80, a loose-jaw bit with interchangeable mouthpiece and continuous silver overlay with inlaid edges (Figures 3-11 and 3-12). The distinctive "EH" mark with rounded letters is shown in Figure 3-13.

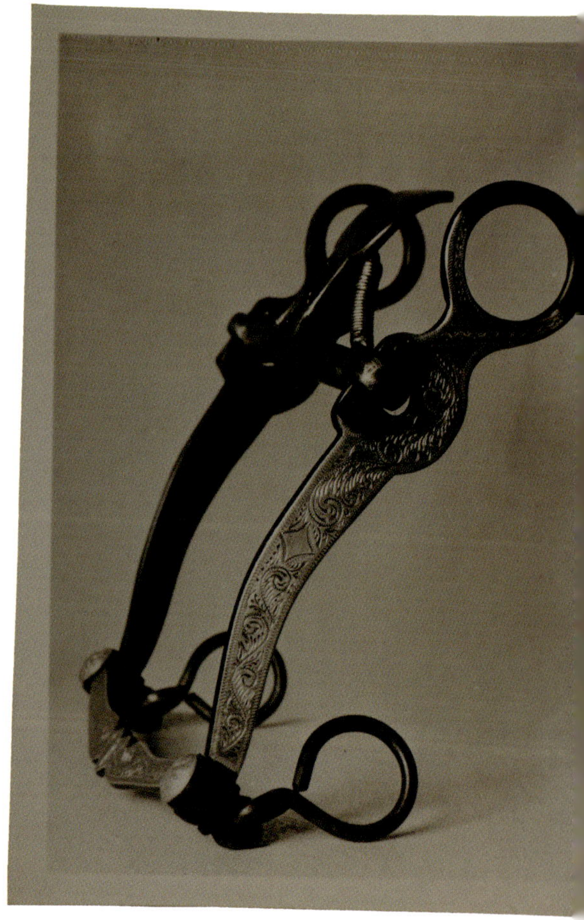

Figure 3-1. Advertising/studio card—Hulbert Bit No. 15. This handsome loose-jaw spade bit with an interchangeable mouthpiece was made with an engraved silver overlay on the cheeks and slobber bar. Hulbert's note (see Figure 3-2) states that a solid bar mouthpiece, with silver conchos, could be substituted for the spade. Card, 5" H x 3.5" W. *Courtesy of R. Wilmot. William Manns photo.*

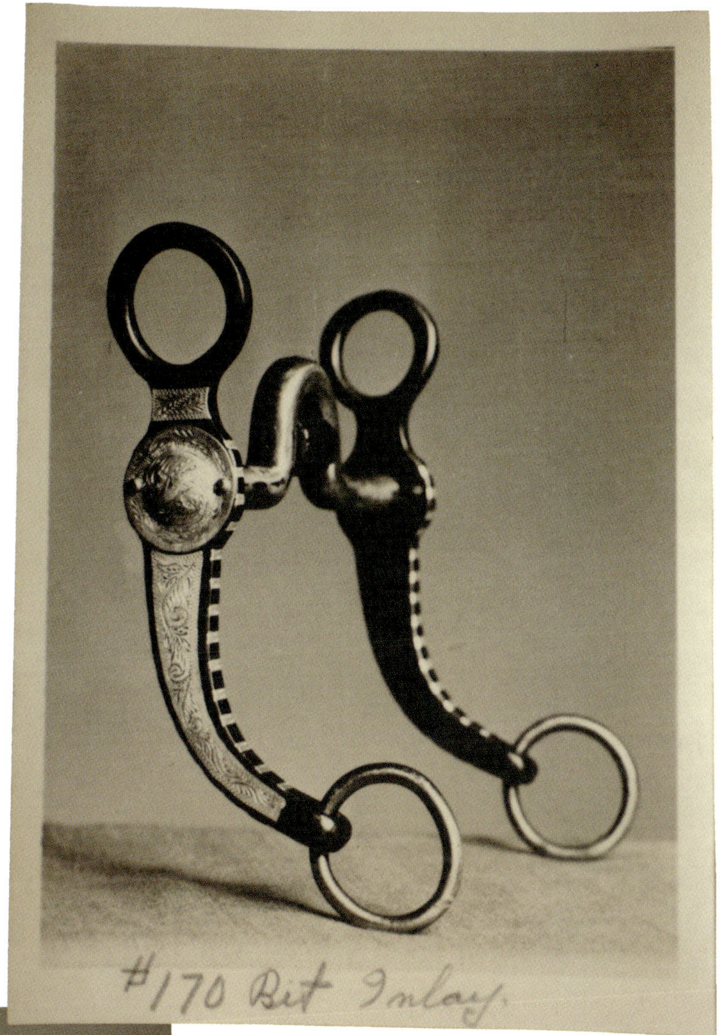

Figure 3-3. Advertising card—Hulbert Bit No. 170. A beautiful bit with engraved silver-inlaid cheeks and fully-striped/inlaid silver edges. The bit was made with conchos, above which were small silver inlays. The mouthpiece is a halfbreed with a cricket (roller). Bit No. 170 was featured in several saddlery catalogs, e.g., Fred Mueller, Otto Ernst, and Hamley & Co. Card, 5" H x 3.5" W. *Courtesy of R. Wilmot. William Manns photo.*

Figure 3-2. Advertising card—Hulbert's description of Bit No. 15 and its modifications (Figure 3-1, verso). *Courtesy of R. Wilmot. William Manns photo.*

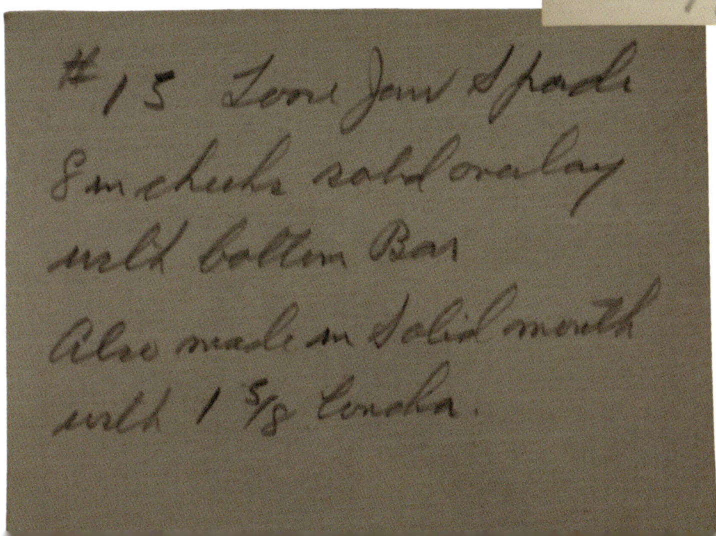
#15 Loose Jaw Spade
8 in cheeks solid overlay
with bottom Bar
Also made in Solid mouth
with 1 5/8 Concha.

Figure 3-4. Advertising card—Hulbert's description of Bit No. 170 (Figure 3-3, verso). *Courtesy of R. Wilmot. William Manns photo.*

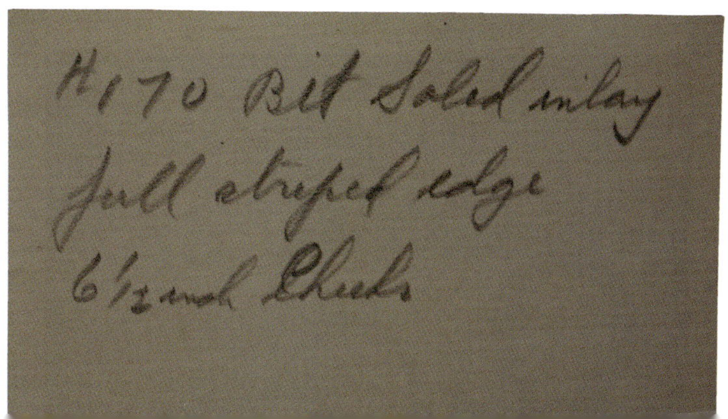
#170 Bit Solid inlay
full striped edge
6 1/2 inch Cheeks

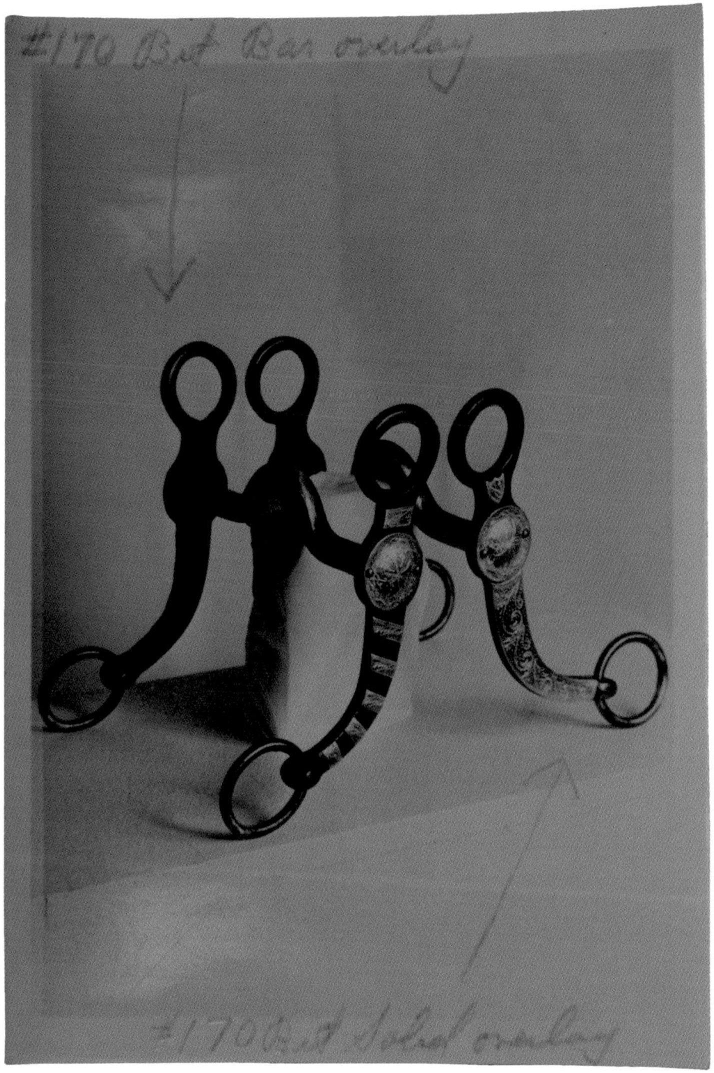

Figure 3-5. Advertising card—Hulbert Bit No. 170 in two styles. The bit on the left exhibits silver bar overlays and 6-1/2" cheeks with engraved silver conchos and small rectangles just below the bridle attachment rings. The bit on the right shows a "solid" overlay of engraved silver on the 7" cheeks, and small shields. Both styles are referred to as "banana cheeks" and have a simple low-port curb (grazing) mouthpiece. Card, 5" H x 3.5" W. *Courtesy of R. Wilmot. William Manns photo.*

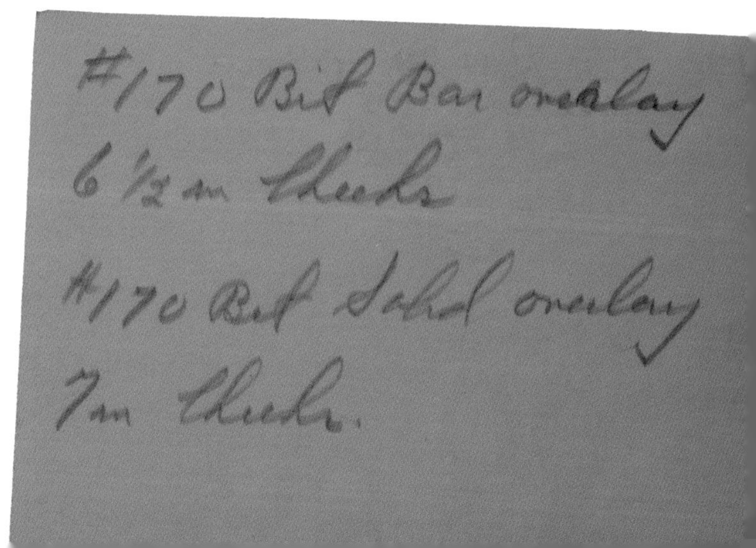

Figure 3-6. Advertising card—Hulbert's description of two variations of Bit No. 170 (Figure 3-5, verso). *Courtesy of R. Wilmot. William Manns photo.*

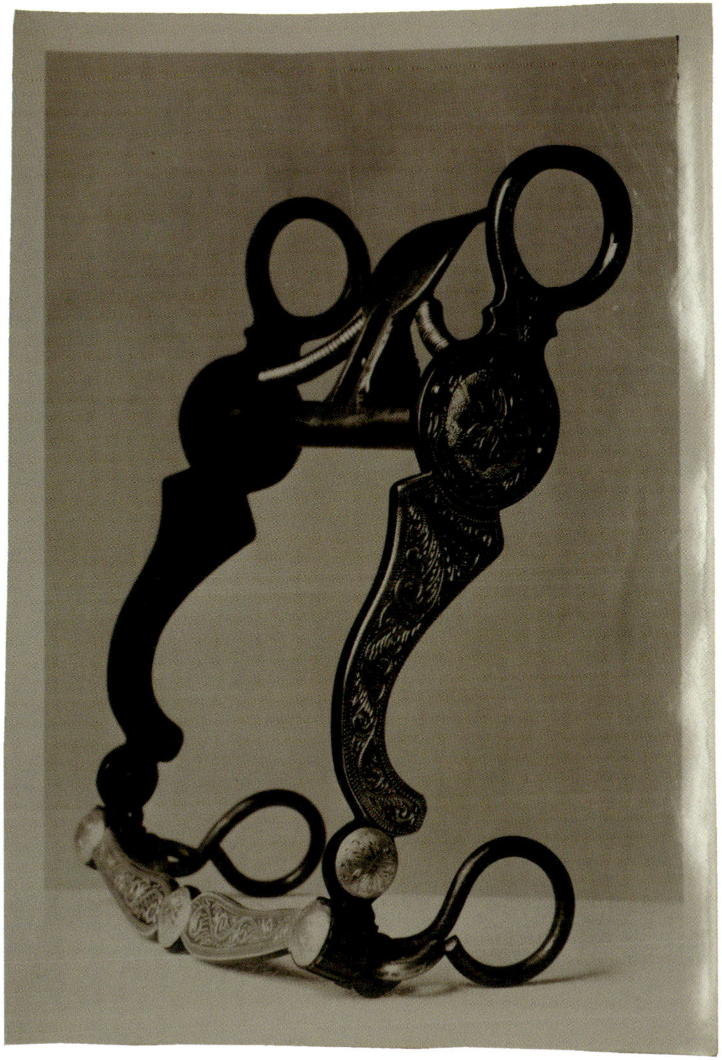

Figure 3-7. Advertising card—Hulbert Bit No. 10. This spade bit exhibits the characteristic Hulbert silver "solid" overlays on the cheeks and slobber bar, as well as conchos and silver almost encircling the bridle attachment rings. Each cheek ends in a silver button. Hulbert states that this bit could be made in a loose or solid jaw style, with a halfbreed or grazing mouthpiece. Card, 5" H x 3.5" W. *Courtesy of R. Wilmot. William Manns photo.*

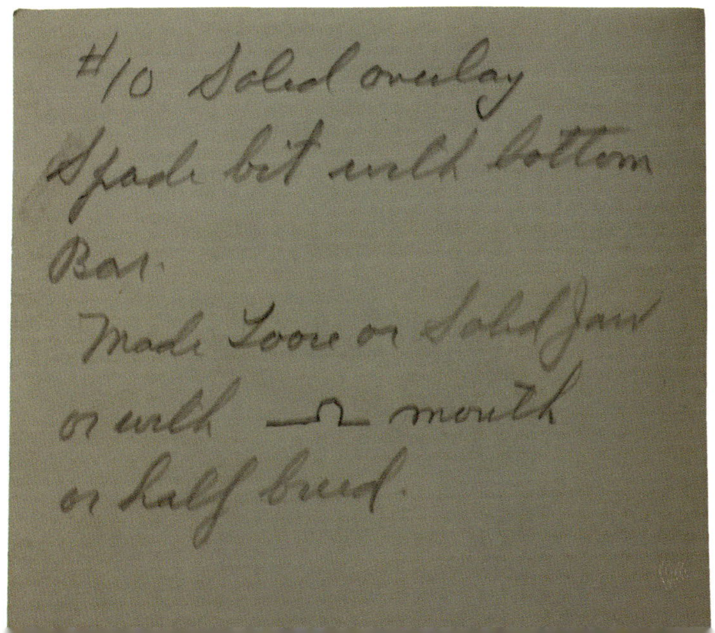

#10 Solid overlay
Spade bit with bottom
Bar.
Made Loose or Solid Jaw
or with mouth
or half breed.

Figure 3-8. Advertising card—Hulbert's description of Bit No. 10 (Figure 3-7, verso). *Courtesy of R. Wilmot. William Manns photo.*

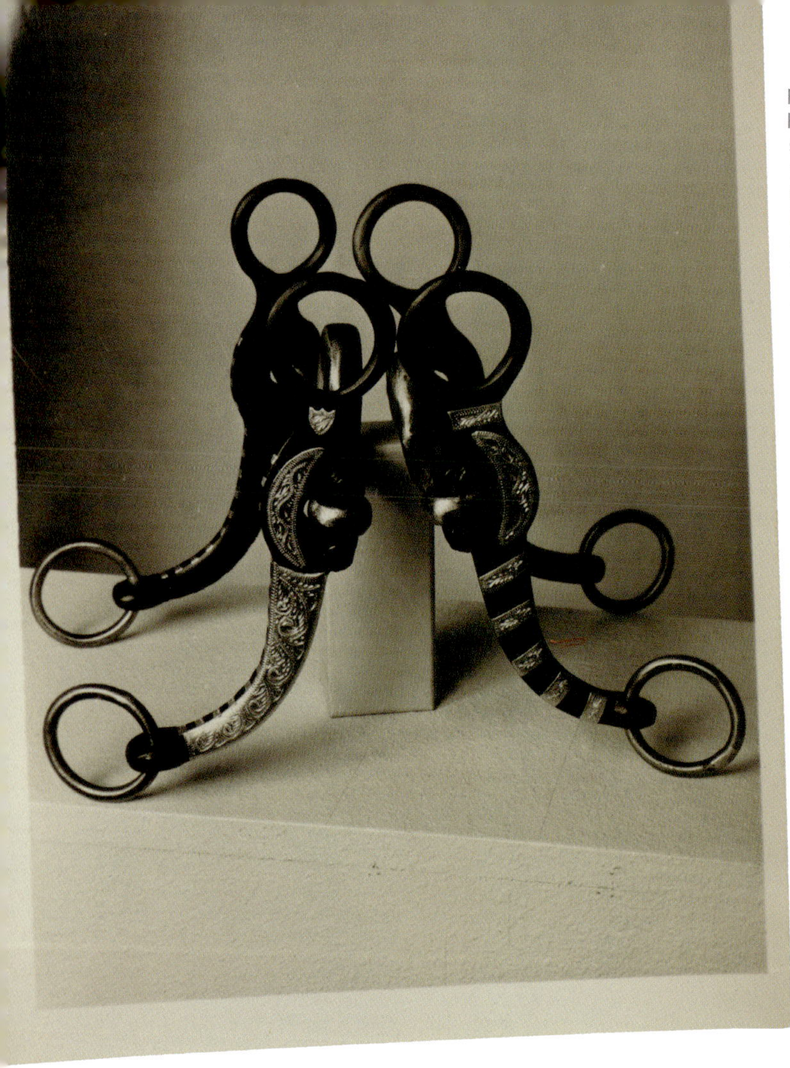

Figure 3-9. Advertising card—Hulbert banana cheek bits with silver crescents and interchangeable mouthpieces. Hulbert describes both bits as loose-jaw styles: that on the left shows a one-piece silver overlay on the 7″ cheeks, inlaid silver edges, and a silver crescent and small shield on each side of the mouthpiece. The bit on the right shows silver bar overlays on the 6-1/2″ cheeks, and a silver crescent rectangle on either side of the mouthpiece. Card, 5″ H x 3.5″ W. *Courtesy of R. Wilmot. William Manns photo.*

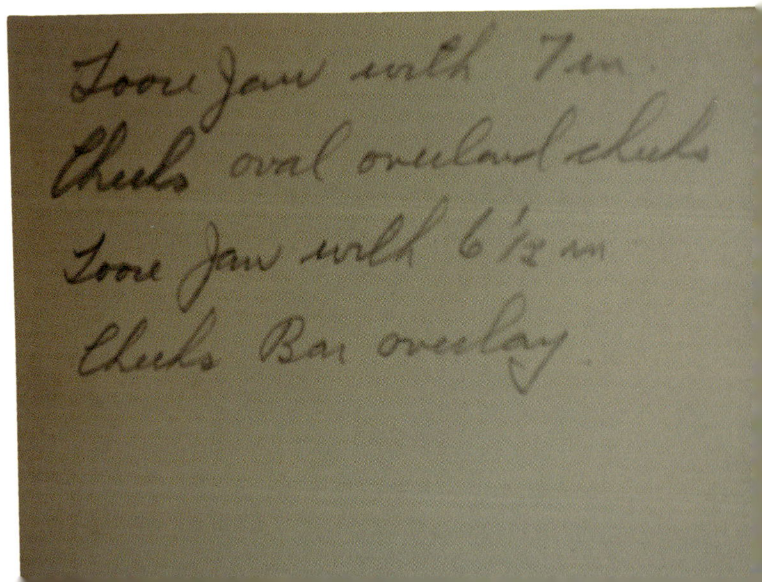

Loose Jaw with 7 in.
Cheeks oval overlaid cheeks
Loose Jaw with 6 1/2 in
Cheeks Bar overlay.

Figure 3-10. Advertising card—Hulbert's description of bits shown in Figure 3-9, verso. *Courtesy of R. Wilmot. William Manns photo.*

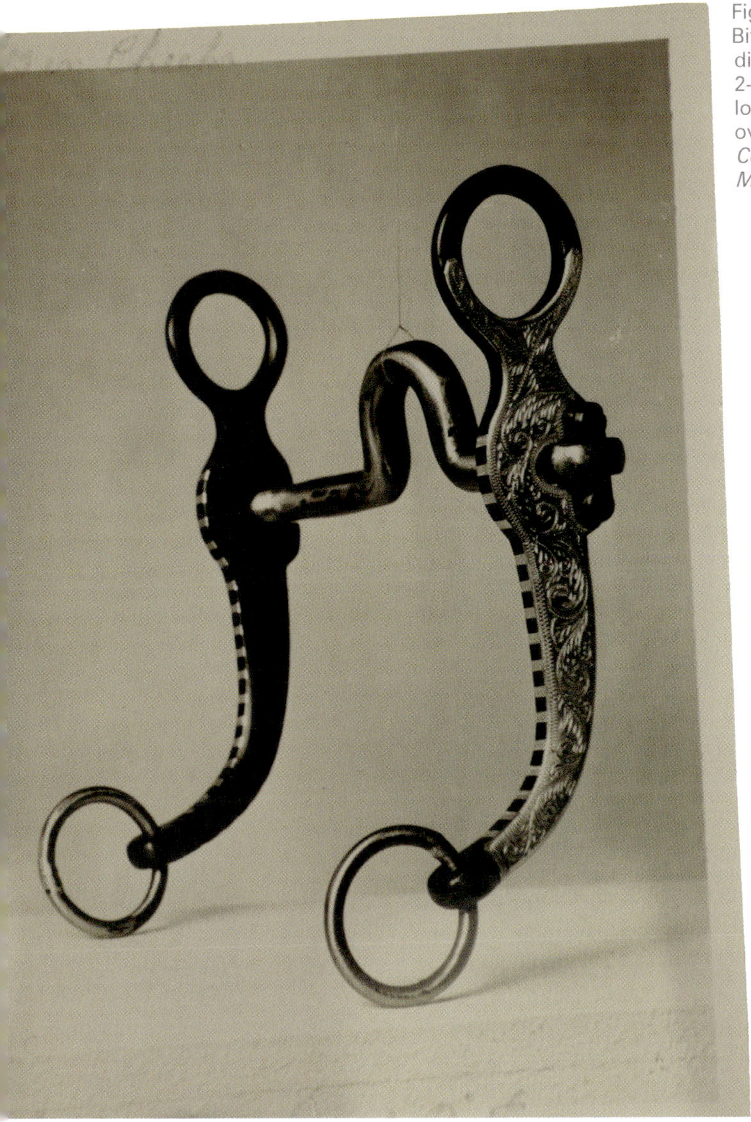

Figure 3-11. Advertising card—Hulbert Bit No. 80. This bit accommodates different mouthpieces, including a 2-1/2″ spade (see Figure 3-12). It is a loose-jaw with engraved silver "solid oval" overlays, and fully-striped edges. *Courtesy of R. Wilmot. William Manns photo.*

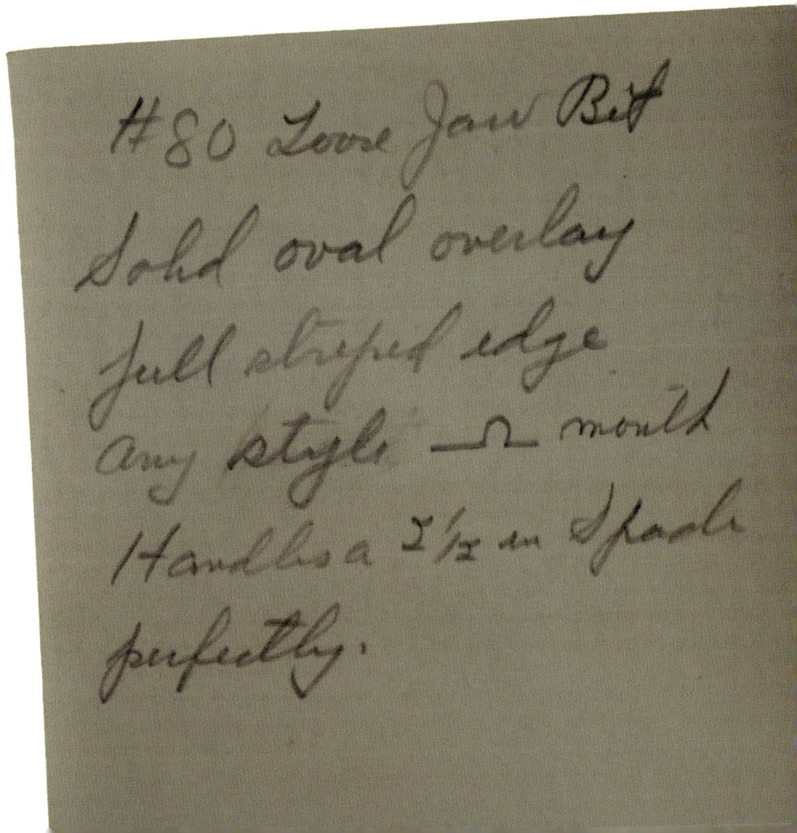

#80 Loose Jaw Bit
Solid oval overlay
full striped edge
any style ⌐ mouth
Handles a 2½ in Spade
perfectly.

Figure 3-12. Advertising card—Hulbert's description of Bit No. 80 (Figure 3-11, verso). *Courtesy of R. Wilmot. William Manns photo.*

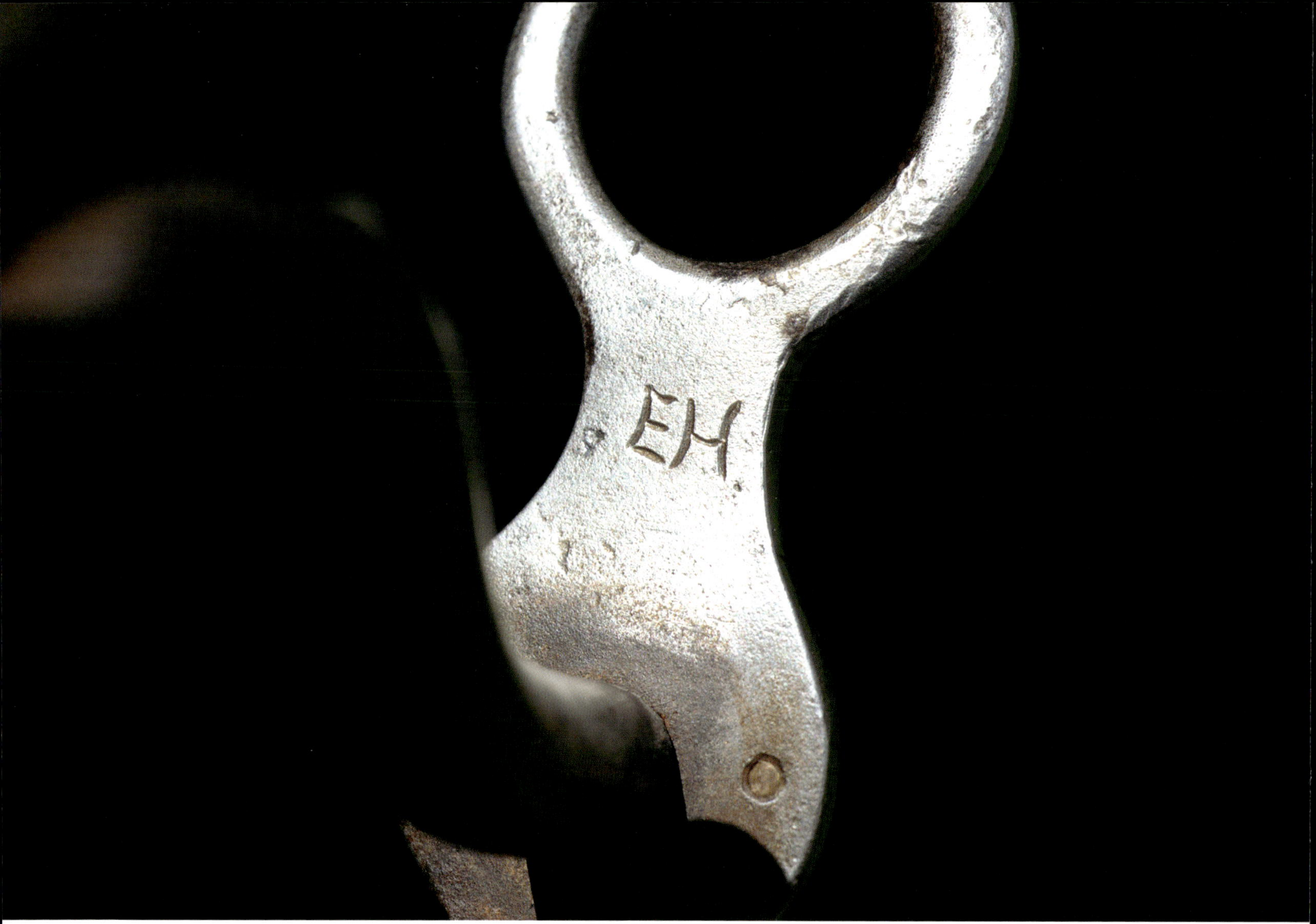

Figure 3-13. Hulbert bits. This photograph shows the Eddy Hulbert (EH) mark in curved letters, on the inside surface of a grazing bit. *Courtesy of R. Wilmot. William Manns photo.*

Examples of Hulbert bits that are different from those pictured on the advertising cards are shown in Figures 3-14 through 3-19. A "3-button" style grazing bit (Figure 3-14), a diamond-inlaid silver banana cheek half-breed bit with cricket (roller, for the horse's tongue) (Figure 3-15), and an interesting modified spade bit with split cheeks, large conchos, and edge inlays (Figure 3-16) attest to the diversity of Hulbert designs. The spade bit with interchangeable mouthpiece and solid silver overlay (Figure 3-17) contrasts with the fixed half-breed bit that matches the 3-button spurs in pattern and engraving style (Figures 3-18 and 3-19).

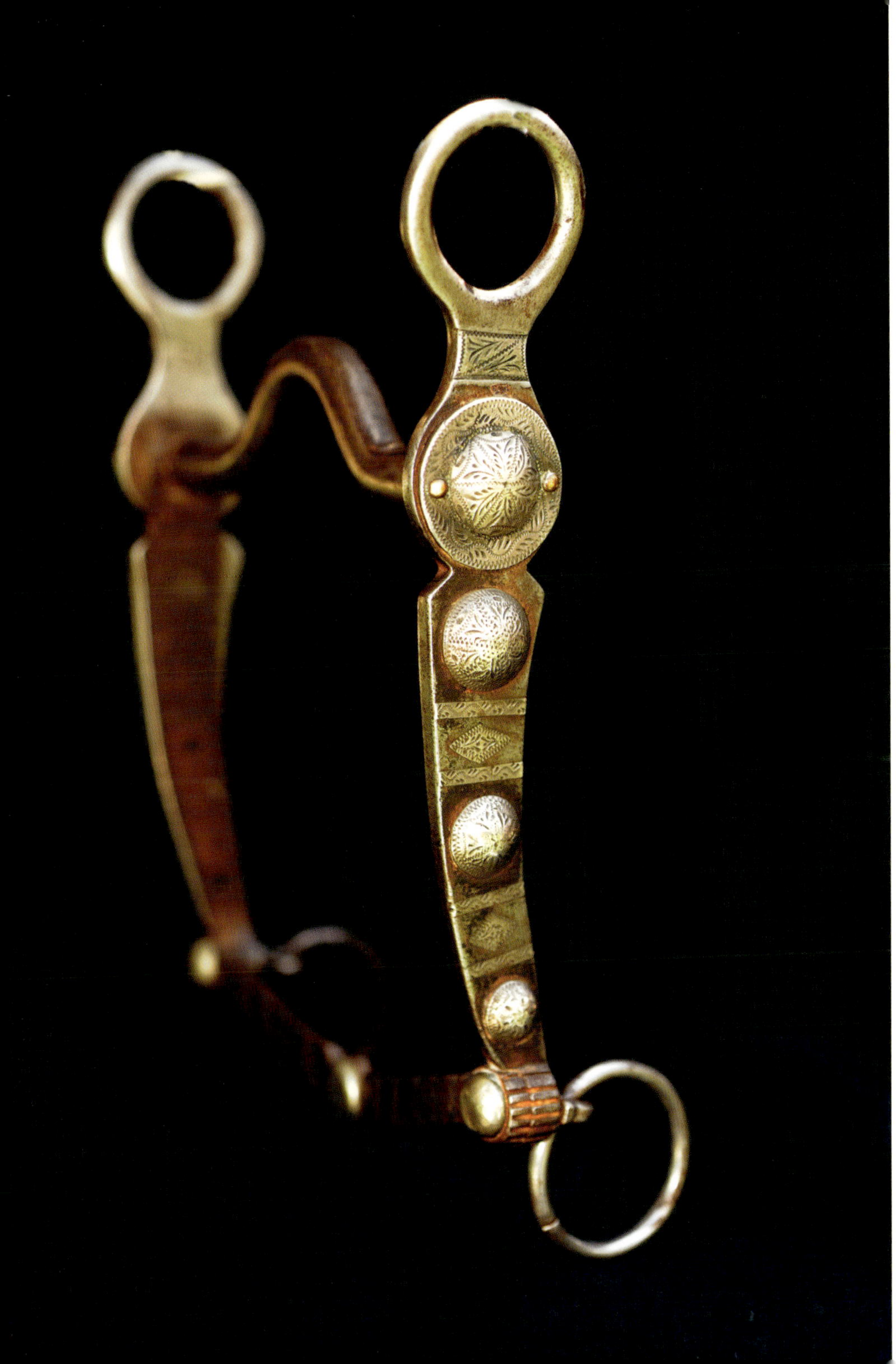

Figure 3-14. Hulbert bits. An attractive grazing bit (low-port curb) in the "3-Button" pattern seen on Hulbert spurs. The slobber bar is inlaid with engraved silver bars. *Courtesy of R. Wilmot. William Manns photo.*

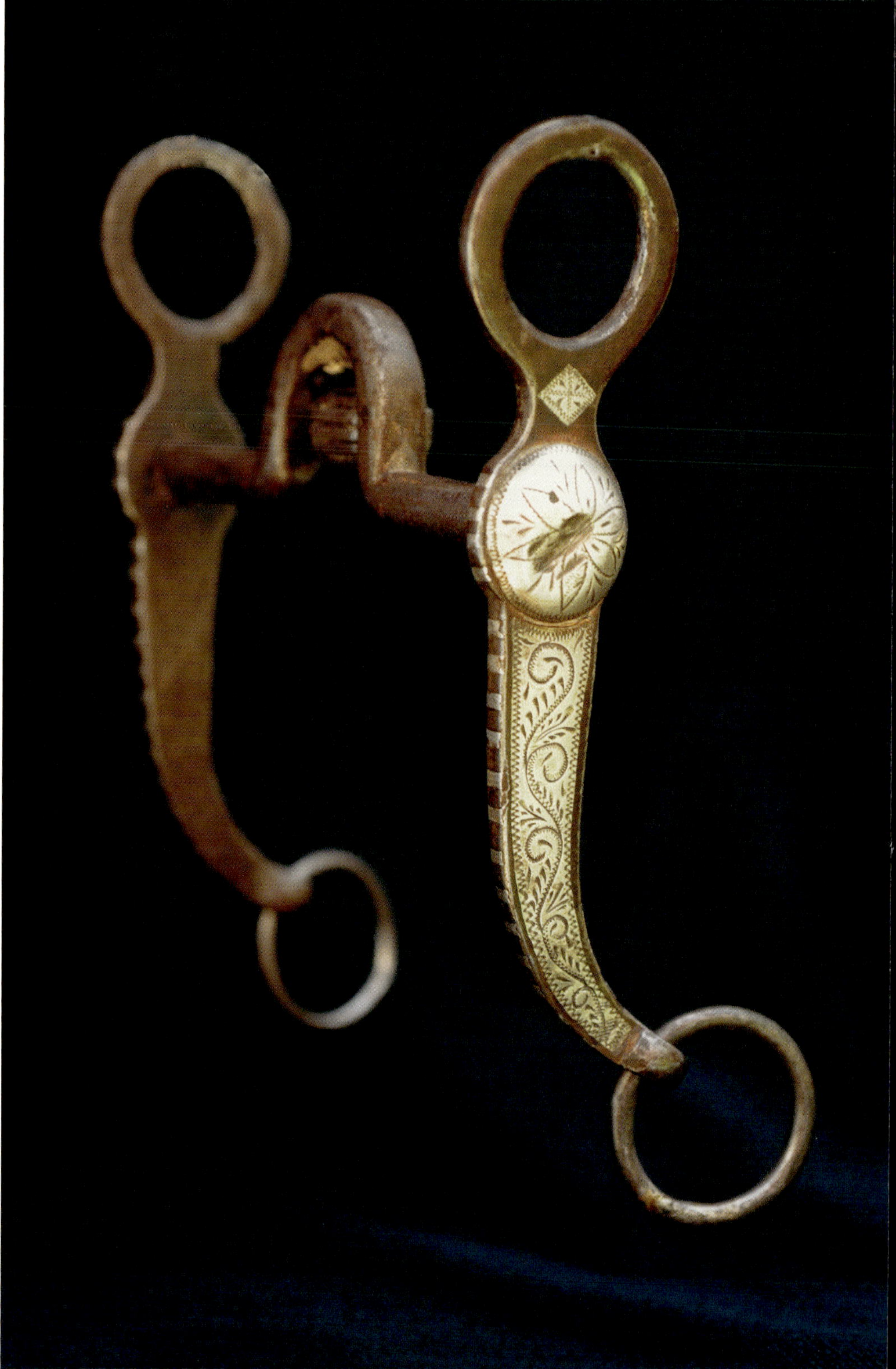

Figure 3-15. Hulbert bits. A silver-inlaid banana cheek halfbreed bit with edge inlays and a small silver diamond above the concho. *Courtesy of R. Wilmot. William Manns photo.*

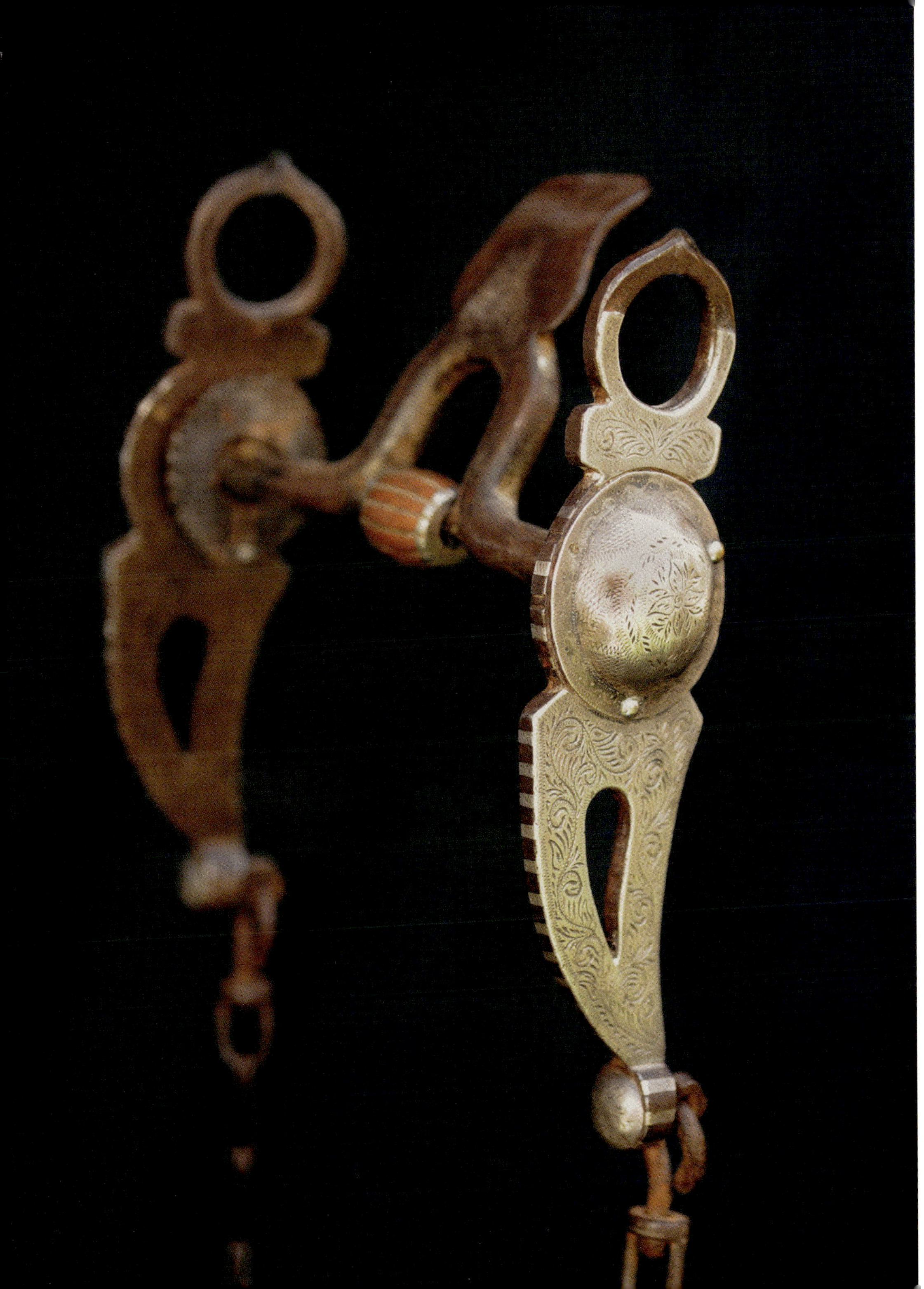

Figure 3-16. Hulbert bits. This unusual spade bit is indicative of a custom order, because the copper barrel-wrapped braces are absent (e.g., as shown on bits in Figures 3-1, 3-7, and 3-17), and the spade appears to be added onto the port of this mouthpiece. The style is also different and shows finely engraved silverwork (note flower on concho) spanning the divided cheeks and bridle attachment rings. The edges are inlaid with rocker-engraved silver bars. *Courtesy of R. Wilmot. William Manns photo.*

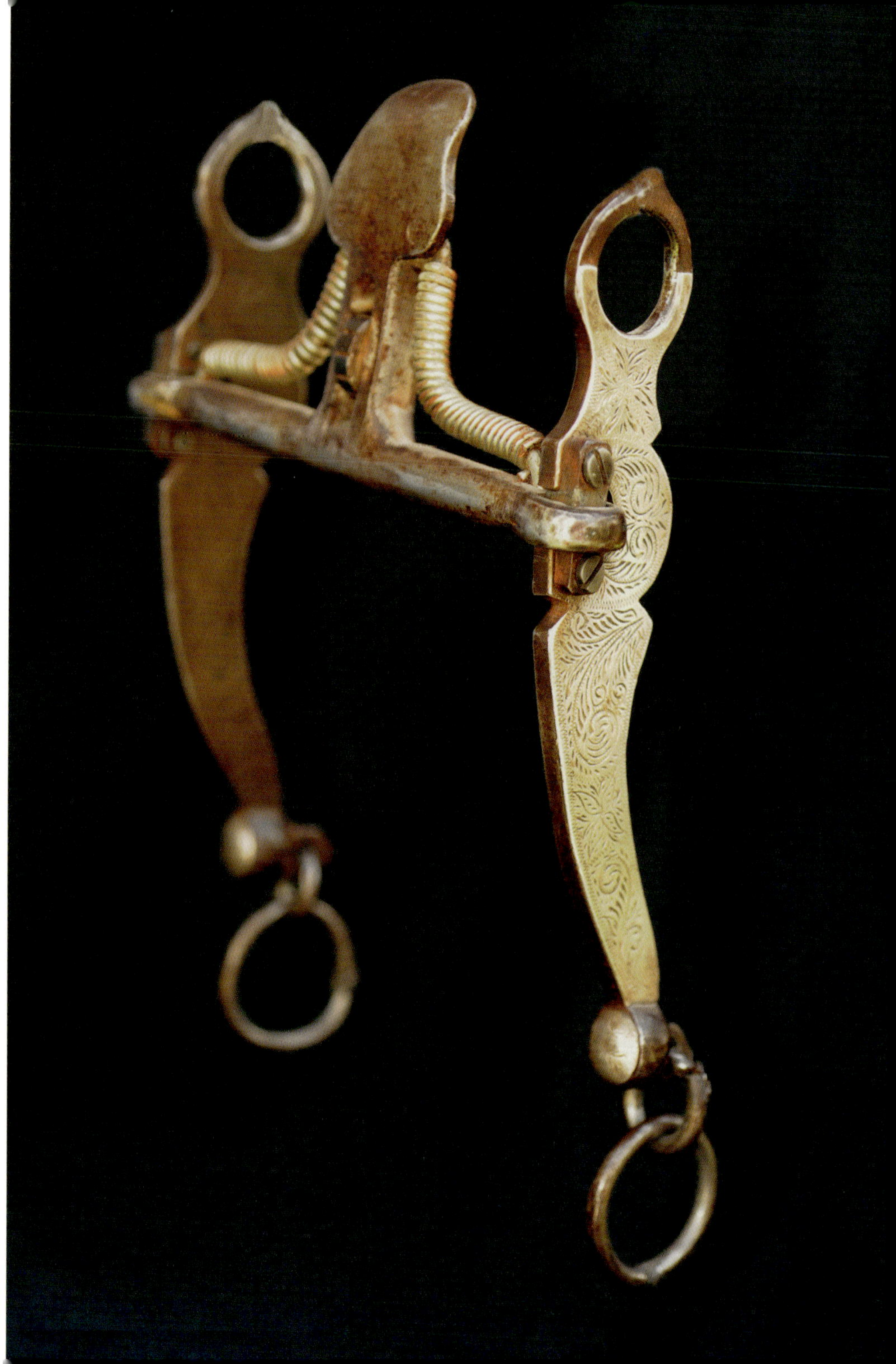

Figure 3-17. Hulbert bits. This silver-overlaid bit exhibits an interchangeable spade mouthpiece, with two screws on either side. *Courtesy of R. Wilmot. William Manns photo.*

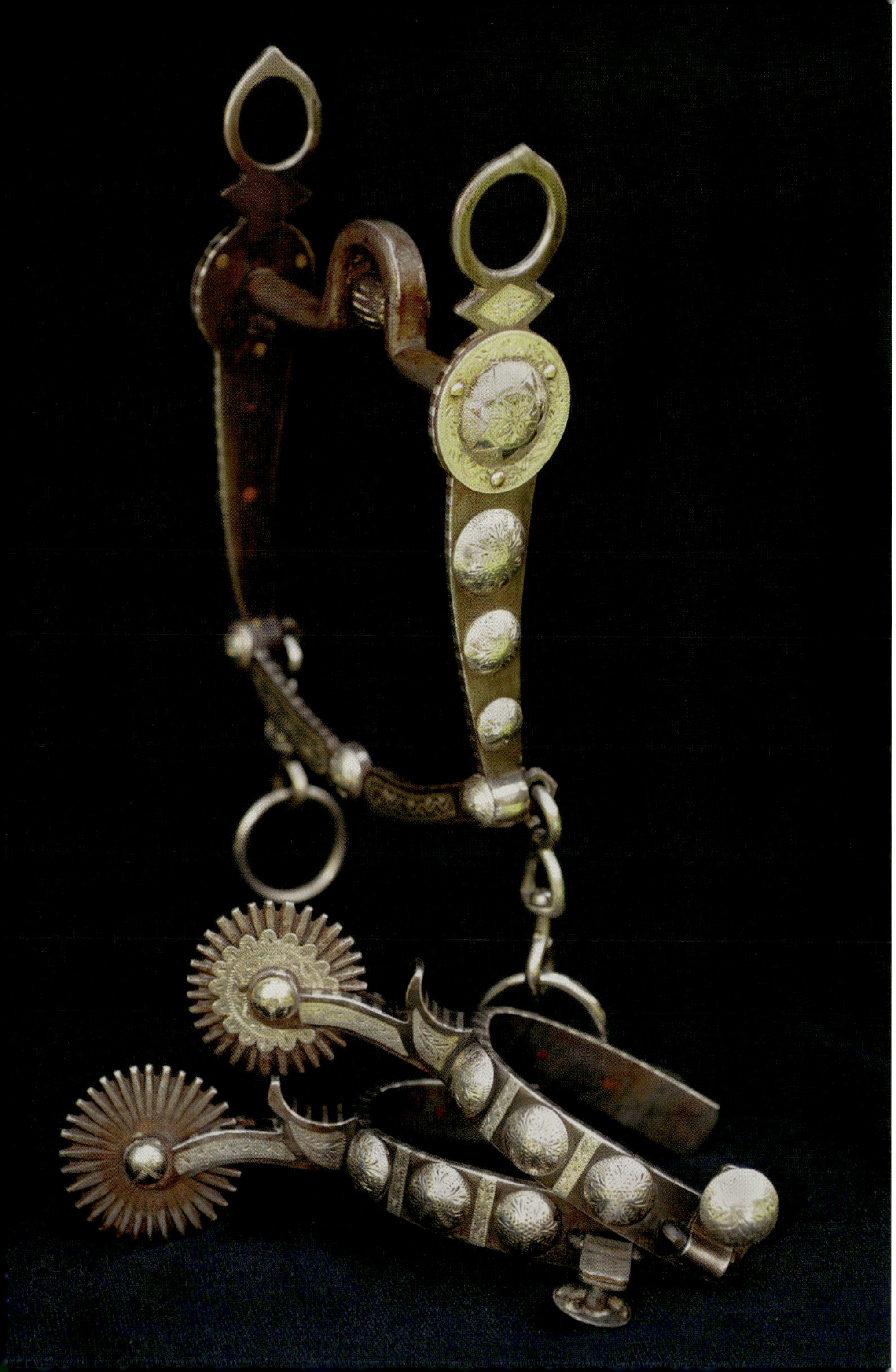

Figure 3-18. Hulbert bits. In this photograph are shown a pair of spurs and matching bit set, done in the "3-Button" pattern (other examples of 3-button silver spurs can be found in Chapter 2). This bit has edge inlays, an inlaid silver slobber bar with buttons, ornate conchos engraved in a star pattern, and small silver diamonds above the conchos. The fancy spurs have matching silver buttons and edge inlays. The rowels are particularly ornate with their engraved silver discs. *Courtesy of R. Wilmot. William Manns photo.*

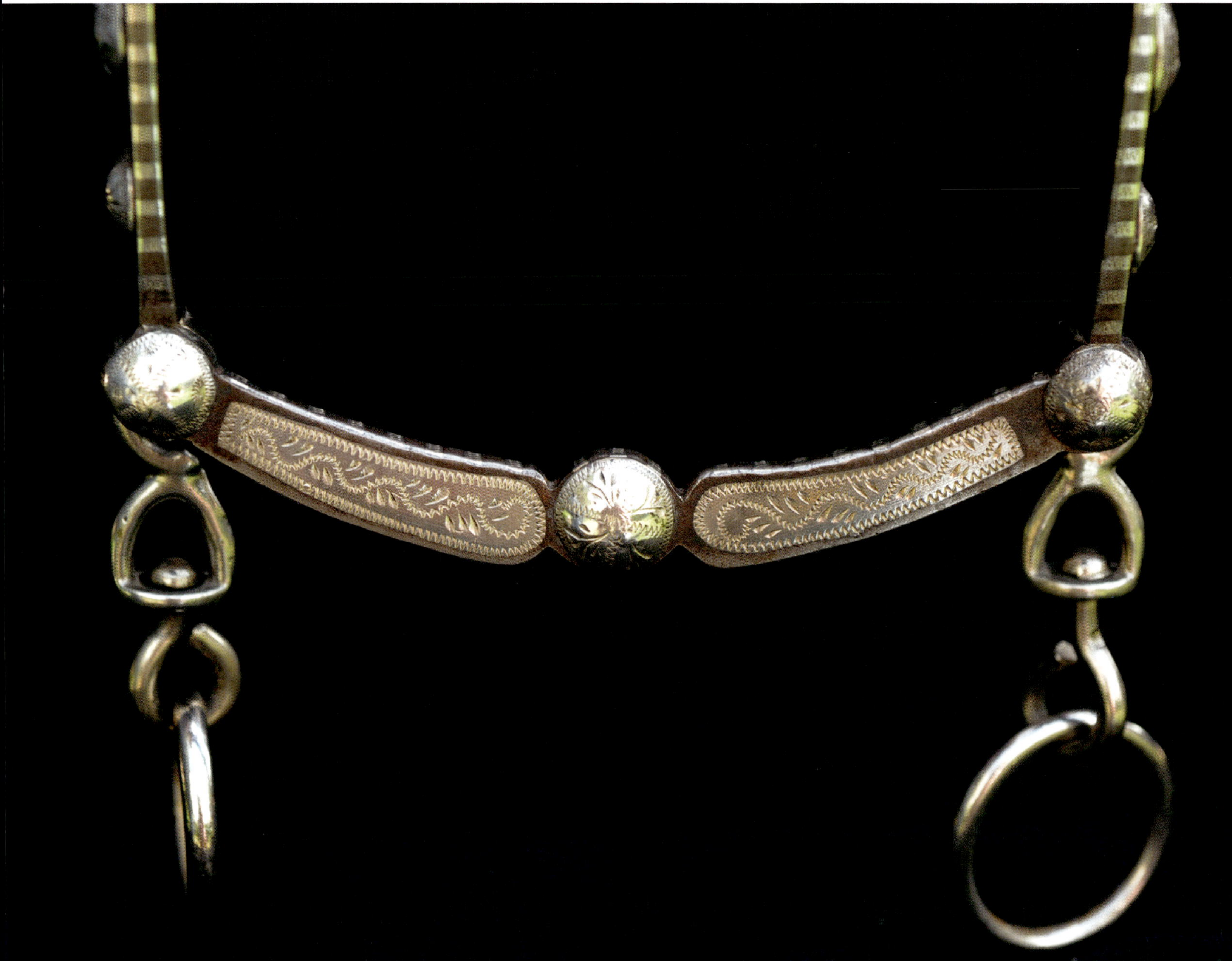

Figure 3-19. Hulbert bits. An enlarged view of the silver-inlaid slobber bar with its three buttons on the bit shown in Figure 3-18. *Courtesy of R. Wilmot. William Manns photo.*

Custom Orders

The "EH" marked bit shown in Figures 3-20 and 3-21 was made for Don Abarr, son of a homesteading family in the Dryhead area who later worked for many ranches as a wrangler and cowboy. His history and life stories have been recorded in *Hoofbeats on the Wind* (Abarr, 1989). The bit, a loose-jaw with silver bar inlays, was personalized by the silver inlaid letters "DON" on both sides of the cheeks where they were screwed onto the interchangeable mouthpiece. Abarr describes his employment at the Pitchfork Ranch (Abarr, 1989), from

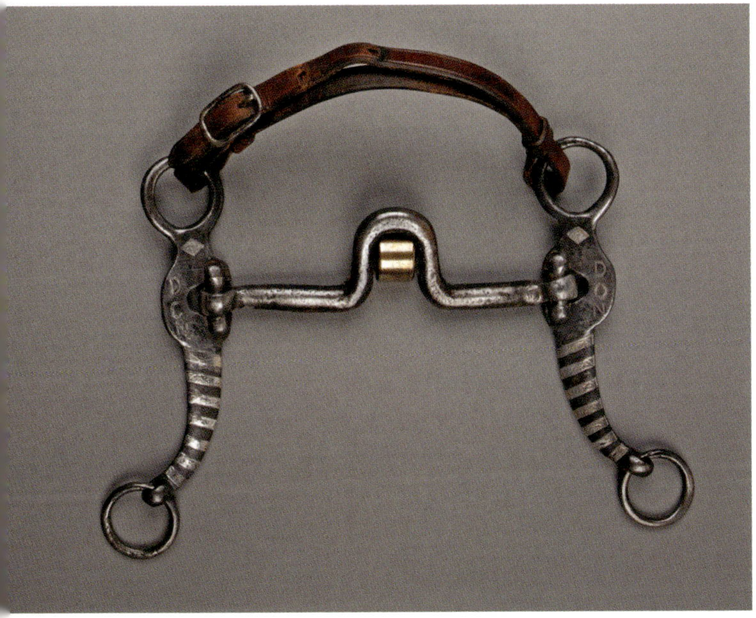

Figure 3-20. Hulbert bits—custom orders. Loose-jaw, silver-bar inlaid bit with interchangeable mouthpiece (a halfbreed with brass cricket is shown). "DON" is inlaid in silver letters on either side where the mouthpiece intersects the cheeks. This bit was made for Don Abarr, of the Pitchfork Ranch (Wyoming). See text for details. The bit is marked "EH." *Photo by D. Congdon-Martin.*

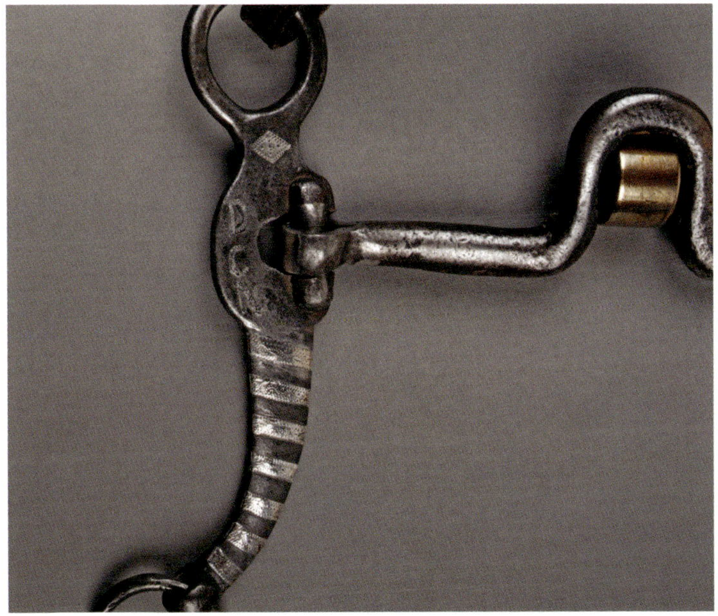

Figure 3-21. Hulbert bits—custom orders. Enlarged view of lettering on Don Abarr's bit shown in Figure 3-20. *Photo by D. Congdon-Martin.*

which this bit was allegedly stolen in the 1960s and reappeared in Buffalo, Wyoming, in the 1980s. Because Hulbert knew Don Abarr as a child at Cedarvale, it is possible that this bit was his gift to a cowboy that he respected and admired. Figures 3-22 and 3-23 show a bit with the "Lazy JD" brand from the Valley Ranch (see Chapter 2). It is an attractive "dude" bit (grazing style, the best bit for beginning riders or those visitors from the East who had not heretofore ridden Western-style) with floral-tooled conchos and silver diamonds.

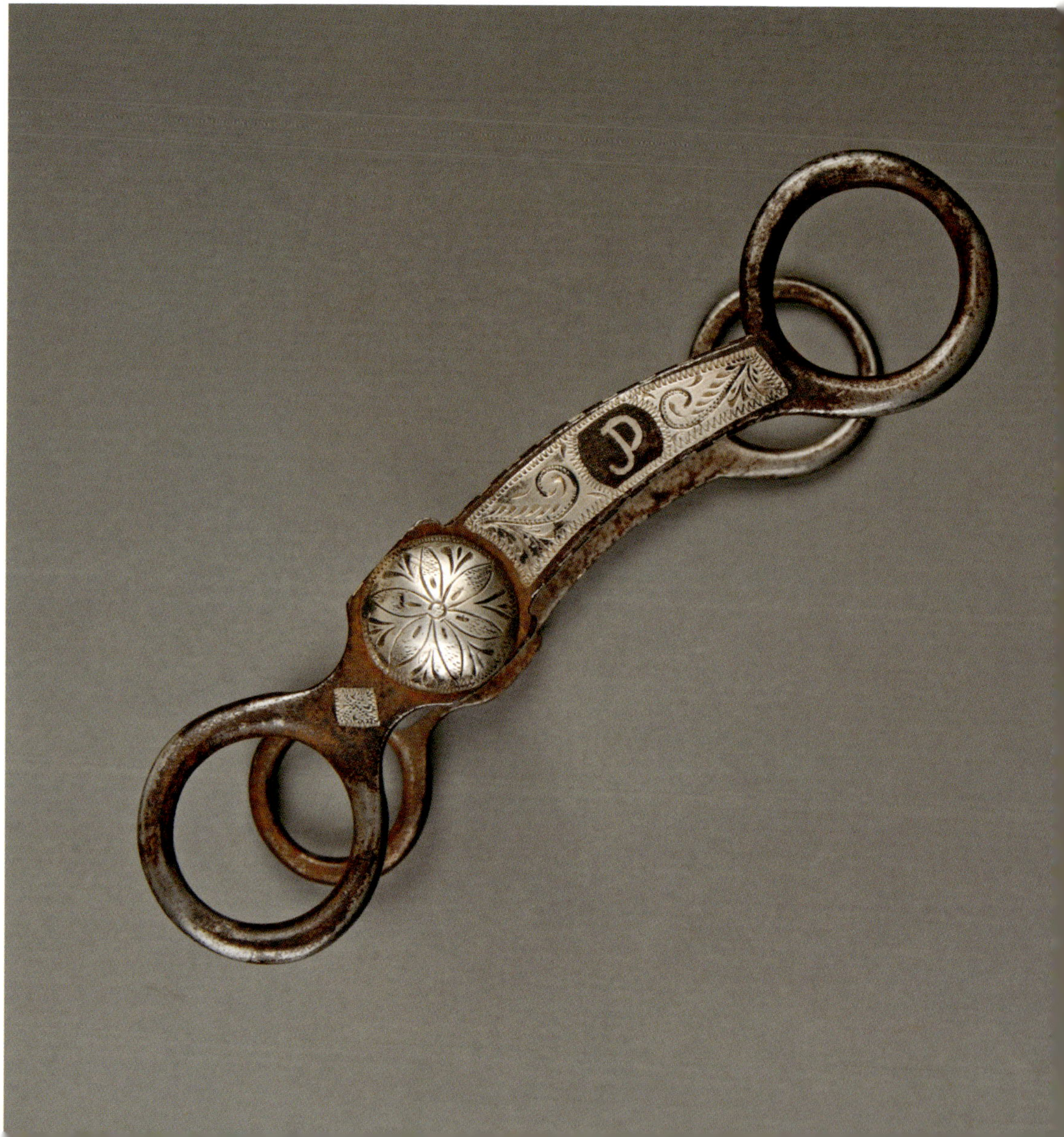

Figure 3-22. Hulbert bits—custom orders. This simple but attractive curb bit bears the "Lazy JD" brand of the Valley Ranch, a dude ranch located on the South Fork of the Shoshone River, in Wyoming (see Chapter 2). The conchos have been engraved with a 6-petaled flower, above which are small silver diamonds. *Photo by D. Congdon-Martin.*

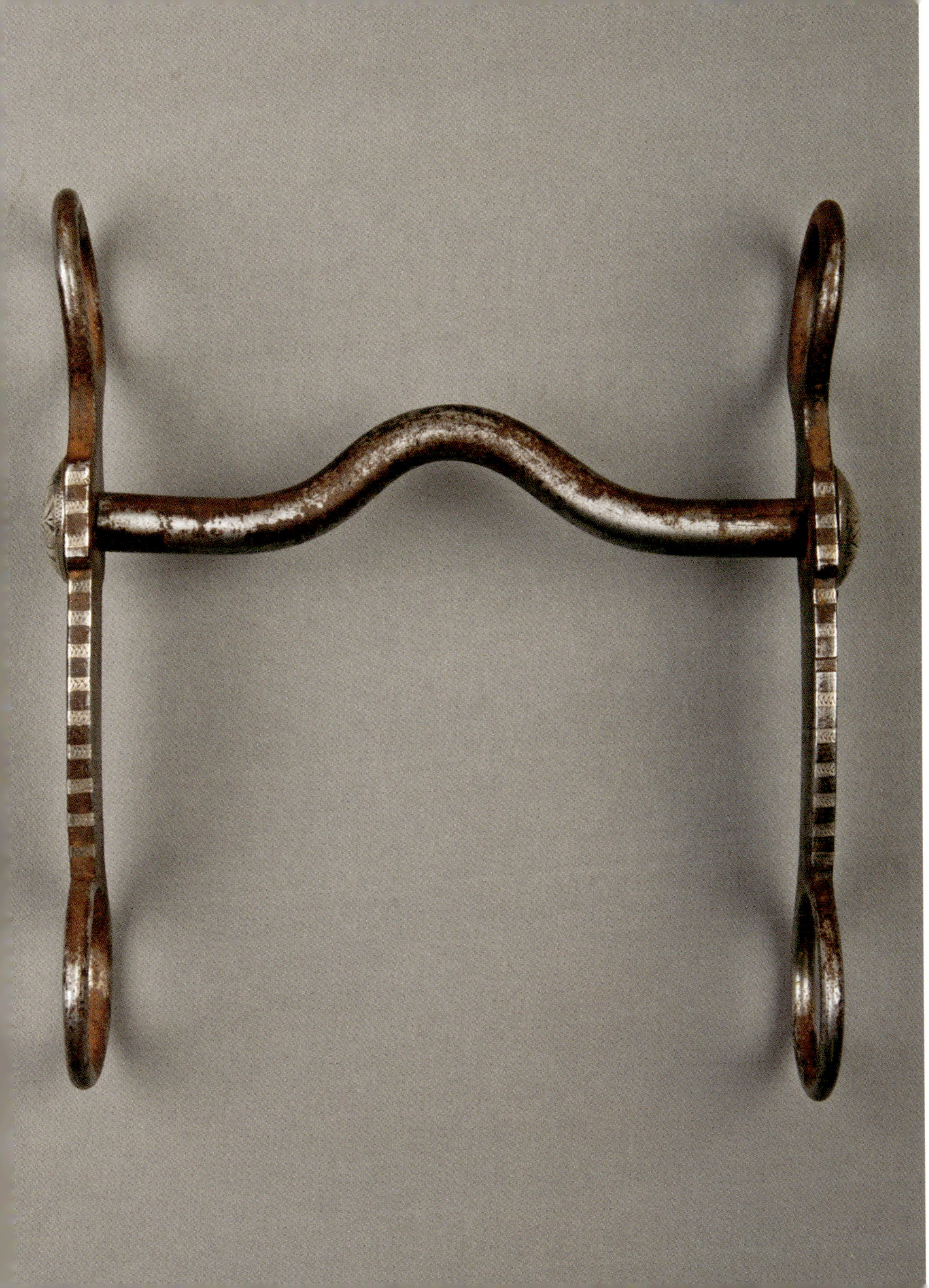

Figure 3-23. Hulbert bits—custom orders. Frontal view of the bit in Figure 3-22, showing low grazing port and silver edge inlays. *Photo by D. Congdon-Martin.*

Silver Bridle Decorations

In this section are shown three bridles that have been embellished with silver ornaments by Eddy Hulbert. The first (Figures 3-24 through 3-30) is a tastefully decorated black leather headstall with engraved silver conchos in graduated sizes (Figures 3-25 and 3-28), matching rosettes with the initials "LT" (Figure 3-26), and a charming longhorn bull (or steer) head at the center of the browband (Figure 3-27). The original bit is a half-breed with floral conchos, silver inlaid edges, and silver banana cheeks (Figures 3-29 and 3-30).

The second bridle (a headstall, without bit and reins) is a true "folk-art" piece, with an interesting story (Figures 3-31 through 3-33). The rosettes are silver four-leaf clovers with the initials "HS" engraved within a central heart. The buckles are heart- or horseshoe-shaped, and each leather tip is covered with silver. The browband is distinguished by a bowing horse named "CHERRY," flanked by hearts and horseshoes (Figure 3-33). Truly a one-of-a-kind creation, the history of this headstall was provided by Arne Esp, son of Hank (Henry L.) Esp and grandson of Henry R. Esp, originally from Lodge Grass, Montana (see frontis for photograph of Henry R. Esp). Harry Sharp, a round-up cook working for the Antler Ranch, owned and trained trick horses for exhibitions at various local rodeos and fairs. In his later years, when he lived in a log cabin in Lodge Grass/Crow Agency, his best horse was named "Cherry." Perhaps this headstall was ordered by Sharp from Eddy Hulbert for Cherry's shows, with his initials "HS."

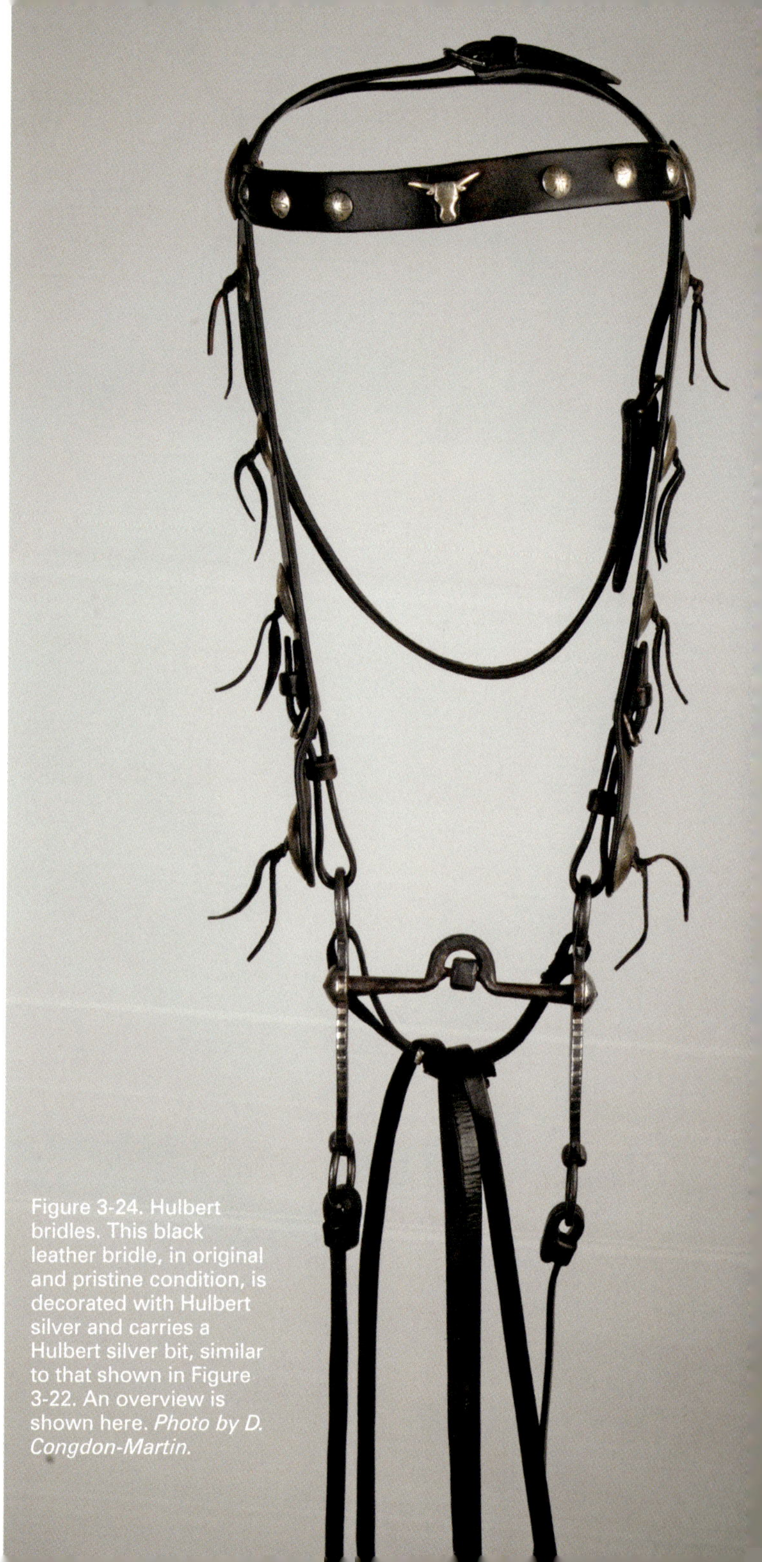

Figure 3-24. Hulbert bridles. This black leather bridle, in original and pristine condition, is decorated with Hulbert silver and carries a Hulbert silver bit, similar to that shown in Figure 3-22. An overview is shown here. *Photo by D. Congdon-Martin.*

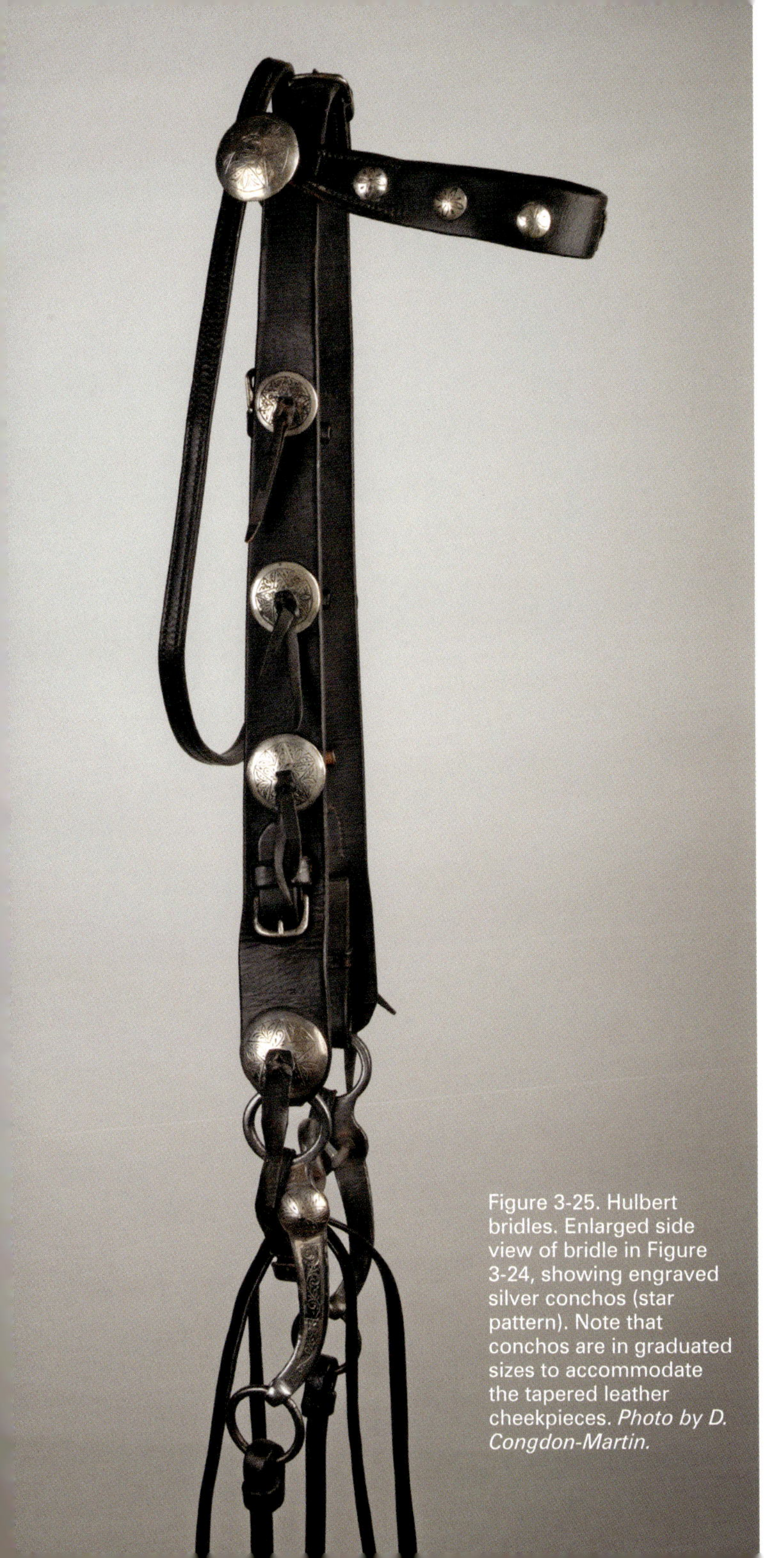

Figure 3-25. Hulbert bridles. Enlarged side view of bridle in Figure 3-24, showing engraved silver conchos (star pattern). Note that conchos are in graduated sizes to accommodate the tapered leather cheekpieces. *Photo by D. Congdon-Martin.*

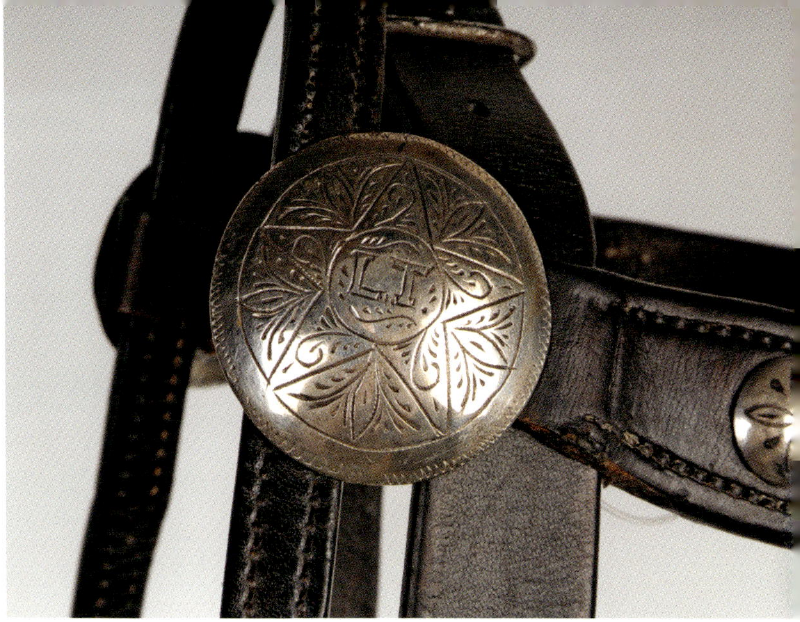

Figure 3-26. Hulbert bridles. Enlarged view of bridle in Figure 3-24, showing bridle rosette engraved in star pattern with the initials "LT." Personalized rosettes are a hallmark of a custom-ordered, silver-decorated bridle. *Photo by D. Congdon-Martin.*

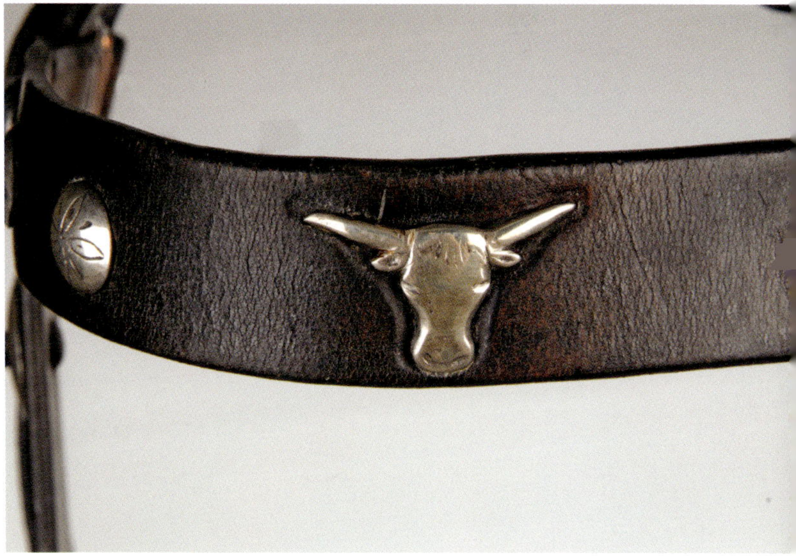

Figure 3-27. Hulbert bridles. Enlarged view of browband on bridle in Figure 3-24, showing silver bull's head in center. *Photo by D. Congdon-Martin.*

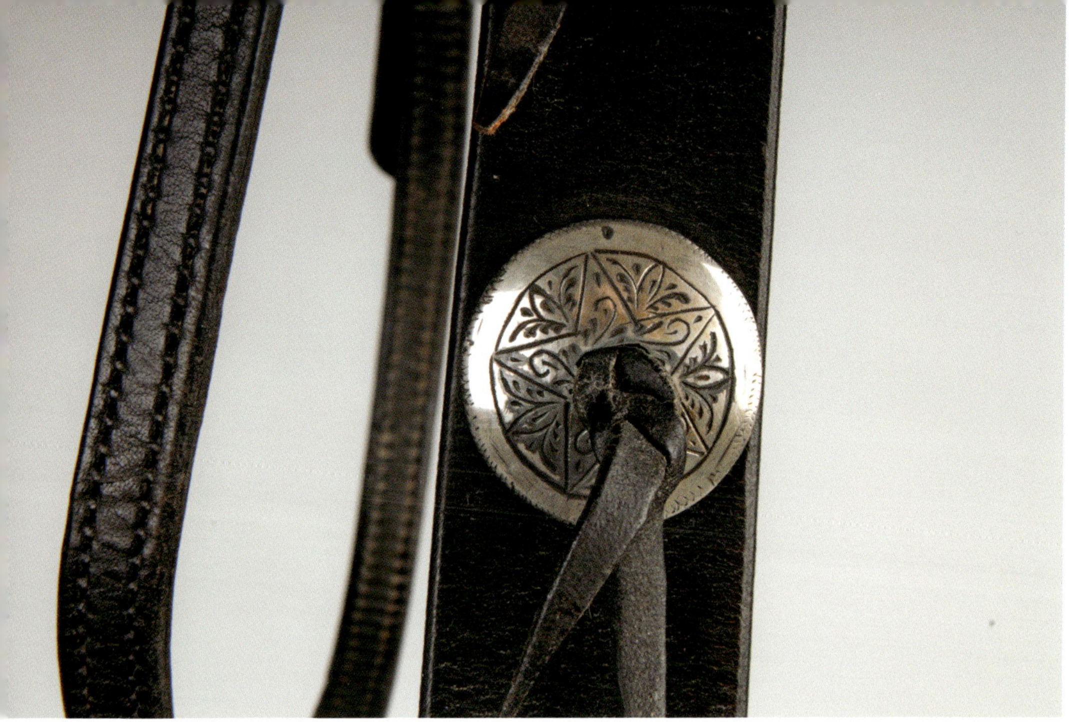

Figure 3-28. Hulbert bridles. Enlarged view of concho on cheekpieces of bridle shown in Figure 3-24. Note star pattern engraving matching that on rosettes. The engraving appears especially bold. *Photo by D. Congdon-Martin.*

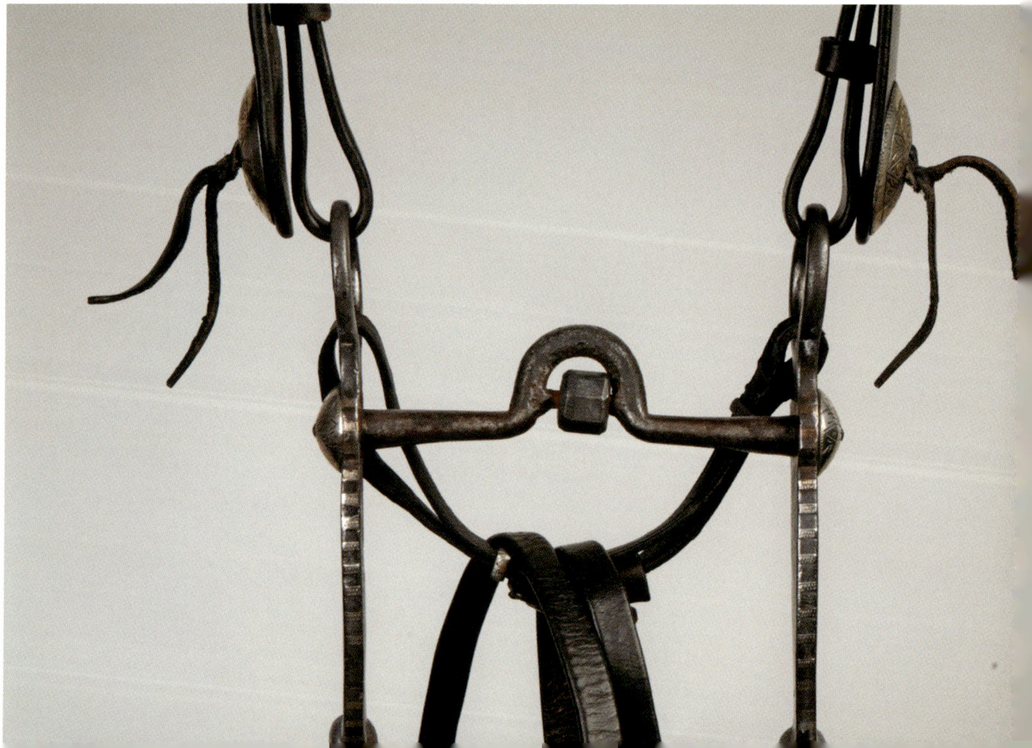

Figure 3-29. Hulbert bridles. Enlarged view of bit on the bridle shown in Figure 3-24. It is a halfbreed with a cricket, and the edges of the cheeks have been inlaid with silver bars. *Photo by D. Congdon-Martin.*

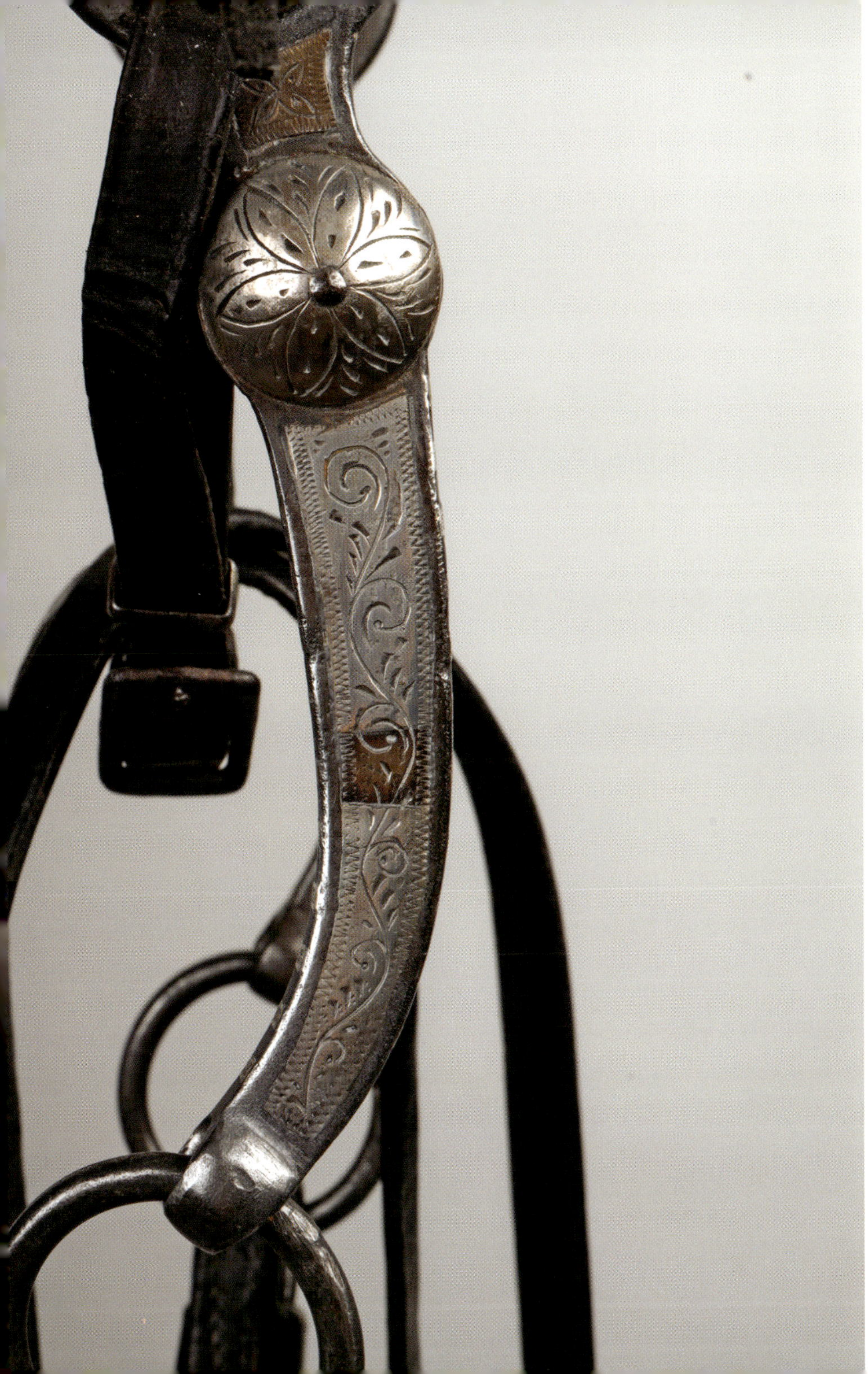

Figure 3-30. Hulbert bridles. Enlarged view of bit on the bridle shown in Figure 3-24. Note the 6-petal flower on the concho, and the engraved silver inlay on the banana cheek. *Photo by D. Congdon-Martin.*

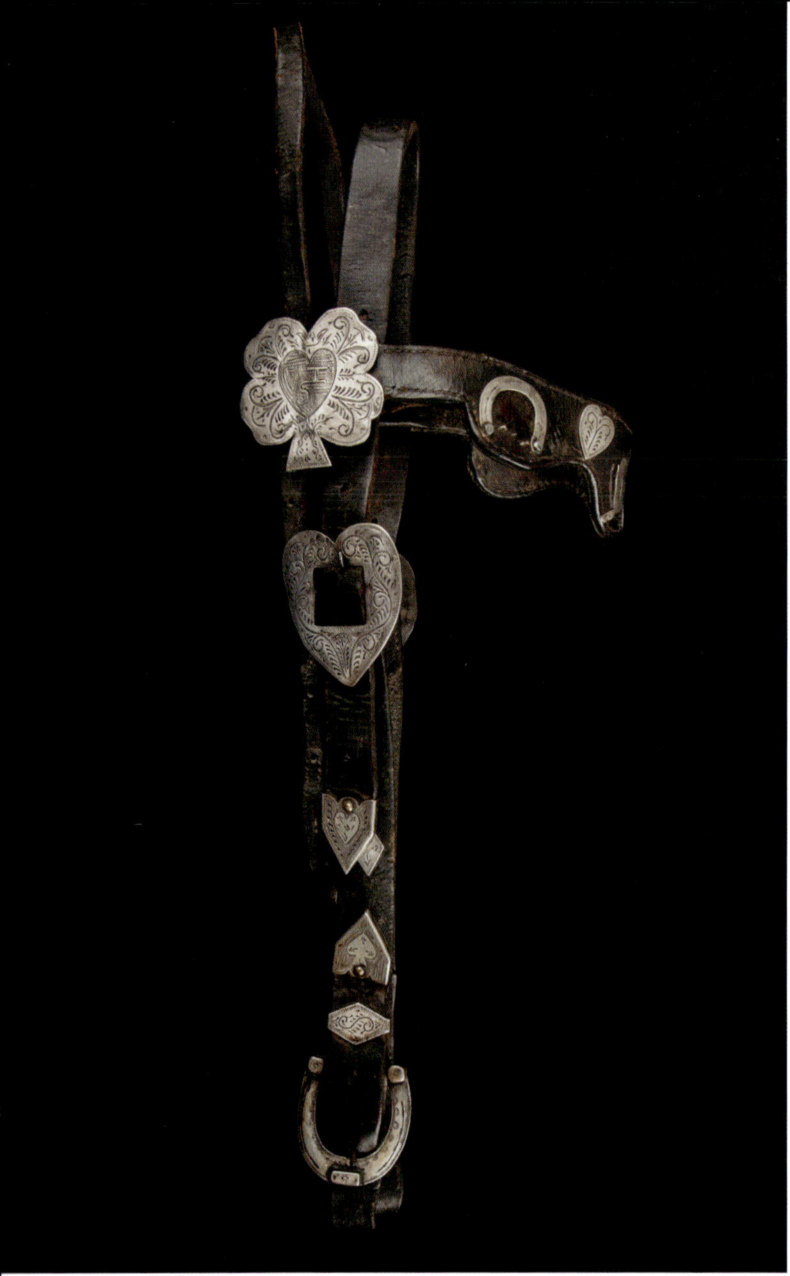

Figure 3-31. Hulbert bridles. This interesting, folk-art-style headstall bears custom Hulbert silver, most of which is unique to this piece. The black leather has been decorated with a horseshoe-style buckle/Ranger set at the bit end and a heart-shaped buckle attaching the cheekpiece to the crownpiece. Additional decorations can be seen on the browband (see Figure 3-33) and the rosettes (see Figure 3-32). *Courtesy of J. Lyndes. Photo by J. Williams.*

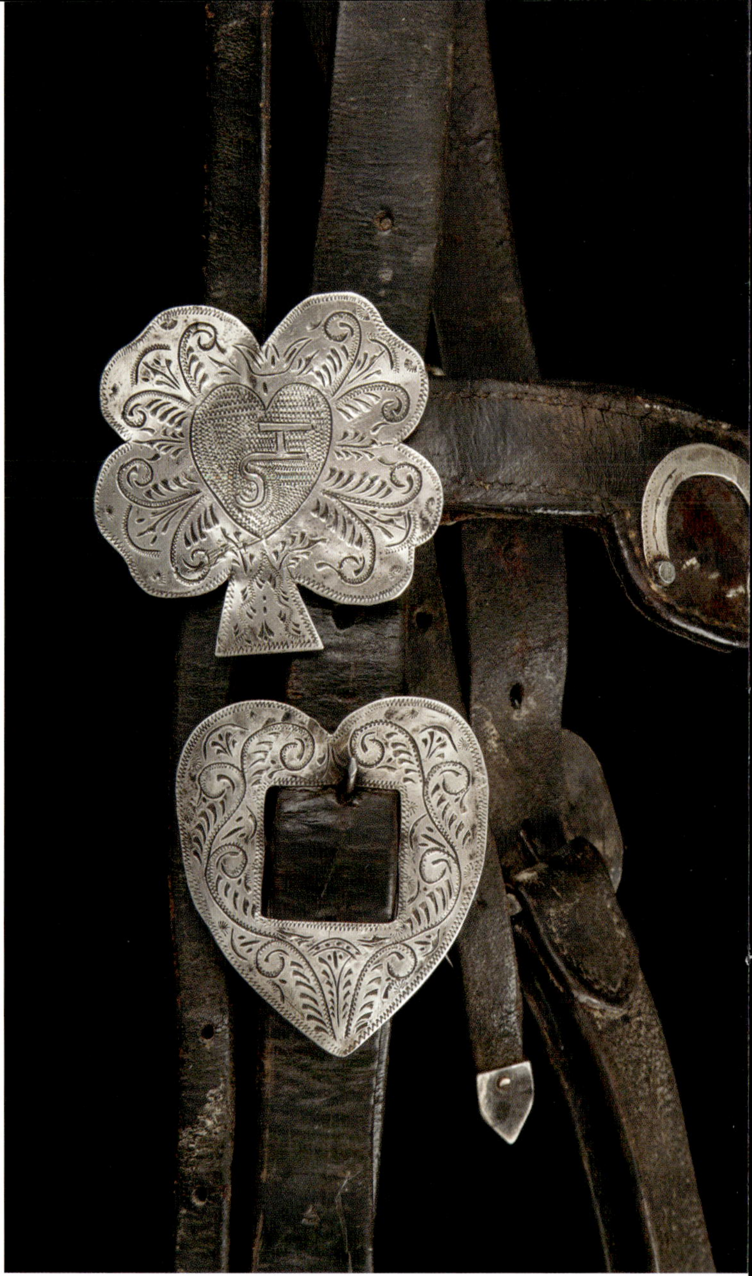

Figure 3-32. Hulbert bridles. Enlarged view of the heart buckle and the shamrock-shaped rosette, the latter engraved with the initials "HS" within a heart, on the bridle shown in Figure 3-31. *Courtesy of J. Lyndes. Photo by J. Williams.*

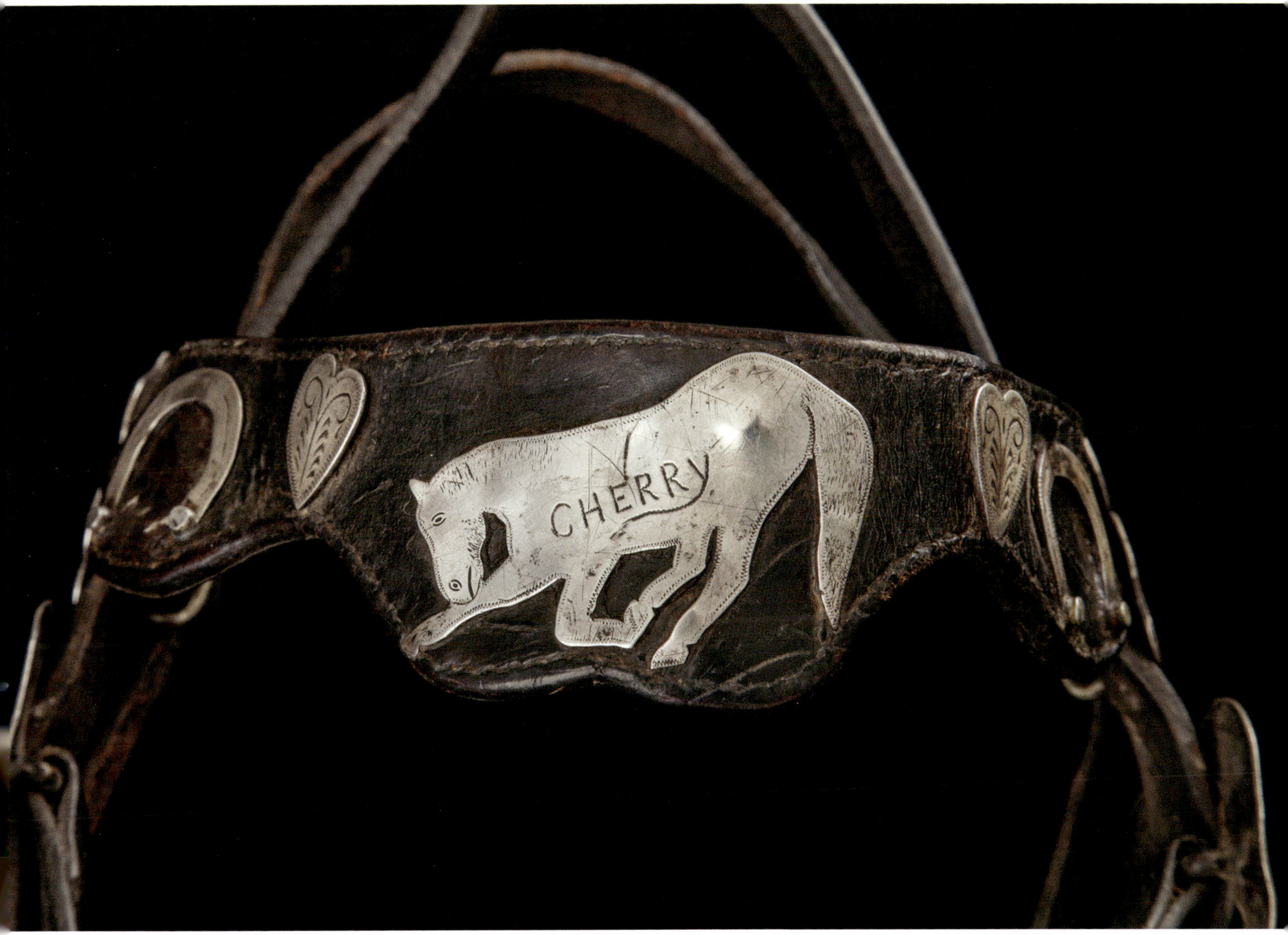

Figure 3-33. Hulbert bridles. Enlarged view of browband on bridle shown in Figure 3-31. A bowing horse, identified as "CHERRY," is flanked on each side by a silver heart and horseshoe. This bridle was owned by Harry Sharp, whose "trick"/performance horse was named "Cherry." See Figures 3-34 through 3-36 and text for details. *Courtesy of J. Lyndes. Photo by J. Williams.*

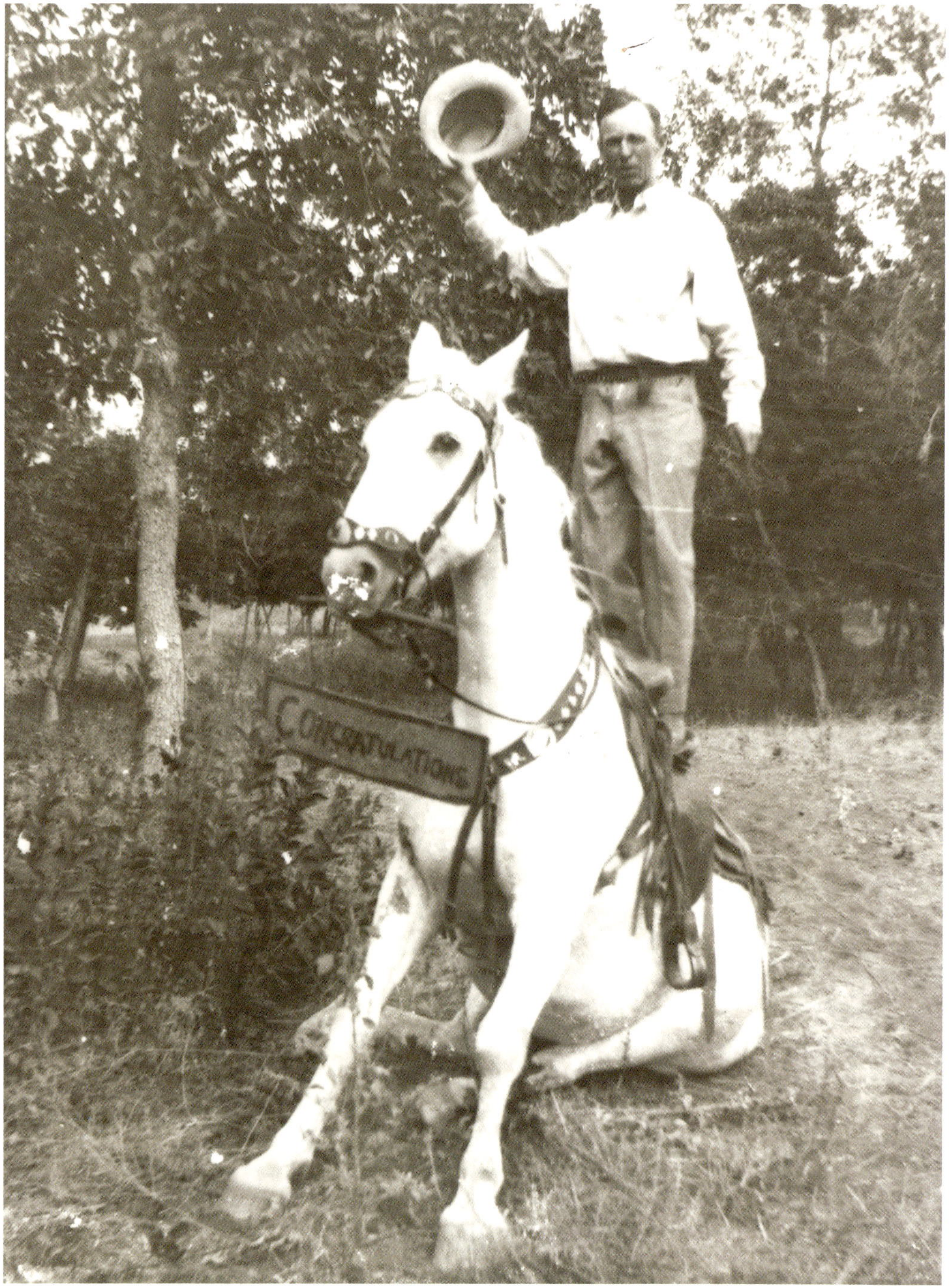

Figure 3-34. Hulbert bridles: Harry Sharp and Cherry. The owner of the bridle shown in Figures 3-31 through 3-33 was Harry Sharp, shown here standing on Cherry, who wears the same bridle (bowing horse can barely be seen on browband) and holds a sign in his or her teeth, "CONGRATULATIONS." Sharp was a round-up cook for the cowboys out on the summer range of the Antler Ranch. *Courtesy of Arne Esp. Photographer unknown.*

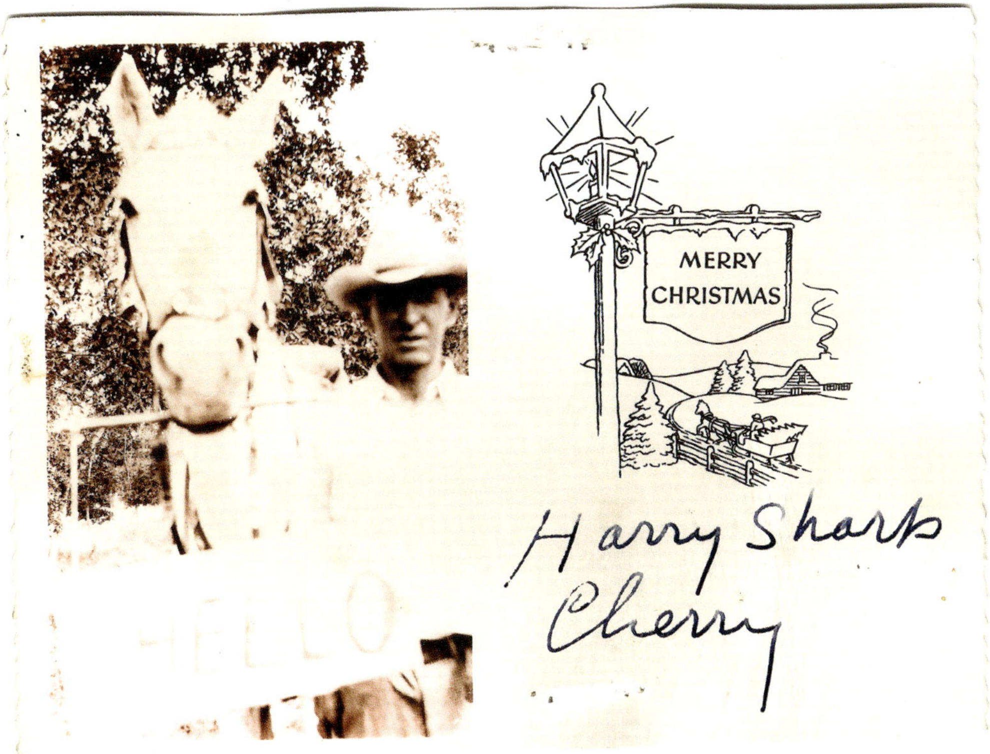

Figure 3-35. Hulbert bridles: Harry Sharp and Cherry. Harry Sharp's Christmas card shows Cherry (holding a sign "HELLO") and Harry, c. late 1930s/early 1940s. *Courtesy of Arne Esp. Photographer unknown.*

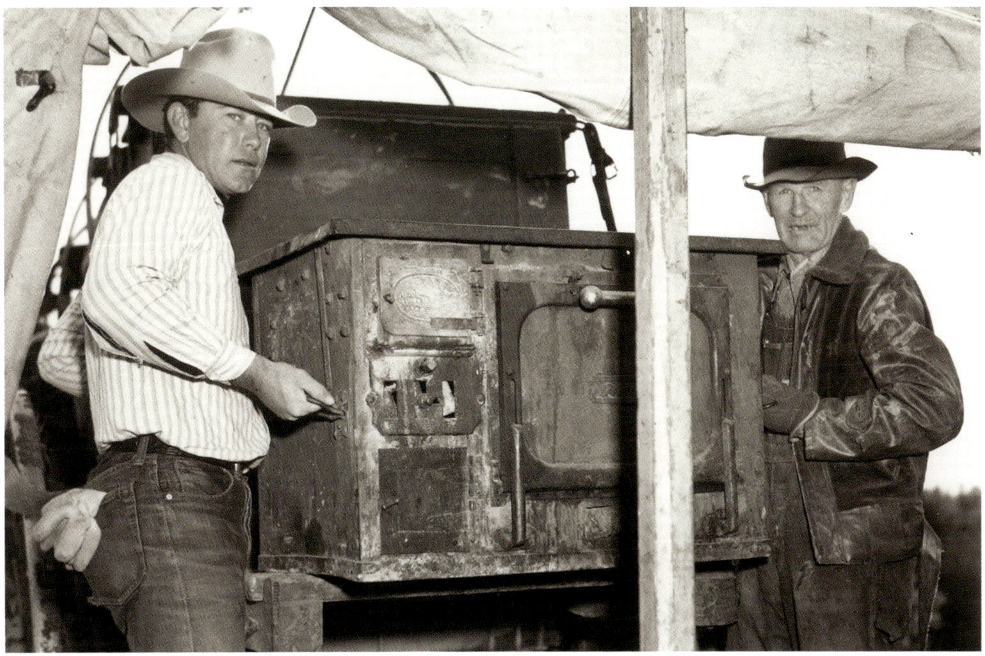

Figure 3-36. Hulbert bridles: Harry Sharp. This later 1940s photograph shows John Hammett (left) and Harry Sharp (right) loading a stove onto a chuck wagon. Both men were working for the Antler Ranch; one of the cow camps in the summer was located across the Big Horn River from Hillsboro (approximately 20 miles distant). For several years Hammett stayed in that camp and became friendly with Eddy Hulbert. *Courtesy of Arne Esp. Photographer unknown.*

Harry Sharp and Cherry are shown in late 1930s photographs in Figures 3-34 and 3-35, and a photograph (c. late 1940s) of John Hammett (see figure caption) and Harry is shown in Figure 3-36. The Antler Ranch (so-called because the brand resembled an antler, but also referred to as the Little Horn because of its location within the environs of the Little Big Horn River), was owned at the time by Matt Tschirgi, who had leased several million acres of the Crow Reservation (see map, Figure 1-1). The Antlers ran tens of thousands of cattle and 50,000 head of sheep. Now a smaller ranch, it is currently known as the Sunlight Ranch. (The author is indebted to Arne Esp for this information.)

The third bridle (minus the reins) (Figures 3-37 through 3-39) also brings forward some interesting local Montana history. It is an elegant piece, with engraved silver conchos in graduated sizes, four large rosettes (at the browband and bit ends), fully decorated browband and caveson (noseband), and a banana cheek bit with interchangeable mouthpiece and a silver crescent and heart complementing the heavily engraved silver cheeks (Figure 3-39). The large silver plate across the caveson has three highlighted letters (in silver relief): "CFC" (Clarks Fork Cattle Co., or possibly, Clarks Fork Café). A paper tag that accompanied the bridle when it was purchased by the present owner identified the piece as having been made by Eddy Hulbert for Mike Capor [*sic*], a rodeo cowboy from Pryor, Montana (see Figure 3-37 caption). Mike Kapor (b. 1930, d. 1996) was active in many endeavors in the Billings area. He owned/ran the Clarks Fork Cattle Company (Clarks Fork Yellowstone River flows from the Gallatin National Forest in southern Montana eastward to the Shoshone National Forest in northwest Wyoming, and back into Montana, passing Belfry and Bridger and rejoining the Yellowstone River), and was active in real estate in his later years. Kapor also owned the Clarks Fork Café and the Clarks Fork Hotel in historic Old Bridger (*Billings Herald*, September 22, 1949) and was president of the Jim Bridger Rodeo in 1953 (*Billings Gazette*, August 30, 1953). He was married

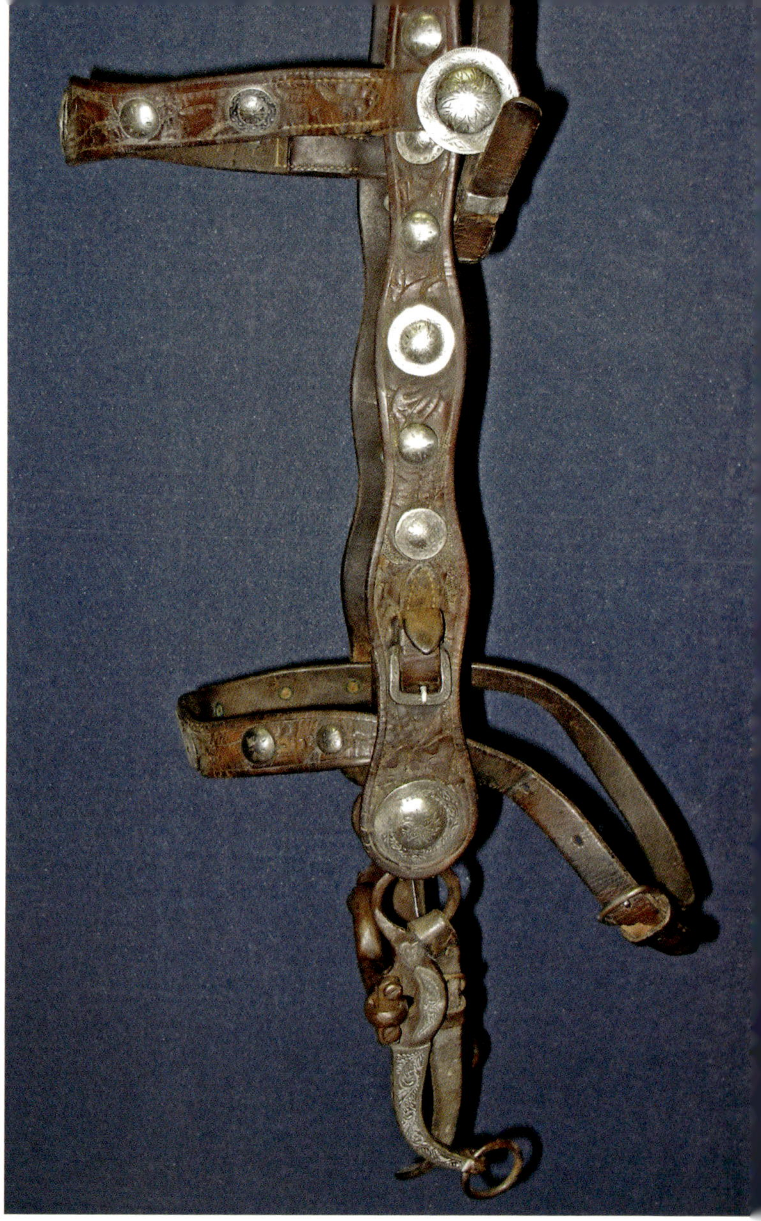

Figure 3-37. Hulbert bridles. This tooled brown leather headstall was outfitted by Hulbert with engraved silver conchos in graduated sizes, silver buttons, and silver rosettes for Mike Kapor, of the Clarks Fork Cattle Co. The browband and noseband (caveson) are decorated as well, and the bit is a silver-overlaid banana cheek curb bit with an interchangeable mouthpiece. The paper tag (not shown) attached to the headstall is handwritten: "Eddy Hulbert Bridle, 3-piece set made for Mike Capor [sic] Rodeo cowboy from Pryor." See Figure 3-38 for confirmation of ownership. *Courtesy of J. Lyndes. Photo by D. Claxton.*

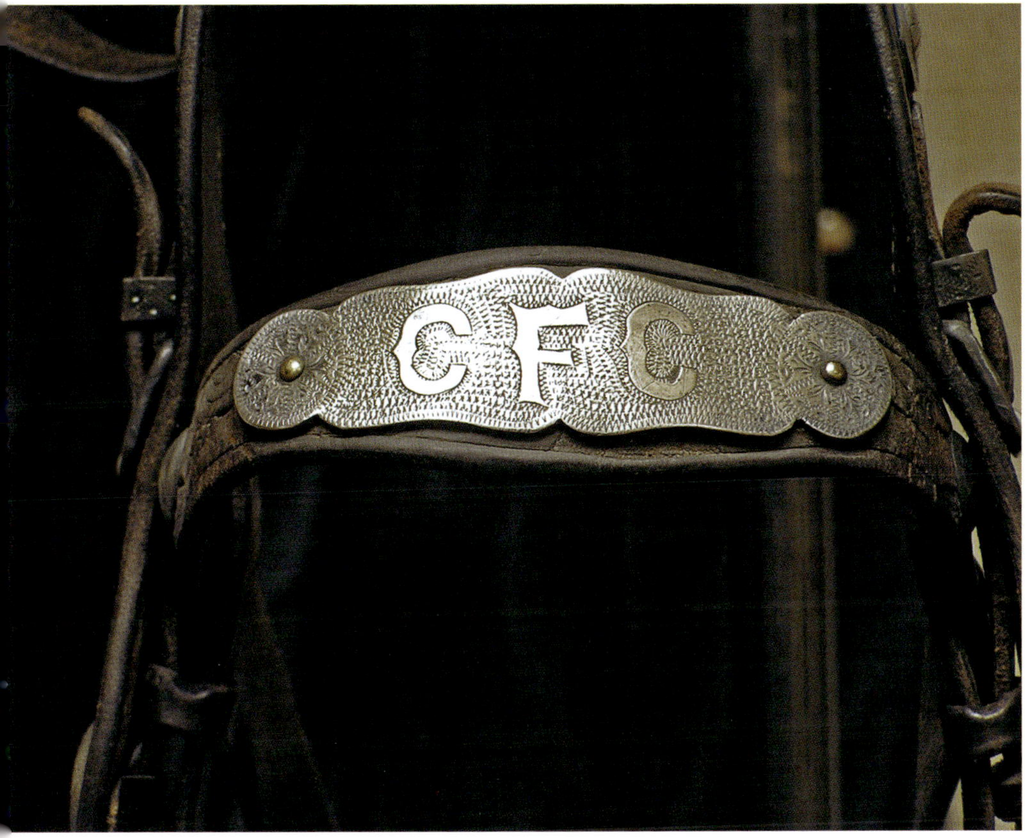

Figure 3-38. Hulbert bridles. The caveson on the bridle shown in Figure 3-37 is nearly covered by an elaborately-engraved silver plate with the initials "CFC" (Clarks Fork Cattle Co.). *Courtesy of J. Lyndes. Photo by D. Claxton.*

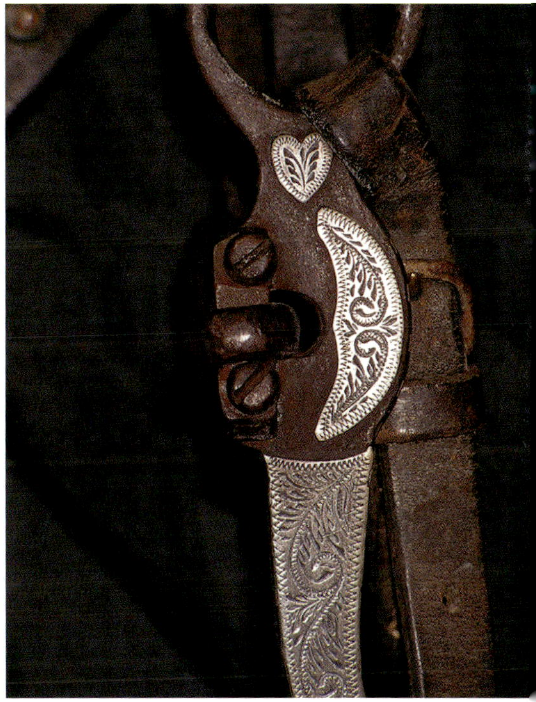

Figure 3-39. Hulbert bridles. Enlarged view of bit shown in Figure 3-37. The characteristic, bold engraving style of Hulbert is apparent on the heart, crescent, and cheek. *Courtesy of J. Lyndes. Photo by D. Claxton.*

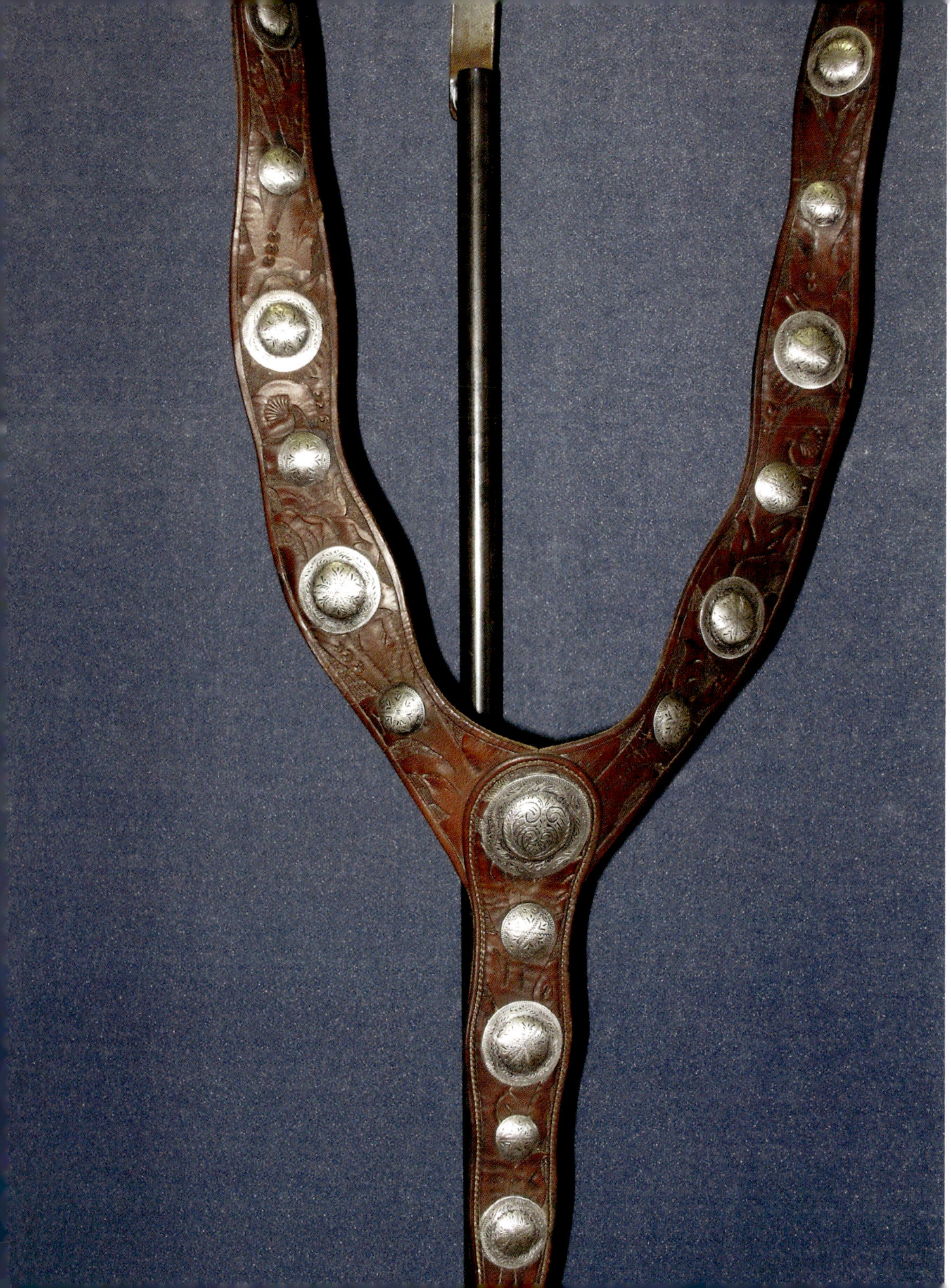

Figure 3-40. Hulbert martingale. Martingales with Hulbert silver are quite rare—this one was part of the "3-piece set" referred to on the tag described in Figure 3-37. The tooled brown leather appears identical to that on the headstall, and the engraved silver conchos match as well. Note the graduated sizes of the conchos, and their separation by smaller silver buttons. *Courtesy of J. Lyndes. Photo by D. Claxton.*

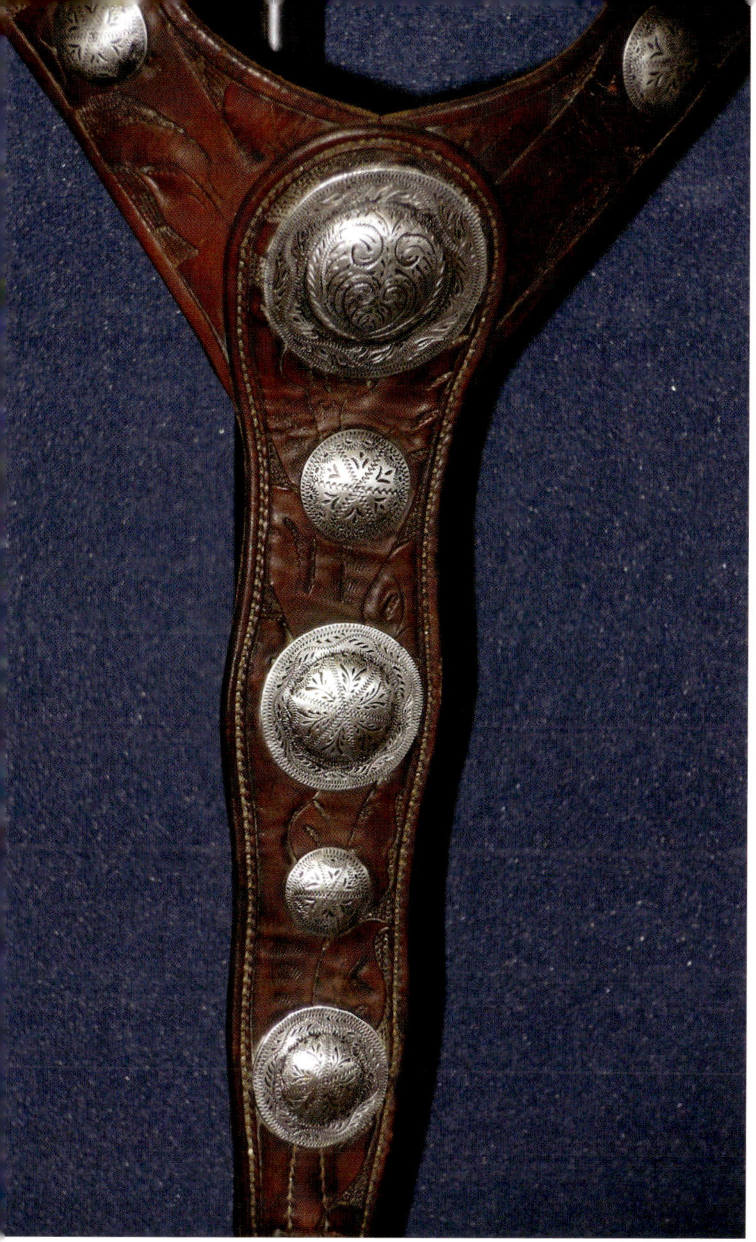

Figure 3-41. Hulbert martingale. Enlarged view of the silver conchos on the yoke of the martingale shown in Figure 3-40. *Courtesy of J. Lyndes. Photo by D. Claxton.*

to Sigrid Kapor (*Billings Gazette*, January 8, 1939), whose belts and jewelry by Eddy Hulbert are described in Chapters 4 and 5, respectively.

A martingale matching the Kapor bridle is shown in Figures 3-40 and 3-41. The floral-tooled leather was decorated with Hulbert's beautifully engraved silver conchos and buttons. This piece was one of Hulbert's few "parade" items and is rare indeed. It sets off the horse in a striking manner (see photo of Hartmam and his parade outfit in Figure 1-21).

Belts and Belt Buckles

Eddy Hulbert became well-known for his artistic, cleverly-designed belt buckles and belts. Some collectors prefer these pieces to any of the other items that Hulbert made. Most of the belt buckles were produced in the 1940s and 1950s, and most of those were custom-ordered for an individual or for rodeos and horse shows. This shift in Hulbert's output reflected the changing times in the country after the second World War—ranches had been threatened during and after the Great Depression, and were later sold, often to land developers. Cowboys found it difficult to secure employment, and the demand for bits and spurs decreased appreciably. Hulbert's talent for jewelry, including belts and buckles, became his mainstay in these later years, before his death in 1960.

Hulbert made silver Ranger sets (a buckle, keeper, and tip) and the rectangular or oval solid buckles (often referred to as the "Rodeo" or "trophy" style) that fitted onto the leather belt by a loop and hook (or stud). Figures 4-1 through 4-10 show various designs of Ranger sets, some of which were personalized. Montana jade (a rare stone in Hulbert's jewelry), Montana pearl-grey agate, and a mixed-brown agate appear, respectively, in the Ranger sets shown in Figures 4-1 through 4-3. The sets are similar in size and style (see figure captions). In Figure 4-4, a second style of buckle, without stones and characterized by a neatly-scalloped edge, can be seen. There is more space for Hulbert's bold and, in this case, exuberant engraving style. Most of his Ranger sets are marked "STERLING" on the back or inside of the buckle.

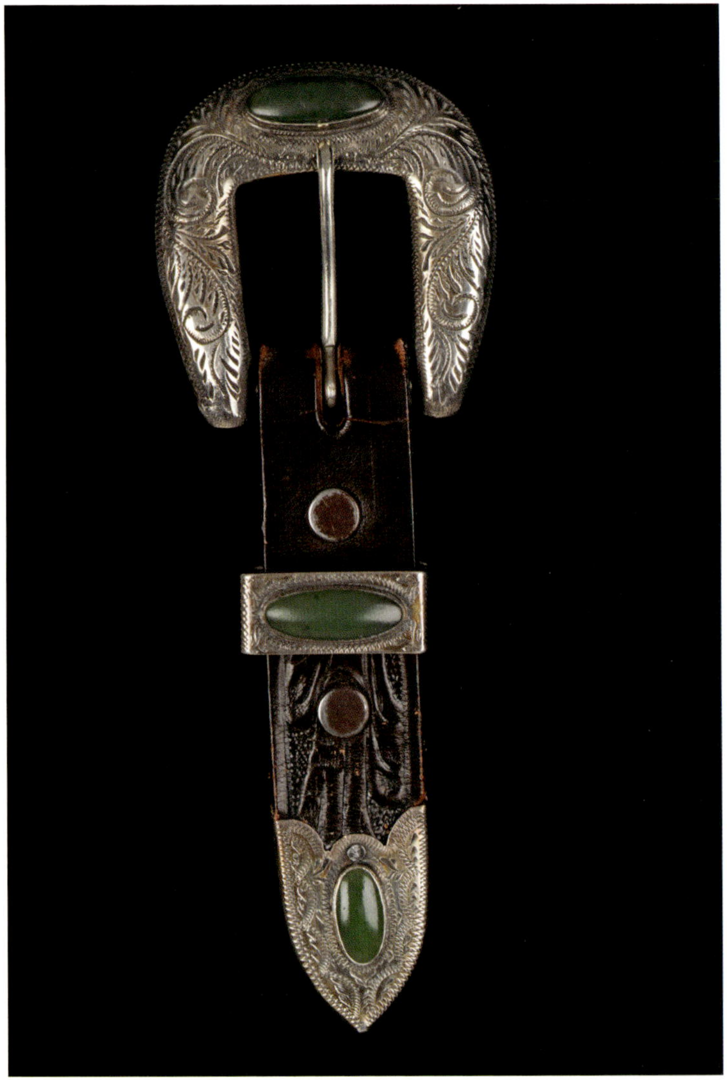

Figure 4-1. Hulbert 3-piece Ranger sets. An engraved silver Ranger set with Wyoming jade stones, marked "STERLING." These stones are rarely seen in Hulbert's work. *Photo by D. Congdon-Martin.*

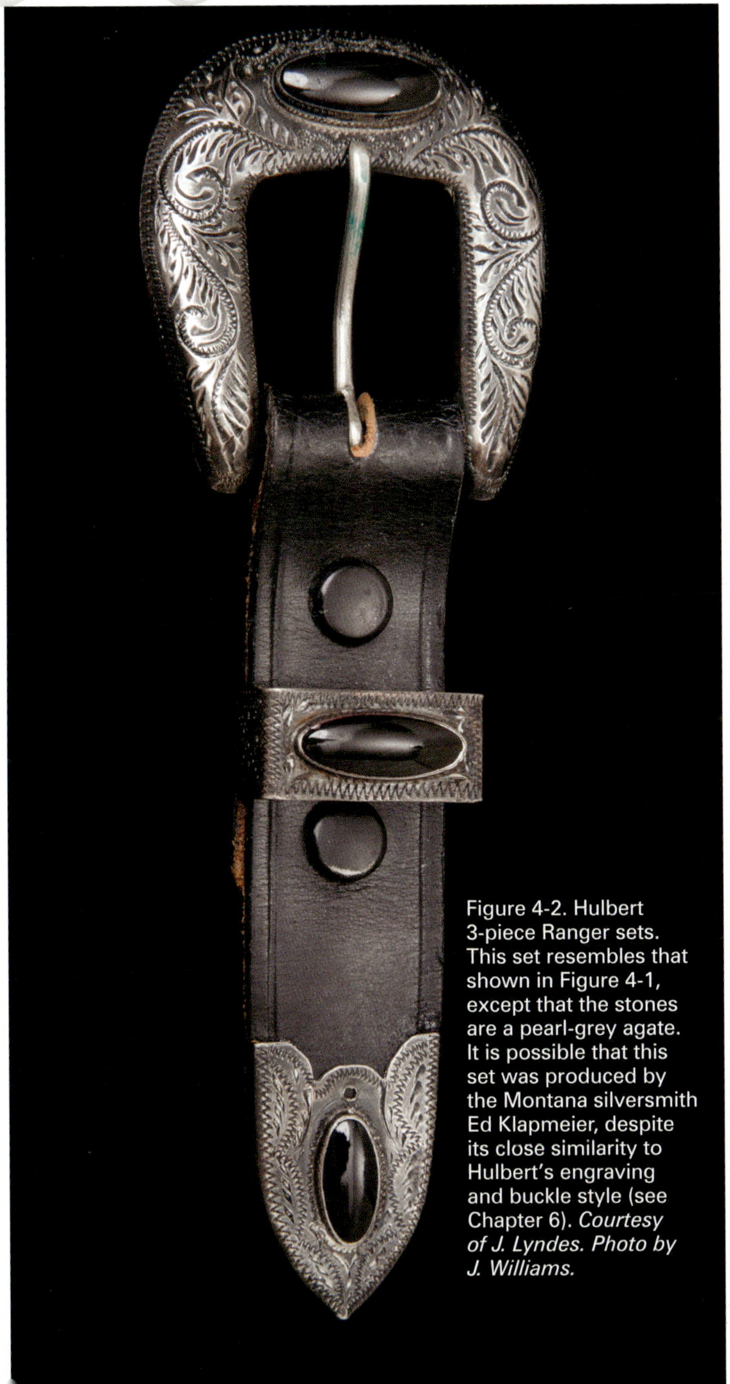

Figure 4-2. Hulbert 3-piece Ranger sets. This set resembles that shown in Figure 4-1, except that the stones are a pearl-grey agate. It is possible that this set was produced by the Montana silversmith Ed Klapmeier, despite its close similarity to Hulbert's engraving and buckle style (see Chapter 6). *Courtesy of J. Lyndes. Photo by J. Williams.*

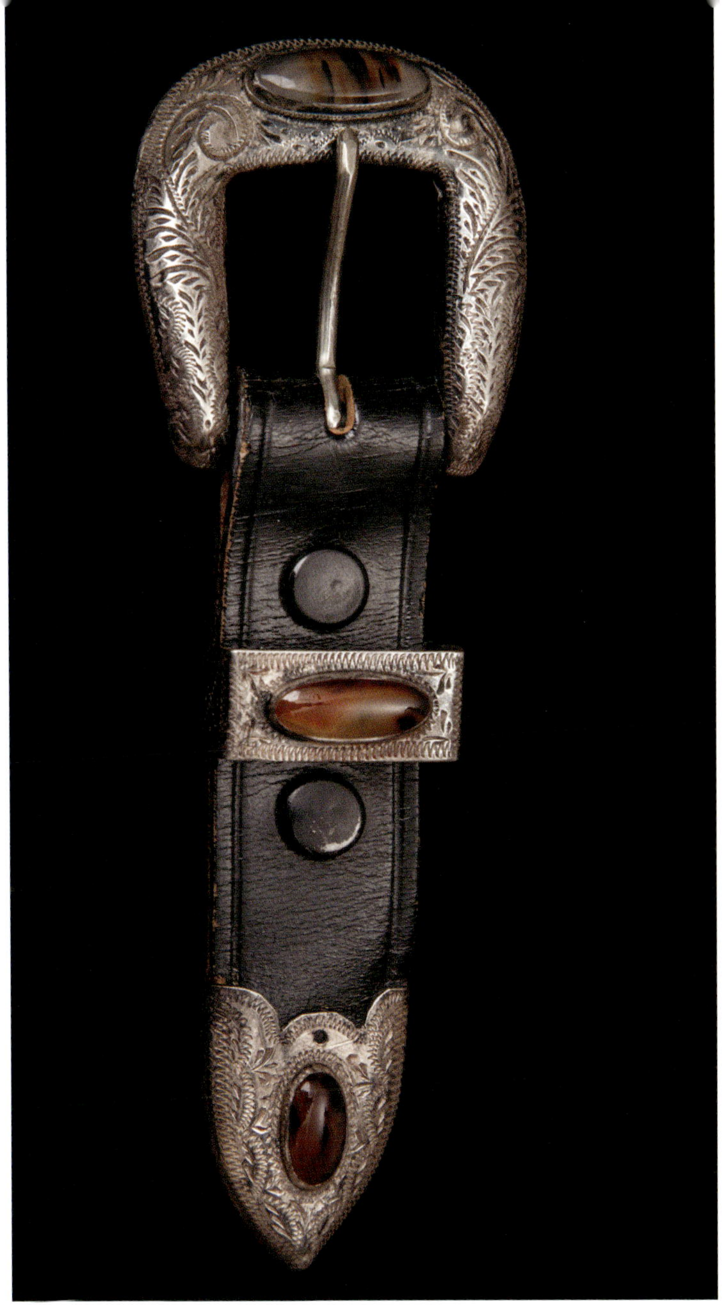

Figure 4-3. Hulbert 3-piece Ranger sets. A third set resembling in style those shown in Figures 4-1 and 4-2, this one with very attractive Montana agates, likely by Hulbert but possibly by Klapmeier. *Courtesy of J. Lyndes. Photo by J. Williams.*

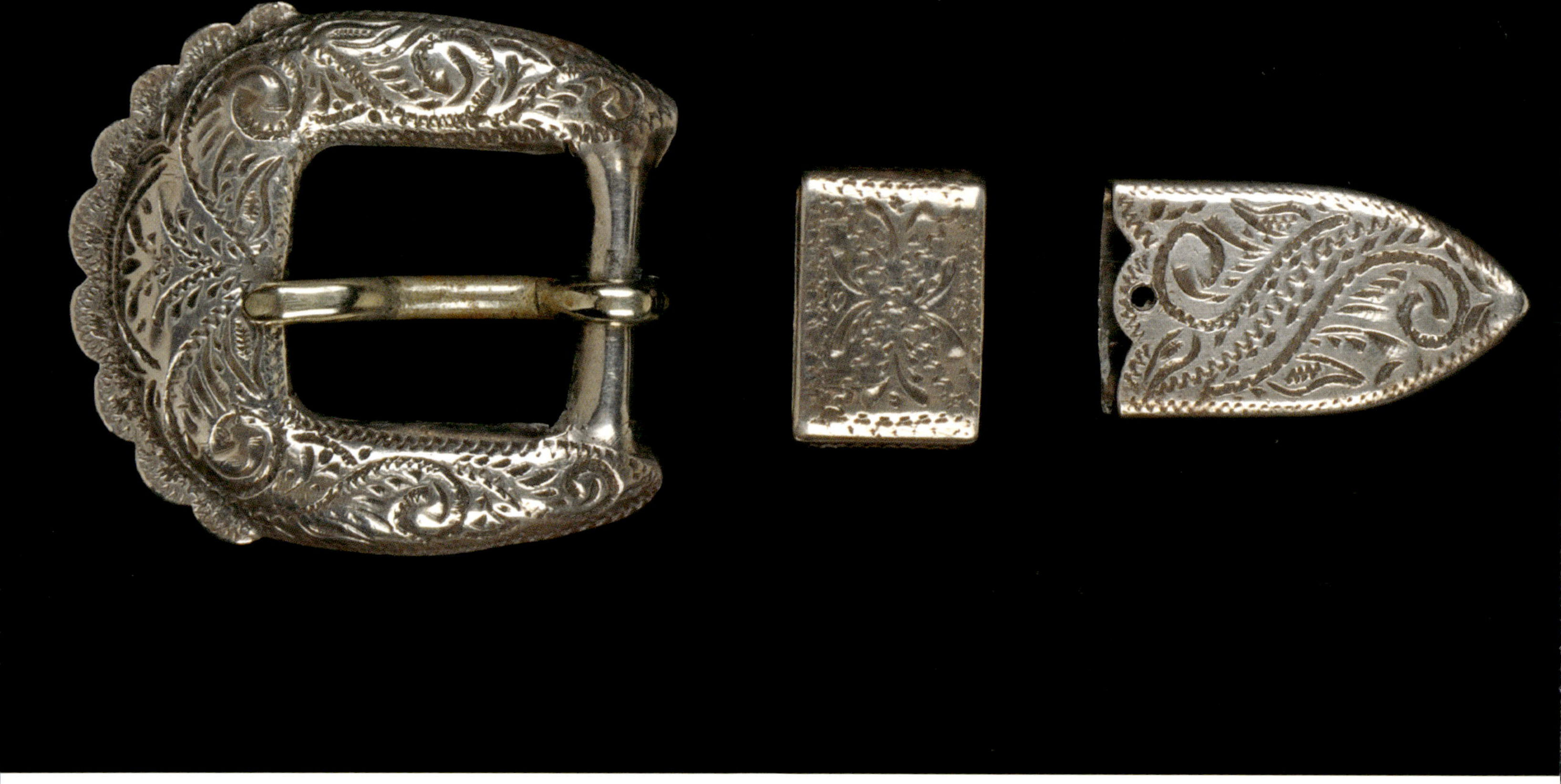

Figure 4-4. Hulbert 3-piece Ranger sets. This medium-sized set (1.5" x 1.5", buckle) shows bold engraving and a scalloped edge on the buckle, hallmarks of Hulbert's work. The inside of the buckle is stamped "STERLING." *Photo by D. Congdon-Martin.*

The "horseshoe" buckle was a totally different style, one made popular by Hulbert. Figure 4-5 is a prime example of the complete Ranger set, finely engraved with gold highlights. The large horseshoe has nail holes, heels, and a toe caulk, and is marked "STERLING," whereas the keeper was accented with a gold horseshoe, and the tip, with a gold heart. Another "horseshoe" buckle, but with customized keeper and tip (and no gold accents), is shown in Figure 4-6. "CLARA" (in silver cut-out letters on the tip) might have referred to the wife of a dentist practicing in Billings at the time—note the heart-shaped keeper with the central cross, and the belt tooled "MONTANA" that accompanied the Ranger set (Figure 4-7).

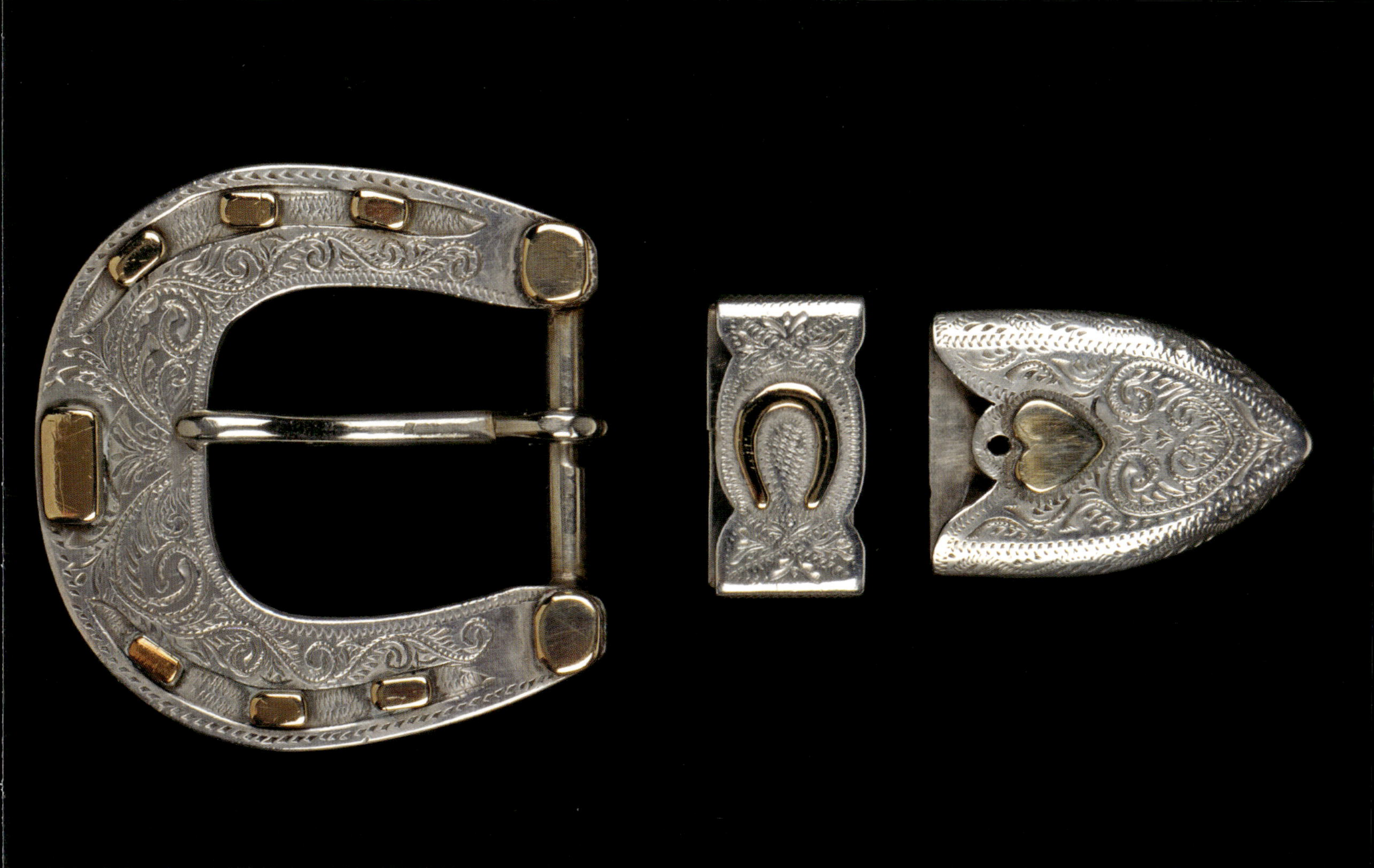

Figure 4-5. Hulbert 3-piece Ranger sets. This large-size horseshoe-shaped belt buckle (2" x 2") is stamped "STERLING" on the inner surface and has been appropriately embellished with gold nails and caulks. A gold horseshoe is shown on the keeper (middle), and a gold heart, on the tip (right). *Photo by D. Congdon-Martin.*

A leather belt marked "HAMLEY AND CO./PENDLETON ORE" was fitted with an unusual buckle and tip (Figure 4-8). Rectangular or square open buckles, with scalloped edges or clipped corners, were less common than the rounded buckles, although both types appear on bridles, spur straps, and other fittings. Note the interesting silver tip with a tulip cut inside. Two additional Ranger sets on tooled leather belts are shown in Figures 4-9 and 4-10. The styles are similar (but not identical) to the sets shown, respectively, in Figures 4-4 and 4-5. The shapes, sizes, and engraving differ between the two similar styles, and the scalloped buckle in Figure 4-10 has a plain section for the owner's initials. This set has been mounted on a leather belt stamped "RUDY MUDRA/

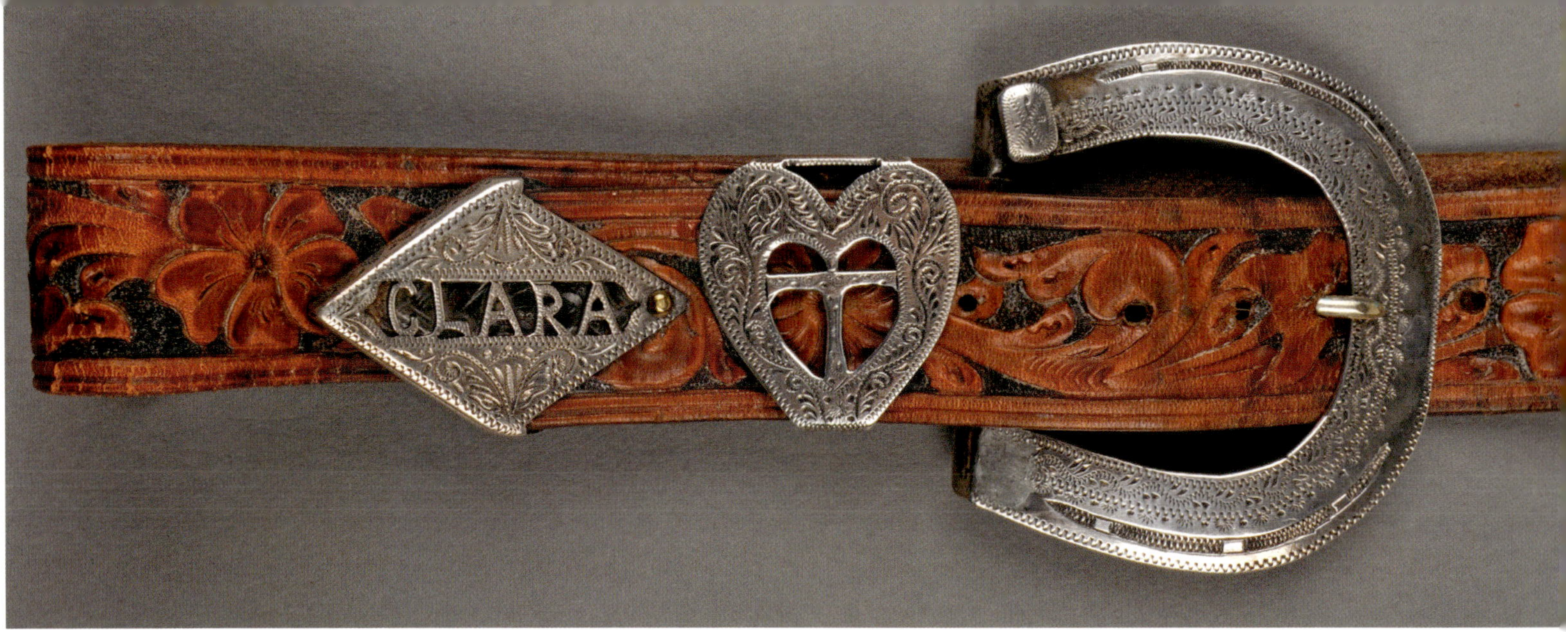

Figure 4-6. Hulbert 3-piece Ranger sets. A custom-ordered set for "CLARA" (cut-out on the tip), claimed to be the wife of a dentist practicing in Billings at the time. The silver buckle is shaped and tooled as a horseshoe, and the keeper is shaped as a heart with a cross inside. This set is extraordinary. *Photo by D. Congdon-Martin.*

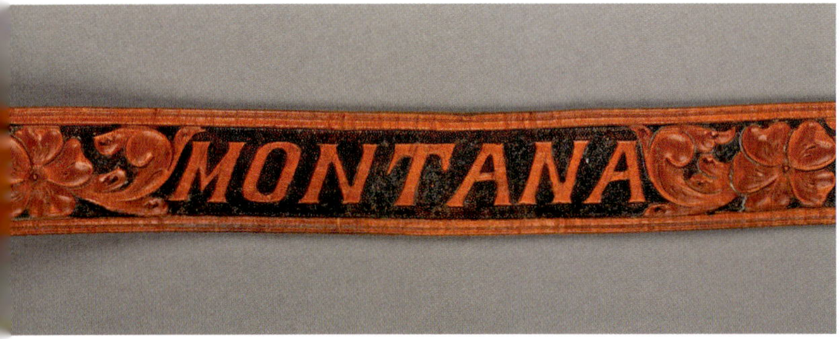

Figure 4-7. Hulbert Ranger sets. This tooled leather belt with "MONTANA" carved in relief across the back accompanied the Ranger set shown in Figure 4-6. *Photo by D. Congdon-Martin.*

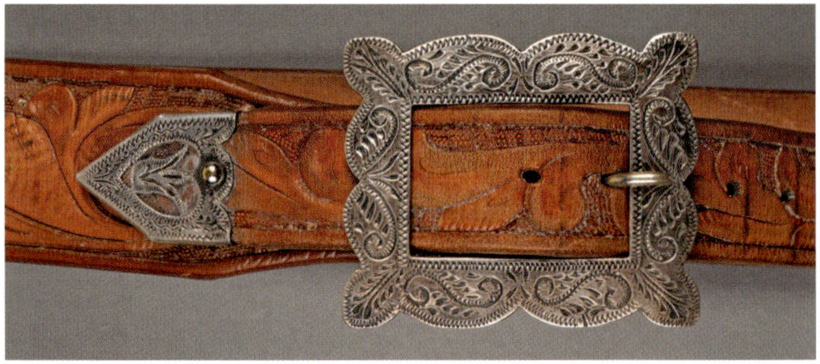

Figure 4-8. Hulbert Ranger sets. This distinctly Hulbert-engraved silver buckle and tip (with tulip cut inside) has been mounted on an elegant, tooled brown leather belt, marked "HAMLEY AND CO./PENDLETON ORE" on the leather section sewn over the buckle tongue. *Photo by D. Congdon-Martin.*

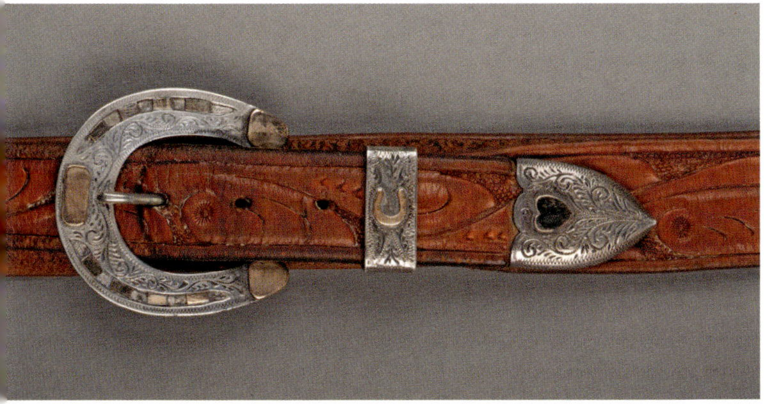

Figure 4-9. Hulbert Ranger sets. A smaller (women's ?) version of the Ranger set shown in Figure 4-5. It has been mounted on a floral tooled brown leather belt. The buckle is marked "10K" and "STERLING." *Photo by D. Congdon-Martin.*

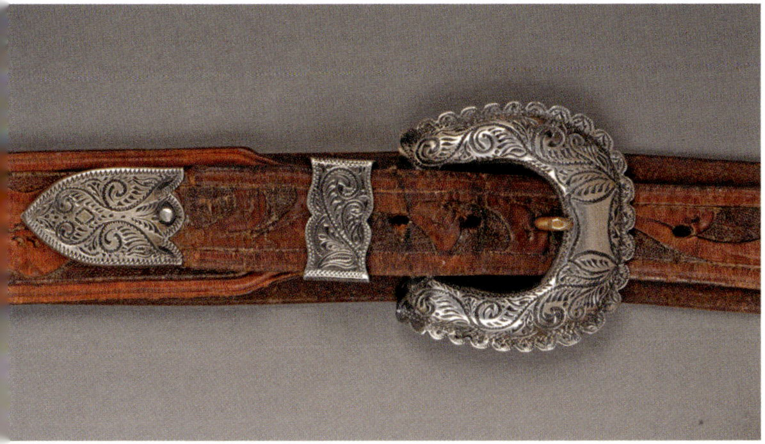

Figure 4-10. Hulbert Ranger sets. This Ranger set resembles that shown in Figure 4-4, with the scalloped edge on the buckle. However, the engraving patterns are quite different, including a plain section for the owner's initials on the buckle. The set has been mounted on a tooled brown leather belt, stamped "RUDY MUDRA/SHERIDAN, WYO." on the attachment sewn over the tongue of the buckle. Mudra was a saddlemaker in Sheridan, Wyoming (see text). *Photo by D. Congdon-Martin.*

SHERIDAN, WYO." Mudra was a famous saddlemaker with a popular "cowtown" shop on Main Street in Sheridan, Wyoming. He trained several renowned saddlemakers including Don King, and operated his shop from 1934–1955, when the leather business was sold to Lloyd Davis. Two years later, Mudra and his wife sold the remainder of the business to Bill Grey, after which it became The Big Horn Saddlery (Gorzalka, 1984). The tooled leather belt and Hulbert's Ranger set were a good marriage.

Custom Orders

Figure 4-11 shows an elegant solid belt buckle marked "10K" and "STERLING" on the back, and highlighted by a silver rope border, deep engraving, a gold shield in each corner, and the initials "HJC" in gold. The owner was Howard Carroll, who ran a Western store in Wyoming, in the 1950s and 1960s. A similar style of solid buckle, but personalized for "VERA" in scalloped gold letters, with a gold heart in each corner, is shown in Figure 4-12. An earlier piece, with rare clipped corners, exhibits Hulbert's bold, somewhat fanciful engraving, a rocker-engraved border, and an agate set in the center (Figure 4-13).

Figures 4-14 and 4-15 are photos of an advertising card and Hulbert's description, *verso*, of an extraordinary belt—very few of this style were made, due to the limitations noted by Hulbert, who felt "they really are something." A silver band was affixed to the leather belt, and in this photo, a fancy silver buckle with "CLARA" and four hearts in gold completes the piece. Could this have been the same Clara whose belt appears in Figure 4-6? A belt of this style was made for Beverly St. John (Figures 4-16 through 4-18) and for Sigrid Kapor (Figures 4-19 through 4-21). Both women were customers of Hulbert's and were wives of ranchers in the area. St. John was particularly close to Eddy Hulbert, as her husband, Claude St. John, was Edith Barry's son (hence

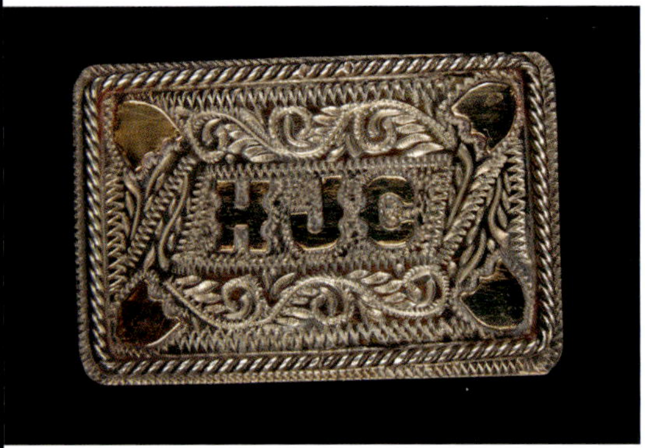

Figure 4-11. Hulbert belt buckles. A custom-ordered silver belt buckle with a rope border, a gold shield in each corner, and the initials of the owner in gold: "HJC." On the back "STERLING" and "10K" are plainly stamped. The owner was Howard "Red" Carroll, of Duncan, Oklahoma, who ran a Western store in Wyoming c1950s–1960s. *Photo by D. Congdon-Martin.*

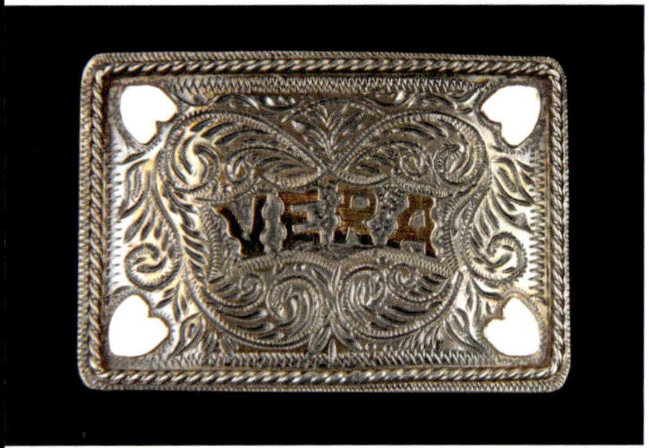

Figure 4-12. Hulbert belt buckles. This rectangular engraved silver belt buckle was made with a rope border and four gold hearts (one in each corner). The name "VERA," in scalloped gold letters, is prominent in the center. "10K" and "STERLING" are stamped on the back. *Photo by D. Congdon-Martin.*

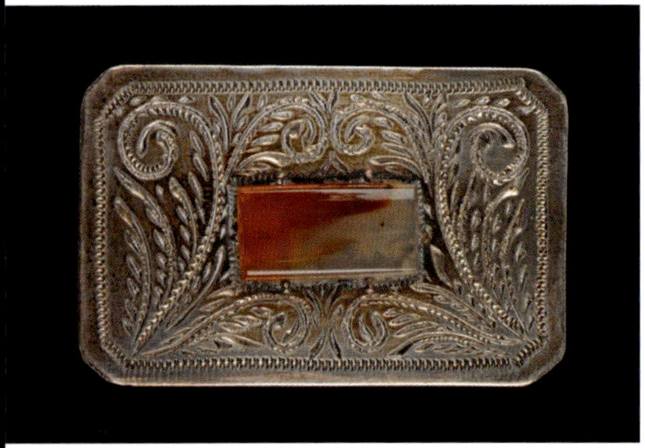

Figure 4-13. Hulbert belt buckles. Boldly-engraved silver belt buckle with a rectangle of Montana agate in the center; "STERLING" is stamped on the back. The corners of this buckle are clipped. *Photo by D. Congdon-Martin.*

"Doc" Barry's stepson, at the Cedarvale Ranch). After Doc Barry's death in 1920, Edith Barry, Claude St. John, and Hulbert managed the Cedarvale Ranch together, and were later joined by Claude's wife, Beverly, after their marriage in 1947 (Table 1). Reid (1998) states that, in 1955, Hulbert surprised Beverly St. John with this silver-banded belt with the longhorn and her initials in gold on the buckle. He was both generous and proud of his work.

Sigrid Kapor's belt, also silver-banded, was fitted with a square "heart motif" buckle showing a gold heart in each corner and an open gold heart in the center with "SIG/CFC" inside (Figure 4-20). Sigrid (b. 1911, d. 1989) married Mike Kapor in 1939, and the couple lived at the Clarks Fork Cattle Co. ranch (see Chapter 3). Her daughter, Michele, was born in 1945 (*The Billings Gazette*, May 4, 1952, describes her seventh birthday party) and also wore a custom-fitted belt by Hulbert (Figures 4-22 and 4-23). The flower-tooled leather is accented with ten alternating conchos, the largest of which serves as a buckle with the initial "M" in gold. A photograph of Michele wearing this belt has been reproduced as Figure 4-24. She knew Hulbert personally and became Rodeo Queen (likely the Bridger Rodeo) in 1961.

An unusual belt and buckle ensemble is shown in Figures 4-25 and 4-26. The Ranger set, by Hulbert, is unusually ornate, with raised 10K gold flowers and the initials "BMS." The belt is elaborately tooled by the noted California worker Sammy Sisco, who added distinctive horse heads encircled by morning glories around the circumference of the belt. Sammy (Samantha) Sisco, her sister Bertha, and her brother Gene were renowned leather artists in the San Francisco area who did work for famous Northern California saddleries, such as Visalia and Olsen-Nolte, from c. 1935 through the late 1960s. The belt shown in Figure 4-25 is thought to have been made for Bertha Sisco.

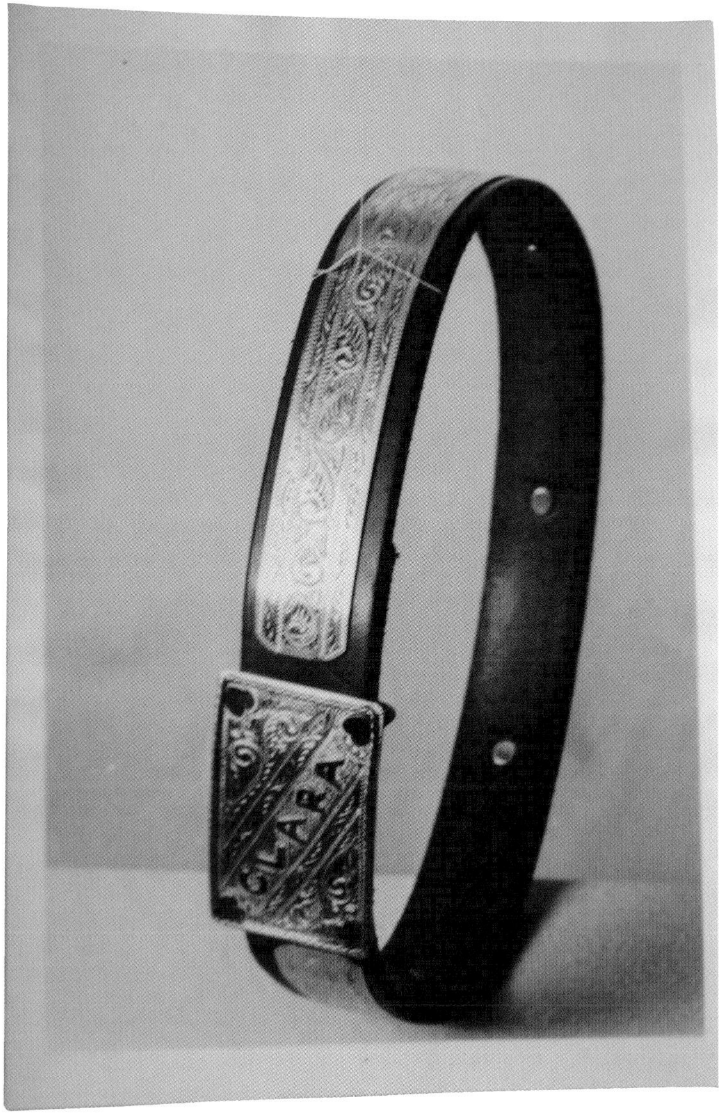

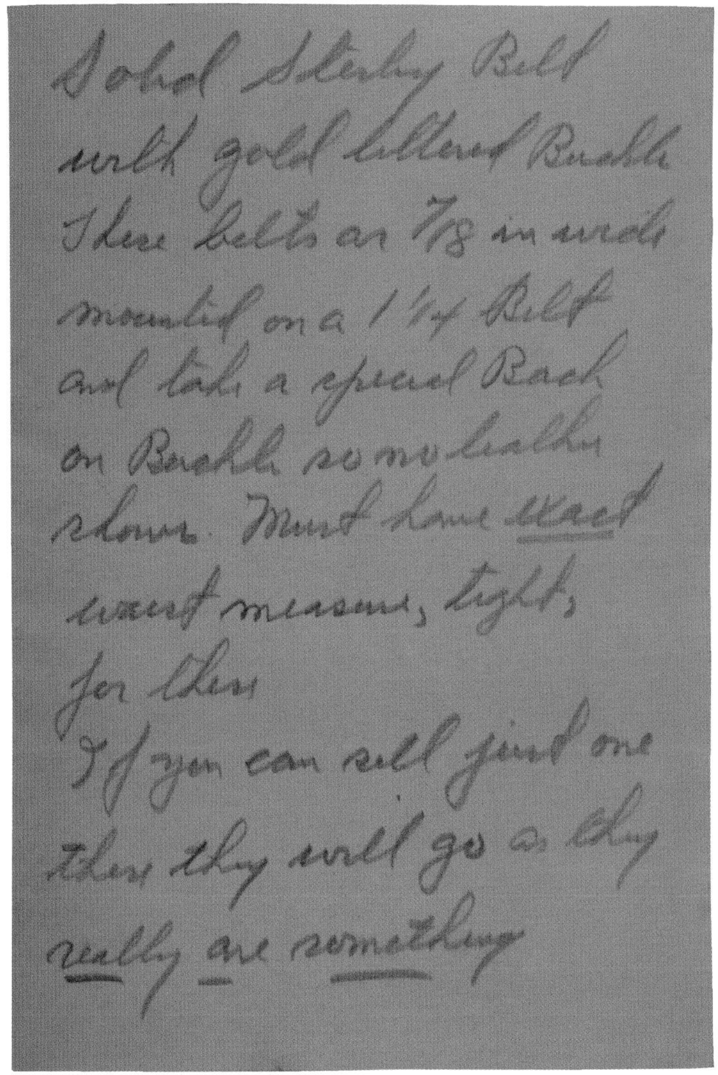

Solid Sterling Belt
with gold lettered Buckle
These belts are 7/8 in wide
mounted on a 1 1/4 Belt
and take a special Back
on Buckle so no leather
shows. Must have exact
waist measure, tight,
for these
If you can sell just one
then they will go as they
really are something

Figure 4-14. Hulbert belt buckles—custom orders (advertising card). This beautiful belt was made with a continuous engraved silver band affixed to the leather, a buckle with a gold heart in each corner, and the name "CLARA" in gold letters on the diagonal. Hulbert, in his accompanying description, states that these belts "really are something" and has designed the buckle such that "no leather shows" (see Figure 4-15). Is this the same Clara whose belt is shown in Figure 4-6? Card dimensions: 5" x 3-1/2". *Courtesy of R. Wilmot. William Manns photo.*

Figure 4-15. Hulbert belts. Hulbert's written description of the belt shown in Figure 4-14. The silver band is 7/8" wide and is mounted on a 1" to 1-1/4" leather strap. Clearly he was proud of this design. *Courtesy of R. Wilmot. William Manns photo.*

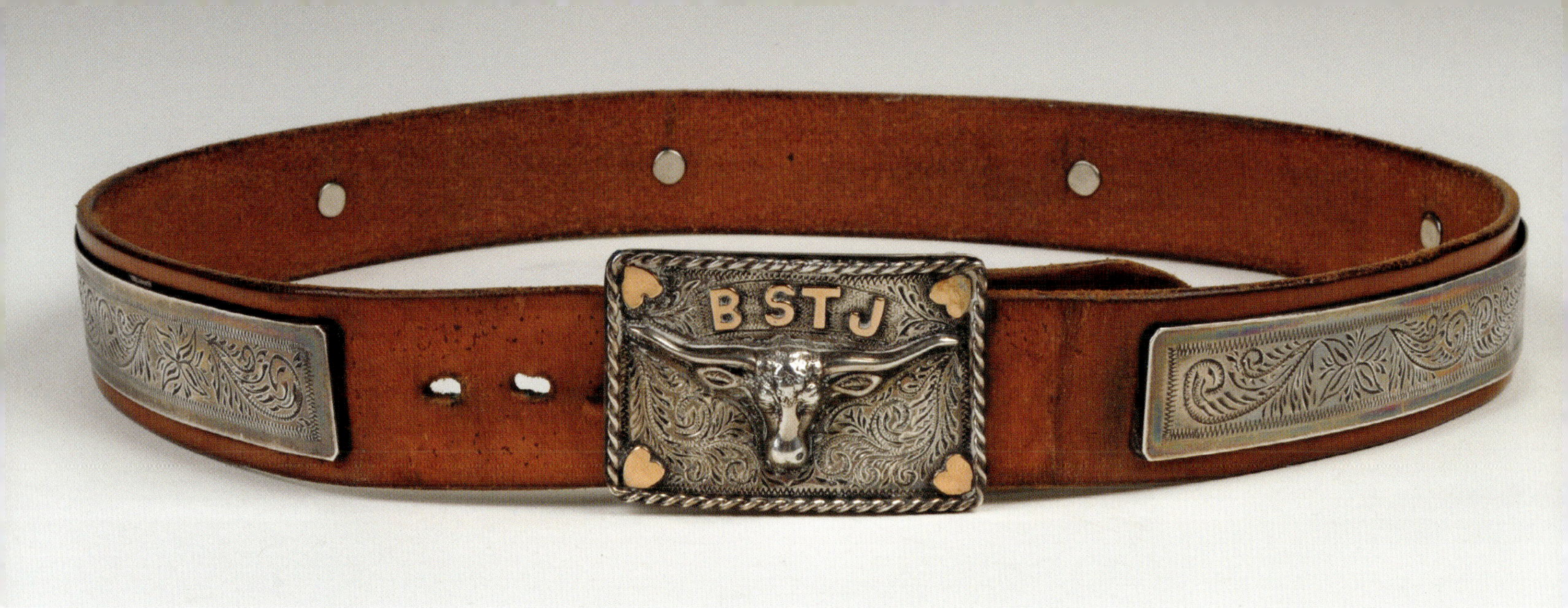

Figure 4-16. Hulbert belts. This fancy belt, which in style resembles that shown in Figure 4-14, was made for Beverly St. John, the wife of Claude St. John (son of Edith Barry) who owned the Cedarvale Ranch. The engraved silver buckle has a rope edge, a gold heart in each corner, the gold initials "B ST J," and a raised silver image of a longhorn cow. The silver band extends continuously around the brown leather belt. *Photo by D. Congdon-Martin.*

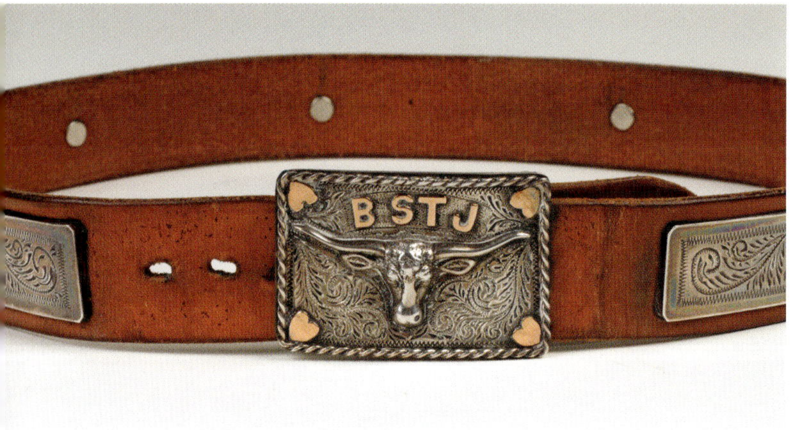

Figure 4-17. Hulbert belts. Enlarged view of the "Longhorn" belt buckle shown in Figure 4-16. *Photo by D. Congdon-Martin.*

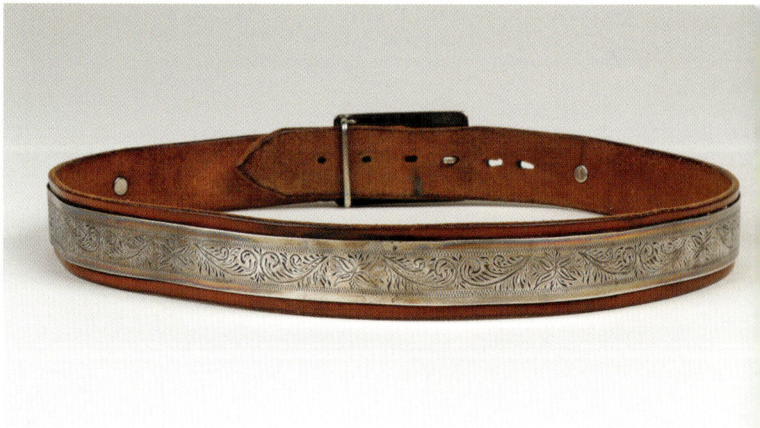

Figure 4-18. Hulbert belts. Verso of belt in Figure 4-16 showing the solid silver band with typical Hulbert engraving. *Photo by D. Congdon-Martin.*

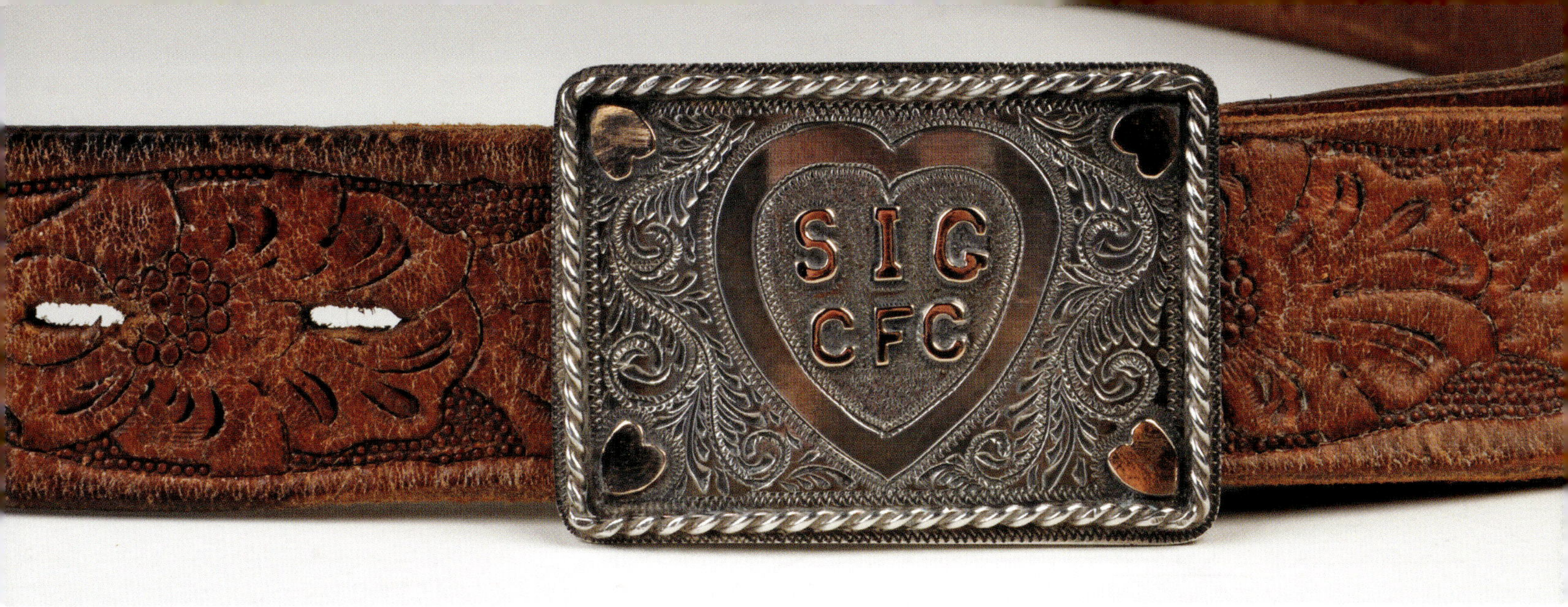

Figure 4-20. Hulbert belts. Enlarged view of the buckle shown in Figure 4-19. *Photo by D. Congdon-Martin.*

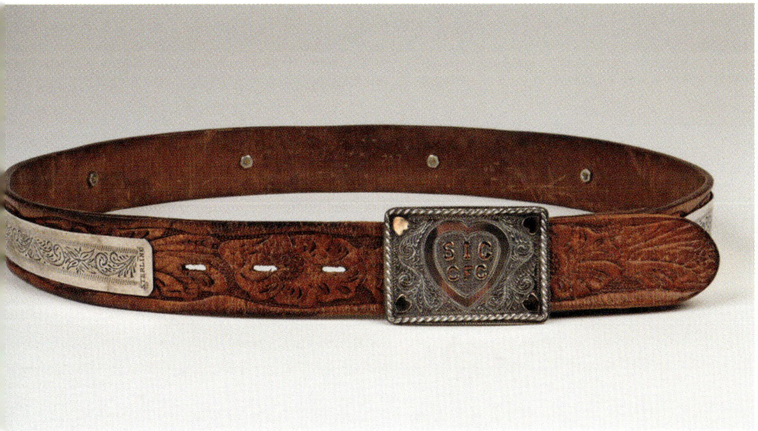

Figure 4-19. Hulbert belts. This custom-ordered belt was made for Sigrid Kapor, of the Clarks Fork Cattle Co., Dryhead, Montana. The banded silver belt has a square, engraved silver buckle with a rope border, a gold heart in each corner, and the names "SIG" and "CFC" (Clarks Fork Cattle Co.) in gold letters within a silver and gold heart. The marks are "STERLING" and "10K." This design is rare, if not exclusive. *Photo by D. Congdon-Martin.*

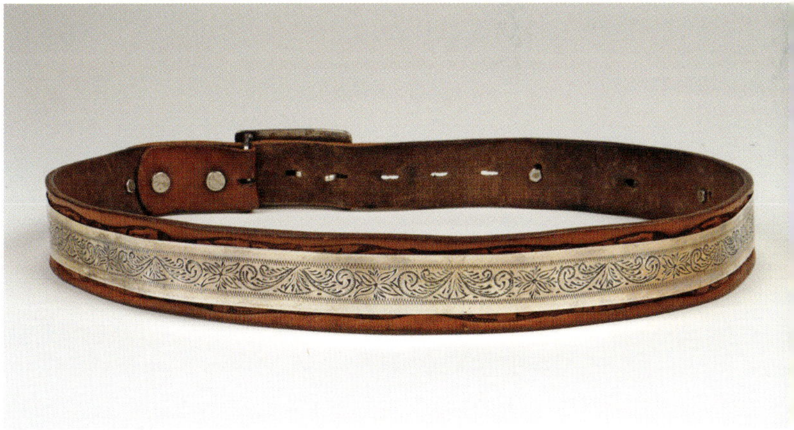

Figure 4-21. View of the engraved silver band encircling the leather belt shown in Figure 4-19. *Photo by D. Congdon-Martin.*

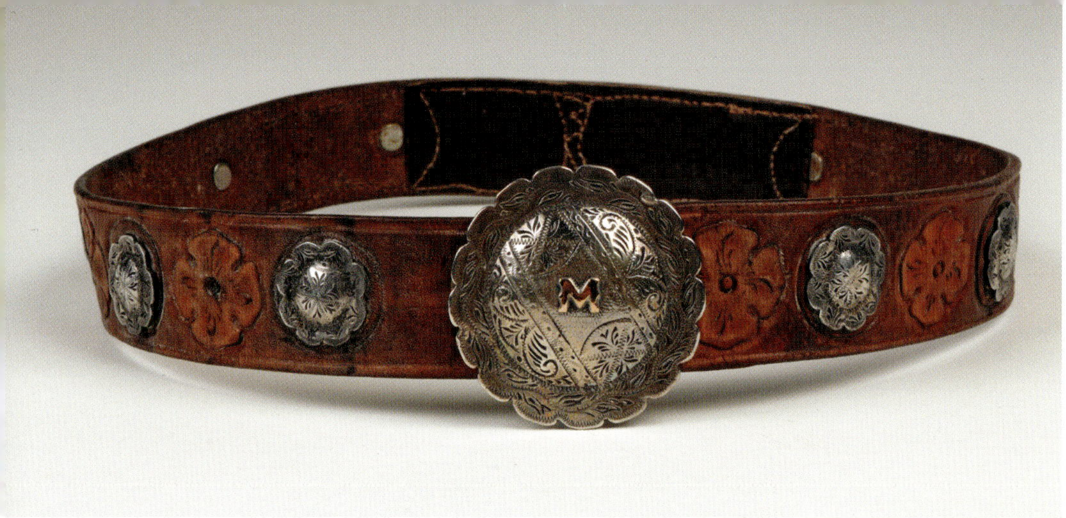

Figure 4-22. Hulbert belts. Engraved silver concho belt made for Michele Kapor (b. 1945), daughter of Mike and Sigrid Kapor (see caption, Figure 4-19). The leather is stamped in individual flowers and accommodates ten alternating silver conchos. The circular (large concho) engraved buckle with Michele's initial "M" in gold is a nice touch. *Photo by D. Congdon-Martin.*

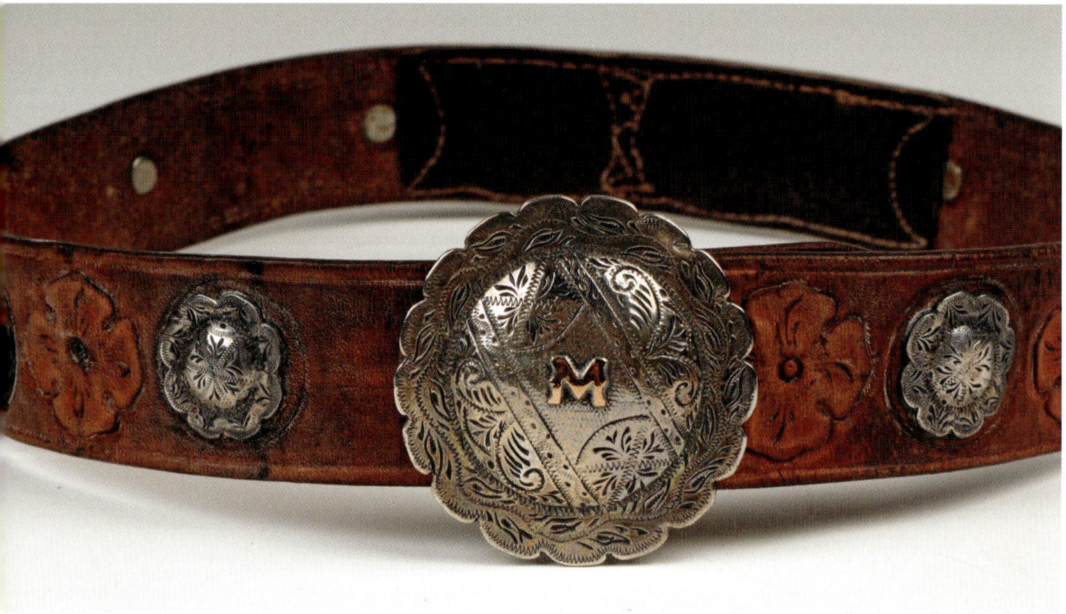

Figure 4-23. Hulbert belts. Enlarged view of belt buckle shown in Figure 4-22. *Photo by D. Congdon-Martin.*

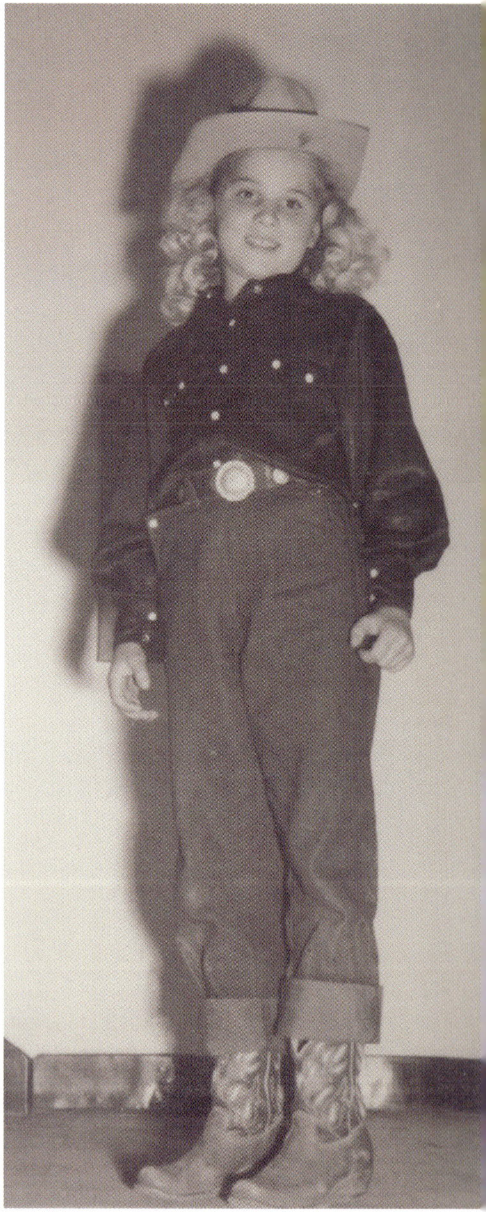

Figure 4-24. Hulbert belts. Photograph of Michele Kapor (at approximately ten years of age), wearing the belt shown in Figure 4-22. Michele, who knew Hulbert personally, was Rodeo Queen in 1961. *Photo by D. Congdon-Martin.*

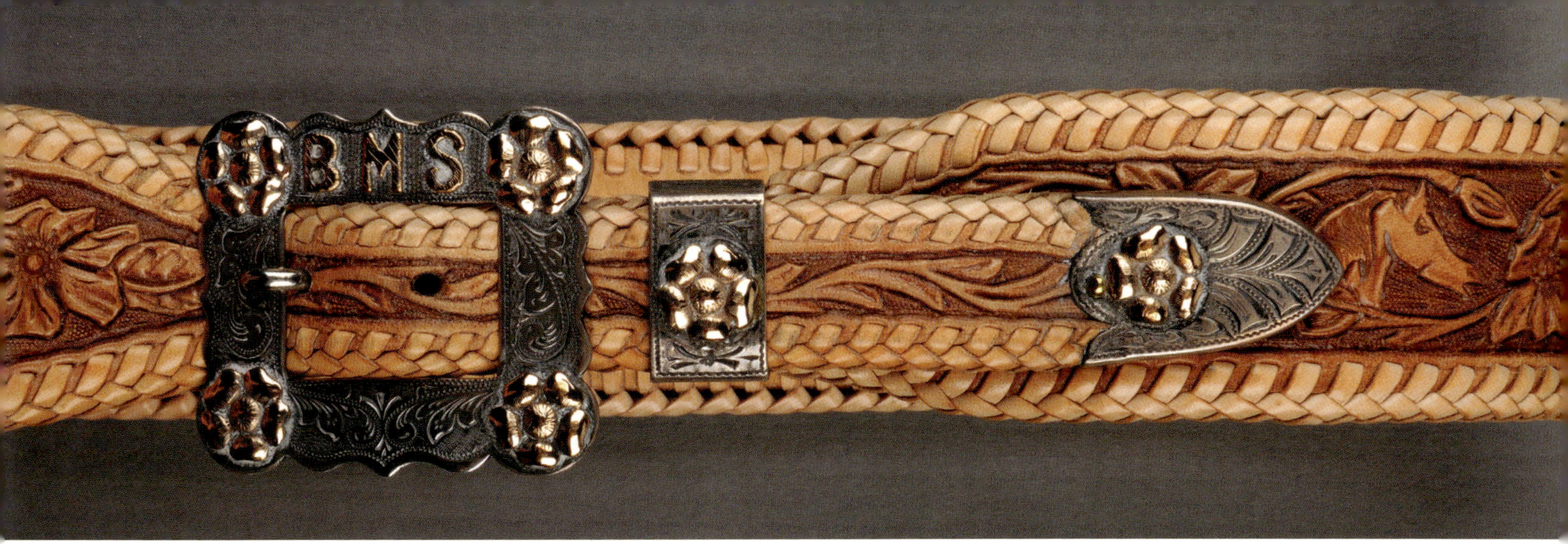

Figure 4-25. Hulbert belts. This laced and artistically tooled leather belt was designed and executed by Sammy Sisco (California; see text for details). It has been fitted with an unusually ornate square engraved sterling silver buckle with a large 10K gold flower in each corner and the initials "BMS" in gold at the top. This belt could have been made for Bertha Sisco, Sammy Sisco's sister. The gold-decorated keeper and tip enhance the elegance of the belt. *Photo by D. Congdon-Martin.*

Hulbert made very few silver concho belts—no doubt they were expensive and had to be custom-ordered for a perfect fit. An outstanding example is shown in Figures 4-27 through 4-29. The engraved silver plates (conchos) are trapezoidal in shape, nicely contoured, and joined by silver links. The belt was adjusted in length by silver rings at the front, and was accented by two diamond-shaped silver conchos. Each plate of the belt was stamped "STERLING," and "HAND MADE" was engraved by Hulbert above the stamp.

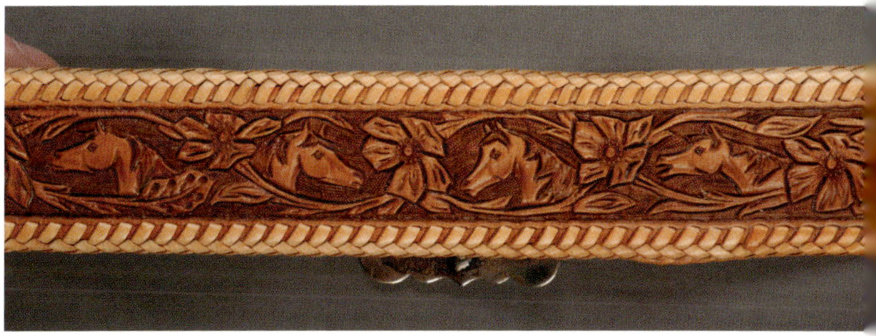

Figure 4-26. Hulbert belts. This figure shows the back of the leather belt (Figure 4-25), tooled in horse heads (each one different) and flowers by Sammy Sisco. *Photo by D. Congdon-Martin.*

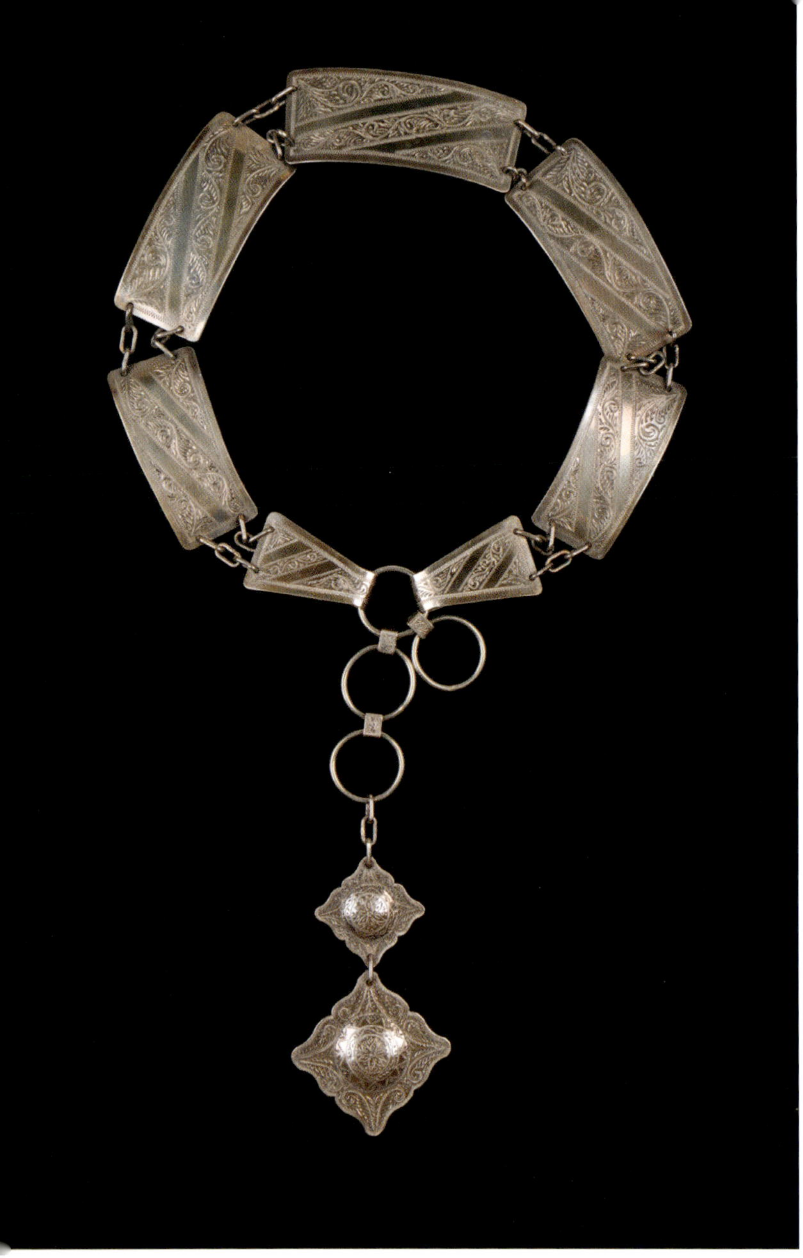

Figure 4-27. Hulbert belts. Hulbert made very few concho belts—this one is beautifully executed in silver and cleverly designed. There are seven engraved silver conchos, trapezoidal in shape, four rings, and two pendant rosettes. Small silver links join the rings, and wire "chain links" join the conchos and rosettes. *Photo by D. Congdon-Martin.*

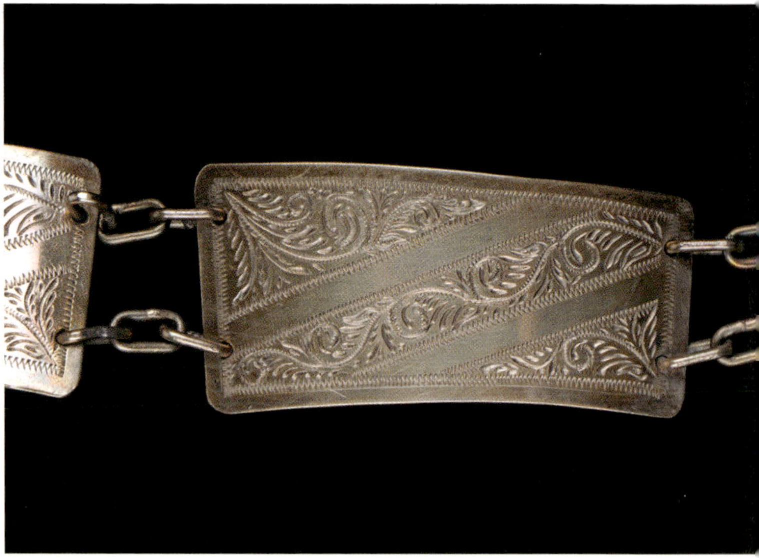

Figure 4-28. Hulbert belts. Enlarged view of one silver plate or concho from the belt shown in Figure 4-27. *Photo by D. Congdon-Martin.*

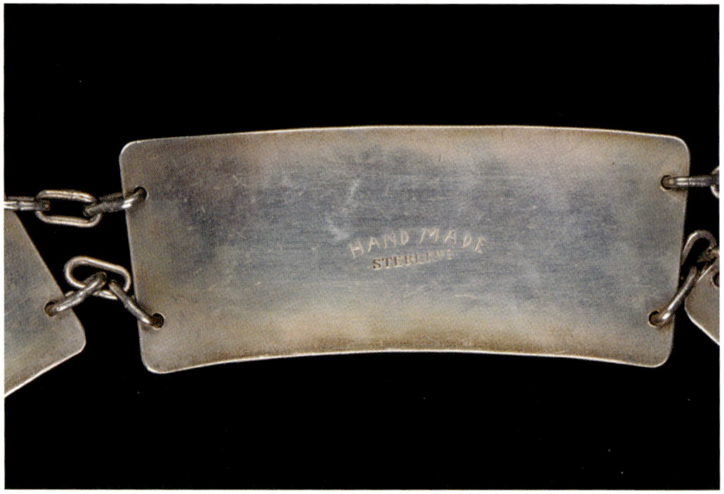

Figure 4-29. Hulbert belts. Verso of silver plate concho shown in Figure 4-28. The stamped mark is "STERLING," and "HAND MADE" is hand-engraved above the stamp. All of the plates are marked similarly. *Photo by D. Congdon-Martin.*

Trophy Buckles

Figures 4-30 through 4-35 show three examples of Hulbert's distinctive trophy buckles. The "longhorn" buckle (Figures 4-30 and 4-31) was made with a blank space for the owner's (or winner's) initials—possibly another owner scratched his initials "RG" on the back. The remaining two buckles were won and owned by Walt Secrest, who in 1955 was both Saddle Bronc Champion and All-Around Cowboy at the Bridger Spring Rodeo (Figures 4-32 through 4-35). The "EH" mark (Figure 4-33) is rarely seen on a buckle, and Hulbert's initials were placed in the upper right-hand corner, above "10K" and "STERLING." This mark is missing from the buckle shown in Figure 4-35, but "STERLING," "10K," and "CAFÉ" are there. Secrest's "All-Around" buckle was probably sponsored by the Bridger Café. Secrest is still living and riding near Hardin, Montana. Hulbert's solid, engraved silver and gold "trophy" buckles have a dramatic appearance and rank among his finest work.

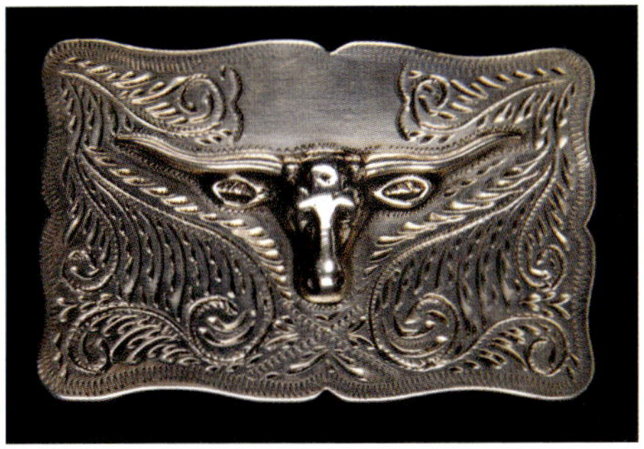

Figure 4-30. Hulbert trophy buckles. This large buckle has a contoured border, bold engraving, and a prominent, raised image of a longhorn steer head. There is a plain area above the steer for a name and/or event and date. Although not strictly a trophy buckle, this one was a model for other pieces made for rodeos and shows. *Photo by D. Congdon-Martin.*

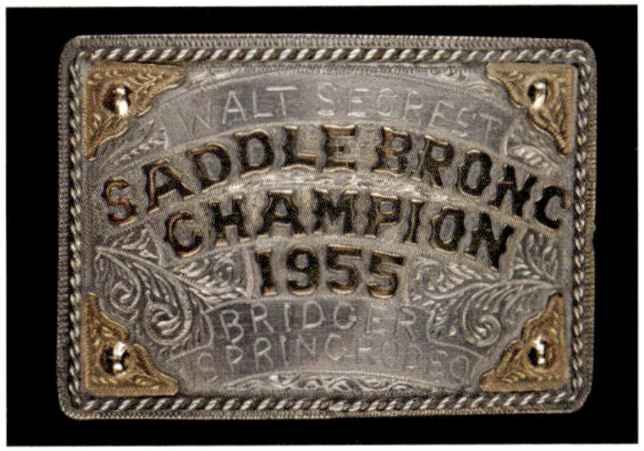

Figure 4-32. Hulbert trophy buckles. This large and impressive buckle has a silver rope border and four gold corners. Gold letters "SADDLE BRONC CHAMPION 1955" are affixed to the buckle, above which is engraved "WALT SECREST" and below, "BRIDGER SPRING RODEO." *Photo by D. Congdon-Martin.*

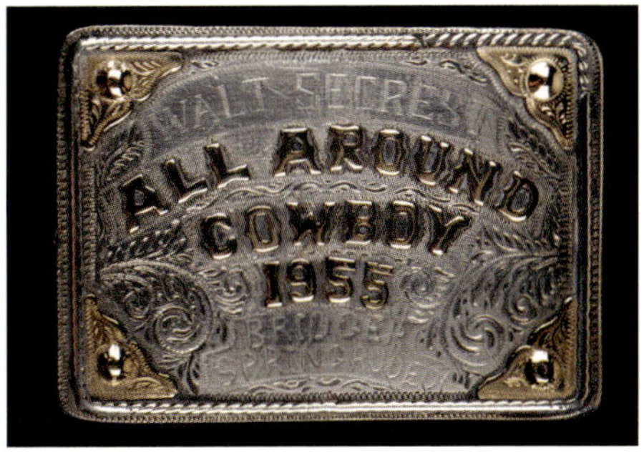

Figure 4-34. Hulbert trophy buckles. This large trophy buckle is a similar style to that shown in Figure 4-32, with gold corners and a silver rope border. "WALT SECREST" and "BRIDGER SPRING RODEO" are engraved above and below, respectively, the gold letters denoting "ALL AROUND COWBOY 1955." *Photo by D. Congdon-Martin.*

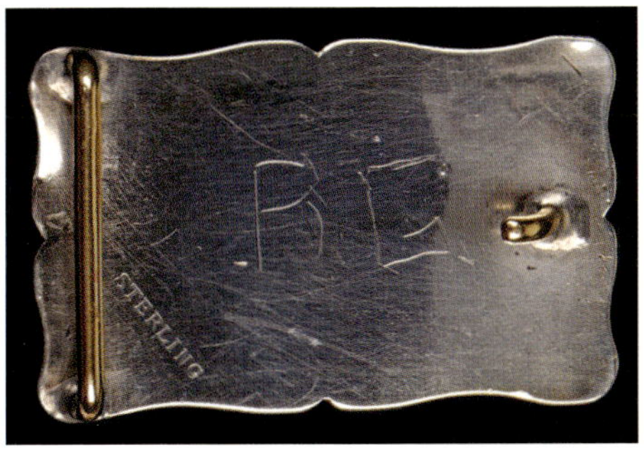

Figure 4-31. Hulbert trophy buckles. Verso of buckle shown in Figure 4-30. The "STERLING" hallmark contrasts strongly with the initials "RG" scratched in the middle. *Photo by D. Congdon-Martin.*

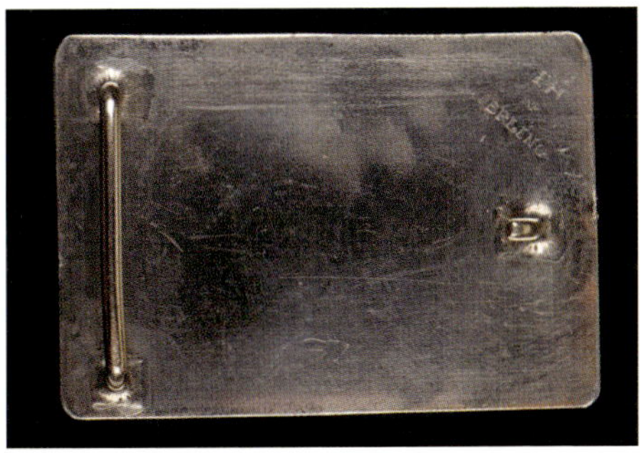

Figure 4-33. Hulbert trophy buckles. Verso of buckle shown in Figure 4-34. The marks are "EH," "10K," and "STERLING." "EH" is a rare mark on a buckle. *Photo by D. Congdon-Martin.*

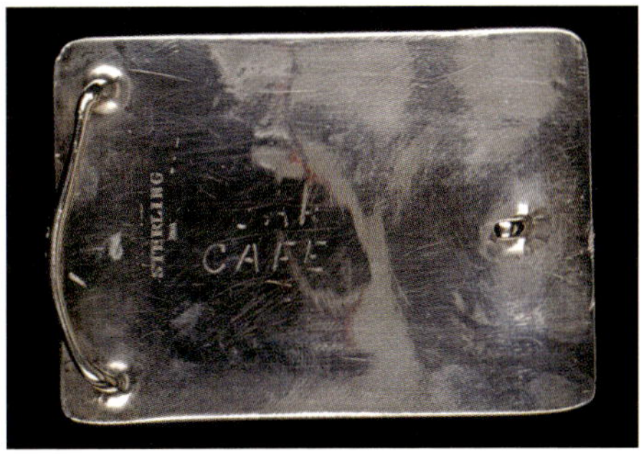

Figure 4-35. Hulbert trophy buckles. Verso of buckle shown in Figure 4-34. "STERLING" and "10K" are clearly stamped near the loop. "CAFÉ" has been engraved in large letters—this buckle was sponsored by the Bridger Café. *Photo by D. Congdon-Martin.*

Jewelry

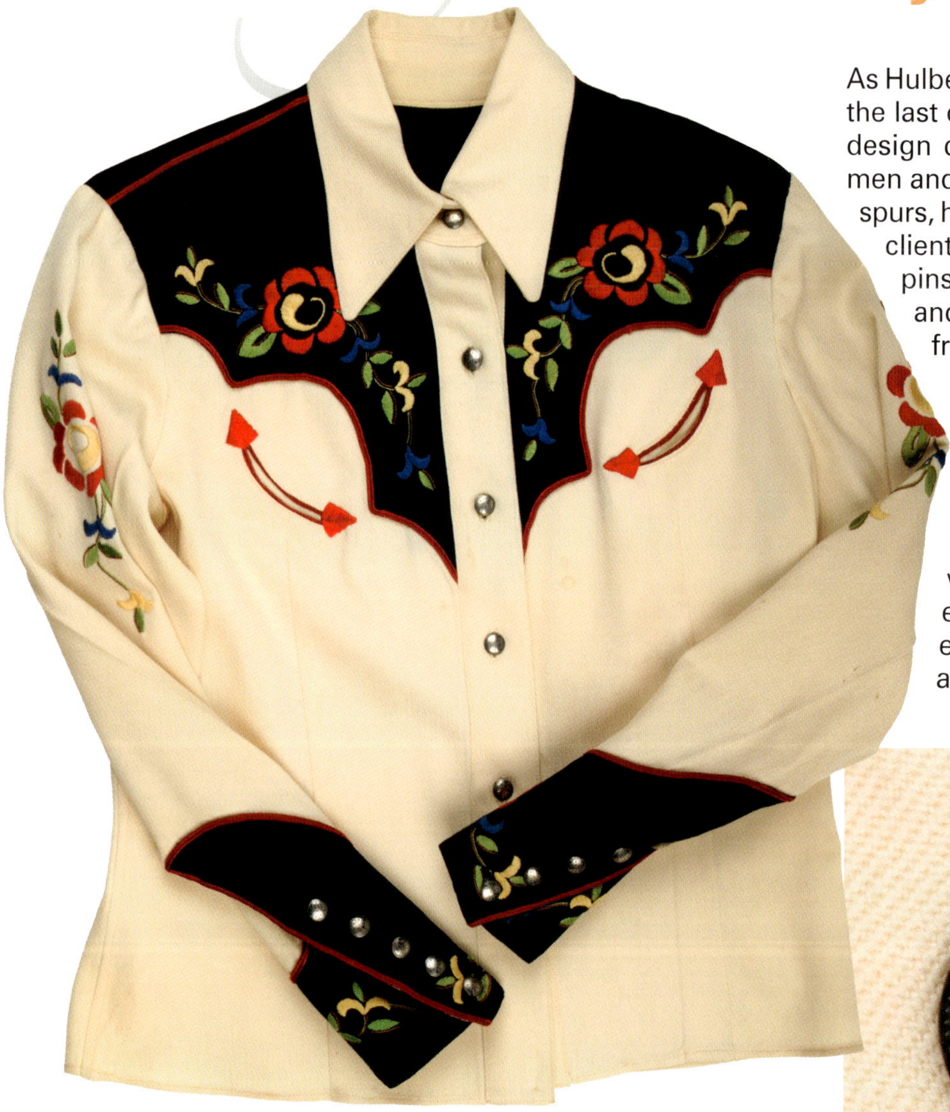

As Hulbert's work increased in demand, especially during the last decade of his life, he turned his artistic skills and design concepts to the production of jewelry for both men and women. At the same time he continued making spurs, his real specialty, and other pieces ordered from his clients. In this chapter are shown examples of buttons, pins, a tie (bolo) clasp, earrings, necklaces, bracelets, and a hat band. Many of the pieces were derived from the Kapor Family collection.

Buttons

The shirt shown in Figure 5-1 (and on the model in Figure 1-13) belonged to Sigrid Kapor, who embroidered it and used Eddy Hulbert's engraved silver buttons for a final touch of elegance. These buttons are quite small and yet are engraved in detail (Figure 5-2).

Figure 5-1. Hulbert jewelry—buttons. This ladies' Western-style shirt was embroidered by Sigrid Kapor, of the Clarks Fork Cattle Co. (see Chapter 4). There are five engraved silver buttons on each sleeve, and six on the placket down the front. *Photo by D. Congdon-Martin.*

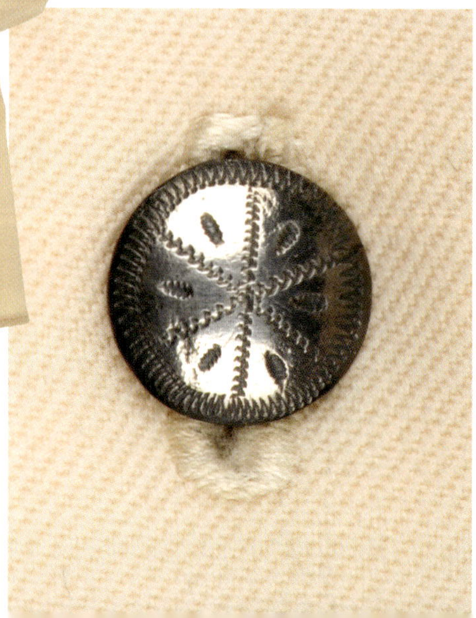

Figure 5-2. Hulbert jewelry—buttons. Enlarged view of engraved silver button on shirt shown in Figure 5-1. *Photo by D. Congdon-Martin.*

Pins

Two engraved sterling silver "rosette" pins, one with a gold heart, are shown in Figure 5-3. These pins belonged to Sigrid Kapor and derive from the Kapor Family collection.

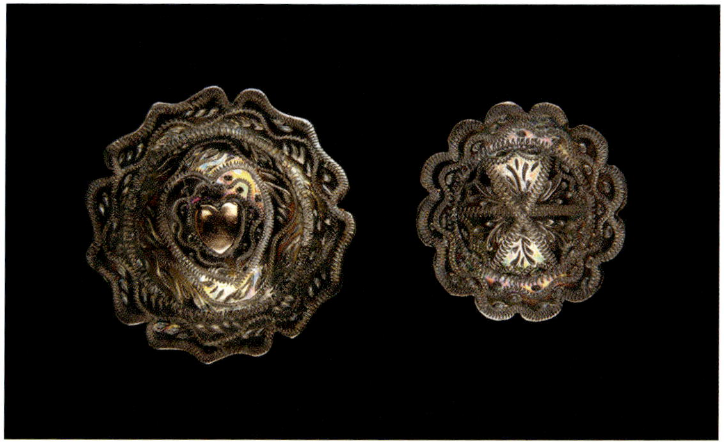

Figure 5-3. Hulbert jewelry—pins. Two engraved rosette pins are shown in this photograph, the larger of which has a gold heart in the center. Both are marked "STERLING." These were part of the Kapor Family collection (see Chapter 4 text for details). *Photo by D. Congdon-Martin.*

Tie/Bolo Clasp

Also from the Kapor Family collection, this engraved clasp with a gold horseshoe and the initials "JK" was probably made for John (Johnny) Kapor, son of Mike and Sigrid Kapor (Figure 5-4).

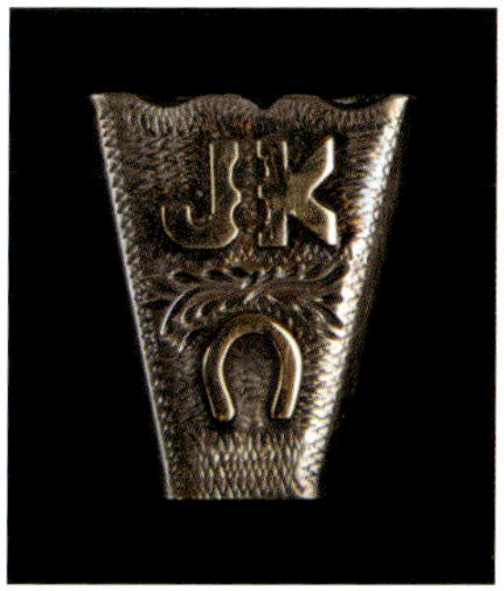

Figure 5-4. Hulbert jewelry—tie clasp. This engraved silver clasp, made for a bolo tie, bears the initials "JK" and a horseshoe in 10K gold. From the Kapor Family collection—"JK" refers to John Kapor, Sigrid and Mike Kapor's son. *Photo by D. Congdon-Martin.*

Earrings

Three different styles of earrings made by Hulbert are shown in Figures 5-5 through 5-7. The "mini-rosette" screwbacks were engraved in a pattern similar to that on the buttons (Figure 5-2) and were owned by either Sigrid or Michele Kapor (see Chapter 4). An interesting pair with lavish, delicate engraving is shown in Figure 5-6. The gold initials "JB" might refer to Julia Brown, the mother of Beverly St. John, of Cedarvale and later, Billings. Hulbert had made a belt buckle for Julia as a child (Reid, 1998, p. 62) and probably kept in touch with this, his only, family after Claude St. John died in 1959. Another pair of screwback earrings belonging to Sigrid Kapor is shown in Figure 5-7. The rosettes or conchos (note the shape is the same as seen in Figure 5-6) are suspended within a silver rope hoop and bear the initials in gold "CFC," for the Clarks Fork Cattle Co.

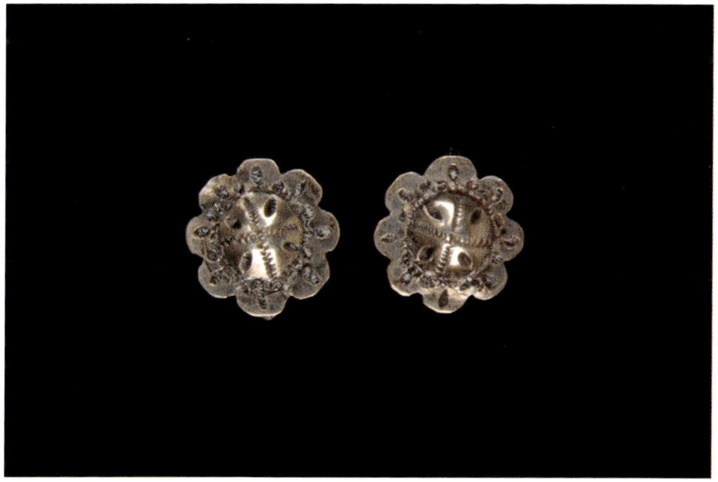

Figure 5-5. Hulbert jewelry—earrings. A pair of screwback mini rosette engraved silver earrings owned by Sigrid Kapor is shown. *Photo by D. Congdon-Martin.*

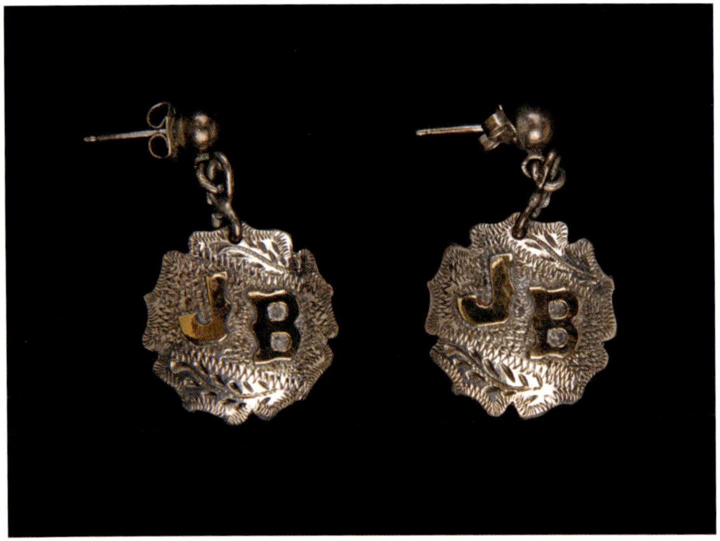

Figure 5-6. Hulbert jewelry—earrings. This pair of elegant, lavishly-engraved silver earrings bears the initials "JB" in gold. They are marked "10K" and "STERLING." Julia Brown, to whom they belonged, was the mother of Beverly St. John, wife of Claude St. John, of Cedarvale (see text for details). *Photo by D. Congdon-Martin.*

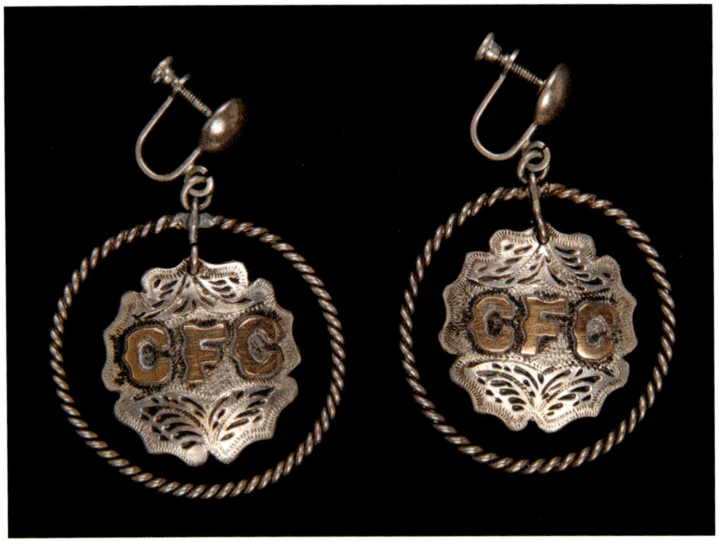

Figure 5-7. Hulbert jewelry—earrings. These handsome screwback earrings bear the initials of the Clarks Fork Cattle Co. in gold. The shaped and engraved rosettes are suspended within a silver rope hoop. Marks are "STERLING" and "10K." *Photo by D. Congdon-Martin.*

Necklaces

The pendant in the shape of a gold-decorated silver-engraved horseshoe (Figure 5-8) was also decorated with "CFC" and was part of the Kapor Family collection. An elegant necklace with these initials or logo on a large rosette, flanked on each side by three matching rosettes of graduated sizes, can be seen in Figure 5-10. It is a beautiful piece of jewelry that once belonged to Sigrid Kapor. Similarly, her "SK" silver horseshoe pendant with gold accents (Figure 5-9) is yet another design modification by Hulbert for this Montana woman.

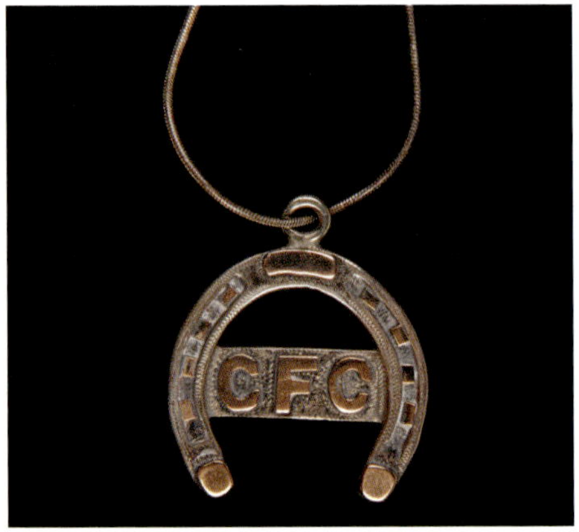

Figure 5-8. Hulbert jewelry—necklaces. A horseshoe-shaped pendant has been decorated with gold toe and heel calks, and the initials "CFC" denoting the Clarks Fork Cattle Co. From the Kapor Family collection. *Photo by D. Congdon-Martin.*

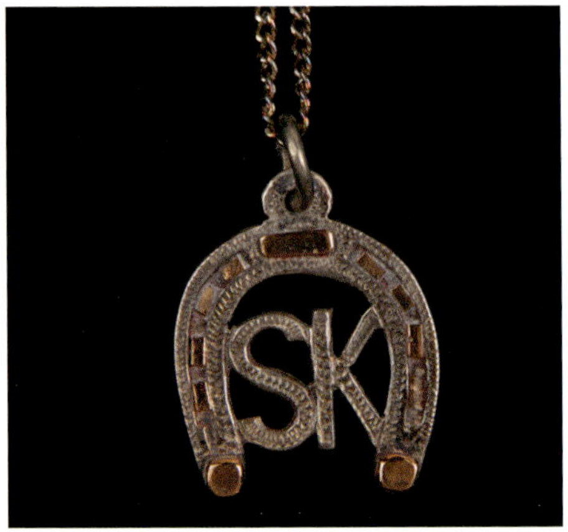

Figure 5-9. Hulbert jewelry—necklaces. An engraved silver horseshoe pendant with gold accents (similar to that shown in Figure 5-8) was made for Sigrid Kapor, with her initials "SK" in the center. From the Kapor Family collection. *Photo by D. Congdon-Martin.*

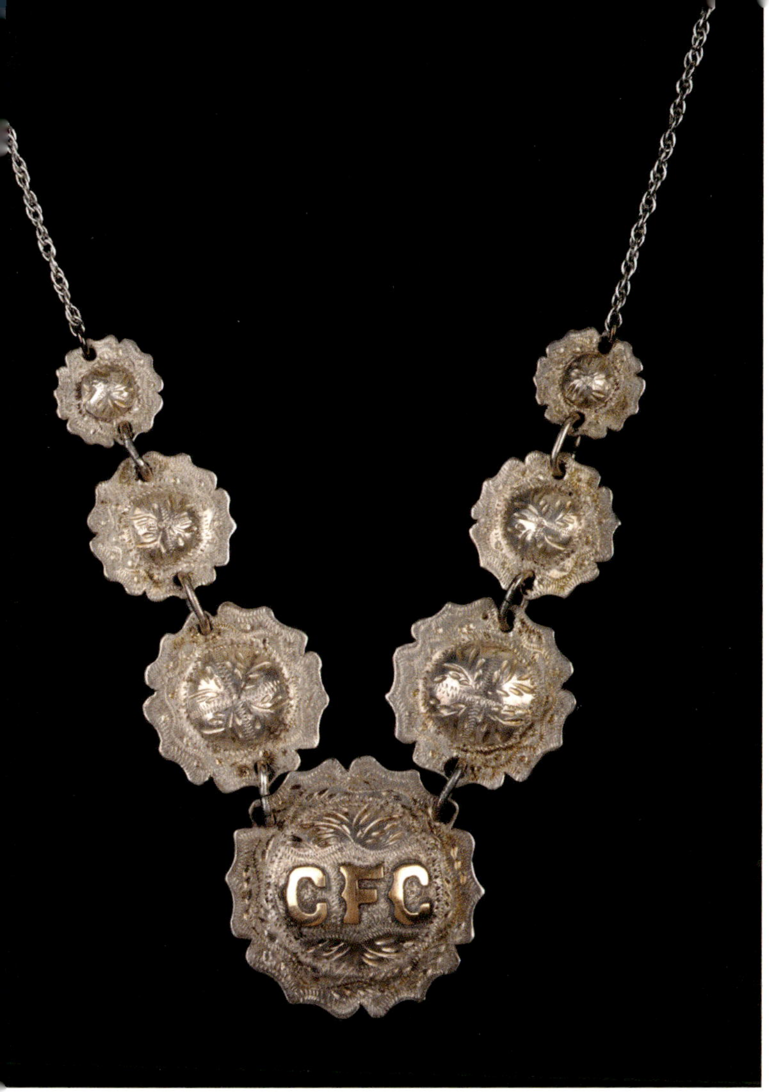

Figure 5-10. Hulbert jewelry—necklaces. The large engraved silver concho bears the "CFC" (Clarks Fork Cattle Co.) logo, and is flanked on either side by three conchos or rosettes of similar style, in graduated sizes. From the Kapor Family collection. *Photo by D. Congdon-Martin.*

Bracelets

Eddy Hulbert's bracelets are cuff-like and form-fitting. A very thin hammered silver cuff, with a blank area for the owner's initials, might have been made for a young girl (Figure 5-11). In contrast, a heavier bracelet with a large, boldly-engraved rosette in the center and flanked by two gold hearts, is shown in Figures 5-12 and 5-13. From the Kapor Family collection, it might have belonged to Michele (compare this bracelet with her belt shown in Chapter 4). The dark agate dominating the cuff shown in Figures 5-14 and 5-15 is also flanked by two gold hearts and bold engraving.

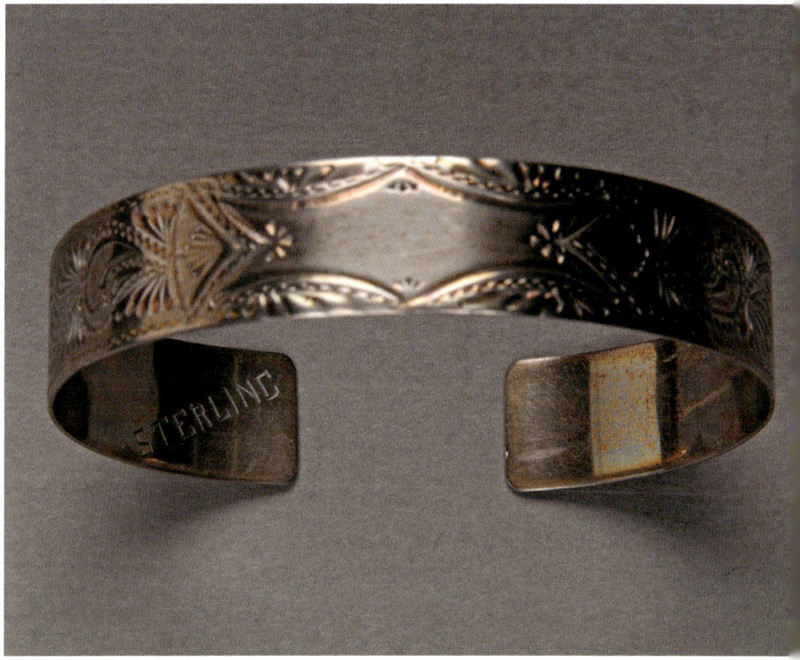

Figure 5-11. Hulbert jewelry—bracelets. A delicate and exceedingly thin bracelet, possibly for a child, with an open area for initials. It is stamped "STERLING" on the inner left side. *Photo by D. Congdon-Martin.*

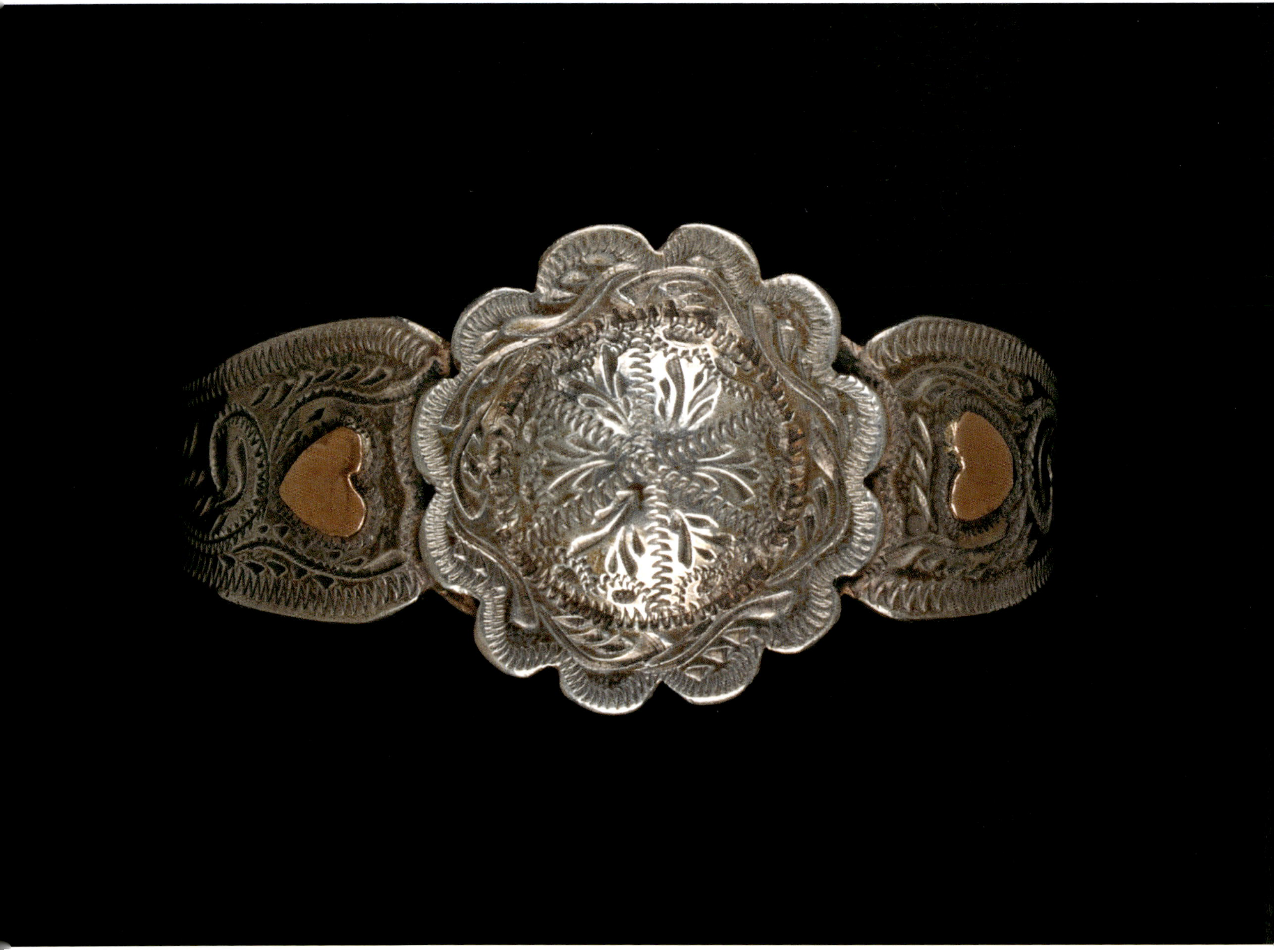

Figure 5-12. Hulbert jewelry—bracelets. A distinctively Hulbert-engraved silver cuff bracelet with a large rosette or concho in the center and a gold heart on each side. From the Kapor Family collection. *Photo by D. Congdon-Martin.*

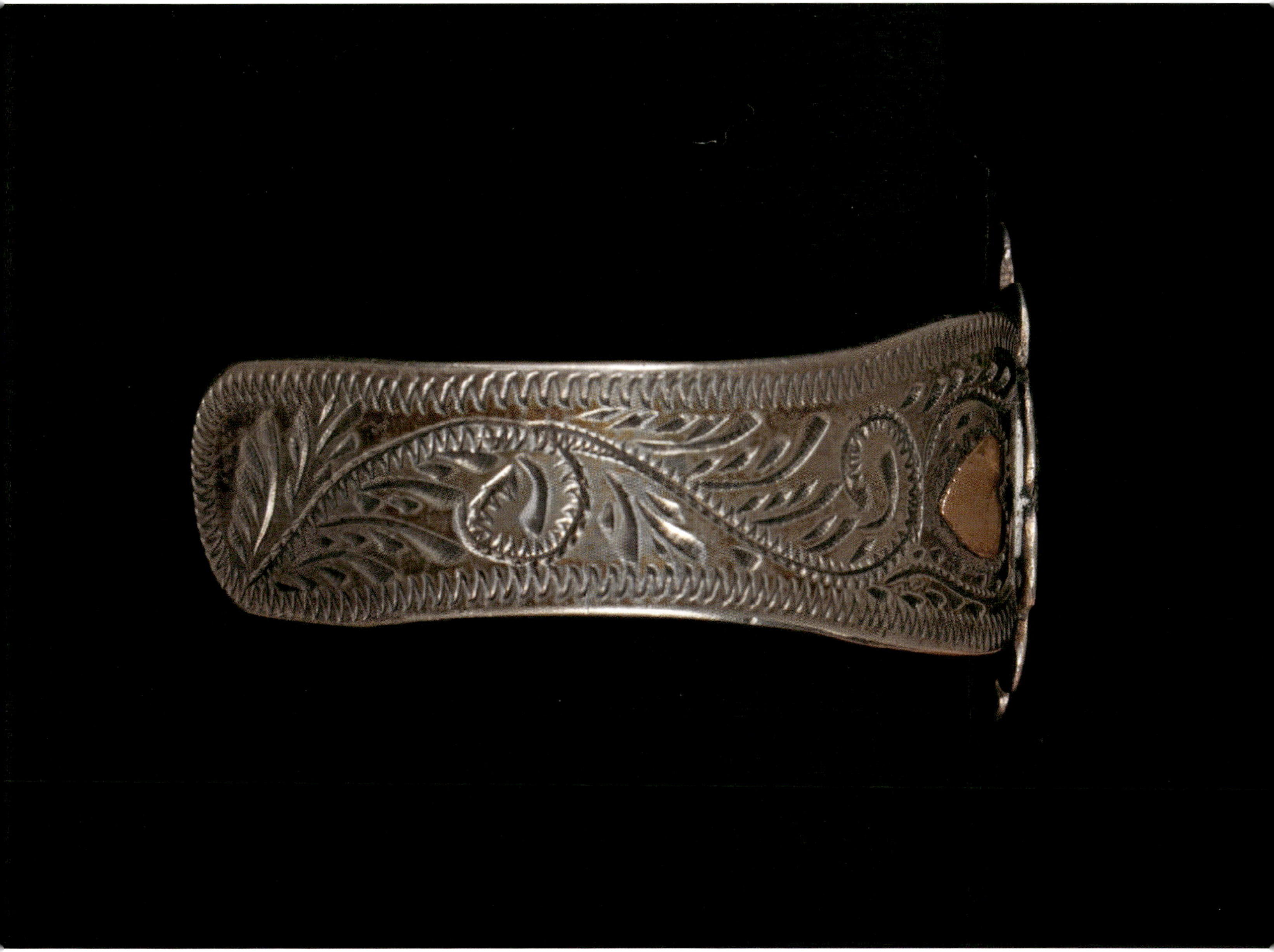

Figure 5-13. Hulbert jewelry—bracelets. Side view of the bracelet shown in Figure 5-12. *Photo by D. Congdon-Martin.*

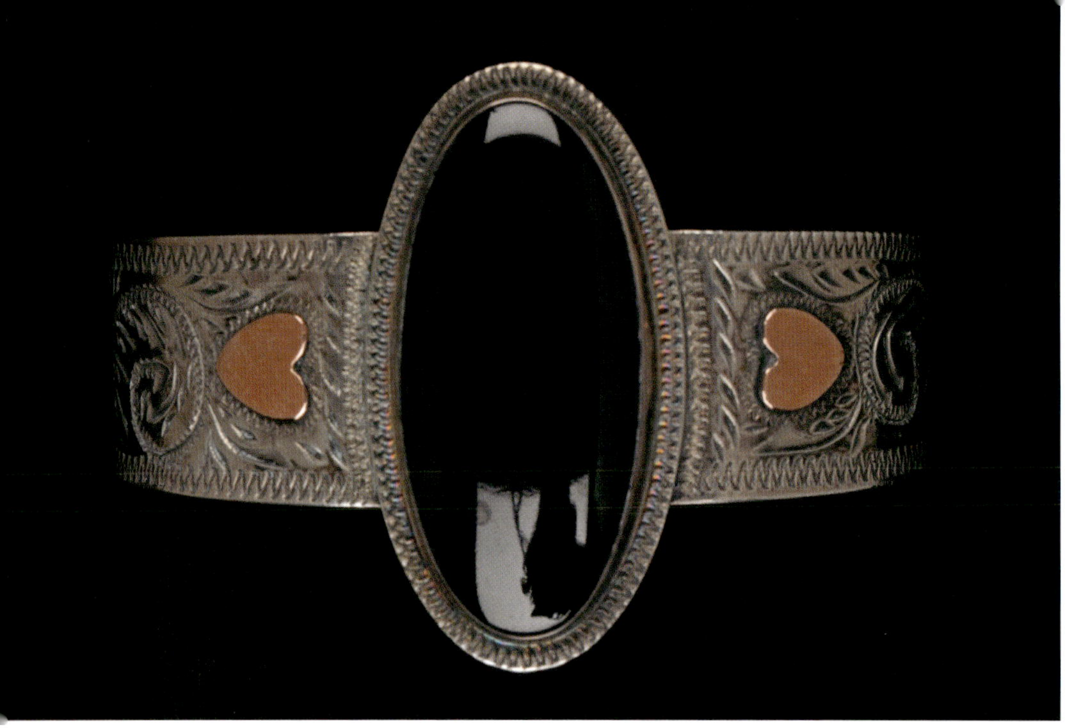

Figure 5-14. Hulbert jewelry—bracelets. A large agate distinguishes this heavily-engraved cuff bracelet, marked "STERLING" and "10K" inside. Two gold hearts flank the center cabochon. *Photo by D. Congdon-Martin.*

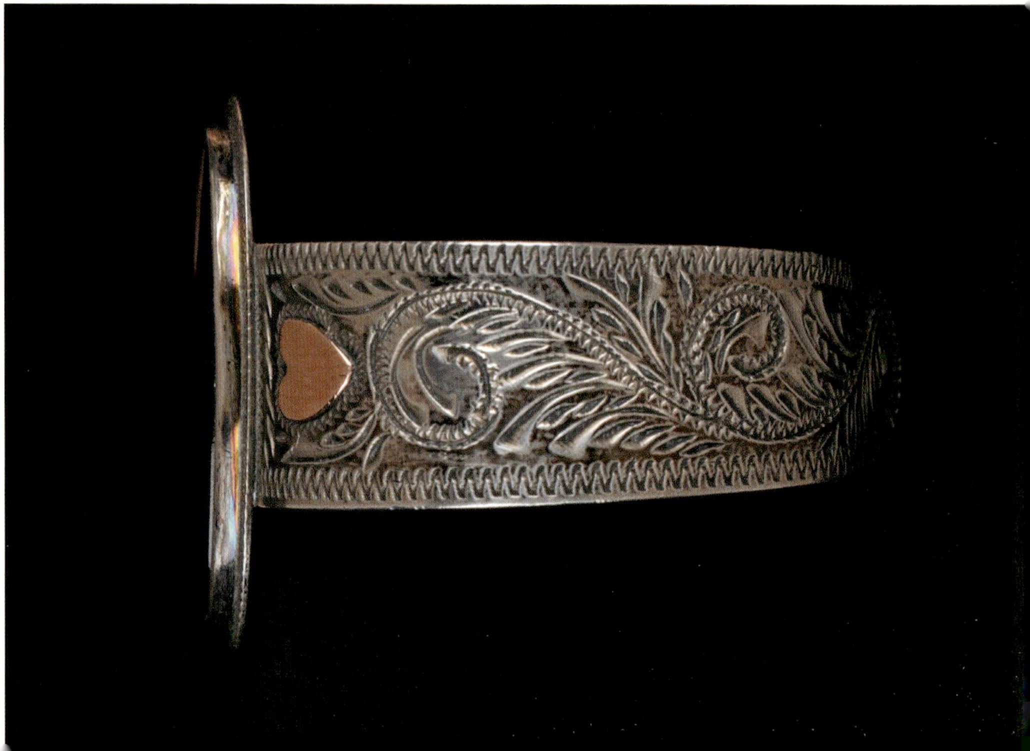

Figure 5-15. Hulbert jewelry—bracelets. Side view of bracelet shown in Figure 5-14. *Photo by D. Congdon-Martin.*

Hat Band

The final three figures in this chapter show an unusual Hulbert creation: an engraved silver hat band (Figures 5-16 through 5-18). The narrow band is adjustable, and the diminutive Ranger set has a gold horseshoe on the solid buckle. On the back of the band was engraved "JIM BRIDGER RODEO 1947." This hat band might have been a trophy, or a souvenir, commissioned by a rodeo official. It is a singular piece showing skill in both design and execution.

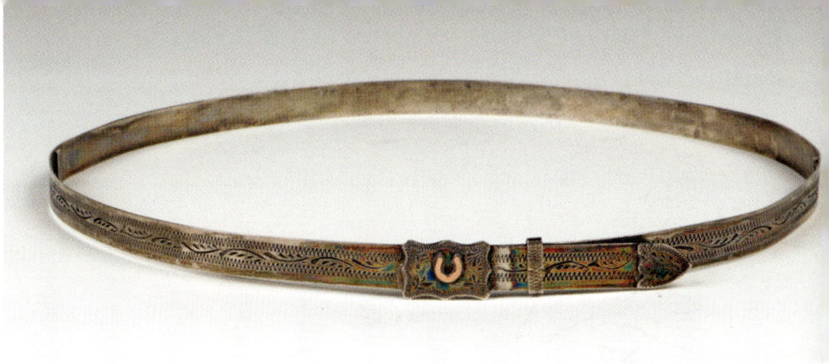

Figure 5-16. Hulbert jewelry—hat band. Hulbert made very few hat bands; this one shows his engraving on a narrow silver band, with a buckle, keeper, and tip. There is a gold horseshoe on the one-prong buckle, and the band is adjustable. It is stamped "STERLING" on the inner surface. *Photo by D. Congdon-Martin.*

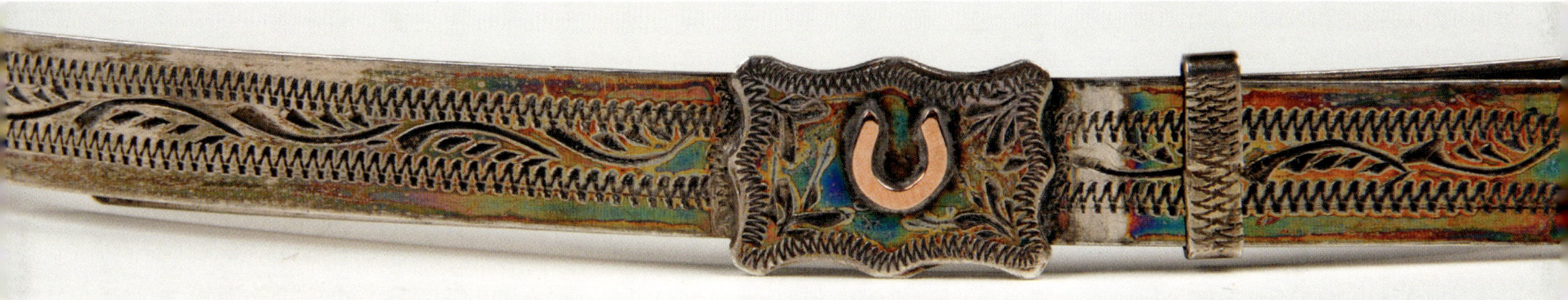

Figure 5-17. Hulbert jewelry—hat band. Enlarged view of buckle and keeper on the band shown in Figure 5-16. *Photo by D. Congdon-Martin.*

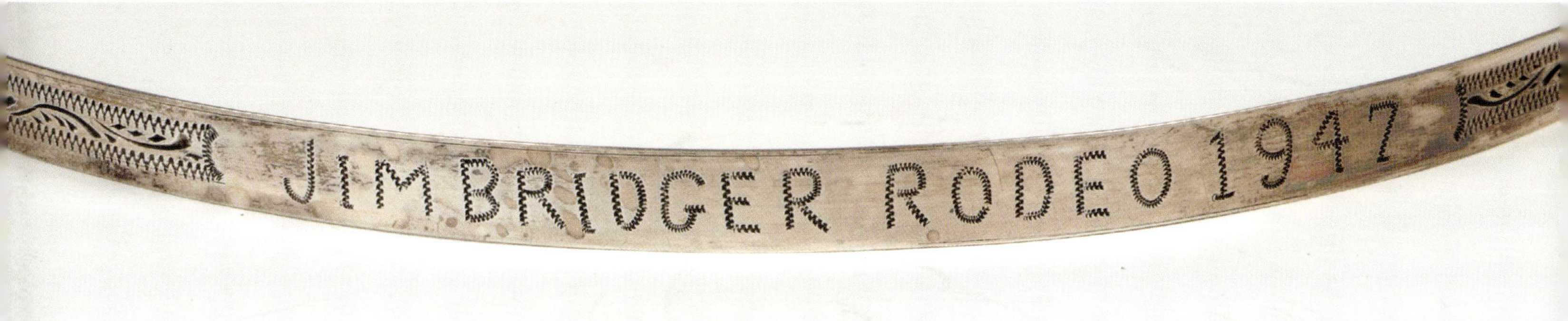

Figure 5-18. Hulbert jewelry—hat band. Back view of band showing inscription: "JIM BRIDGER RODEO 1947." This hat band was a commissioned trophy. *Photo by D. Congdon-Martin.*

MONTANA SILVERSMITHS OF HULBERT'S ERA: Klapmeier and O'Such

In this final chapter are presented two of Eddy Hulbert's contemporaries, both in time and place, who worked and sold silver in the extended area between Billings and Miles City, Montana (Carbon and Custer Counties). It is more than likely that Hulbert was familiar with their work and might even have been influenced by certain aspects of their designs. In similar fashion, Hulbert's work was known in the area and, although his engraving style was never duplicated, his bit and spur designs, and possibly belt buckles, were without a doubt influential as well.

Ed Klapmeier

Ed Klapmeier (1896–1983), originally from Nebraska, owned a ranch north of Miles City, where he began producing bits and spurs for local horsemen. His best work began in the late 1930s, when he sold his ranch and moved to Miles City. A pair of his spurs, made for Jack Peters c. 1935, resides in the Grant-Kohrs Ranch Museum, National Historic Site. They show an earlier, workman-like style, atypical of his later work, which was characterized by beautifully engraved silver and his use of Montana agates, many of which resembled landscapes. Klapmeier's bits and spurs are few, but throughout the 1950s–early 1970s he became well-known for his interesting and exquisite jewelry, including belt buckles. He displayed his work at several silver/gold/gem shows (*Montana Standard*, Butte, Montana, August 2, 1964; *Billings Gazette*, Billings, Montana, July 23, 1971), and was written up in the *Billings Gazette* (June 30, 1963) for his creation of an agate fireplace! Much of Klapmeier's work was stamped (or hand-lettered) "KLAPMEIER/MILES CITY, MONT."

C.E. O'Such

C.E. (Charles Edward) O'Such is far more enigmatic, and details of his life and work have been elusive. He was a saddlemaker and silver engraver who lived approximately one block from Klapmeier in Miles City. At this point, due to our lack of information, it is probably inappropriate to refer to O'Such as a silversmith, although his mark "C.E. O'SUCH/MILES CITY, MONT/STERLING" appears on a few items, two of which (belt buckles) are shown at the end of this chapter. It is also possible that Klapmeier made the buckles (or Eddy Hulbert, or an unidentified silversmith?), and O'Such marked and sold them in his saddlery shop (see discussion below).

Klapmeier – Overview

Montana collector Jay Lyndes graciously contributed most of the Klapmeier pieces shown in this chapter. His extensive and representative collection, seen in overview in Figures 6-1 through 6-3, includes many types of jewelry, a concho belt, bolo ties, a dagger handle, spur straps, and a bit. Labeled "Hand wrought mountings/ scenic Montana moss agate," the collection includes a fascinating subset of pins as animal images (Figure 6-2) and tree-lined lakes and pastures (Figure 6-3).

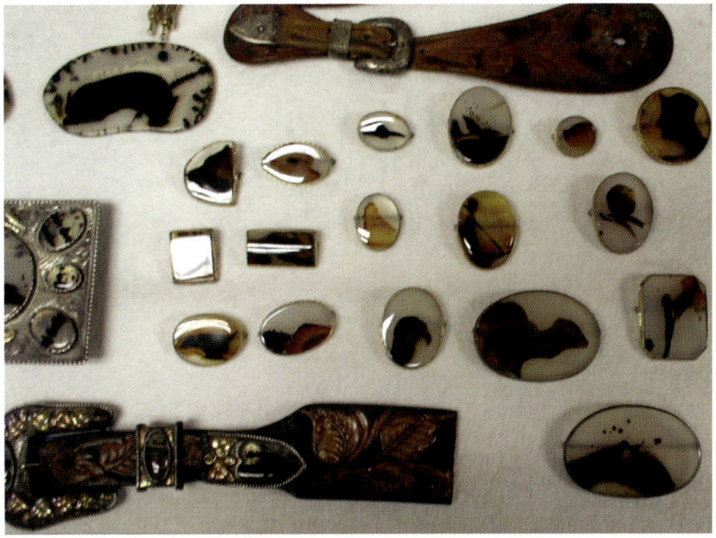

Figure 6-2. Klapmeier—overview. A subset of the Lyndes collection shown in Figure 6-1. Note the "animal agates," e.g., a camel, vulture, butterfly, bear, bird, and a man's head. *Courtesy of J. Lyndes. Photo by D. Claxton.*

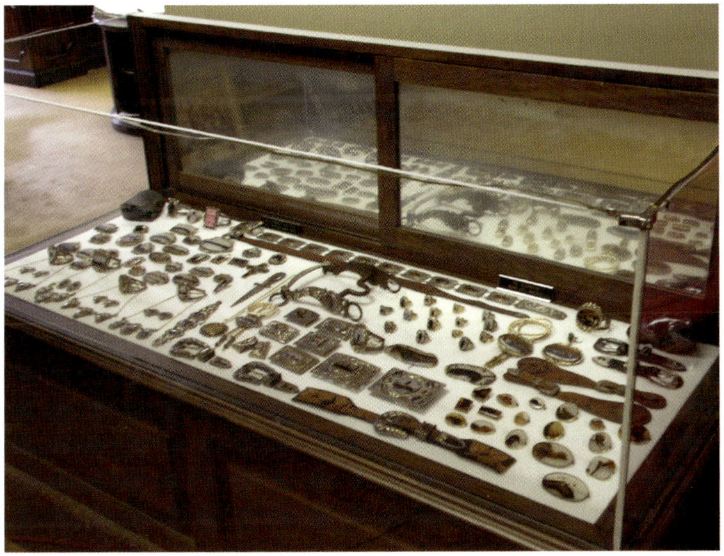

Figure 6-1. Klapmeier—overview. An extensive collection of Ed Klapmeier's work (Miles City, Montana). The scope and quality of this collection are unequalled. *Courtesy of J. Lyndes. Photo by D. Claxton.*

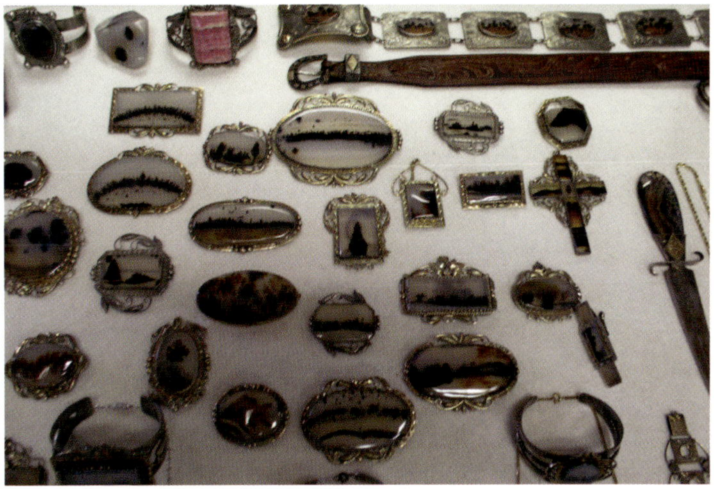

Figure 6-3. Klapmeier—overview. A subset of the Lyndes collection shown in Figure 6-1. Note the "scenic Montana moss agate" pins, pendants, rings, dagger handle, tie clip, and incredible silver concho belt. *Courtesy of J. Lyndes. Photo by D. Claxton.*

Klapmeier – Necklace and Earring Sets

Figures 6-4 through 6-6 show three exquisite necklaces with matching earrings. The agate stones match in each piece, and are set off by distinctive silver bezels or frames, two of which are separated by gold hearts.

A single example of a Klapmeier bracelet is shown in Figure 6-7. One of the more stunning of his agates, with its "sunset" over a forest of trees, this silver cuff-style bracelet is highlighted in gold leaves and berries. An agate tie tac with an interesting mark *verso* and set within a silver horseshoe is shown in Figures 6-8 and 6-9.

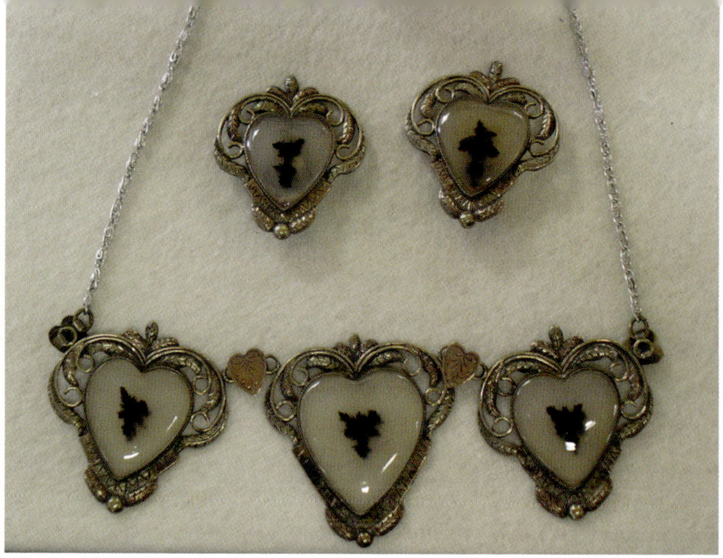

Figure 6-5. Klapmeier jewelry—necklace and earring sets. A unique design with three heart-shaped pictorial agates set in silver mounts and separated by gold hearts. The matching earrings recapitulate this design. *Courtesy of J. Lyndes. Photo by D. Claxton.*

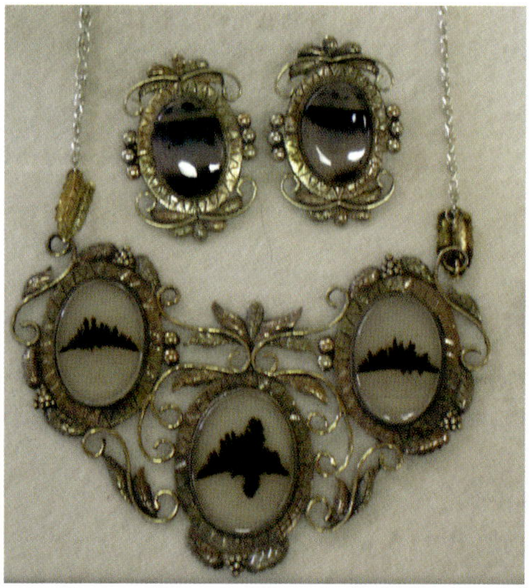

Figure 6-4. Klapmeier jewelry—necklace and earring sets. This fancy three-cabochon necklace and its matching earrings are delicately wrought and beautifully balanced. *Courtesy of J. Lyndes. Photo by D. Claxton.*

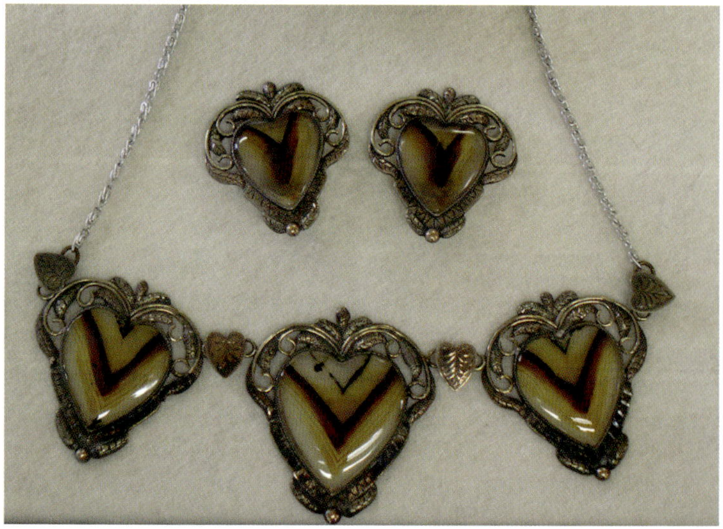

Figure 6-6. Klapmeier jewelry—necklace and earring sets. The agates with their "double V" colors impart a dramatic effect to these pieces of jewelry. The Vs fit nicely into the heart settings, which on the necklace are separated by small gold hearts. *Courtesy of J. Lyndes. Photo by D. Claxton.*

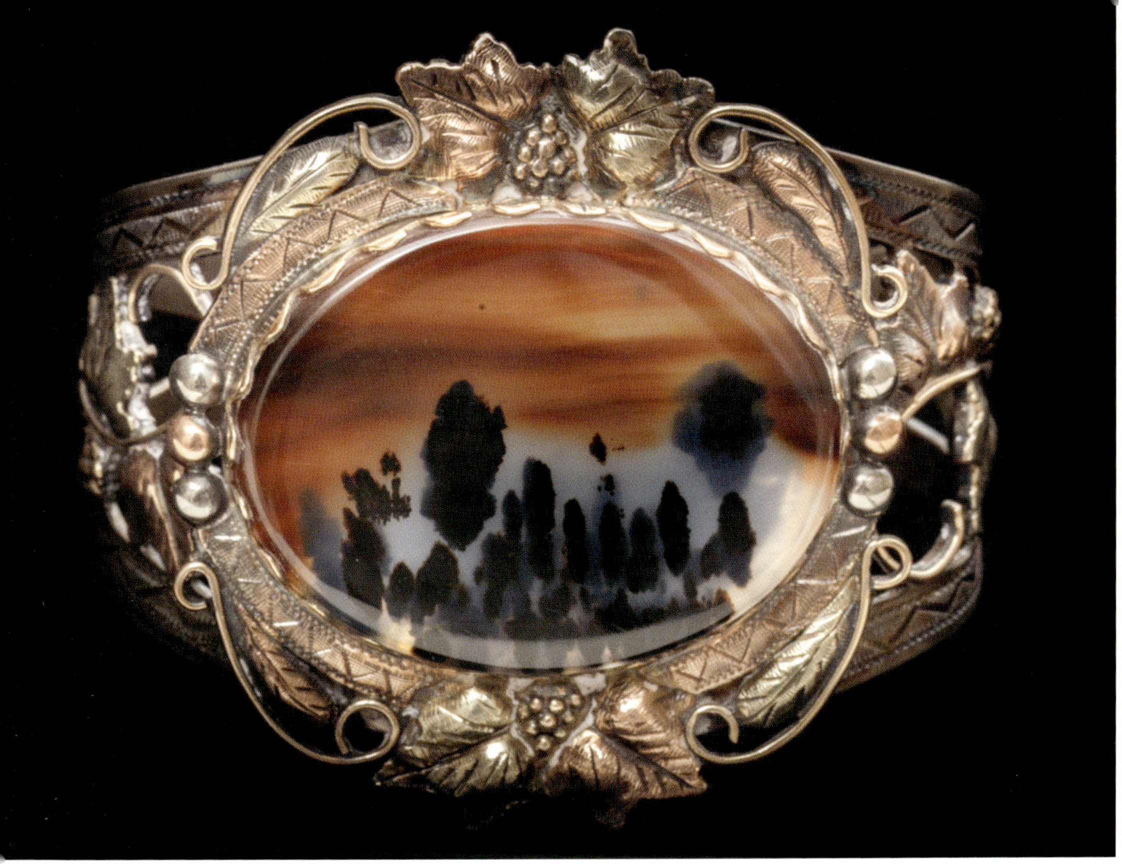

Figure 6-7. Klapmeier jewelry—bracelet. This silver cuff bracelet was made with a pictorial agate reminiscent of trees and a sunset, offset by a gold surround of leaves and berries. *Photo by J. Williams.*

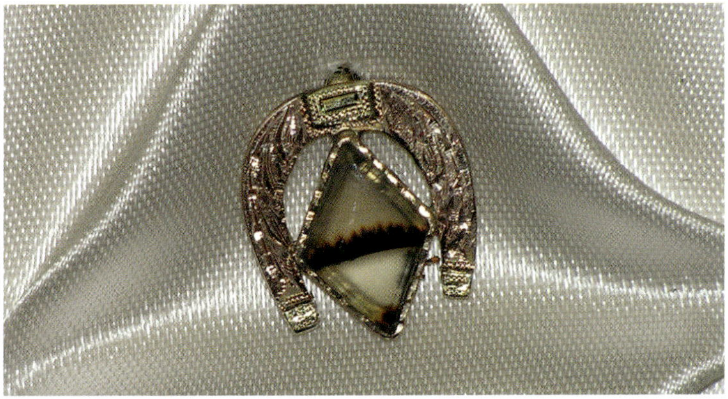

Figure 6-8. Klapmeier jewelry—tie tac. A beautifully engraved silver tie tac in the shape of a horseshoe, with a diamond-shaped agate resembling a line of trees on a lake and a sunset above. *Courtesy of J. Lyndes. Photo by D. Claxton.*

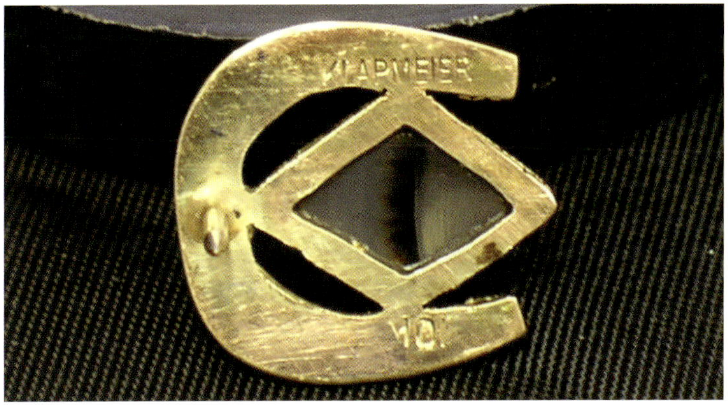

Figure 6-9. Klapmeier jewelry—tie tac. Verso of the tie tac shown in Figure 6-8. The stamp "KLAPMEIER" and an unidentified mark opposite can be seen. *Courtesy of J. Lyndes. Photo by D. Claxton.*

Klapmeier – Ranger Sets and Belt Buckles

Figures 6-10 through 6-13 are two examples of unusual Ranger sets, the first of which has three matched agates within engraved silver and accented by silver rope and gold leaves. An earlier set (Figures 6-11 through 6-13) exhibits the same design executed in a less ornate style, without gold or silver rope. The mark is hand-wrought rather than stamped (Figure 6-12), also perhaps indicative of an earlier piece. The leather belt with this Ranger set is tooled in the owner's name "OTTO MILLER."

Klapmeier's true artistic sense is epitomized in his solid silver belt buckles. Figures 6-14 and 6-15 show an impressive piece with a "mountain scene square agate" embedded within a masterfully engraved silver rectangle embellished with clusters of golden grapes and leaves. The gold "spittoon" at the top of the buckle was probably a ranch brand, but research has revealed nothing regarding its identity. This buckle bears the typical marks "KLAPMEIER/MILES CITY, MONT./10K/ STERLING" (Figure 6-15). Additional silver, gold, and agate belt buckles, similar in style but each distinctive, are shown in Figures 6-16 through 6-20. The open-engraved filigree work of the buckle in Figure 6-20 leaves little doubt that Klapmeier was a master designer and silversmith. The Montana pictorial agate was clearly chosen as an outstanding image complementing the engraving and open-work of the buckle.

Figure 6-10. Klapmeier jewelry—Ranger sets. Engraved silver buckle, keeper, and tip with silver rope edge and gold leaf accents. Each piece is set with a matching Montana pictorial agate. Note the heart-shaped cutout on the tip, into which the agate was embedded, to allow clearance of the tip through the keeper. *Courtesy of J. Lyndes. Photo by J. Williams.*

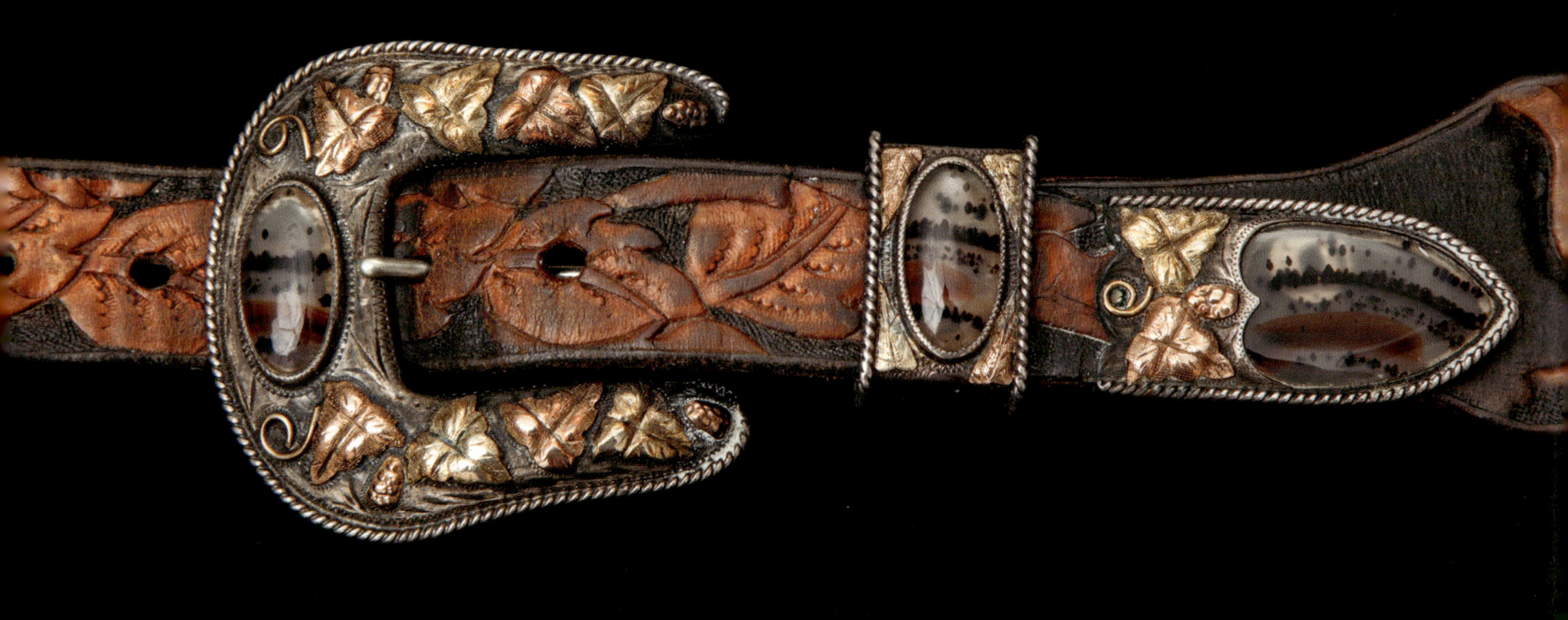

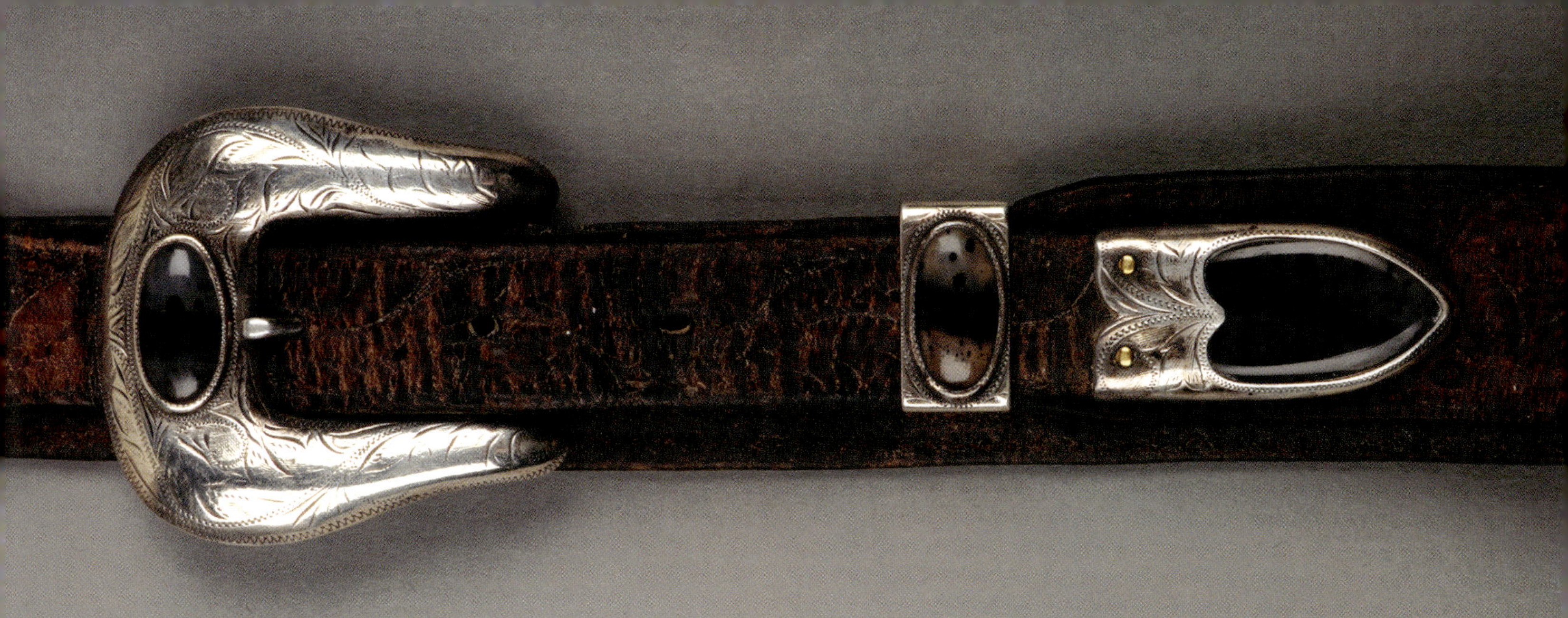

Figure 6-11. Klapmeier jewelry—Ranger sets. A heavy and masculine buckle of engraved silver, with a pictorial agate that matches those in the keeper and tip. Note heart-shaped cutout on the tip, as seen in Figure 6-10. *Photo by D. Congdon-Martin.*

It is not known how many bits Klapmeier turned out, but very few have surfaced. That shown in Figure 6-21 is certainly a prime example of his work. The blank might have come from another shop (perhaps Hulbert's?), but the moss agate concho and the engraved silver card suits on the cheeks are clearly Klapmeier's, as confirmed by his mark on the inner side of the slobber bar.

Figure 6-12. Klapmeier jewelry—Ranger sets. Verso of tip shown on the set in Figure 6-11. The mark, "KLAPMEIER/ MILES CITY/MONT.," was done by hand, letter-by-letter, in contrast to later marks which were stamped (e.g., Figure 6-15). *Photo by D. Congdon-Martin.*

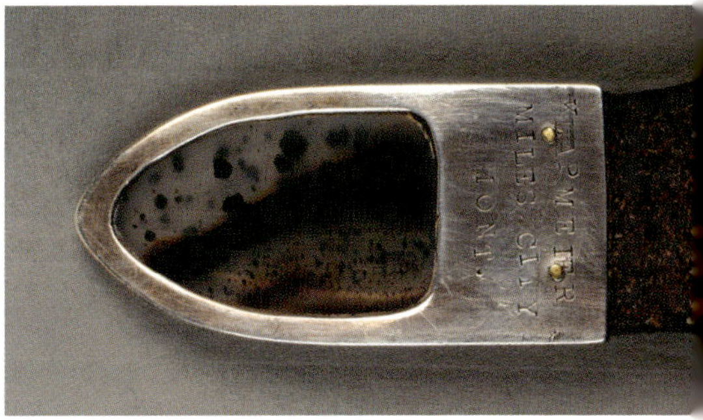

Figure 6-13. Klapmeier jewelry—Ranger sets. The leather belt with the Ranger s et shown in Figure 6-11 is tooled in the owner's name: "OTTO MILLER." *Photo by D. Congdon-Martin.*

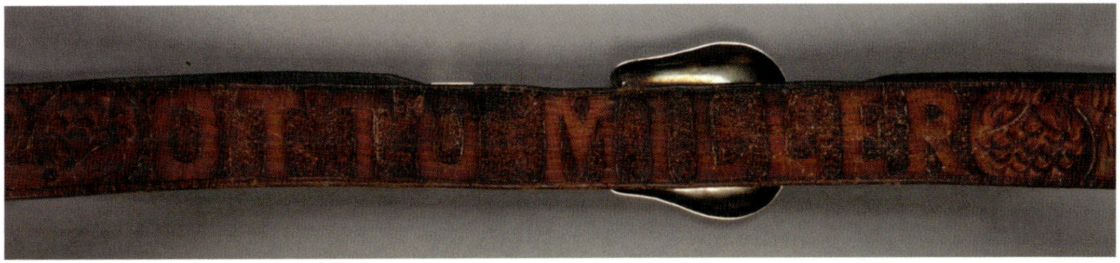

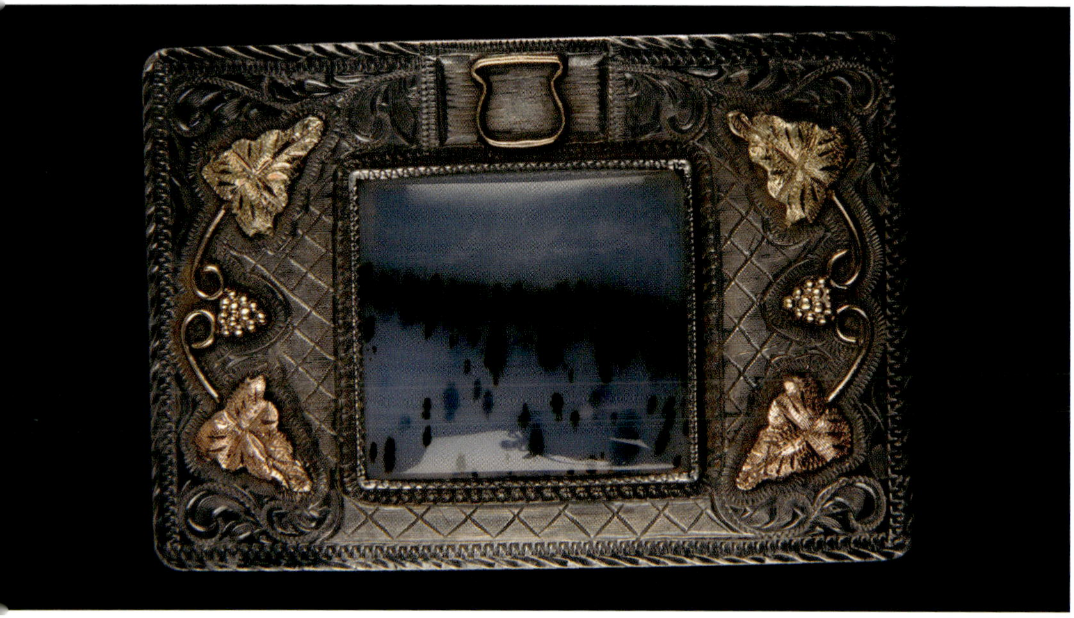

Figure 6-14. Klapmeier jewelry—belt buckles. This marked, engraved silver belt buckle shows Klapmeier's artistry—there is a "mountain scene" (pines on a snow-covered ridge ?) agate set in the center of the buckle, and gold leaves and grapes on the sides. Of interest is the gold "spittoon" at the top, perhaps a Ranch brand. *Photo by D. Congdon-Martin.*

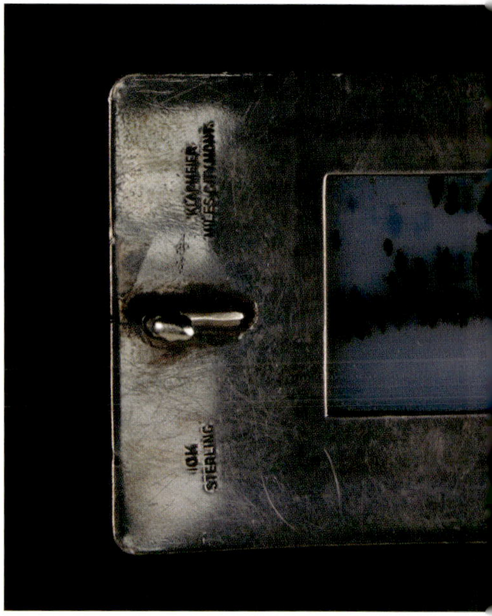

Figure 6-15. Klapmeier jewelry—belt buckles. Verso of buckle shown in Figure 6-14; stamped marks "10K/STERLING" and "KLAPMEIER/MILES CITY, MONT." are evident. *Photo by D. Congdon-Martin.*

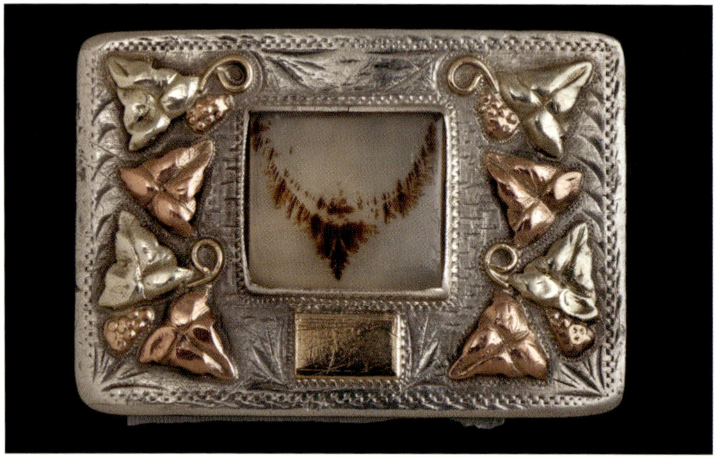

Figure 6-16. Klapmeier jewelry—belt buckles. A buckle in a style similar to that shown in Figure 6-14, with an unusual pictorial agate, and gold and copper leaves and grapes. There is a gold rectangle in a space that could have been reserved for a brand or initials. *Courtesy of J. Lyndes. Photo by J. Williams.*

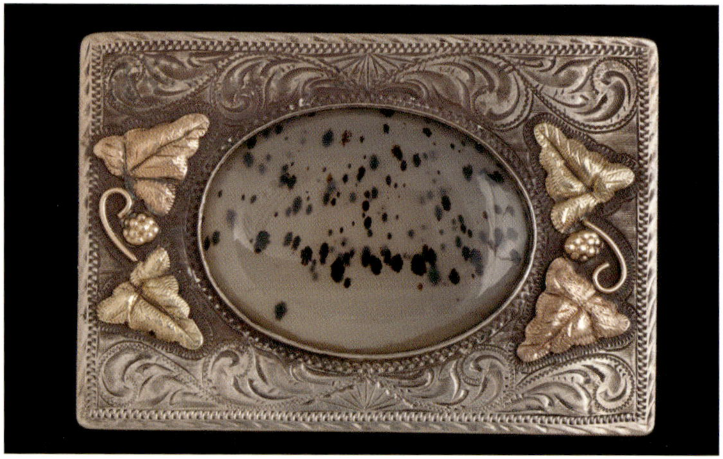

Figure 6-17. Klapmeier jewelry—belt buckles. A beautifully engraved silver buckle with a gold pair of leaves and grapes, and center oval agate. *Courtesy of J. Lyndes. Photo by J. Williams.*

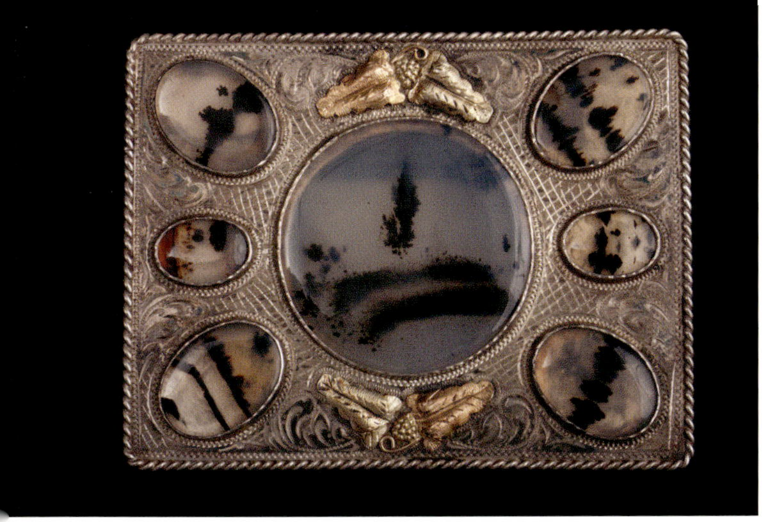

Figure 6-18. Klapmeier jewelry—belt buckles. This buckle encompasses all the elements of the exquisite Klapmeier design: lavishly-engraved silver in two styles (floral and geometric), gold grape leaf clusters, central pictorial agate, and six surrounding, smaller oval agates of intriguing, complementary patterns. *Courtesy of J. Lyndes. Photo by J. Williams.*

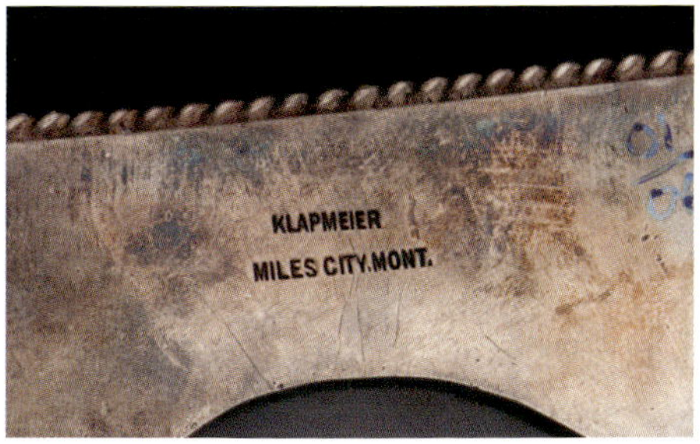

Figure 6-19. Klapmeier jewelry—belt buckles. Verso of buckle shown in Figure 6-18. "KLAPMEIER/ MILES CITY, MONT." is clearly seen, and "10K/ STERLING" appears on the opposite side (not shown). *Courtesy of J. Lyndes. Photo by J. Williams.*

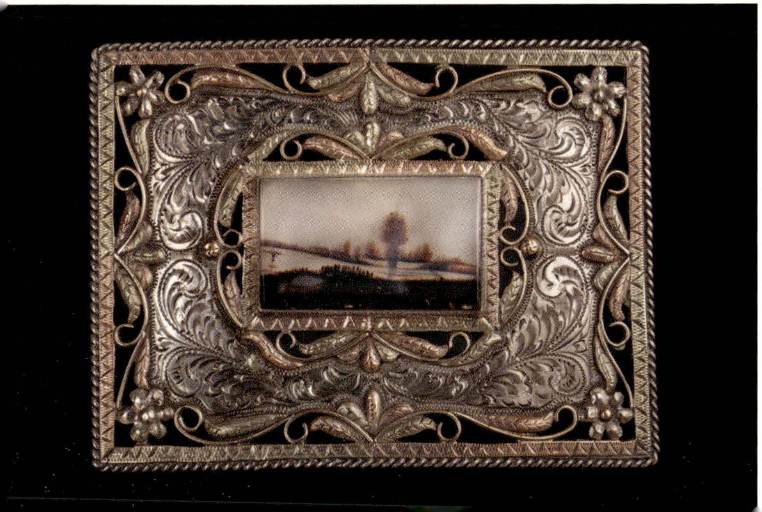

Figure 6-20. Klapmeier jewelry—belt buckles. This open, engraved silver filigree buckle ranks among Klapmeier's finest work. The silver rope edge surrounds a solid silver border with a flower in each corner. The same border offsets a scenic Montana agate that is reminiscent of a Western countryside. *Courtesy of J. Lyndes. Photo by J. Williams.*

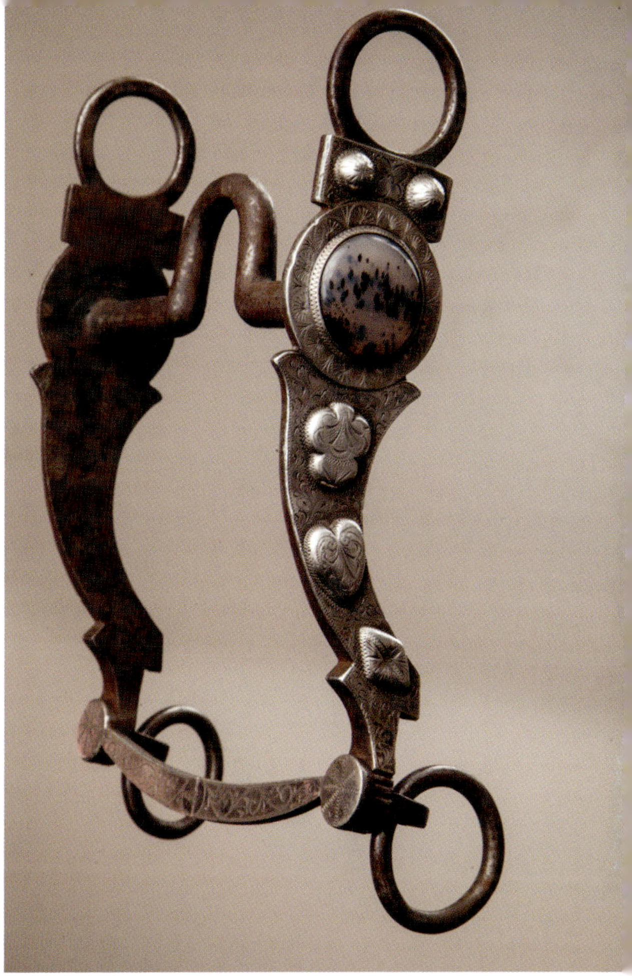

Figure 6-21. Klapmeier jewelry—bit. The maker of the blank steel bit is not known (perhaps Hulbert?), but the agate and patterned silver overlays (heart, spade, and diamond in relief) are unmistakably Klapmeier's work. This piece is likely one-of-a-kind. *Courtesy of J. Lyndes. Photo by J. Williams.*

O'Such – Belt Buckles

The solid silver engraved buckle shown in Figures 6-22 and 6-23 is marked "C.E. O'SUCH/ MILES CITY, MONT/ STERLING." The engraving resembles that of Klapmeier but is clearly different, and the agate cowboy boot might have been an original design. A nearly identical buckle can be seen online (http://estatesalesblog.blogspot.com/), but it has been attributed to Klapmeier. The striking similarity between the two pieces leads one to speculate on a possible collaborative interaction between the two men, who were neighbors in Miles City.

The differences in the engraving, however, might also indicate that O'Such employed a silversmith in his shop whose identity remains unknown. Figures 6-24 and 6-25 show another O'Such-marked silver buckle, this one with detailed engraving and a well-executed gold Western saddle in the center.

The final figures in this chapter (6-26 and 6-27) present a bit of a mystery—is this outstanding silver belt buckle with a center medallion Klapmeier's, O'Such's, or another's work? It is marked "HE/STERLING" and "78/12," and is beautifully executed, the cowboy riding the bronc especially so. The reverse side of the medallion bears the brand of the "NINE QUARTER CIRCLE RANCH" and, on the periphery, "REMEMBER THE BIG SKY COUNTRY/ GALLATIN GATEWAY MONTANA." This item was a promotional for a dude ranch, founded in 1912 and active today, located on the Taylor Fork of the Gallatin River (near the northwest corner of Yellowstone Park). This handsome piece should stimulate further research on the talented silversmiths of Ed Klapmeier's and Eddy Hulbert's era.

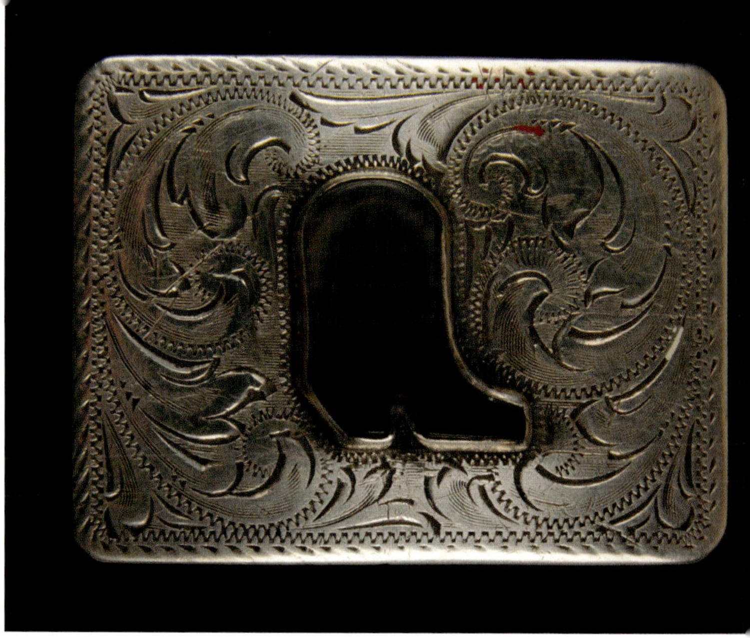

Figure 6-22. O'Such jewelry—belt buckles. O'Such's work is scarce; this engraved silver buckle has what appears to be a rocker-engraved border and floral interior, and is accented by an agate cowboy boot. *Photo by D. Congdon-Martin.*

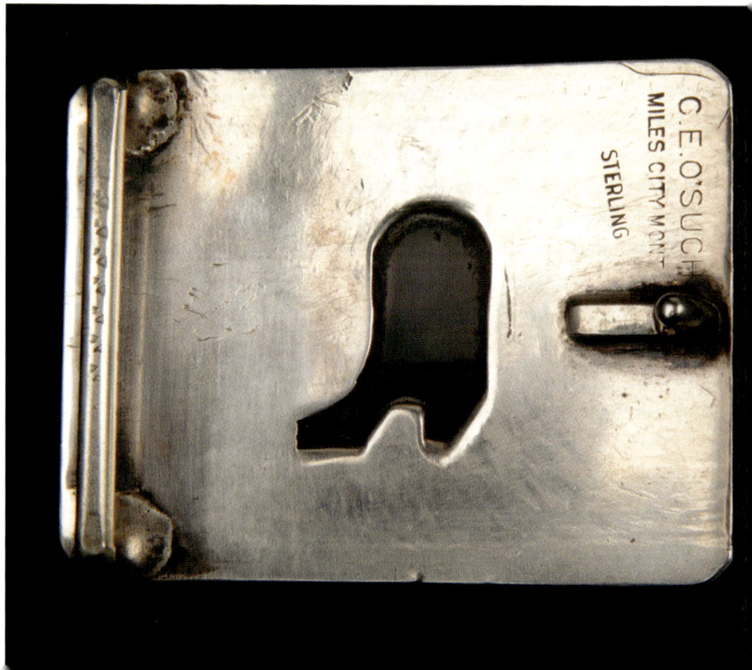

Figure 6-23. O'Such jewelry—belt buckles. Verso of the buckle shown in Figure 6-22. The mark is "C.E. O'SUCH/MILES CITY, MONT./STERLING." *Photo by D. Congdon-Martin.*

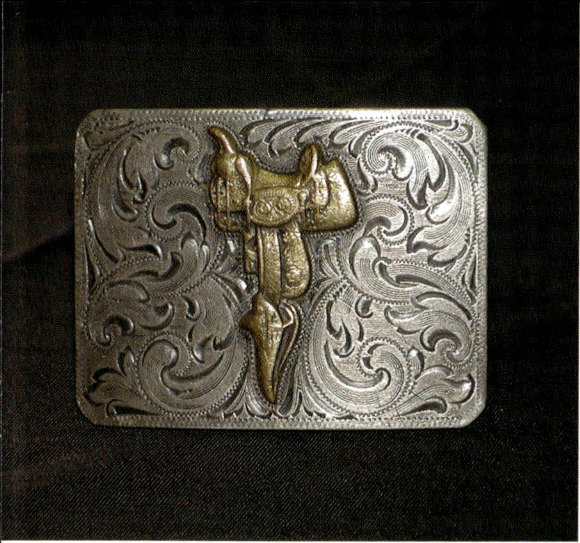

Figure 6-24. O'Such jewelry—belt buckles. This buckle exhibits an engraving style and pattern similar to that shown in Figure 6-22. There is a gold Western saddle in the center. *Courtesy of J. Lyndes. Photo by J. Williams.*

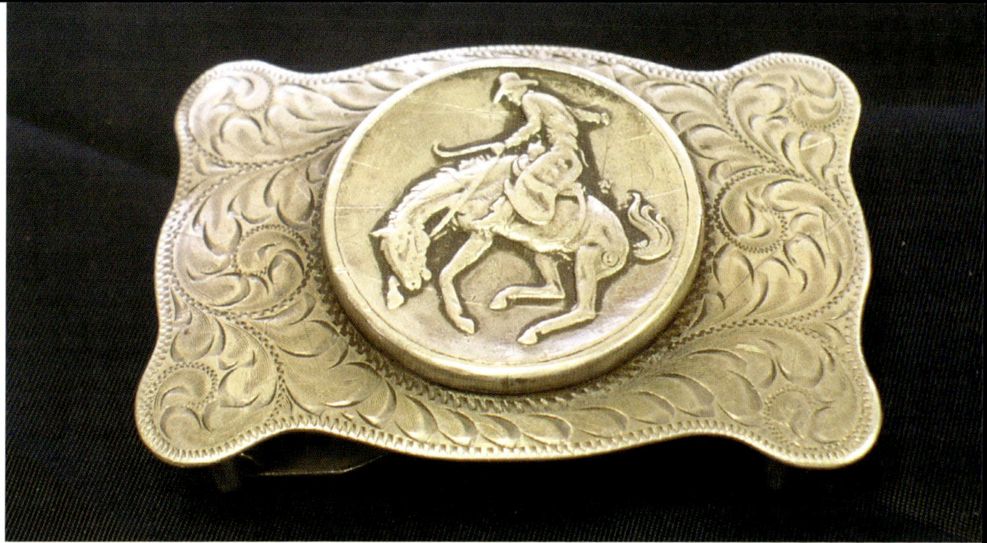

Figure 6-26. Klapmeier or O'Such—belt buckle. The engraving on this buckle is similar, but not identical to that shown on the O'Such buckle in Figure 6-24. The center medallion shows a cowboy on a bucking horse, the reverse of which can be seen on the back of the buckle (see Figure 6-27). Because the buckle bears neither O'Such's nor Klapmeier's mark, it might well have been made by another silversmith who at this time remains unidentified. *Courtesy of J. Lyndes. Photo by J. Williams.*

Figure 6-25. O'Such jewelry—belt buckles. Verso of the buckle shown in Figure 6-24. The mark is "C.E. O'SUCH/MILES CITY, MONT./STERLING."

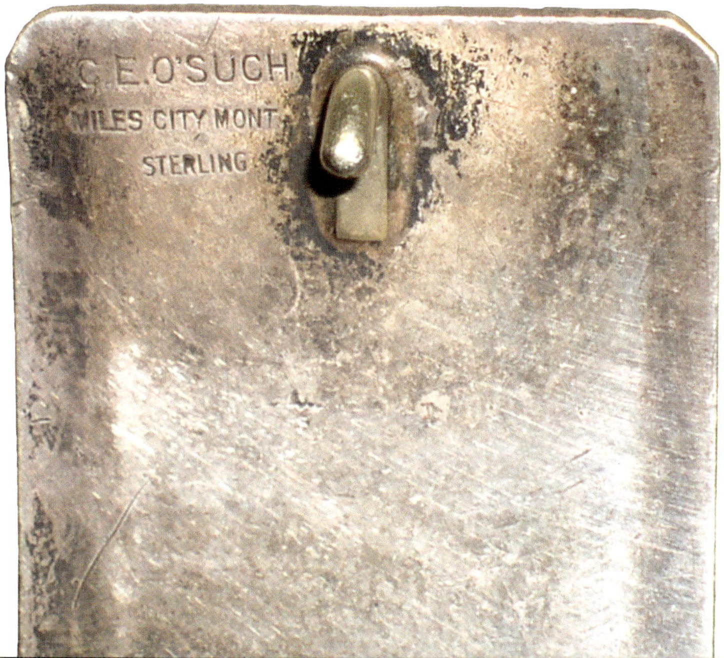

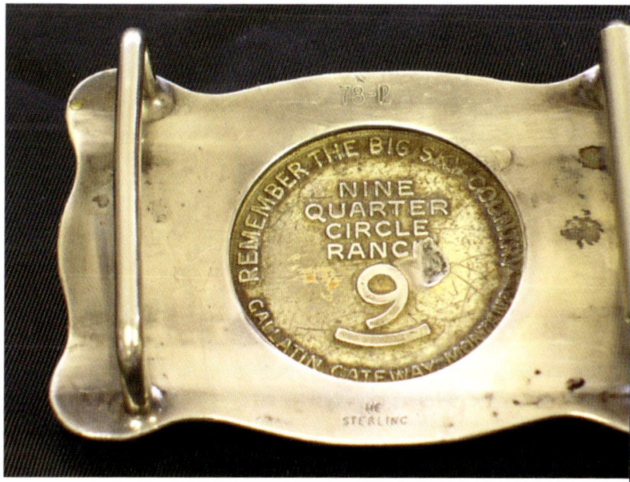

Figure 6-27. Klapmeier or O'Such—belt buckle. Verso of the buckle shown in Figure 6-26. The medallion was struck for the "NINE QUARTER CIRCLE RANCH," with its brand, and on the periphery appears "REMEMBER THE BIG SKY COUNTRY/GALLATIN GATEWAY, MONTANA." The marks are "78-12" and "HE/STERLING." This buckle was a promotional item for a dude ranch, founded in 1912 and active today, located on the Taylor Fork of the Gallatin River. *Courtesy of J. Lyndes. Photo by J. Williams.*

Books

Abarr, Don. *Hoofbeats on the Wind – Tales of a Sagebrush Cowboy*. (Columbus, Montana: The Stillwater Sun, 1989).

Furman, Necah Stewart. *Caroline Lockhart – Her Life and Legacy.* (Cody, Wyoming: The Buffalo Bill Historical Center, and Seattle, Washington: The University of Washington Press, 1994).

Gorzalka, Ann. *The Saddlemakers of Sheridan, Wyoming*. (Boulder, Colorado: Pruett Publishing Co., 1984).

Graham, Gretchen and Mike Graham. *Old Cowboy Saddles and Spurs (7th edition)*. (Manitou Springs, Colorado: Old West Trading Co., 2003, p. 173).

Hicks, Lucille Patrick. *Caroline Lockhart – Liberated Lady – 1870-1962*. (Cheyenne, Wyoming: Pioneer Printing and Stationery Col., 1984).

Hutchins, Dan and Sebie Hutchins. *Old Cowboy Saddles and Spurs*. (Santa Fe, New Mexico, 1991).

Mackin, Bill. *Cowboy and Gunfighter Collectibles – A Photographic Encyclopedia with Price Guide and Makers Index.* (Missoula, Montana: Mountain Press Publishing Co., 1995).

Maul, Patrice and Jack Ferguson, with Mike and Gretchen Graham. *Canon City Spur – Colorado Prison Spurs and the Men Who Made Them*. (Colorado Springs, Colorado: Canon City Spur Co. and Old West Trading Co., 1995).

Patrick, Lucille Nichols. *The Candy Kid: James Calvin "Kid" Nichols, 1883–1962.* (Cheyenne, Wyoming: Flintock Publishing Co., 1969).

Pattie, Jane. *Cowboy Spurs and Their Makers*. (College Station, Texas: Texas A&M University Press, 1994).

Reid, Shell. *Eddy Hulbert – Montana Silversmith*. (Bozeman, Montana: Artcraft Printers, 1998).

Sanderson, Nathan B. *Dean of the Range: George Edward Lemmon, Open Range Cattle Ranching and the Development of the Northern Great Plains.* (Lincoln, Nebraska: University of Nebraska Ph.D. dissertation, Department of History, 2011)

Schmidt, Phyllis. *The West as I Lived It: Stories by Ed Lemmon.* (Pierre, South Dakota: State Publishing Co., 2007)

Yost, N.S. *Boss Cowman: The Recollections of Ed Lemmon, 1857-1946.* (Lincoln, Nebraska: University of Nebraska Press, 1969)

Catalogs

Cowboy Clothing and Gear – The Complete Hamley Catalog of 1942 – Hamley & Company. (New York: Dover Publications, Inc., 1995).

Hamley's Cowboy Catalog No. 36. (Pendleton, Oregon: Hamley & Company, 1936).

Hamley & Company – Cowboy Outfitters, Catalog No. 22. (Pendleton, Oregon: Hamley & Company, 1922).

Fred Mueller Saddle & Harness Co., Catalog No. 70. (Denver, Colorado: The Fred Mueller Saddle & Harness Co., 1934).

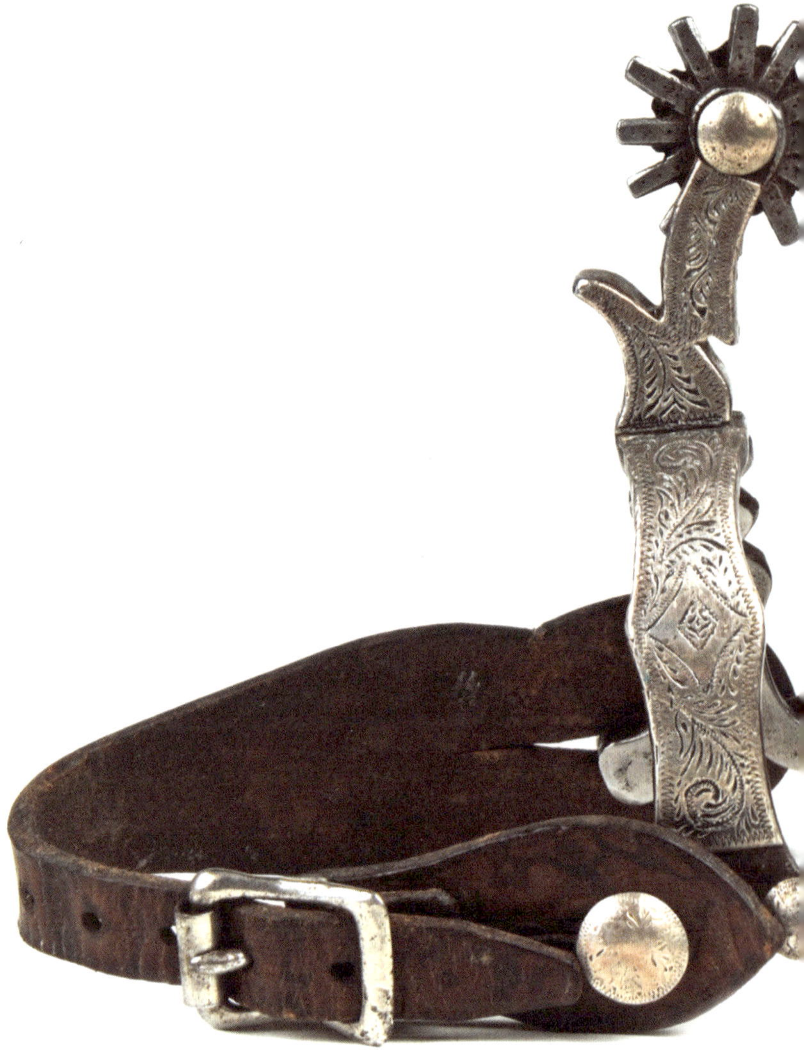